HORI-san and MIYAMURA-KUN

# HORIMIYA

HERO

×

DAISUKE HAGIWARA

08

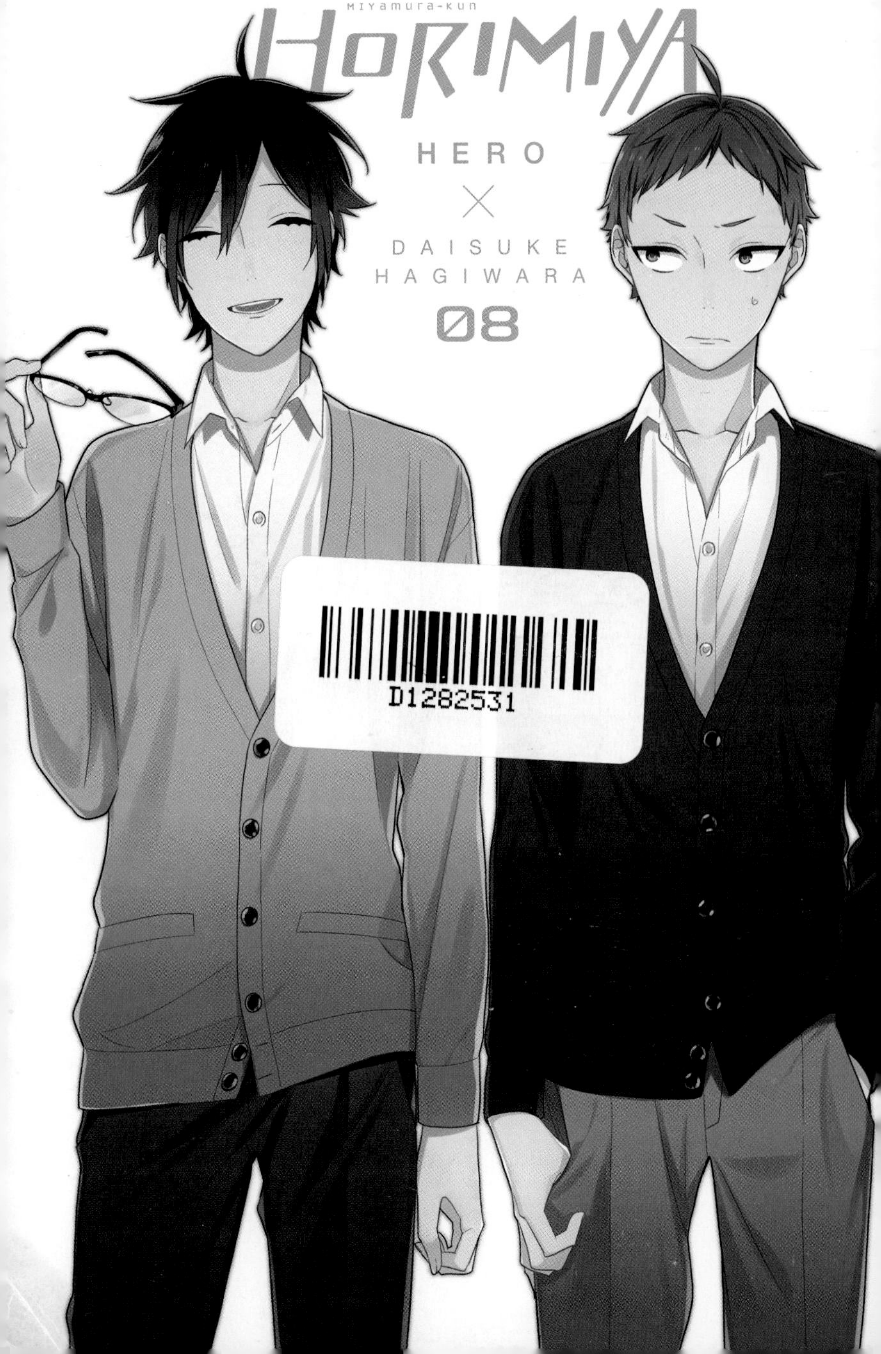

HORI-san and
MIYAMURA-kun

# HORIMIYA

## 08

# Contents ★

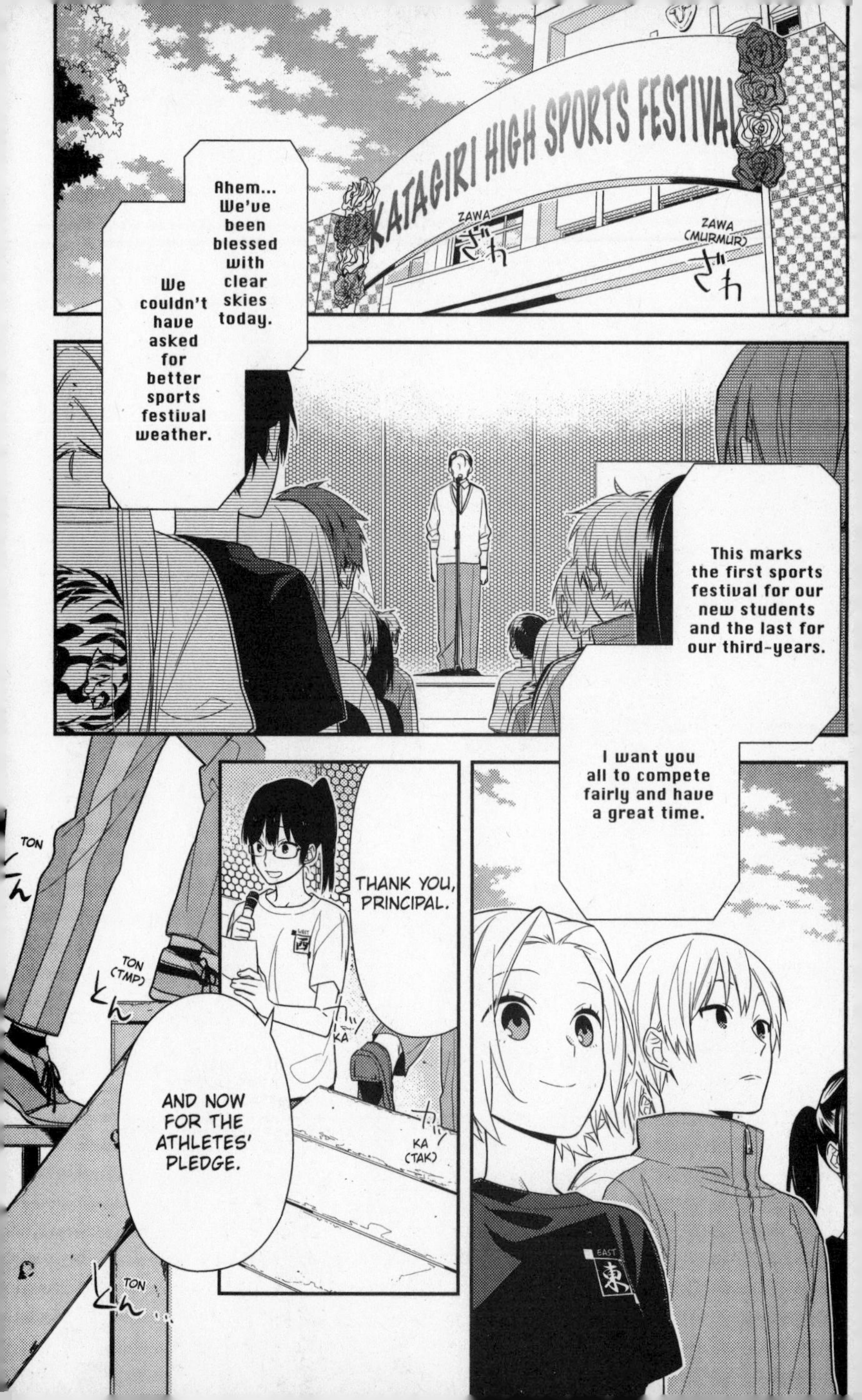
KATAGIRI HIGH SPORTS FESTIVAL
ZAWA (MURMUR) ざわ
ZAWA ざわ
Ahem... We've been blessed with clear skies today.
We couldn't have asked for better sports festival weather.
This marks the first sports festival for our new students and the last for our third-years.
I want you all to compete fairly and have a great time.
THANK YOU, PRINCIPAL.
KA
AND NOW FOR THE ATHLETES' PLEDGE.
KA (TAK)
TON とん
TON (TMP) とん
TON とん...

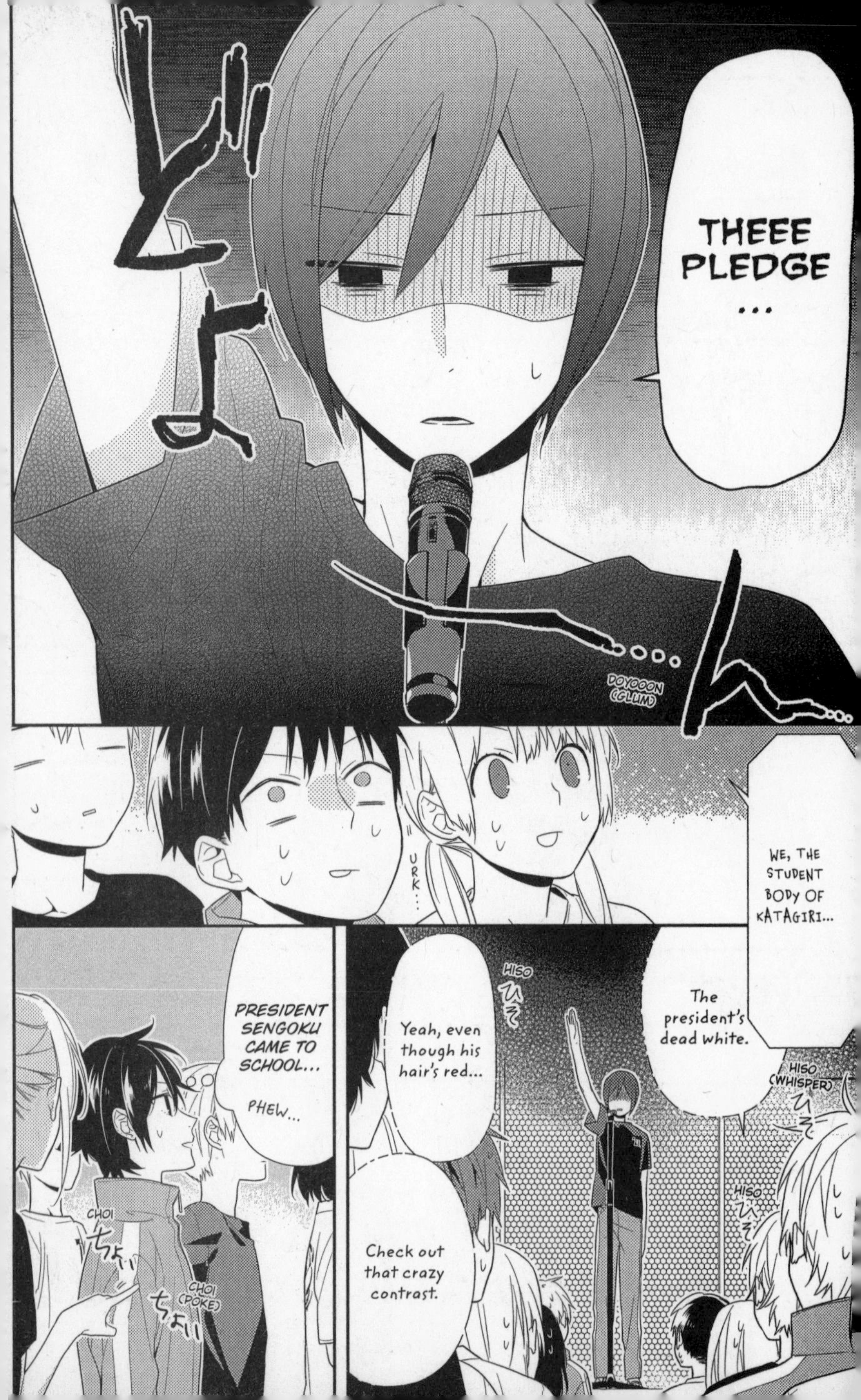
THEEE PLEDGE ...
DOYOOON (GLUM)
WE, THE STUDENT BODY OF KATAGIRI...
URK...
The president's dead white.
HISO (WHISPER) ひそ
HISO ひそ
Yeah, even though his hair's red...
HISO ひそ
Check out that crazy contrast.
PRESIDENT SENGOKU CAME TO SCHOOL...
PHEW...
CHOI ちょい
CHOI (POKE) ちょい

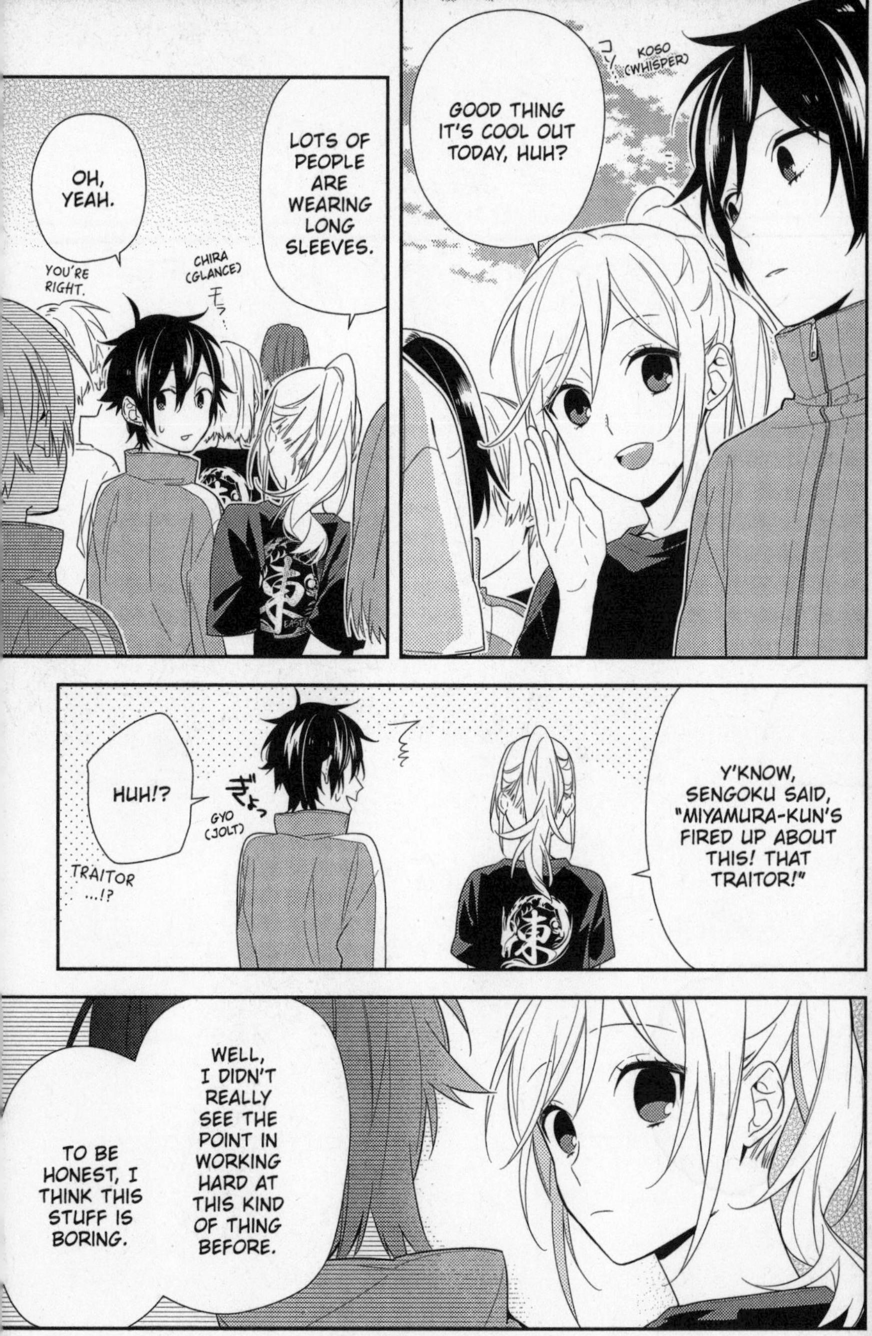
KOSO (WHISPER)
GOOD THING IT'S COOL OUT TODAY, HUH?
LOTS OF PEOPLE ARE WEARING LONG SLEEVES.
CHIRA (GLANCE)
OH, YEAH.
YOU'RE RIGHT.
Y'KNOW, SENGOKU SAID, "MIYAMURA-KUN'S FIRED UP ABOUT THIS! THAT TRAITOR!"
ぎょっ
GYO (JOLT)
HUH!?
TRAITOR ...!?
WELL, I DIDN'T REALLY SEE THE POINT IN WORKING HARD AT THIS KIND OF THING BEFORE.
TO BE HONEST, I THINK THIS STUFF IS BORING.

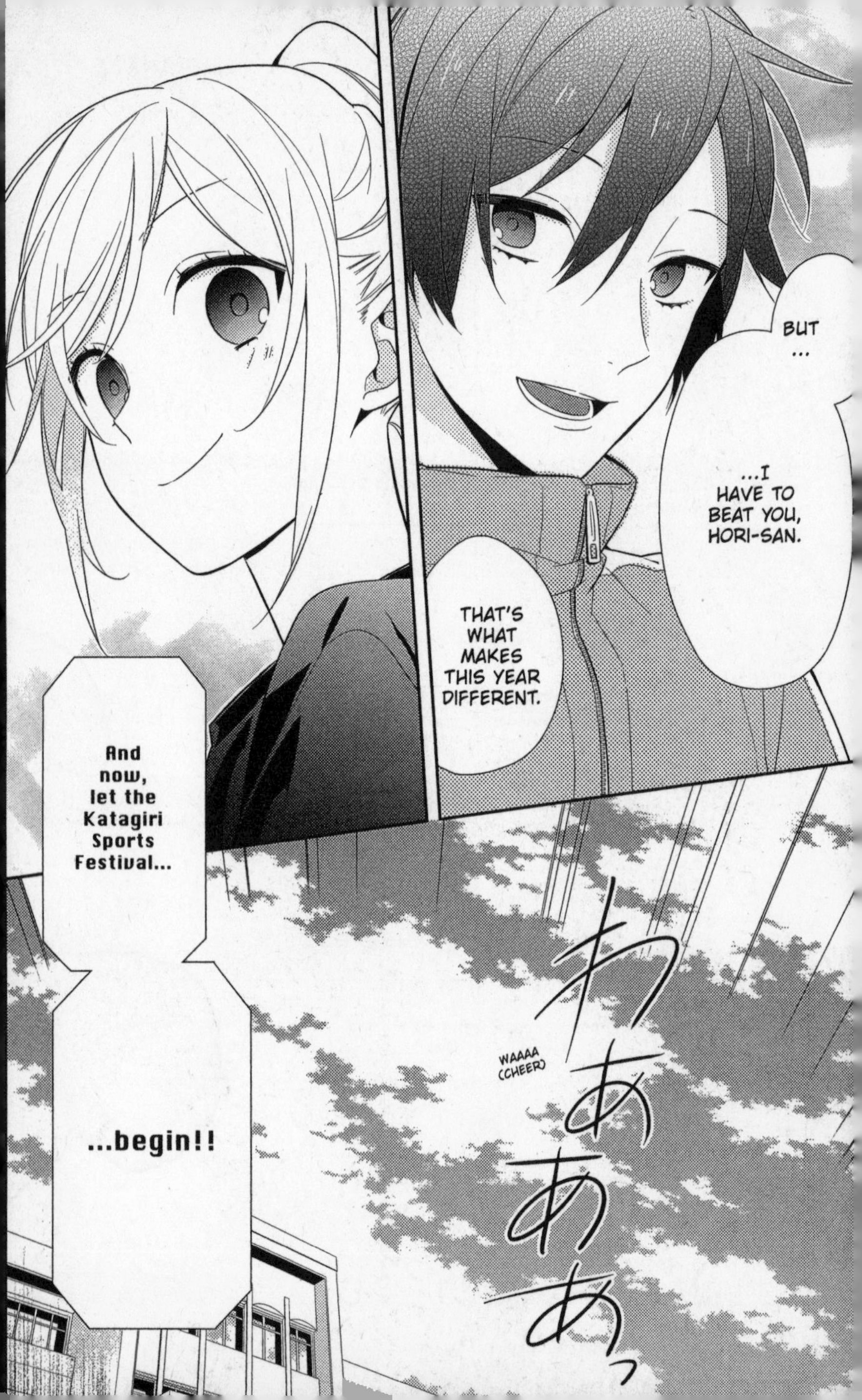
BUT ...
...I HAVE TO BEAT YOU, HORI-SAN.
THAT'S WHAT MAKES THIS YEAR DIFFERENT.
And now, let the Katagiri Sports Festival...
...begin!!
わあああっ
WAAAA (CHEER)

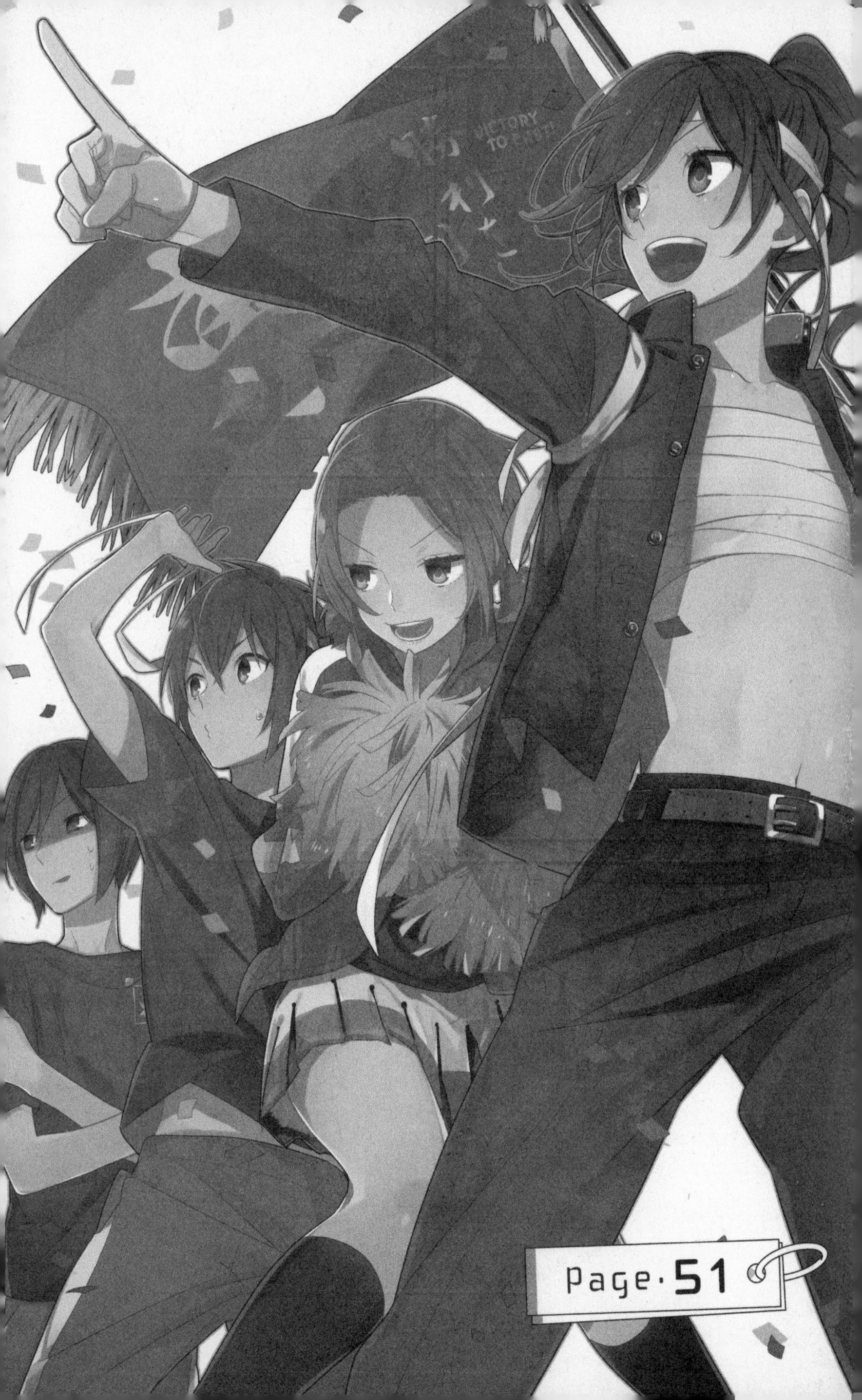
VICTORY TO ENEMY
Page·51

HORIMIYA

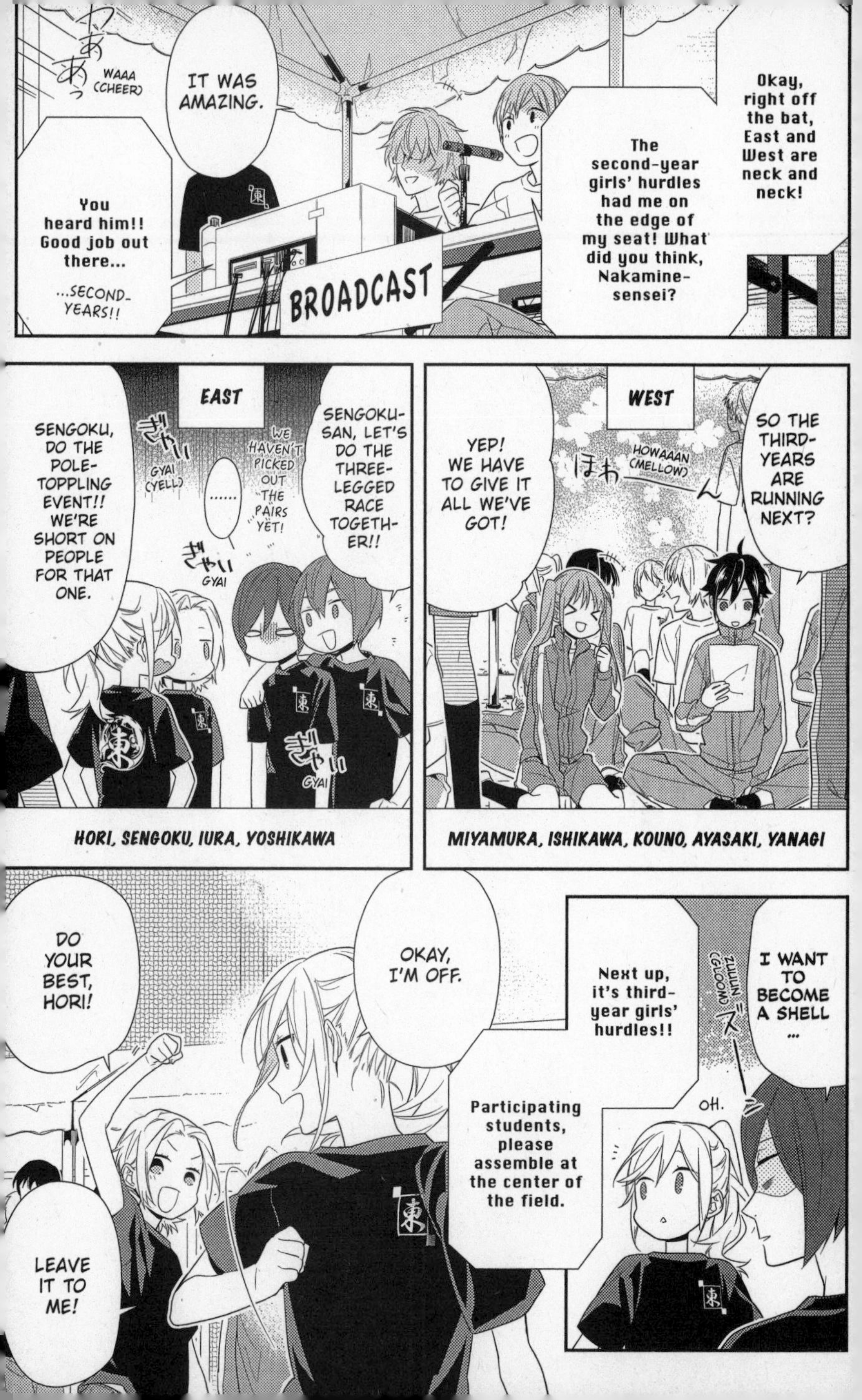
Okay, right off the bat, East and West are neck and neck!
The second-year girls' hurdles had me on the edge of my seat! What did you think, Nakamine-sensei?
IT WAS AMAZING.
WAAA (CHEER)
You heard him!! Good job out there...
...SECOND-YEARS!!
BROADCAST
WEST
SO THE THIRD-YEARS ARE RUNNING NEXT?
YEP! WE HAVE TO GIVE IT ALL WE'VE GOT!
HOWAAAN (MELLOW)
MIYAMURA, ISHIKAWA, KOUNO, AYASAKI, YANAGI
EAST
SENGOKU-SAN, LET'S DO THE THREE-LEGGED RACE TOGETHER!!
WE HAVEN'T PICKED OUT THE PAIRS YET!
......
SENGOKU, DO THE POLE-TOPPLING EVENT!! WE'RE SHORT ON PEOPLE FOR THAT ONE.
GYAI (YELL)
GYAI
GYAI
HORI, SENGOKU, IURA, YOSHIKAWA
I WANT TO BECOME A SHELL...
ZUUUN (GLOOM)
Next up, it's third-year girls' hurdles!!
Participating students, please assemble at the center of the field.
OH.
OKAY, I'M OFF.
DO YOUR BEST, HORI!
LEAVE IT TO ME!

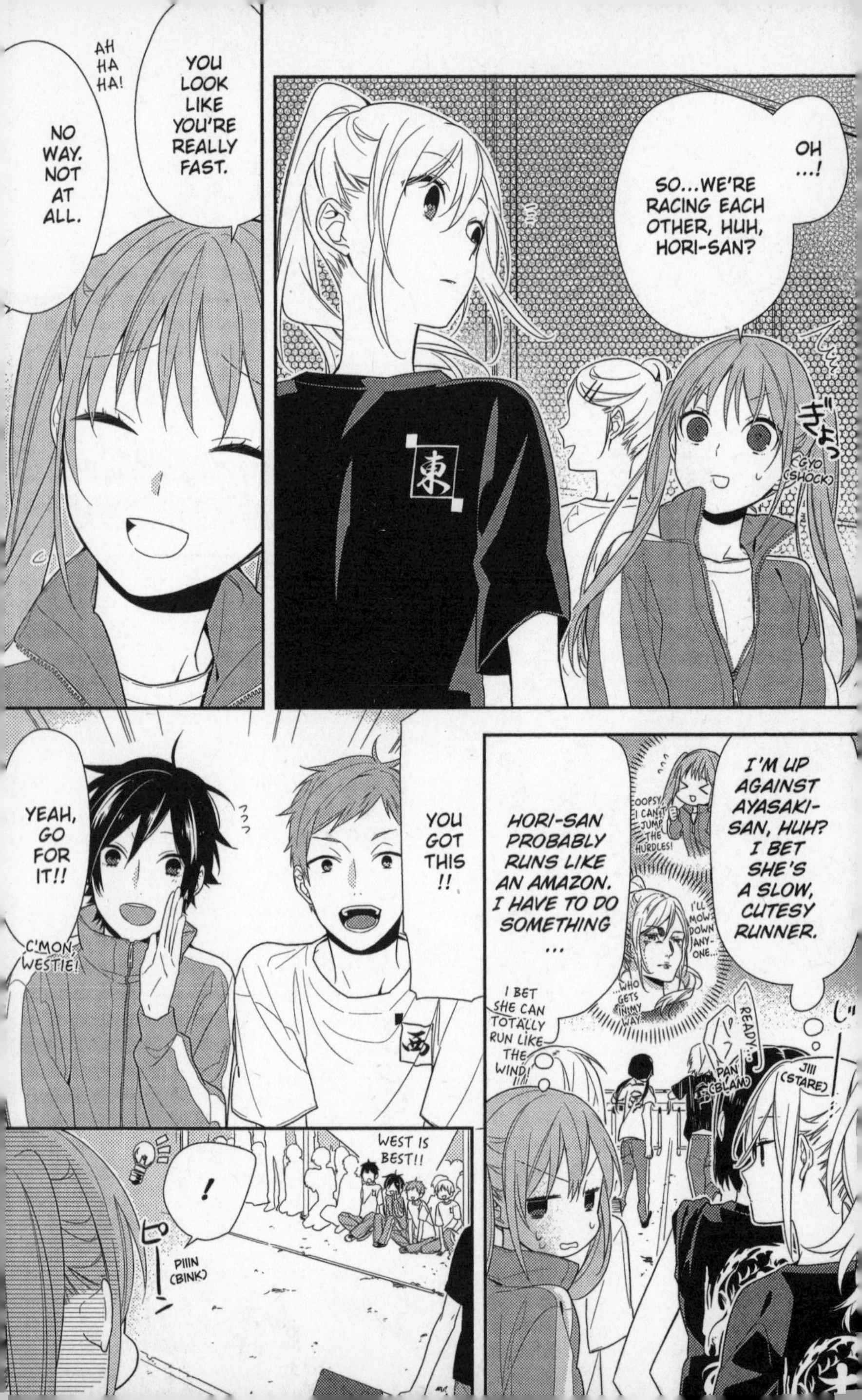
OH ...!
SO...WE'RE RACING EACH OTHER, HUH, HORI-SAN?
ぎょっ
GYO (SHOCK)
YOU LOOK LIKE YOU'RE REALLY FAST.
AH HA HA!
NO WAY. NOT AT ALL.
I'M UP AGAINST AYASAKI-SAN, HUH? I BET SHE'S A SLOW, CUTESY RUNNER.
OOPSY I CAN'T JUMP THE HURDLES!
HORI-SAN PROBABLY RUNS LIKE AN AMAZON. I HAVE TO DO SOMETHING ...
I'LL MOW DOWN ANY-ONE...
...WHO GETS IN MY WAY
I BET SHE CAN TOTALLY RUN LIKE THE WIND!
READY...
PAN (BLAM)
JIII (STARE)
YOU GOT THIS !!
YEAH, GO FOR IT!!
C'MON, WESTIE!
WEST IS BEST!!
!
PIIIN (BINK)

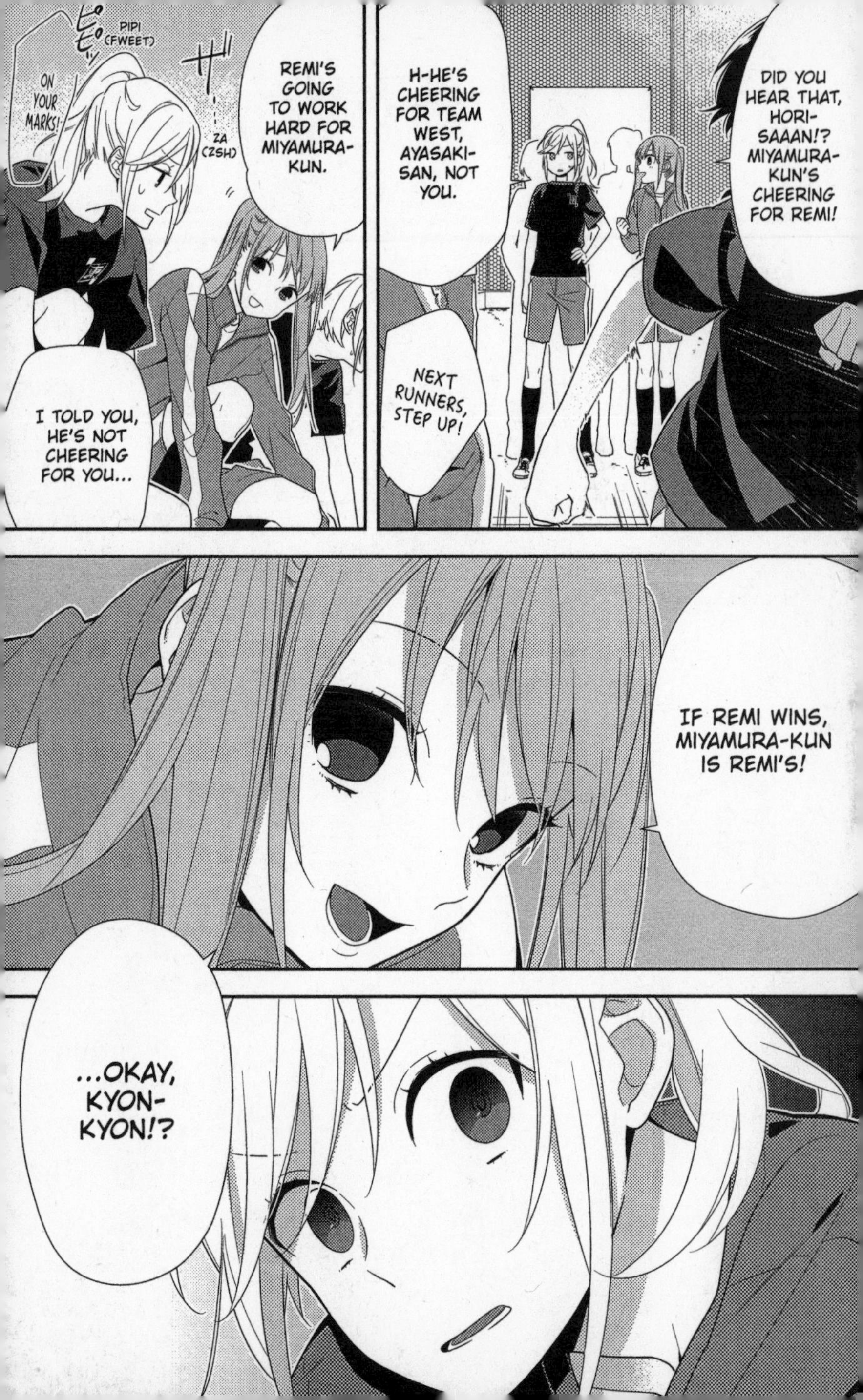
DID YOU HEAR THAT, HORI-SAAAN!? MIYAMURA-KUN'S CHEERING FOR REMI!
H-HE'S CHEERING FOR TEAM WEST, AYASAKI-SAN, NOT YOU.
NEXT RUNNERS, STEP UP!
REMI'S GOING TO WORK HARD FOR MIYAMURA-KUN.
ZA (ZSH)
PIPI (FWEET)
ON YOUR MARKS!
I TOLD YOU, HE'S NOT CHEERING FOR YOU...
IF REMI WINS, MIYAMURA-KUN IS REMI'S!
...OKAY, KYON-KYON!?

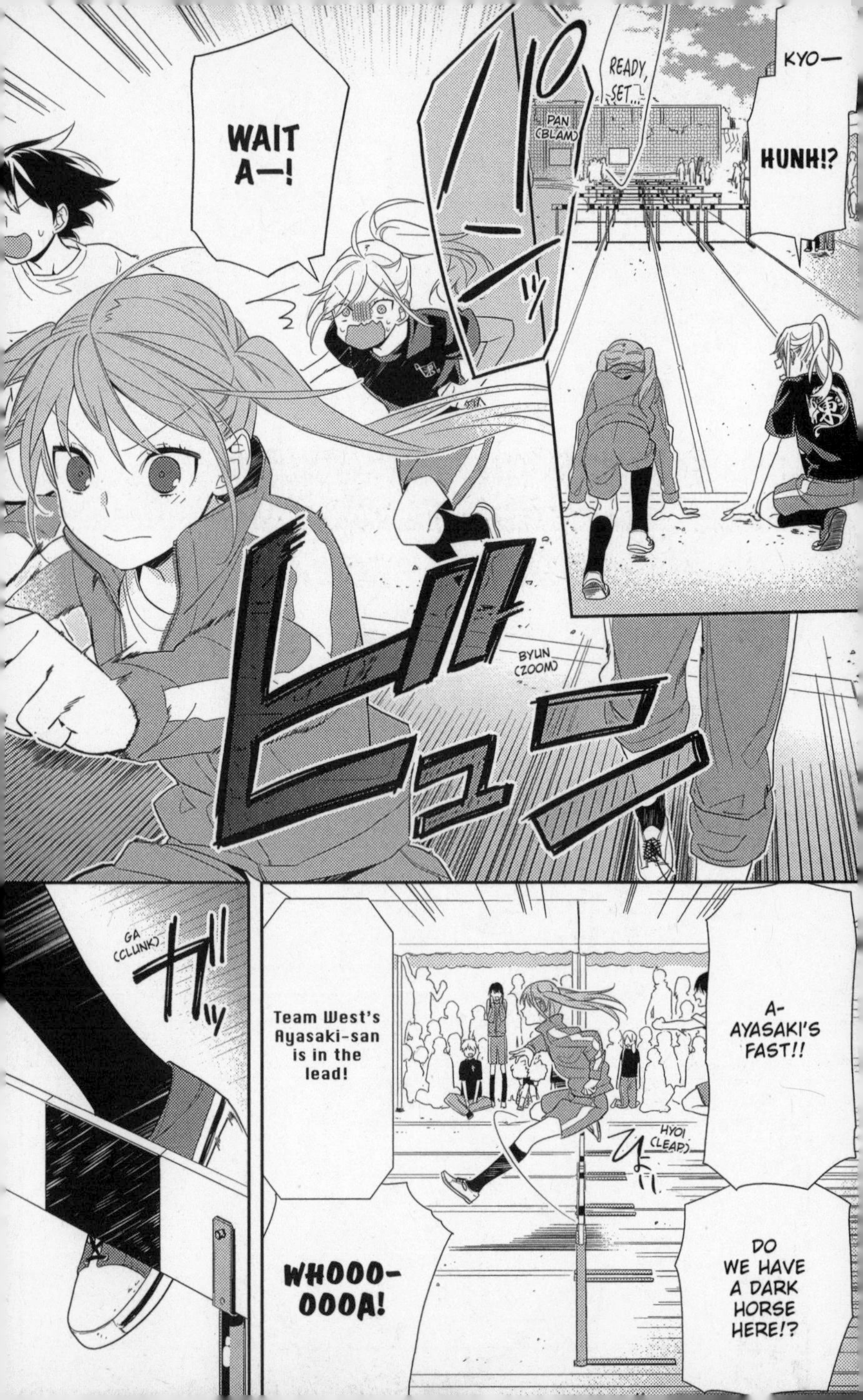
KYO—
HUNH!?
READY, SET...
PAN (BLAM)
WAIT A—!
BYUN (ZOOM)
A-AYASAKI'S FAST!!
Team West's Ayasaki-san is in the lead!
HYOI (LEAP)
DO WE HAVE A DARK HORSE HERE!?
WHOOO-OOOA!
GA (CLUNK)

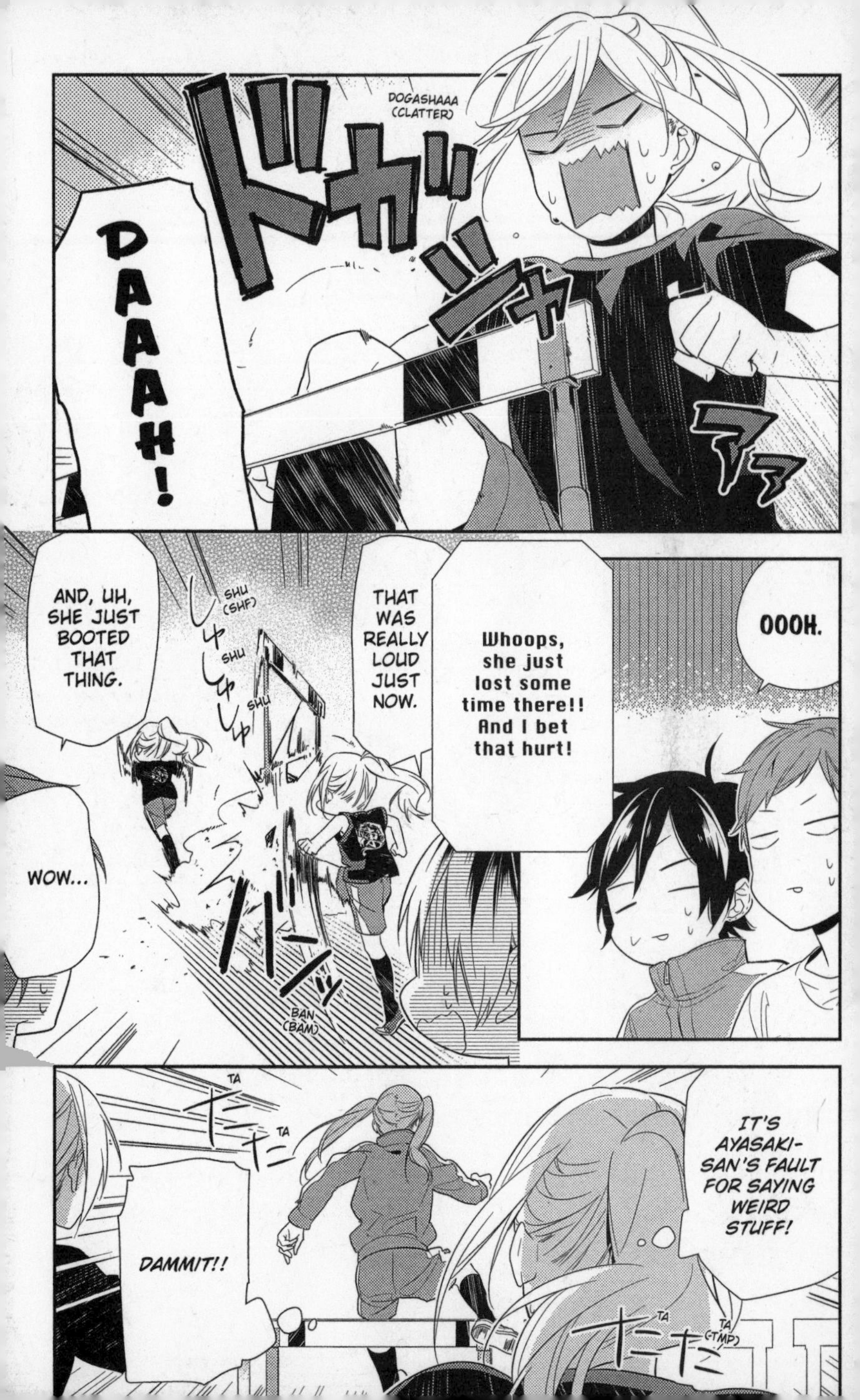
DOGASHAAA (CLATTER)
DAAAAH!
OOOH.
Whoops, she just lost some time there!! And I bet that hurt!
THAT WAS REALLY LOUD JUST NOW.
SHU (SHF)
SHU
SHU
AND, UH, SHE JUST BOOTED THAT THING.
WOW...
BAN (BAM)
IT'S AYASAKI-SAN'S FAULT FOR SAYING WEIRD STUFF!
TA
TA (TMP)
TA
TA
DAMMIT!!

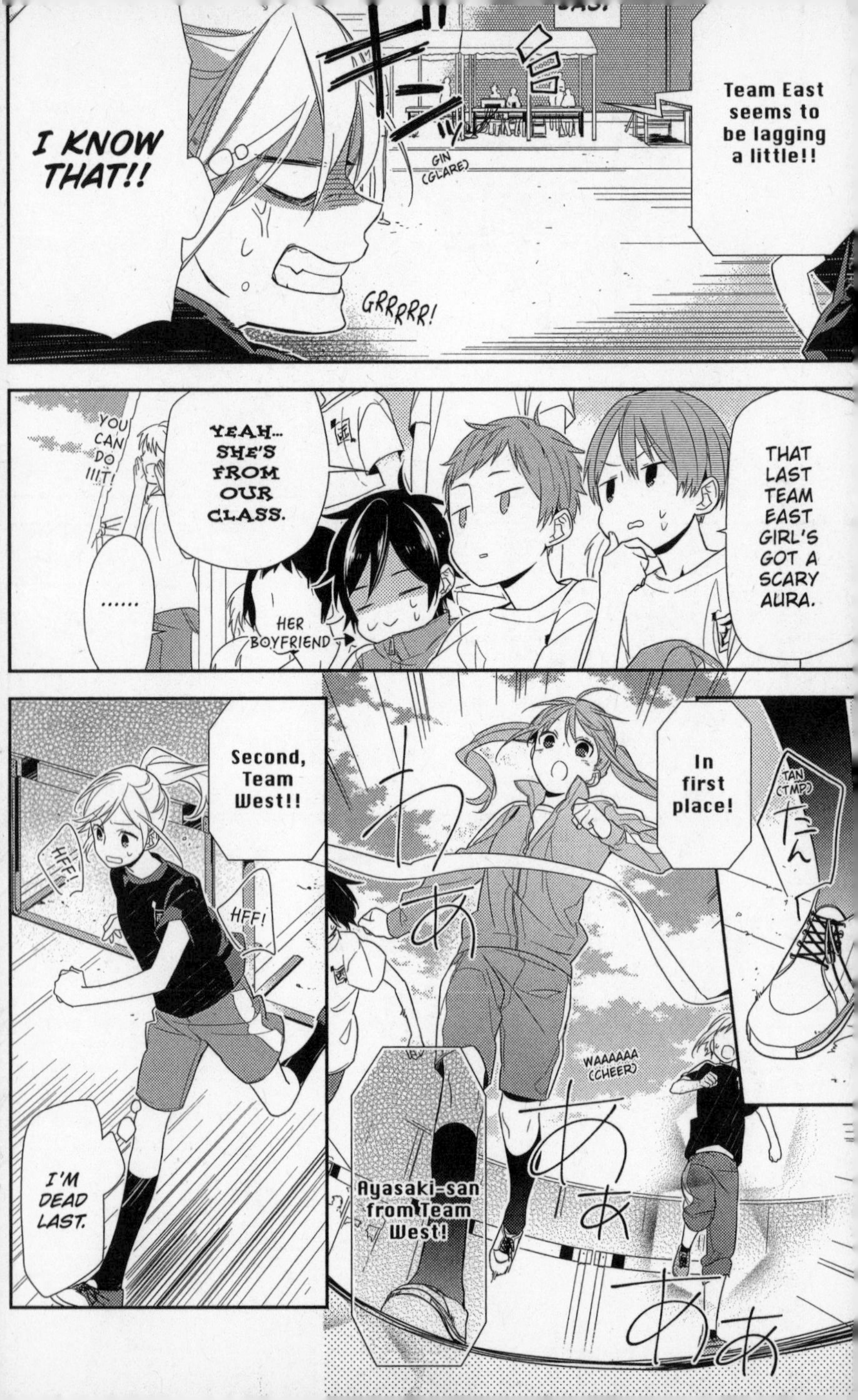

Team East seems to be lagging a little!!
GIN (GLARE)
I KNOW THAT!!
GRRRRR!
THAT LAST TEAM EAST GIRL'S GOT A SCARY AURA.
YEAH... SHE'S FROM OUR CLASS.
HER BOYFRIEND
YOU CAN DO IIIT!
......
TAN (TMP)
たん
In first place!
Ayasaki-san from Team West!
WAAAAAA (CHEER)
Second, Team West!!
HFF!
HFF!
I'M DEAD LAST.

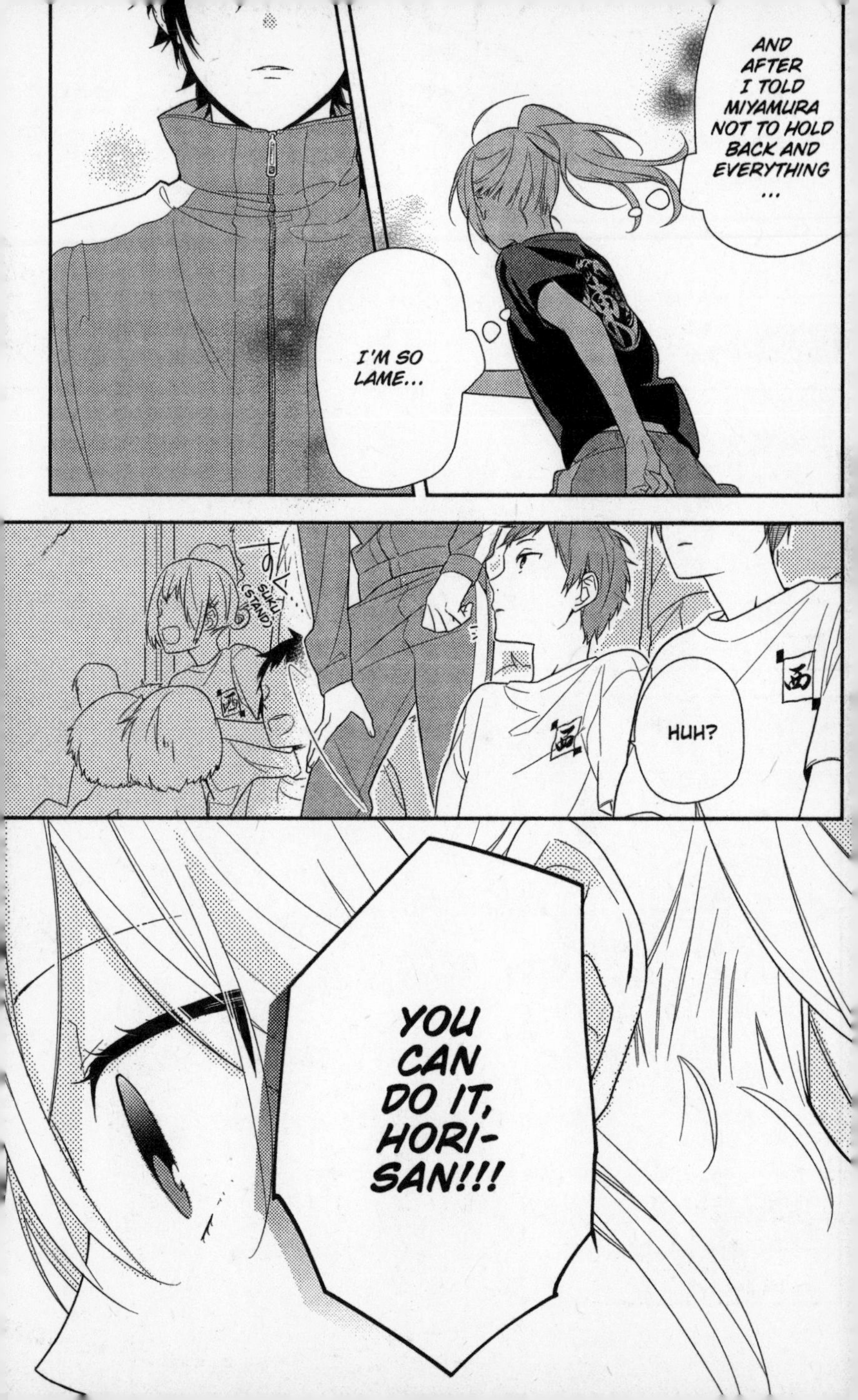
AND AFTER I TOLD MIYAMURA NOT TO HOLD BACK AND EVERYTHING ...
I'M SO LAME...
HUH?
SUKU (STAND)
YOU CAN DO IT, HORI-SAN!!!

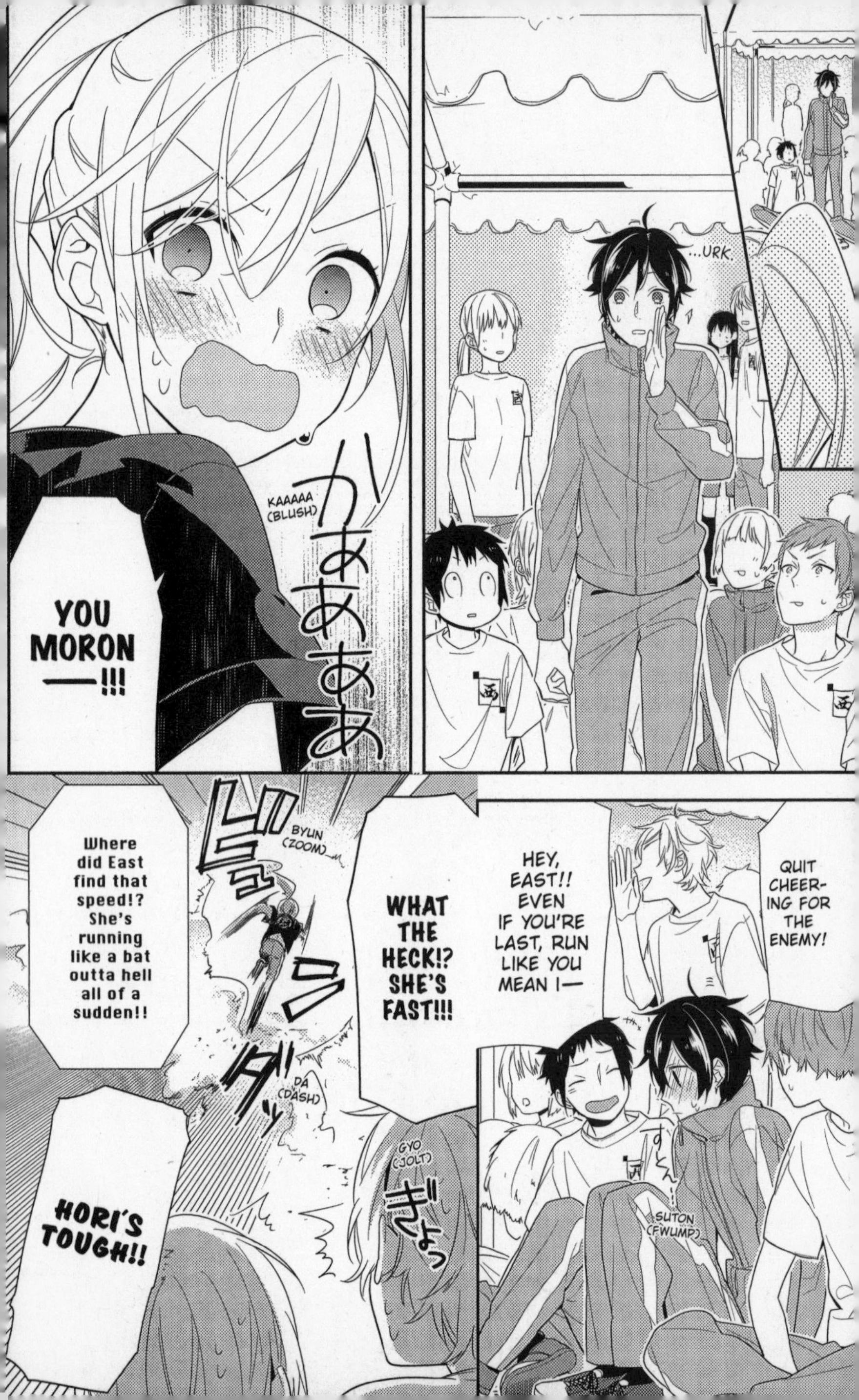
...URK.
かあああああ
KAAAAA (BLUSH)
YOU MORON—!!!
HEY, EAST!! EVEN IF YOU'RE LAST, RUN LIKE YOU MEAN I—
QUIT CHEERING FOR THE ENEMY!
すとん
SUTON (FWUMP)
WHAT THE HECK!? SHE'S FAST!!!
びゅん
BYUN (ZOOM)
Where did East find that speed!? She's running like a bat outta hell all of a sudden!!
ダッ
DA (DASH)
ぎょっ
GYO (JOLT)
HORI'S TOUGH!!

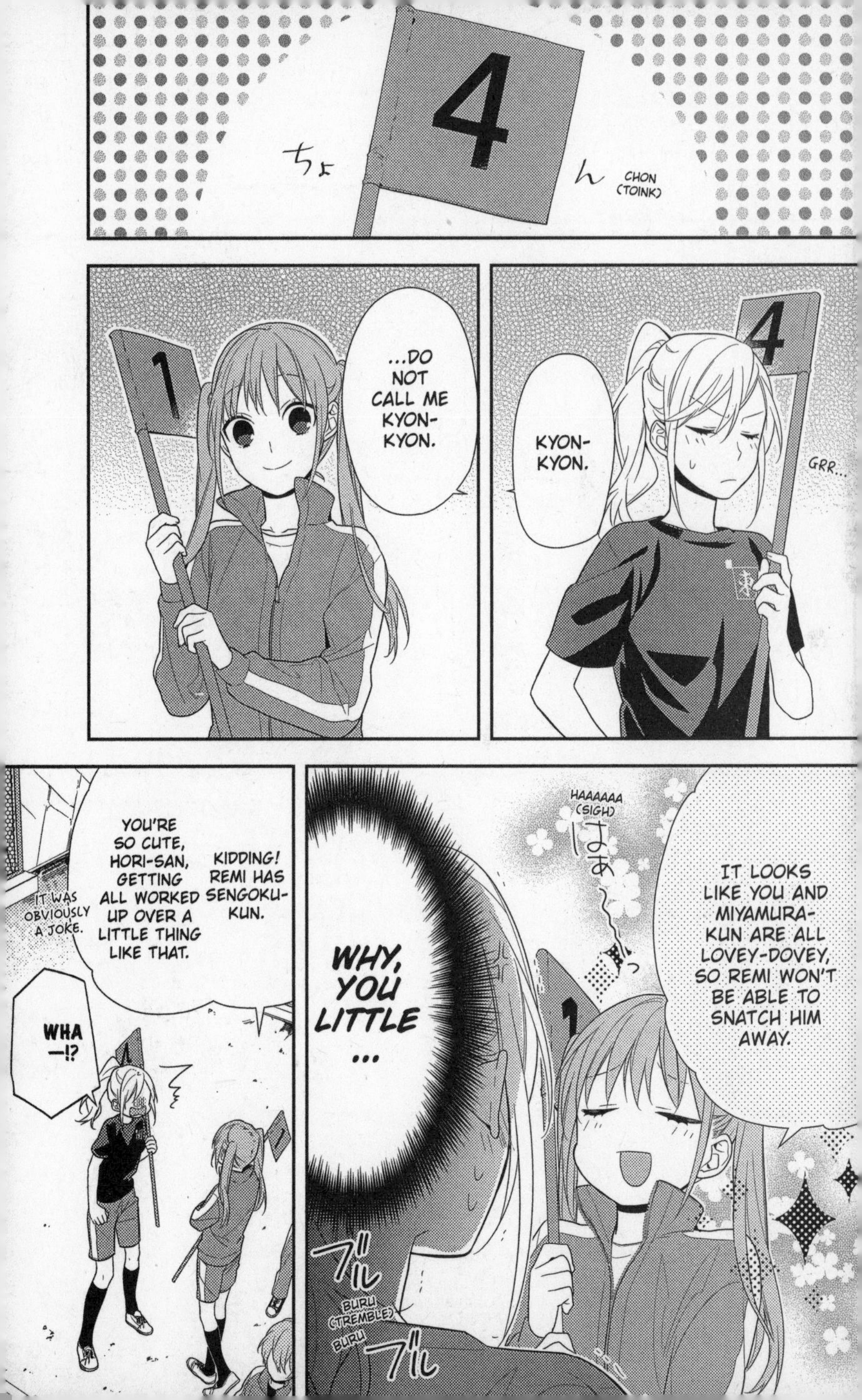
ちょん
CHON (TOINK)
KYON-KYON.
GRR...
...DO NOT CALL ME KYON-KYON.
はぁ~
HAAAAAA (SIGH)
IT LOOKS LIKE YOU AND MIYAMURA-KUN ARE ALL LOVEY-DOVEY, SO REMI WON'T BE ABLE TO SNATCH HIM AWAY.
WHY, YOU LITTLE...
ブル ブル
BURU (TREMBLE) BURU
KIDDING! REMI HAS SENGOKU-KUN.
YOU'RE SO CUTE, HORI-SAN, GETTING ALL WORKED UP OVER A LITTLE THING LIKE THAT.
IT WAS OBVIOUSLY A JOKE.
WHA—!?

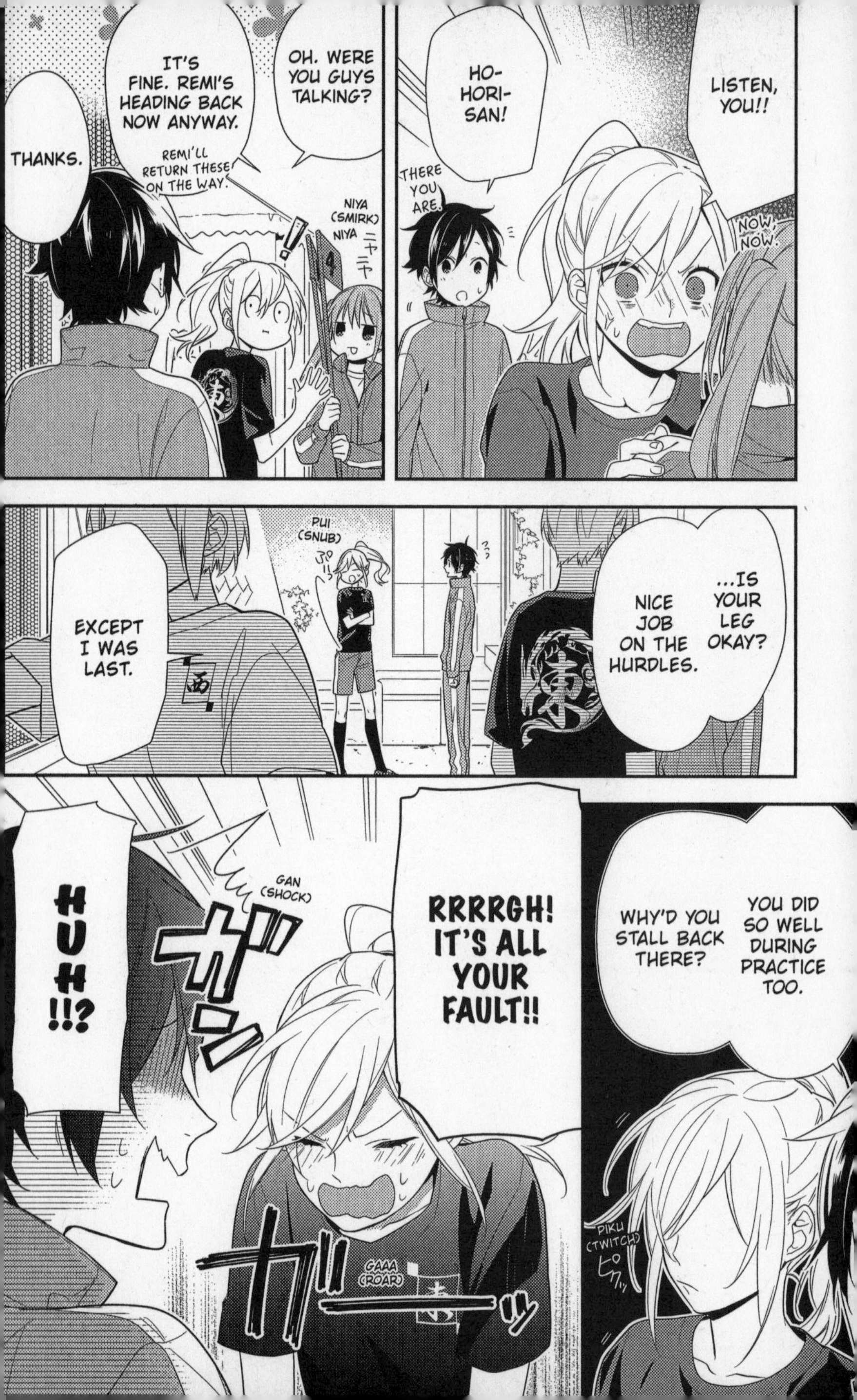
LISTEN, YOU!!
HO-HORI-SAN!
NOW, NOW.
THERE YOU ARE.
OH. WERE YOU GUYS TALKING?
IT'S FINE. REMI'S HEADING BACK NOW ANYWAY.
REMI'LL RETURN THESE ON THE WAY.
NIYA (SMIRK) NIYA
ニヤニヤ
THANKS.
...IS YOUR LEG OKAY?
NICE JOB ON THE HURDLES.
PUI (SNUB)
ぷい
EXCEPT I WAS LAST.
YOU DID SO WELL DURING PRACTICE TOO.
WHY'D YOU STALL BACK THERE?
PIKU (TWITCH)
RRRRGH! IT'S ALL YOUR FAULT!!
GAN (SHOCK)
GAAA (ROAR)
HUH!!?

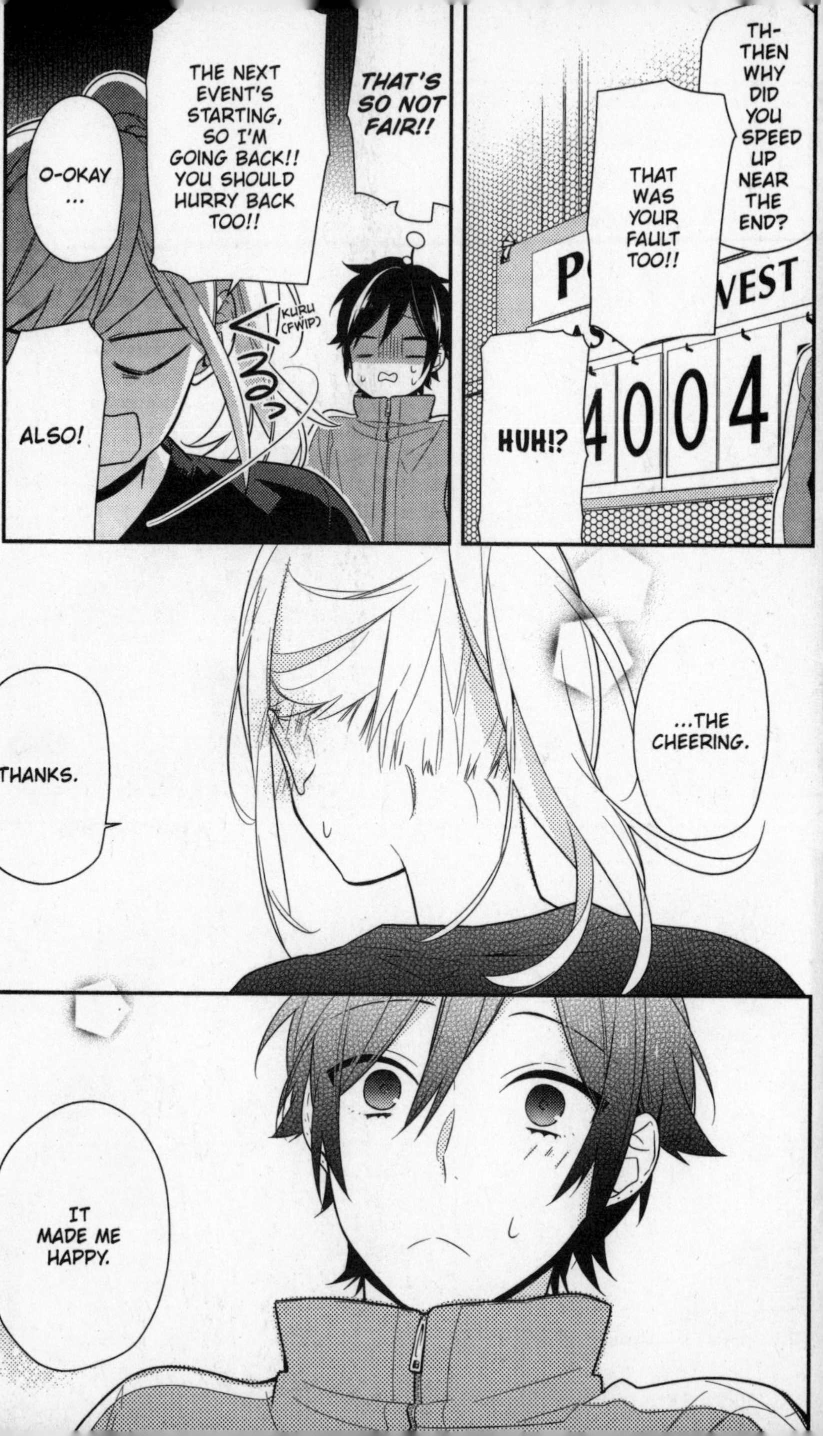
TH-THEN WHY DID YOU SPEED UP NEAR THE END?
THAT WAS YOUR FAULT TOO!!
HUH!?
4004
THAT'S SO NOT FAIR!!
THE NEXT EVENT'S STARTING, SO I'M GOING BACK!! YOU SHOULD HURRY BACK TOO!!
O-OKAY ...
KURU (FWIP)
ALSO!
...THE CHEERING.
THANKS.
IT MADE ME HAPPY.

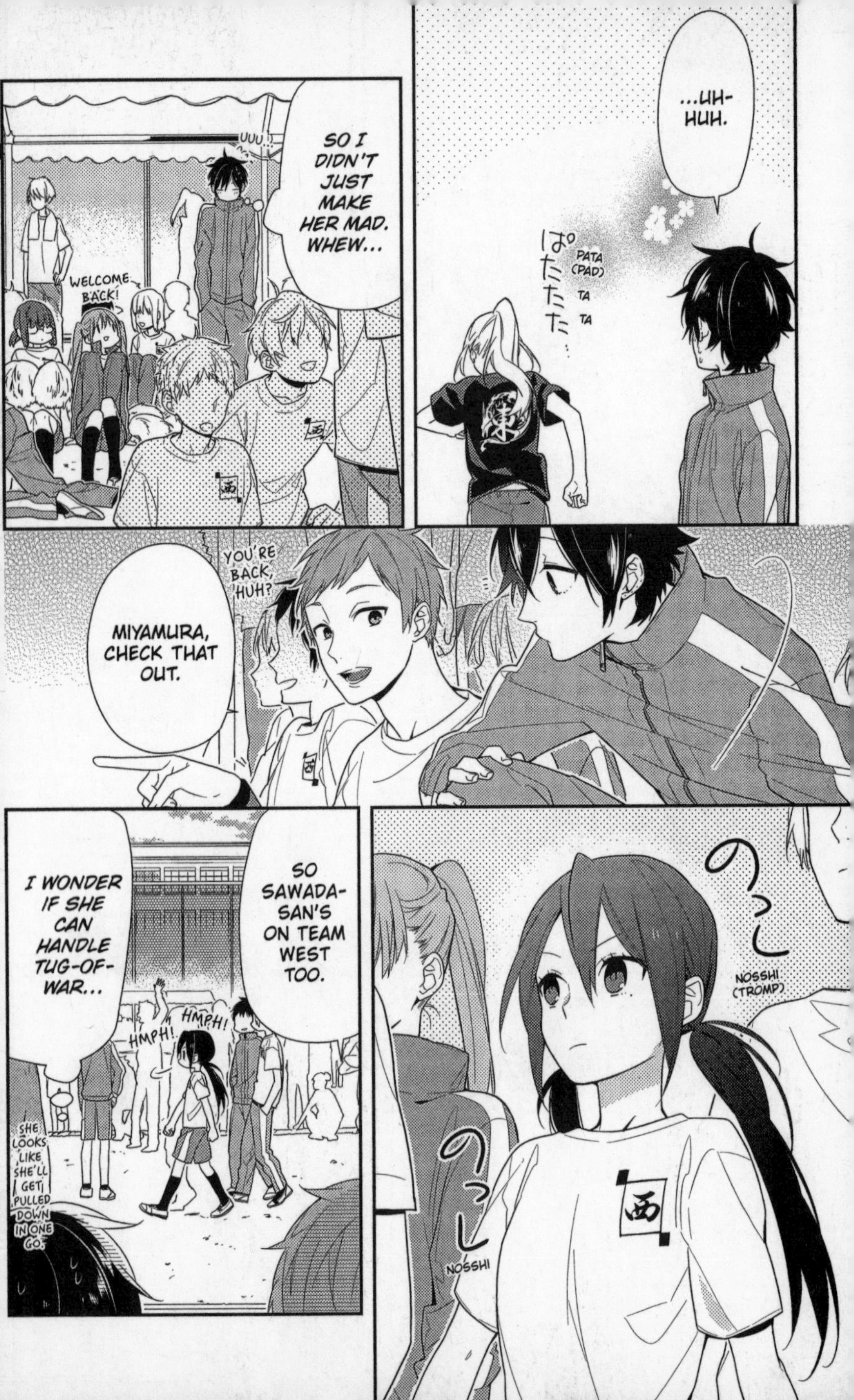

...UH-HUH.
ぱたたた
PATA (PAD) TA TA
SO I DIDN'T JUST MAKE HER MAD. WHEW...
UUU...!!
WELCOME BACK!
YOU'RE BACK, HUH?
MIYAMURA, CHECK THAT OUT.
のっし
NOSSHI (TROMP)
のっし
NOSSHI
SO SAWADA-SAN'S ON TEAM WEST TOO.
I WONDER IF SHE CAN HANDLE TUG-OF-WAR...
HMPH!
HMPH!
SHE LOOKS LIKE SHE'LL GET PULLED DOWN IN ONE GO.

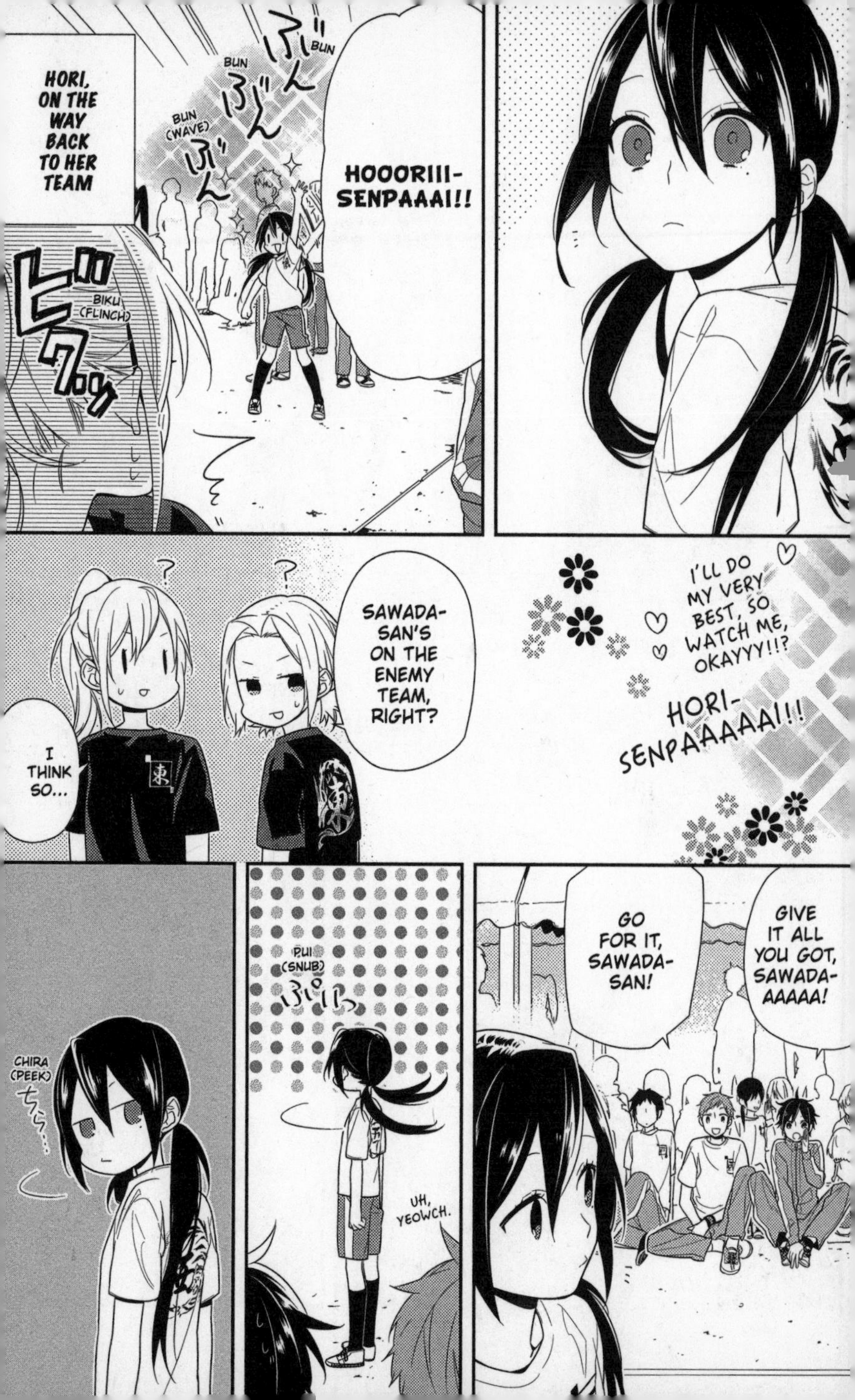
HOOORIII-SENPAAAI!!
ぶん BUN
ぶん BUN
ぶん BUN (WAVE)
HORI, ON THE WAY BACK TO HER TEAM
ビクッ BIKU (FLINCH)
I'LL DO MY VERY BEST, SO WATCH ME, OKAYYY!!?
HORI-SENPAAAAAI!!
SAWADA-SAN'S ON THE ENEMY TEAM, RIGHT?
I THINK SO...
GIVE IT ALL YOU GOT, SAWADA-AAAAA!
GO FOR IT, SAWADA-SAN!
ぷいっ PUI (SNUB)
UH, YEOWCH.
ちら… CHIRA (PEEK)

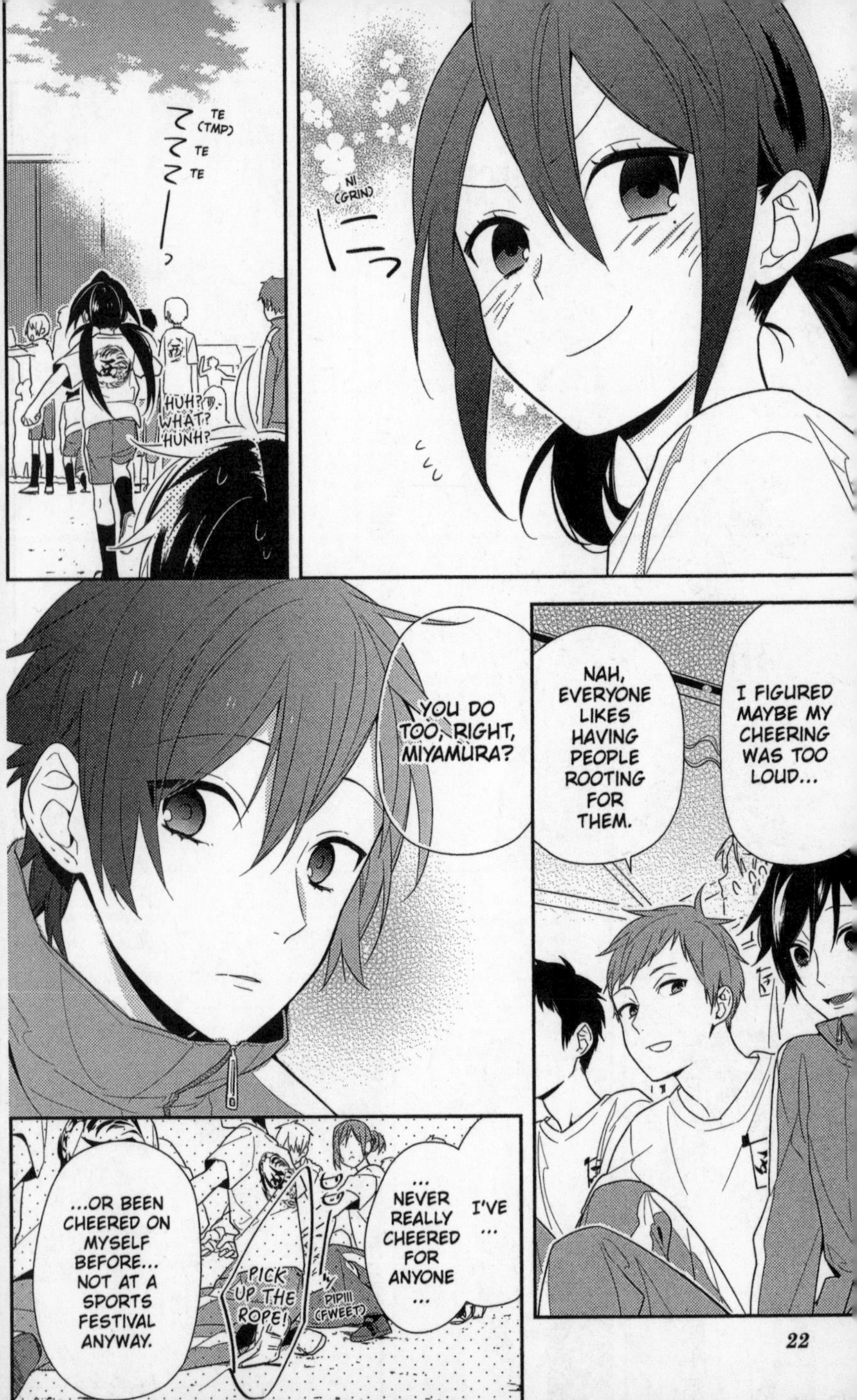
NI (GRIN)
TE (TMP) TE TE
HUH? WHAT? HUNH?
I FIGURED MAYBE MY CHEERING WAS TOO LOUD...
NAH, EVERYONE LIKES HAVING PEOPLE ROOTING FOR THEM.
YOU DO TOO, RIGHT, MIYAMURA?
I'VE...
...NEVER REALLY CHEERED FOR ANYONE...
PIPIII (FWEET)
PICK UP THE ROPE!
...OR BEEN CHEERED ON MYSELF BEFORE... NOT AT A SPORTS FESTIVAL ANYWAY.

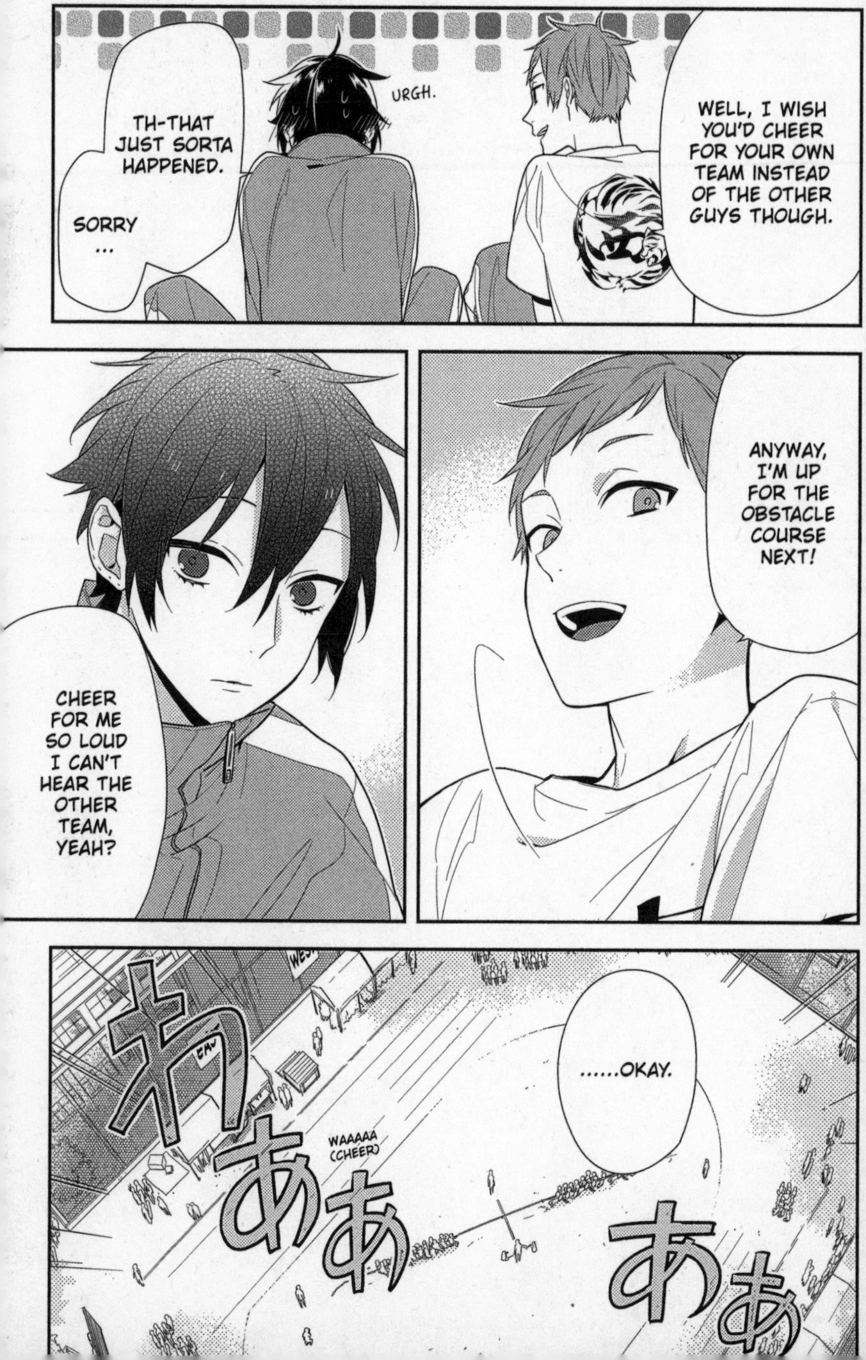
WELL, I WISH YOU'D CHEER FOR YOUR OWN TEAM INSTEAD OF THE OTHER GUYS THOUGH.
URGH.
TH-THAT JUST SORTA HAPPENED.
SORRY ...
ANYWAY, I'M UP FOR THE OBSTACLE COURSE NEXT!
CHEER FOR ME SO LOUD I CAN'T HEAR THE OTHER TEAM, YEAH?
......OKAY.
わあああ
WAAAAA (CHEER)

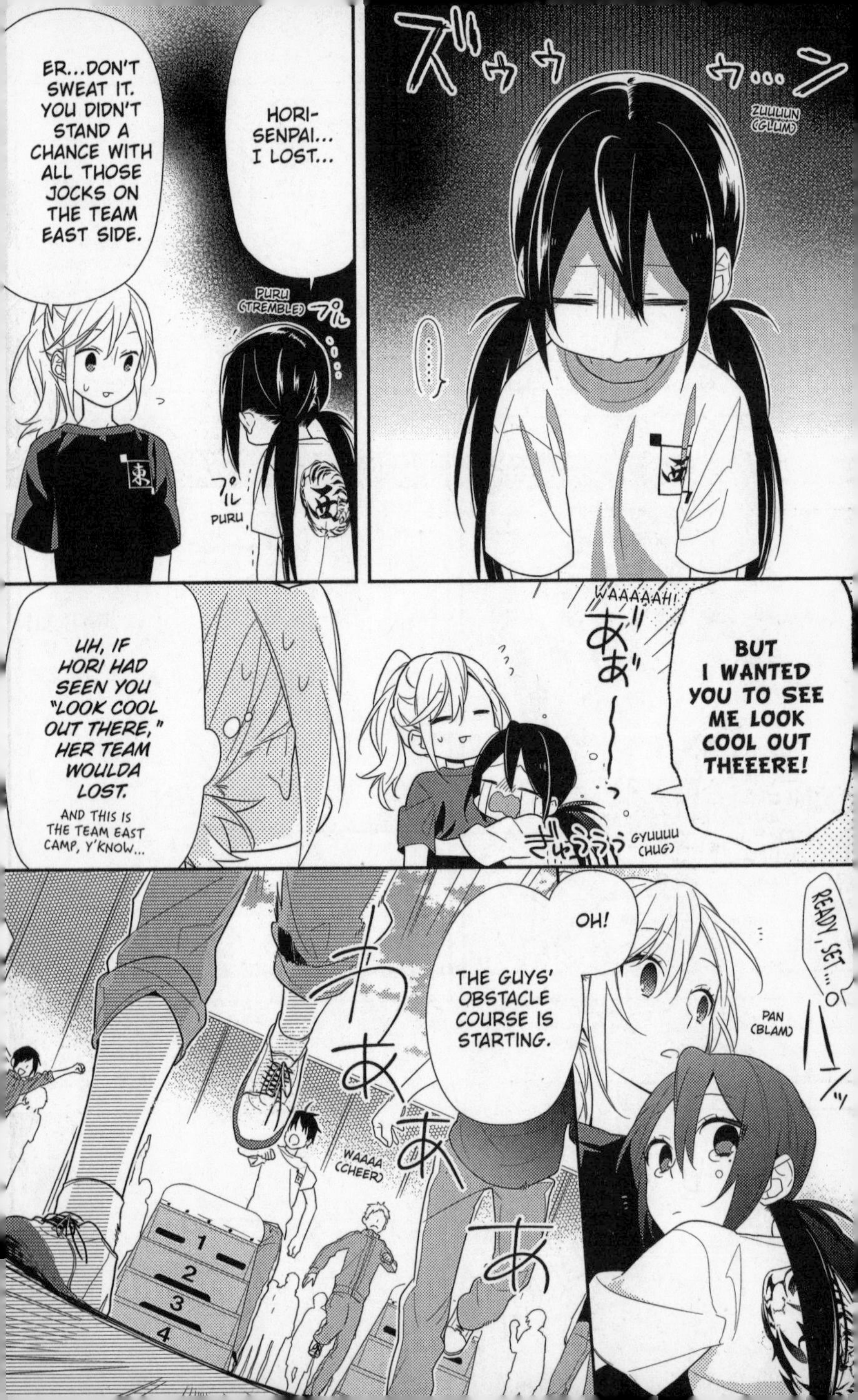
ズゥゥゥゥ…ン
ZUUUUN (GLUM)
......
HORI-SENPAI... I LOST...
PURU (TREMBLE) プル
プル PURU
ER...DON'T SWEAT IT. YOU DIDN'T STAND A CHANCE WITH ALL THOSE JOCKS ON THE TEAM EAST SIDE.
BUT I WANTED YOU TO SEE ME LOOK COOL OUT THEEERE!
あ゛あ゛ー
WAAAAAH!
ぎゅううう GYUUUU (HUG)
UH, IF HORI HAD SEEN YOU "LOOK COOL OUT THERE," HER TEAM WOULDA LOST.
AND THIS IS THE TEAM EAST CAMP, Y'KNOW...
READY, SET...
パーン
PAN (BLAM)
OH!
THE GUYS' OBSTACLE COURSE IS STARTING.
わああああ
WAAAA (CHEER)
1
2
3
4

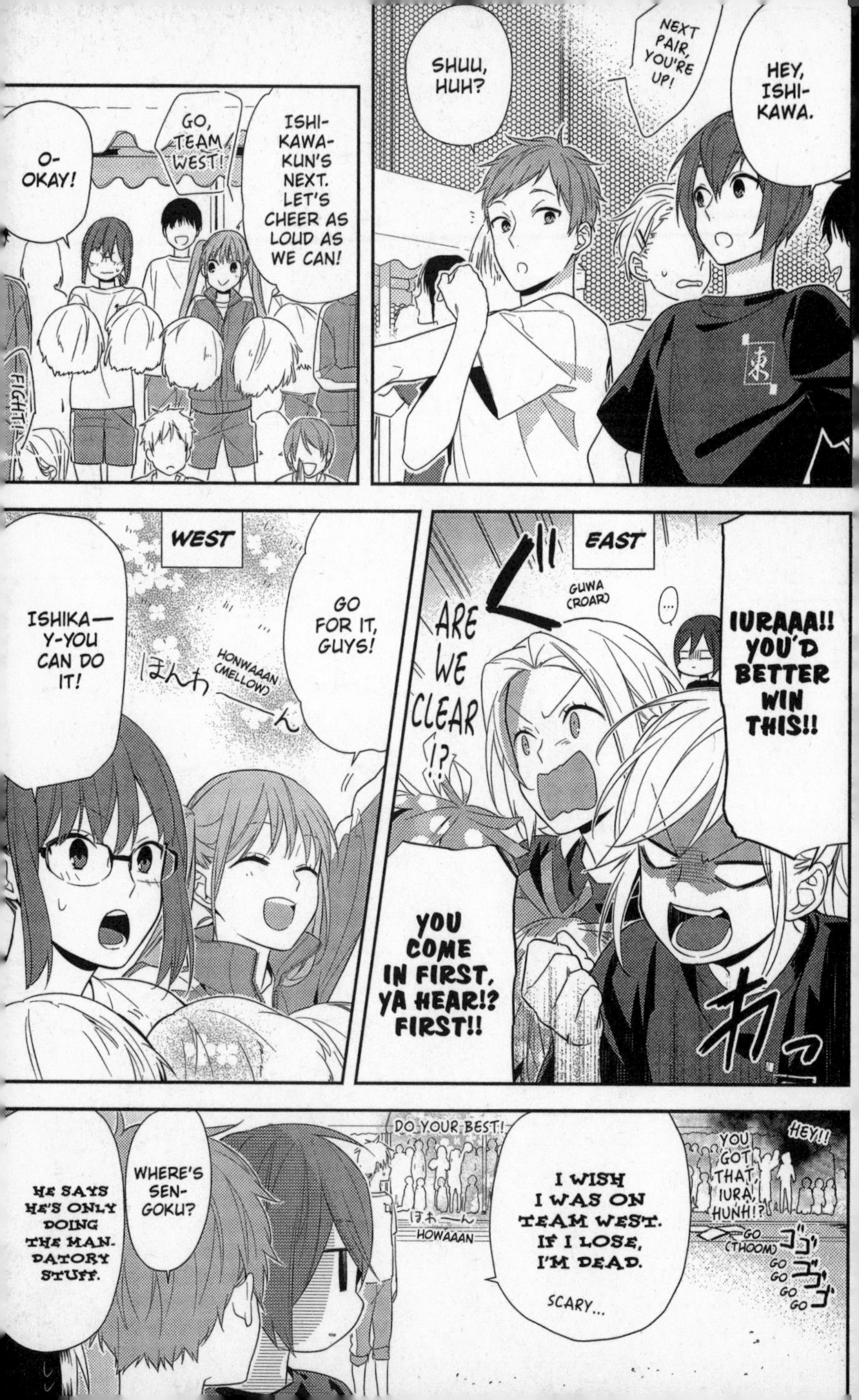
HEY, ISHIKAWA.
NEXT PAIR, YOU'RE UP!
SHUU, HUH?
ISHIKAWA-KUN'S NEXT. LET'S CHEER AS LOUD AS WE CAN!
GO, TEAM WEST!
O-OKAY!
FIGHT!
EAST
IURAAA!! YOU'D BETTER WIN THIS!!
...
GUWA (ROAR)
ARE WE CLEAR!?
YOU COME IN FIRST, YA HEAR!? FIRST!!
WEST
GO FOR IT, GUYS!
HONWAAAN (MELLOW)
ほんわ〜ん
ISHIKA— Y-YOU CAN DO IT!
HEY!!
YOU GOT THAT, IURA, HUNH!?
GO (THOOM) GO GO GO GO
DO YOUR BEST!
ほわ〜ん
HOWAAAN
I WISH I WAS ON TEAM WEST. IF I LOSE, I'M DEAD.
SCARY...
WHERE'S SENGOKU?
HE SAYS HE'S ONLY DOING THE MANDATORY STUFF.

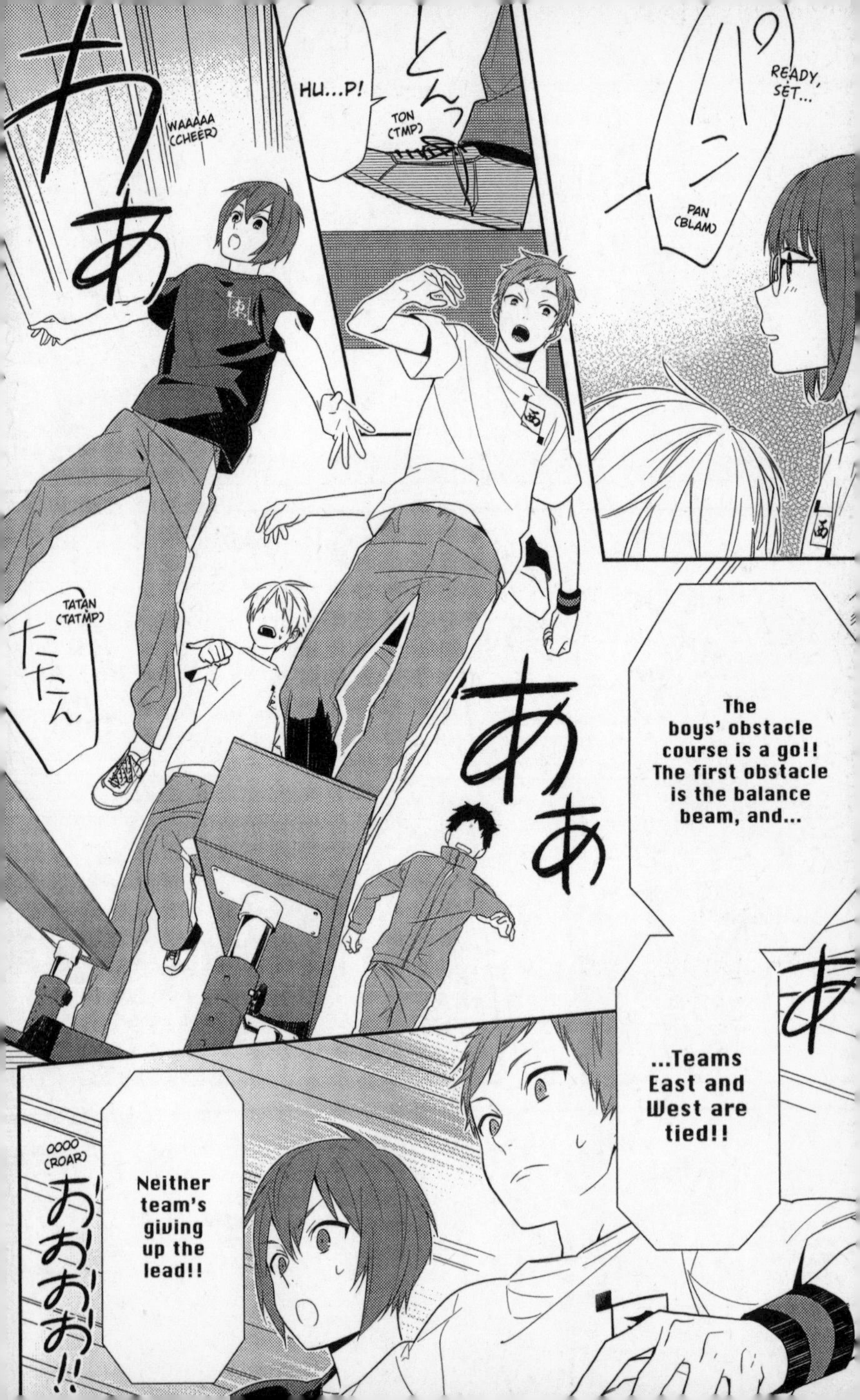
READY, SET...
パン
PAN (BLAM)
HU...P!
とんっ
TON (TMP)
わあああ
WAAAAA (CHEER)
たたん
TATAN (TATMP)
The boys' obstacle course is a go!! The first obstacle is the balance beam, and...
...Teams East and West are tied!!
Neither team's giving up the lead!!
おおおお!!
OOOO (ROAR)

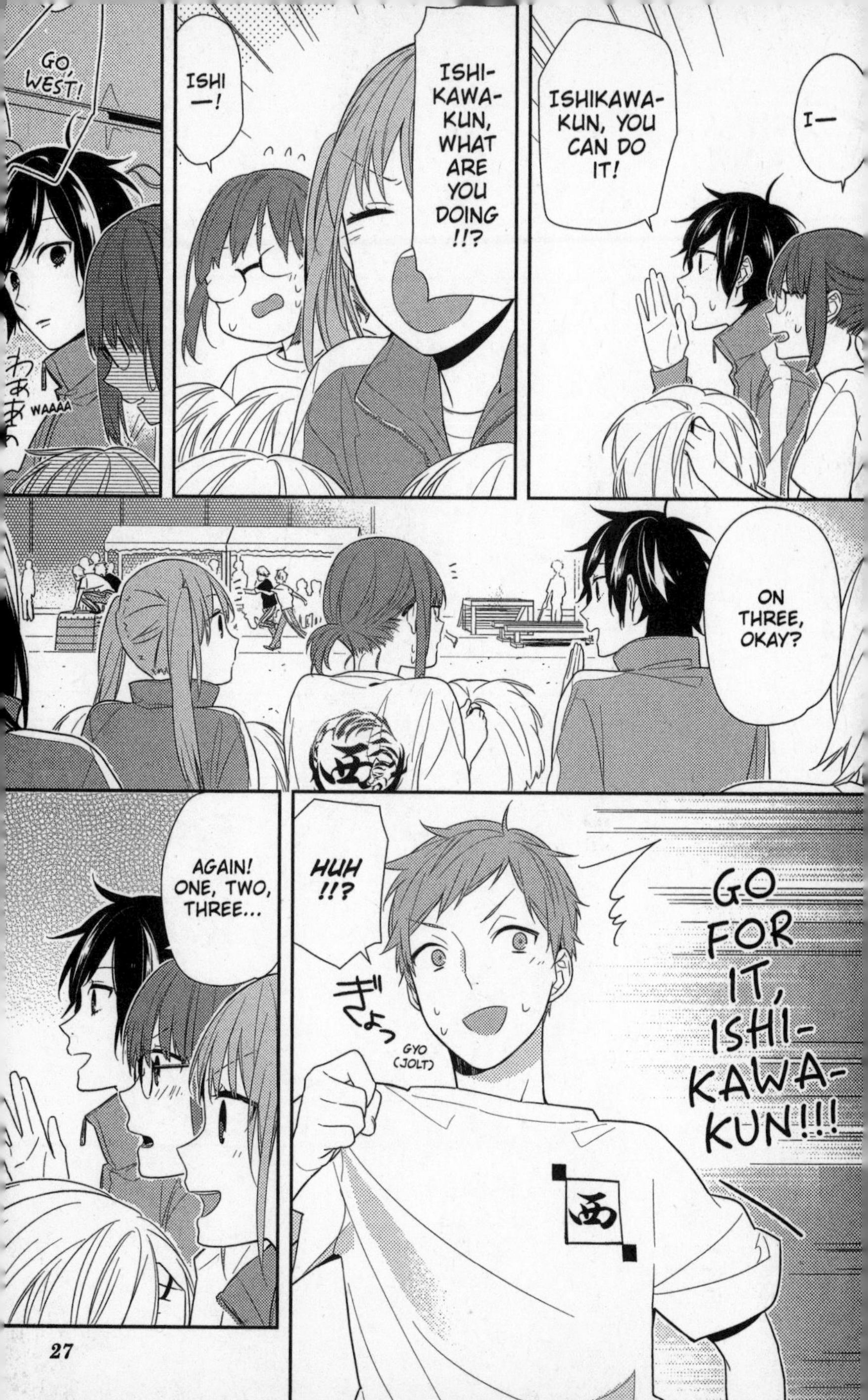
I—
ISHIKAWA-KUN, YOU CAN DO IT!
ISHI-KAWA-KUN, WHAT ARE YOU DOING!!?
ISHI—!
GO, WEST!
わぁぁ
WAAAA
ON THREE, OKAY?
GO FOR IT, ISHI-KAWA-KUN!!!
HUH!!?
ぎょっ
GYO (JOLT)
AGAIN! ONE, TWO, THREE...

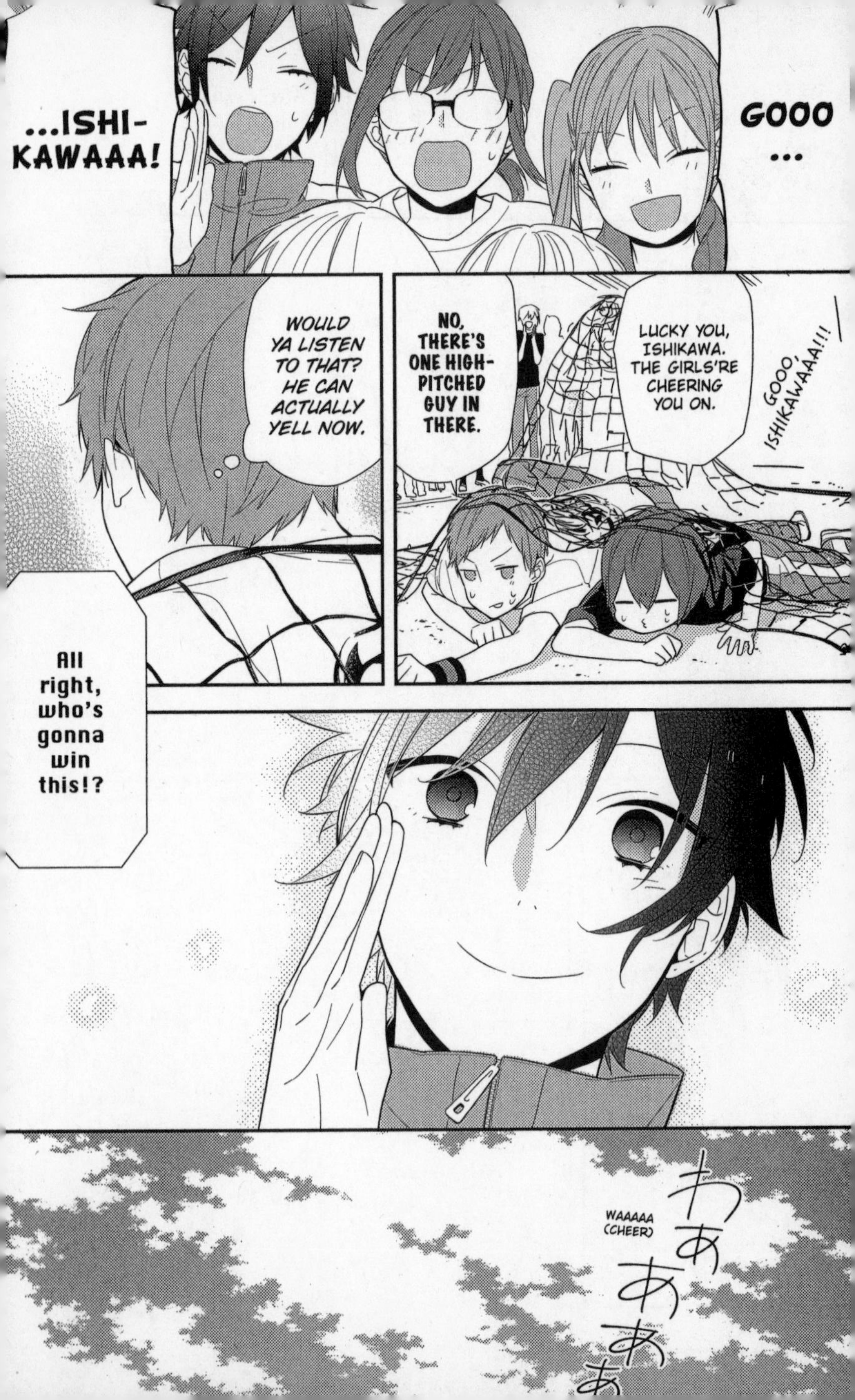
GOOO...
...ISHI-KAWAAA!
GOOO, ISHIKAWAAA!!!
LUCKY YOU, ISHIKAWA. THE GIRLS'RE CHEERING YOU ON.
NO, THERE'S ONE HIGH-PITCHED GUY IN THERE.
WOULD YA LISTEN TO THAT? HE CAN ACTUALLY YELL NOW.
All right, who's gonna win this!?
わあああ
WAAAAA (CHEER)

HORIMIYA

HORIMIYA

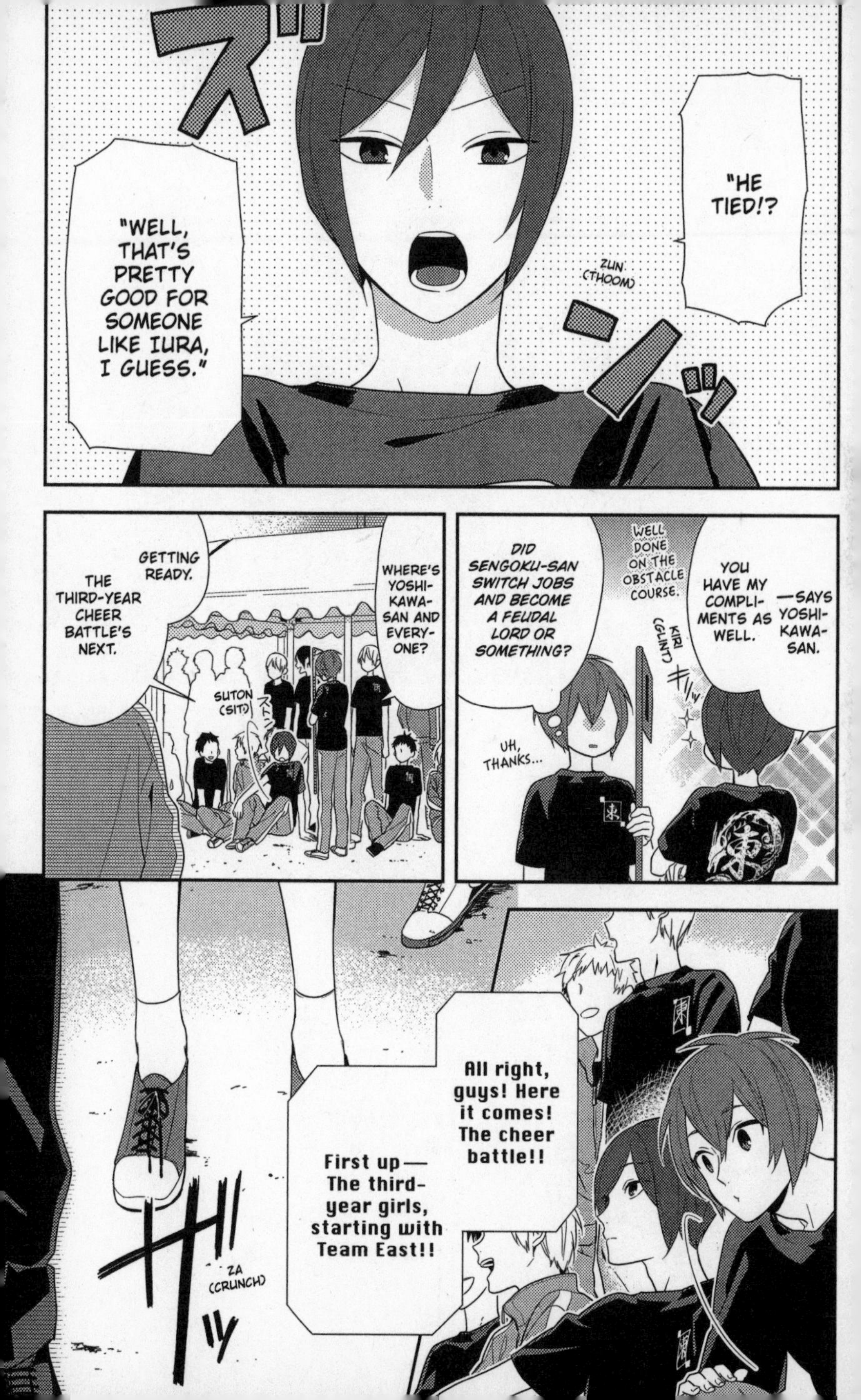
"HE TIED!?
ZUN (THOOM)
"WELL, THAT'S PRETTY GOOD FOR SOMEONE LIKE IURA, I GUESS."
WELL DONE ON THE OBSTACLE COURSE.
YOU HAVE MY COMPLIMENTS AS WELL. —SAYS YOSHIKAWA-SAN.
KIRI (GLINT)
DID SENGOKU-SAN SWITCH JOBS AND BECOME A FEUDAL LORD OR SOMETHING?
UH, THANKS...
WHERE'S YOSHIKAWA-SAN AND EVERYONE?
GETTING READY.
THE THIRD-YEAR CHEER BATTLE'S NEXT.
SUTON (SIT)
All right, guys! Here it comes! The cheer battle!!
First up— The third-year girls, starting with Team East!!
ZA (CRUNCH)

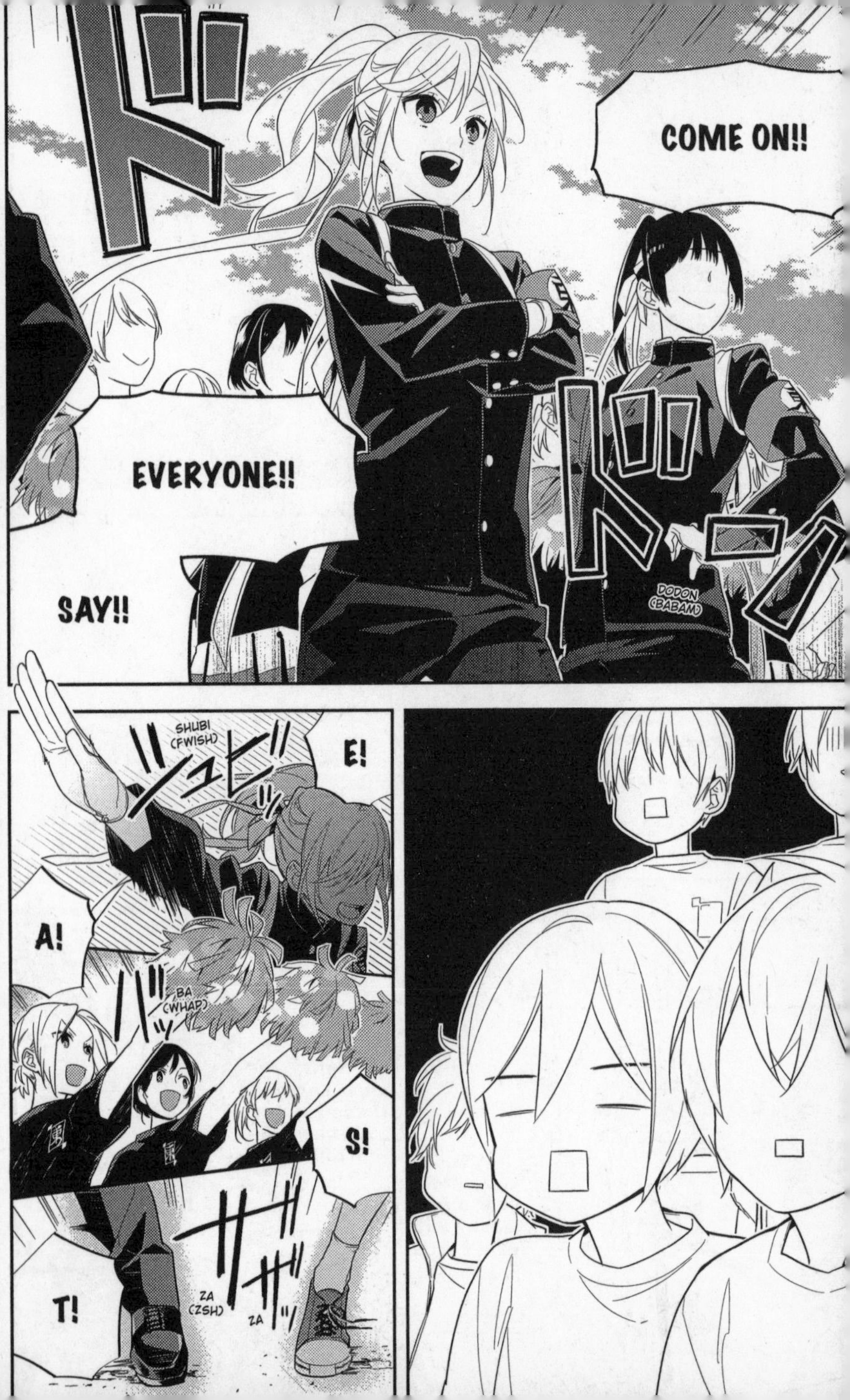
COME ON!!
DODON (BABAN)
EVERYONE!!
SAY!!
E!
SHUBI (FWISH)
A!
BA (WHAP)
S!
T!
ZA (ZSH)
ZA

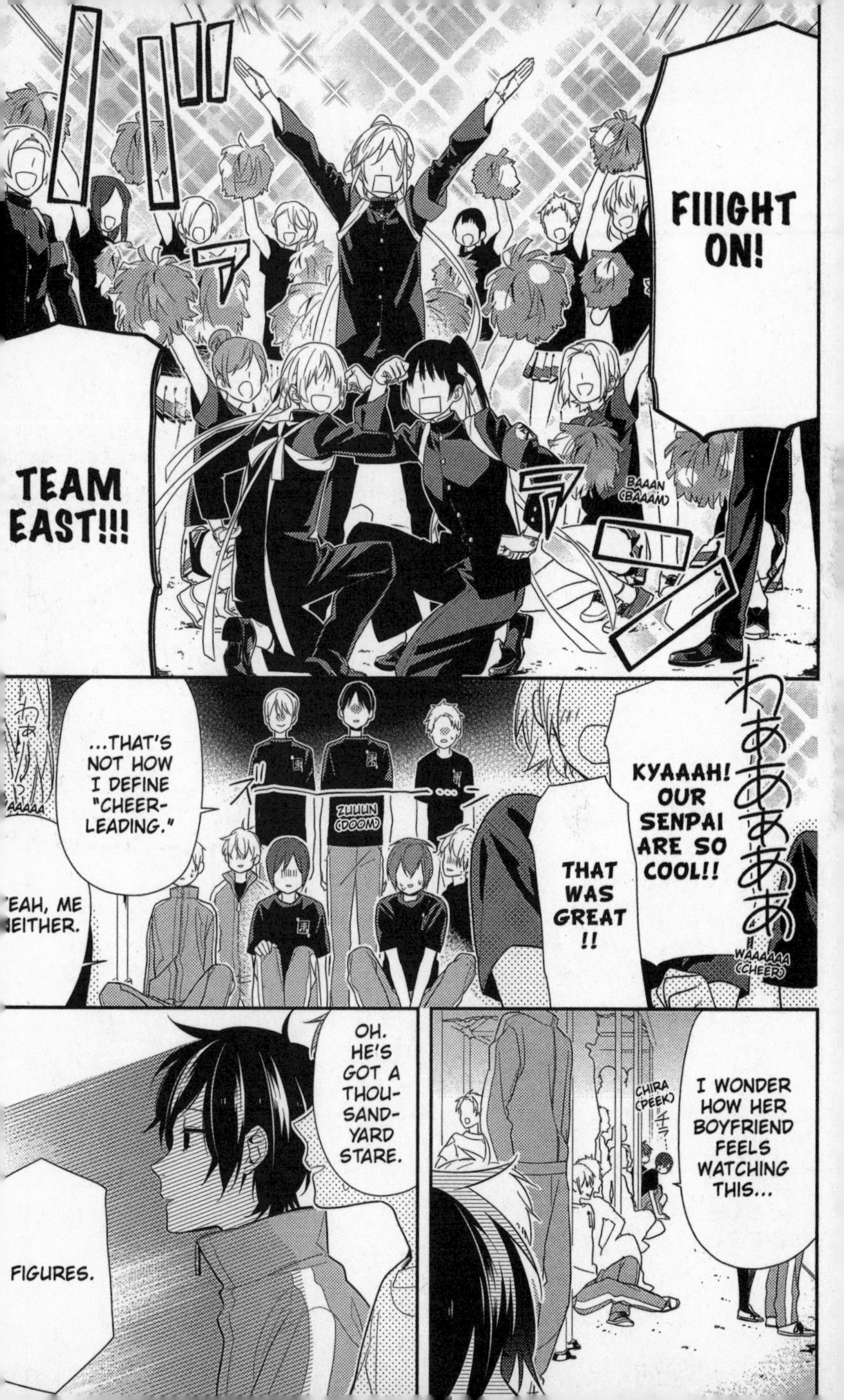
FIIIGHT ON!
BAAAN (BAAAM)
TEAM EAST!!!
わあああああ
WAAAAAA (CHEER)
KYAAAH! OUR SENPAI ARE SO COOL!!
THAT WAS GREAT!!
ZUUUN (DOOM)
...THAT'S NOT HOW I DEFINE "CHEER-LEADING."
EAH, ME EITHER.
I WONDER HOW HER BOYFRIEND FEELS WATCHING THIS...
CHIRA (PEEK)
チラ
OH. HE'S GOT A THOUSAND-YARD STARE.
FIGURES.

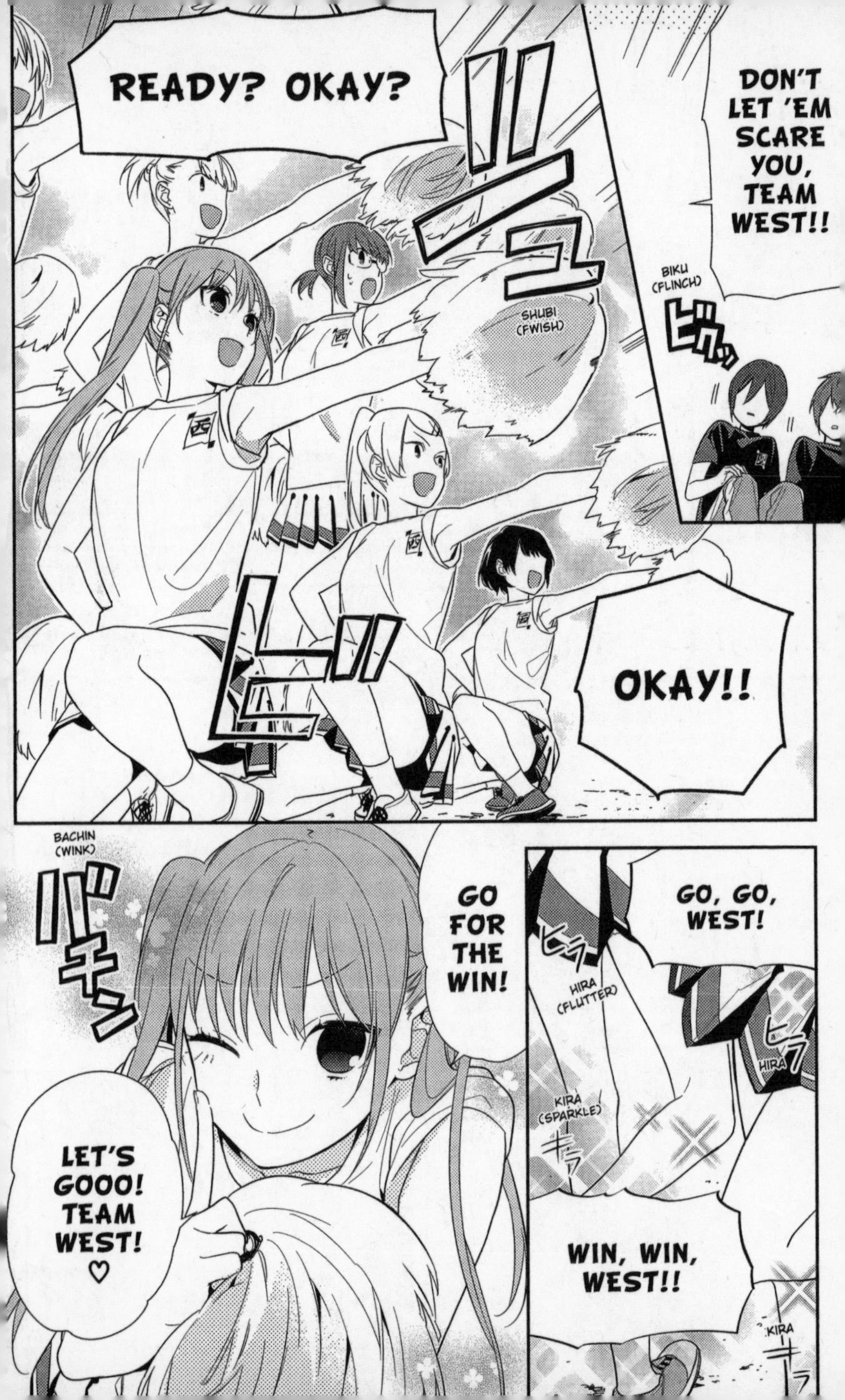
DON'T LET 'EM SCARE YOU, TEAM WEST!!
BIKU (FLINCH)
READY? OKAY?
SHUBI (FWISH)
OKAY!!
GO, GO, WEST!
HIRA (FLUTTER)
HIRA
KIRA (SPARKLE)
WIN, WIN, WEST!!
KIRA
BACHIN (WINK)
GO FOR THE WIN!
LET'S GOOO! TEAM WEST! ♡

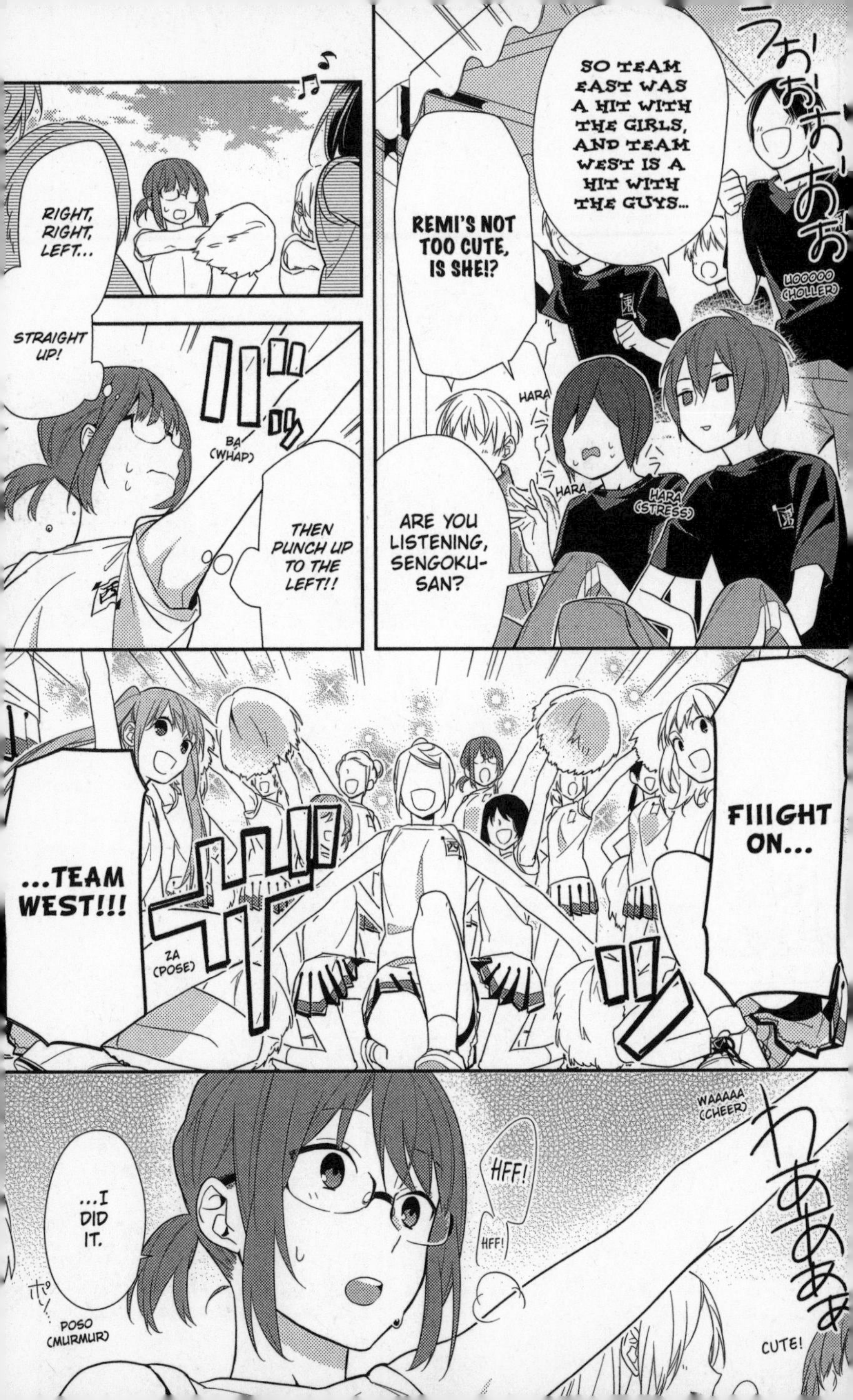

UOOOOO (HOLLER)
SO TEAM EAST WAS A HIT WITH THE GIRLS, AND TEAM WEST IS A HIT WITH THE GUYS...
REMI'S NOT TOO CUTE, IS SHE!?
HARA
HARA
HARA (STRESS)
ARE YOU LISTENING, SENGOKU-SAN?
RIGHT, RIGHT, LEFT...
STRAIGHT UP!
BA (WHAP)
THEN PUNCH UP TO THE LEFT!!
FIIIGHT ON...
...TEAM WEST!!!
ZA (POSE)
WAAAAA (CHEER)
CUTE!
HFF!
HFF!
...I DID IT.
POSO (MURMUR)

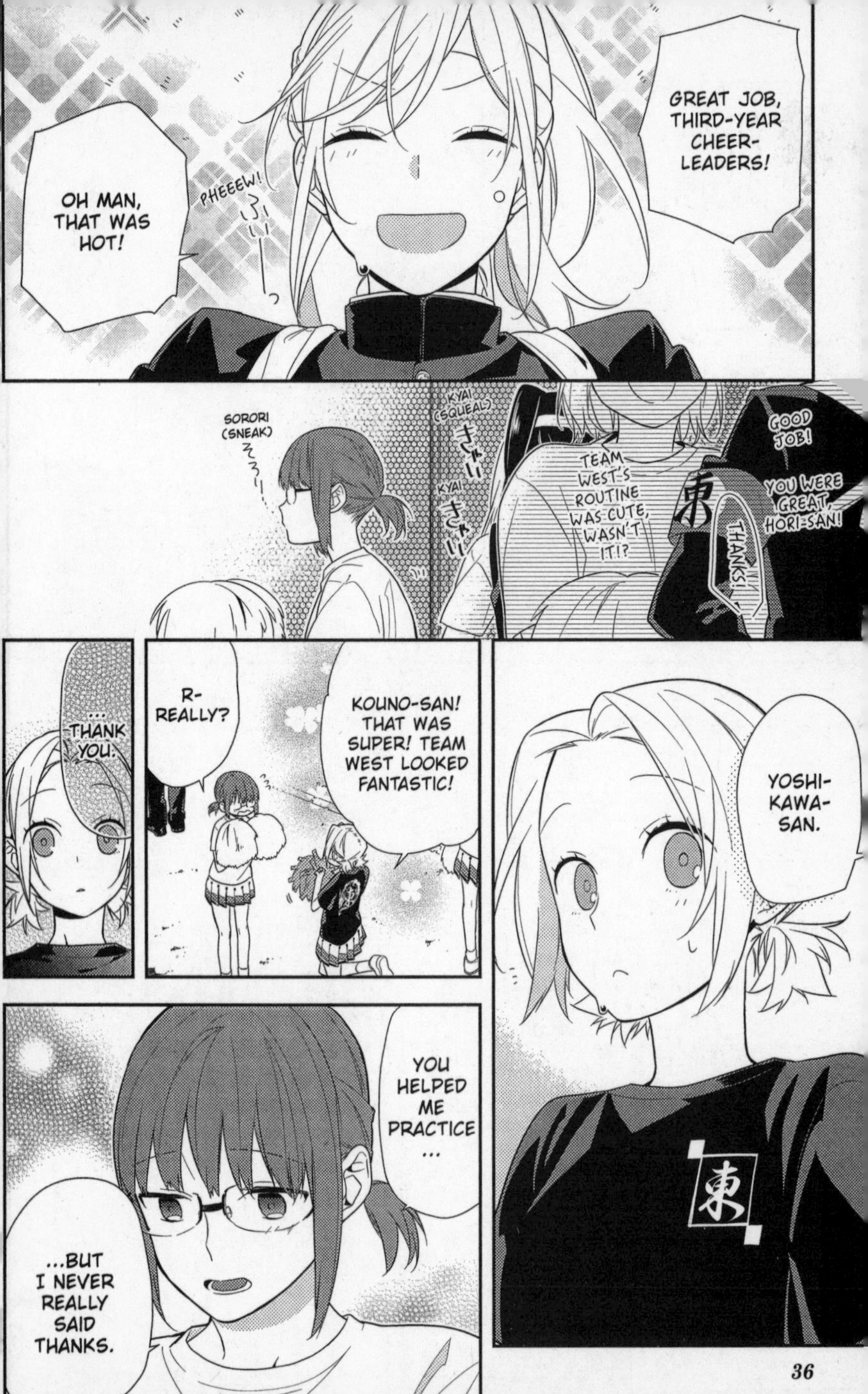
GREAT JOB, THIRD-YEAR CHEER-LEADERS!
PHEEEW!
OH MAN, THAT WAS HOT!
GOOD JOB!
YOU WERE GREAT, HORI-SAN!
THANKS!
TEAM WEST'S ROUTINE WAS CUTE, WASN'T IT!?
KYAI (SQUEAL)
KYAI
SORORI (SNEAK)
YOSHI-KAWA-SAN.
KOUNO-SAN! THAT WAS SUPER! TEAM WEST LOOKED FANTASTIC!
R-REALLY?
...THANK YOU.
YOU HELPED ME PRACTICE...
...BUT I NEVER REALLY SAID THANKS.

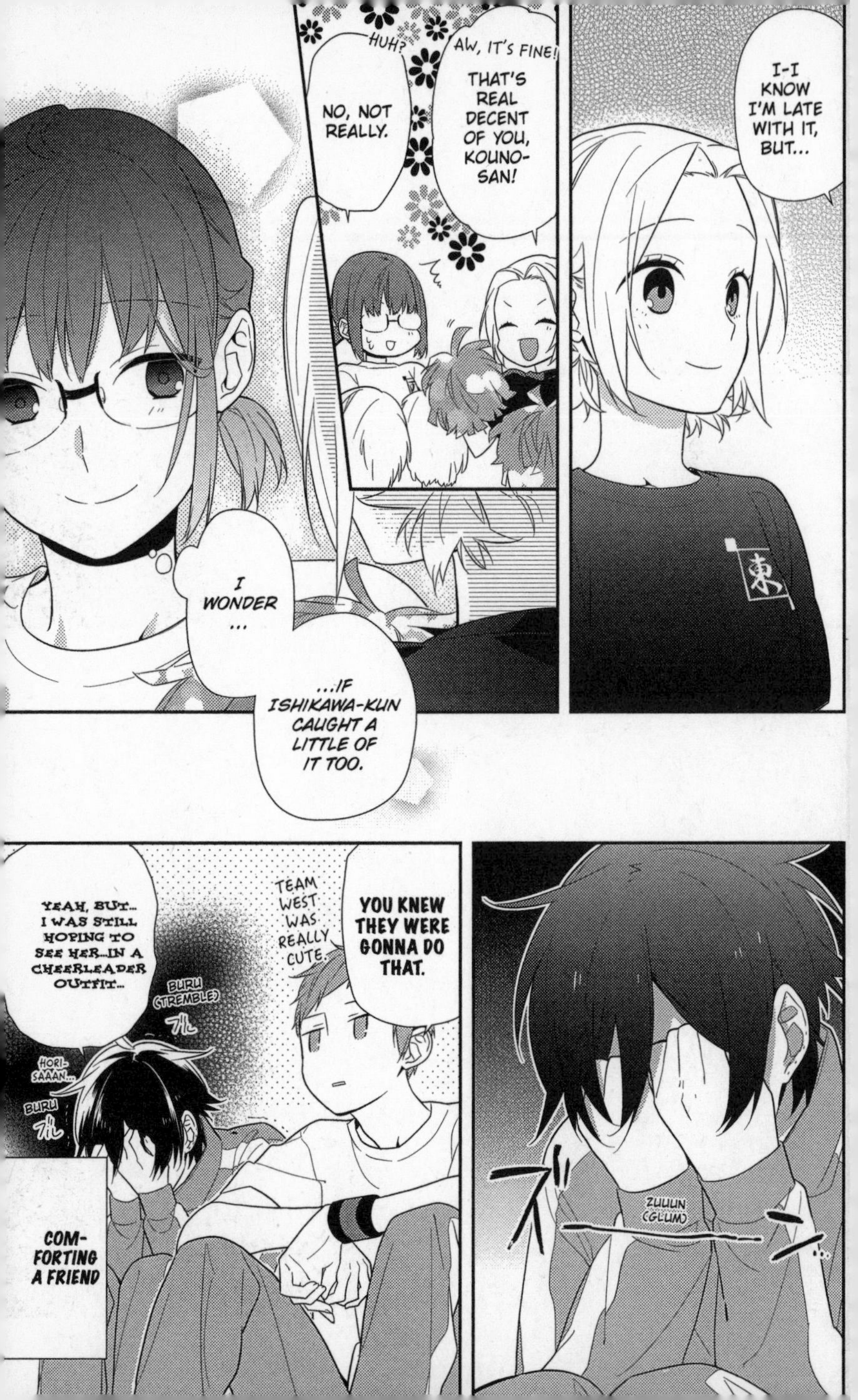
I-I KNOW I'M LATE WITH IT, BUT...
AW, IT'S FINE!
THAT'S REAL DECENT OF YOU, KOUNO-SAN!
HUH?
NO, NOT REALLY.
I WONDER...
...IF ISHIKAWA-KUN CAUGHT A LITTLE OF IT TOO.
ZUUUN (GLUM)
YOU KNEW THEY WERE GONNA DO THAT.
TEAM WEST WAS REALLY CUTE.
YEAH, BUT... I WAS STILL HOPING TO SEE HER...IN A CHEERLEADER OUTFIT...
BURU (TREMBLE)
HORI-SAAAN...
BURU
COMFORTING A FRIEND

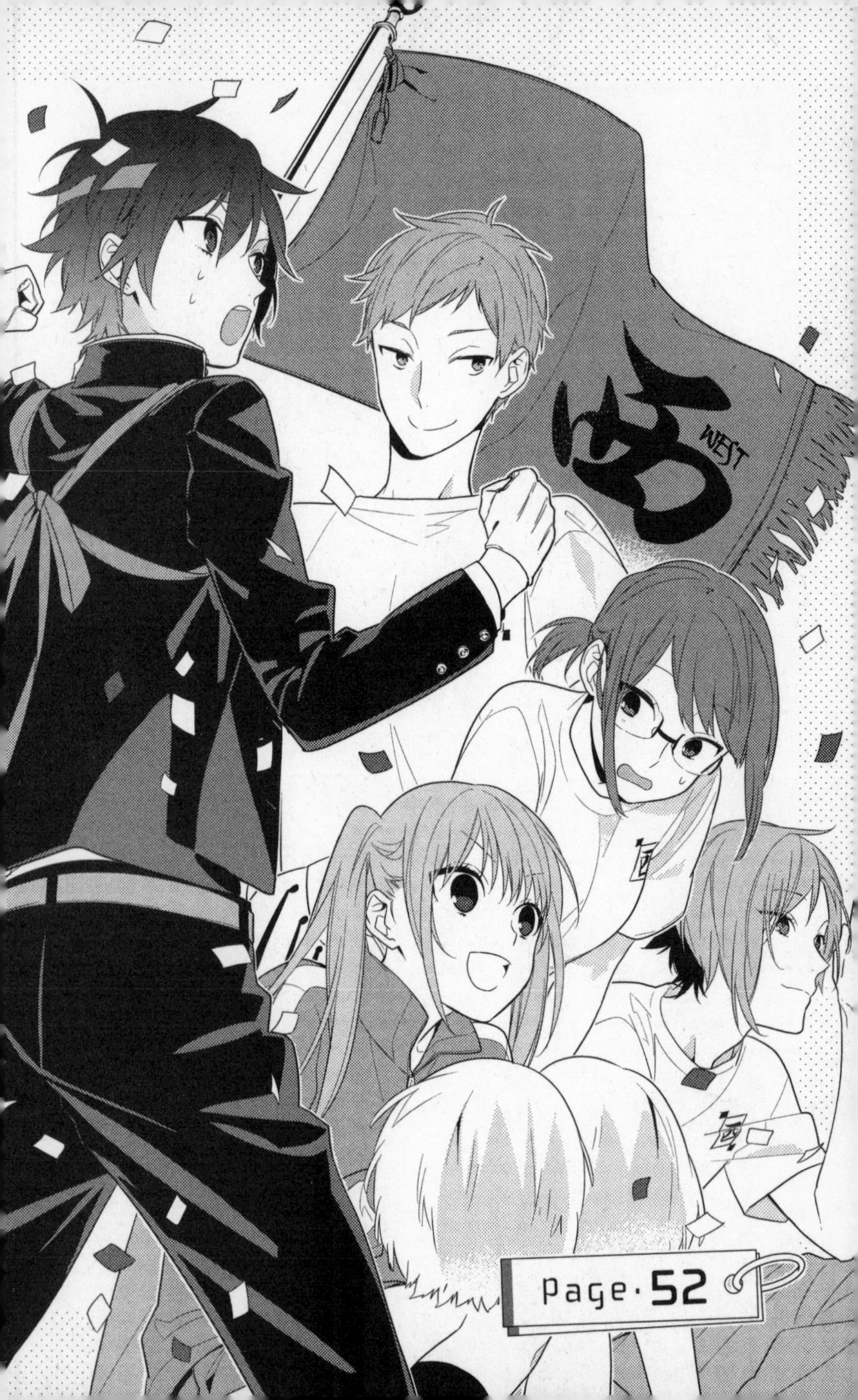
WEST
page.52

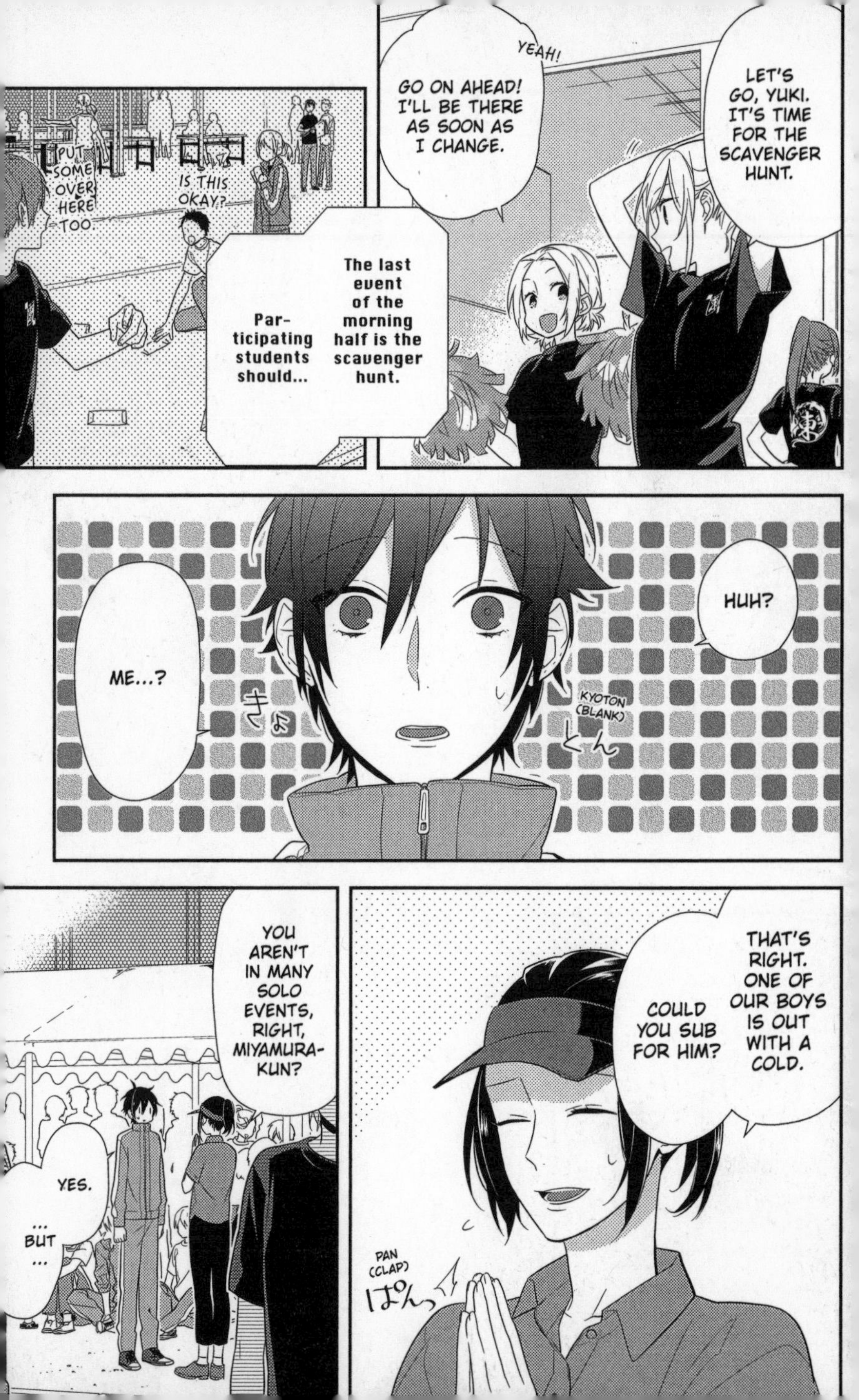
LET'S GO, YUKI. IT'S TIME FOR THE SCAVENGER HUNT.
YEAH!
GO ON AHEAD! I'LL BE THERE AS SOON AS I CHANGE.
The last event of the morning half is the scavenger hunt.
Par-ticipating students should...
IS THIS OKAY?
PUT SOME OVER HERE TOO.
HUH?
KYOTON (BLANK)
きょとん
ME...?
THAT'S RIGHT. ONE OF OUR BOYS IS OUT WITH A COLD.
COULD YOU SUB FOR HIM?
PAN (CLAP)
ぱんっ
YOU AREN'T IN MANY SOLO EVENTS, RIGHT, MIYAMURA-KUN?
YES.
... BUT ...

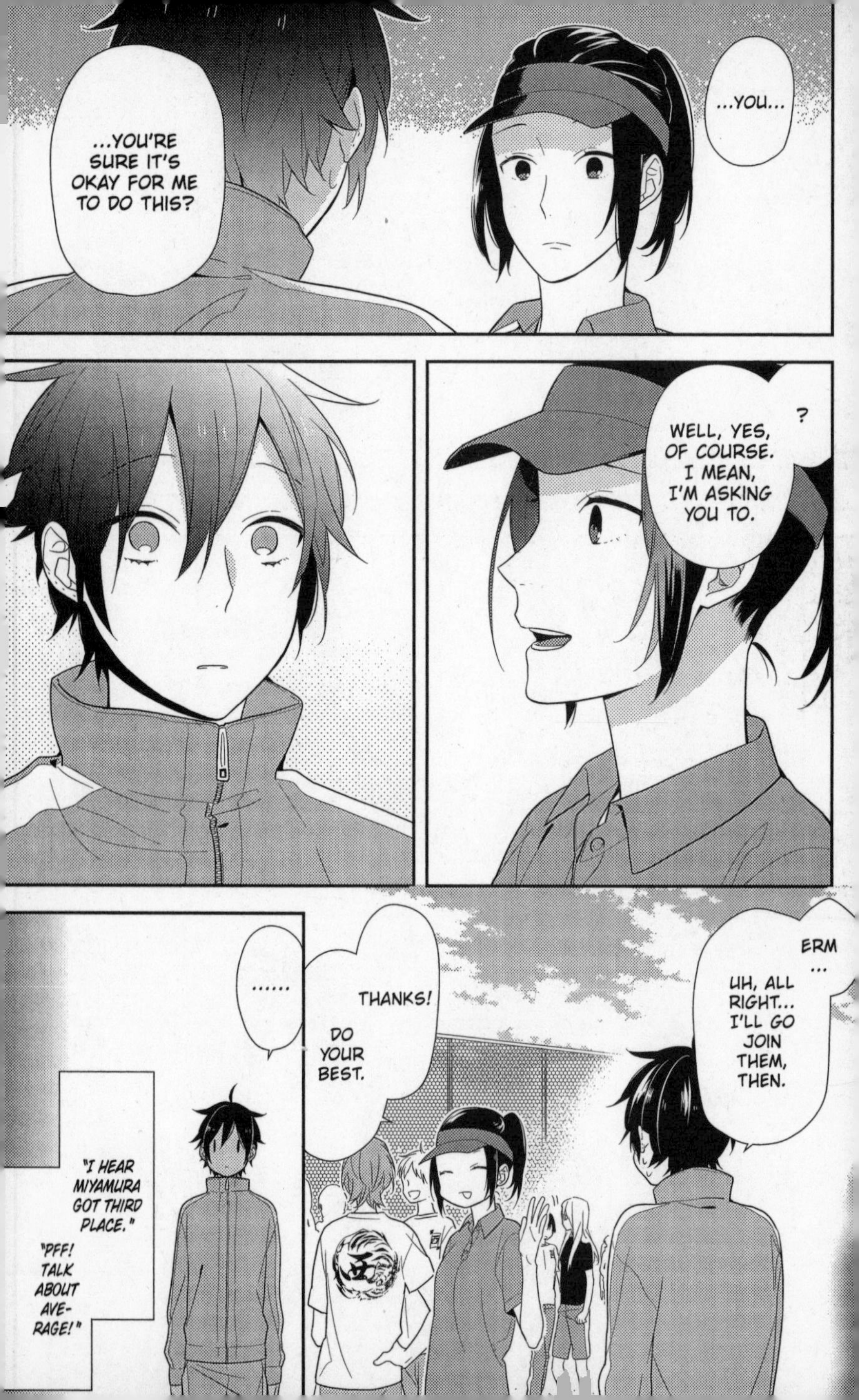
...YOU...
...YOU'RE SURE IT'S OKAY FOR ME TO DO THIS?
?
WELL, YES, OF COURSE. I MEAN, I'M ASKING YOU TO.
ERM ...
UH, ALL RIGHT... I'LL GO JOIN THEM, THEN.
THANKS!
DO YOUR BEST.
......
"I HEAR MIYAMURA GOT THIRD PLACE."
"PFF! TALK ABOUT AVE-RAGE!"

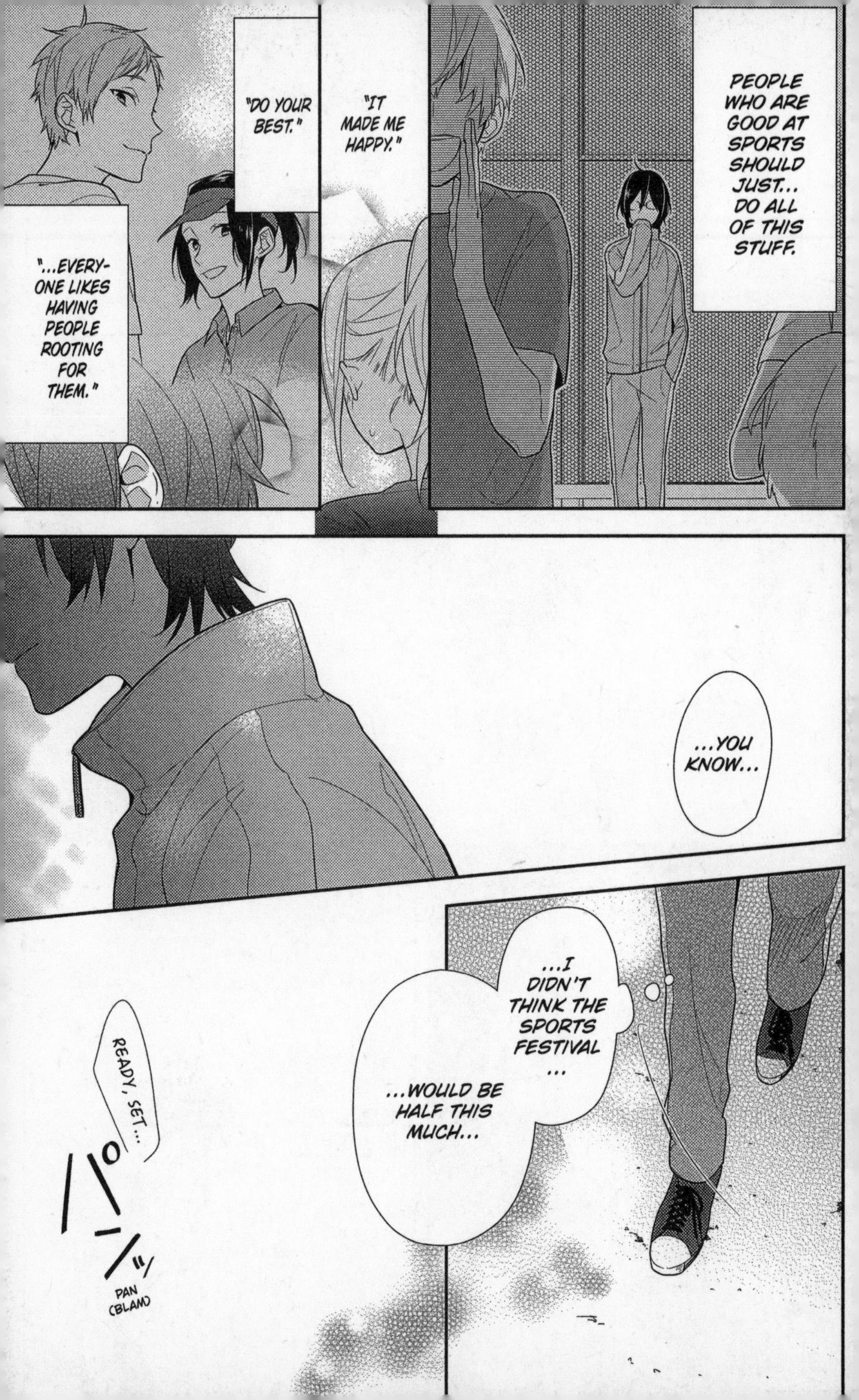
PEOPLE WHO ARE GOOD AT SPORTS SHOULD JUST... DO ALL OF THIS STUFF.
"IT MADE ME HAPPY."
"DO YOUR BEST."
"...EVERY-ONE LIKES HAVING PEOPLE ROOTING FOR THEM."
...YOU KNOW...
...I DIDN'T THINK THE SPORTS FESTIVAL...
...WOULD BE HALF THIS MUCH...
READY, SET...
PAN (BLAM)

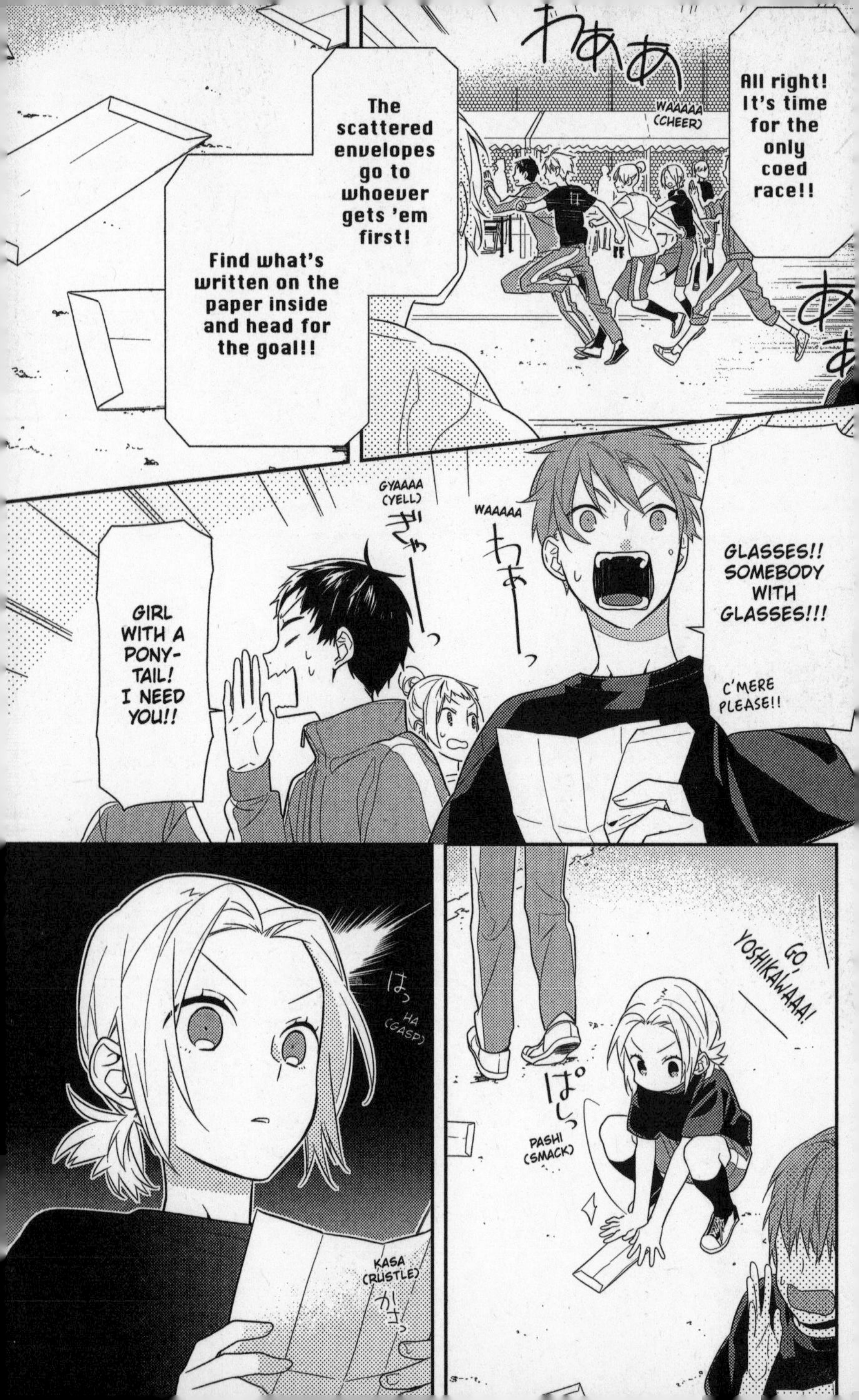
All right! It's time for the only coed race!!
わあああ
WAAAAA (CHEER)
The scattered envelopes go to whoever gets 'em first!
Find what's written on the paper inside and head for the goal!!
GLASSES!! SOMEBODY WITH GLASSES!!!
C'MERE PLEASE!!
WAAAAA
わぁーっ
GYAAAA (YELL)
ぎゃーっ
GIRL WITH A PONY-TAIL! I NEED YOU!!
GO, YOSHIKAWAAAA!
PASHI (SMACK)
ぱしっ
はっ
HA (GASP)
KASA (RUSTLE)
かさっ

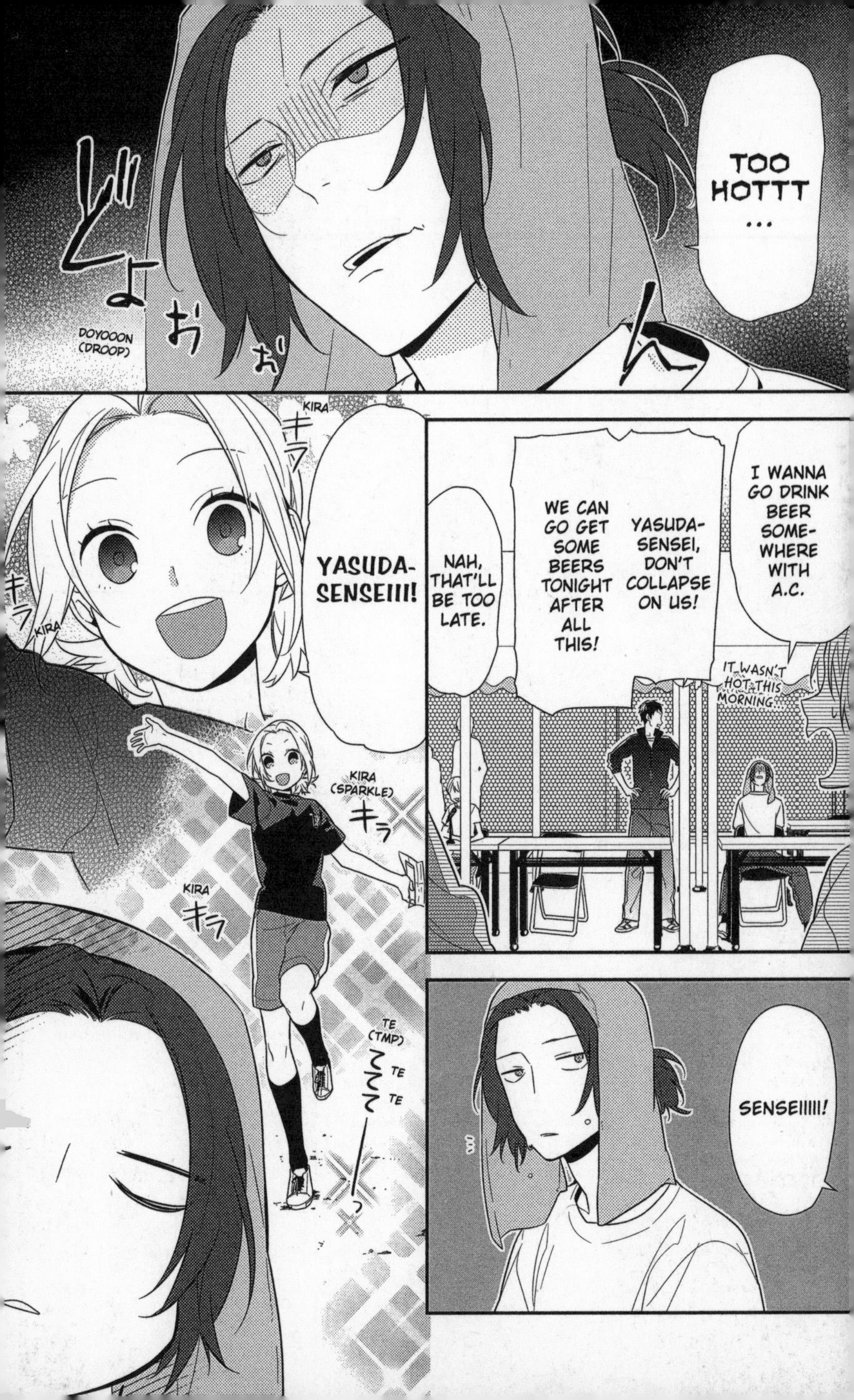
TOO HOTTT ...
DOYOOON (DROOP)
I WANNA GO DRINK BEER SOME-WHERE WITH A.C.
IT WASN'T HOT THIS MORNING...
YASUDA-SENSEI, DON'T COLLAPSE ON US!
WE CAN GO GET SOME BEERS TONIGHT AFTER ALL THIS!
NAH, THAT'LL BE TOO LATE.
SENSEIIIII!
YASUDA-SENSEIIII!
KIRA
KIRA
KIRA (SPARKLE)
KIRA
TE (TMP)
TE
TE

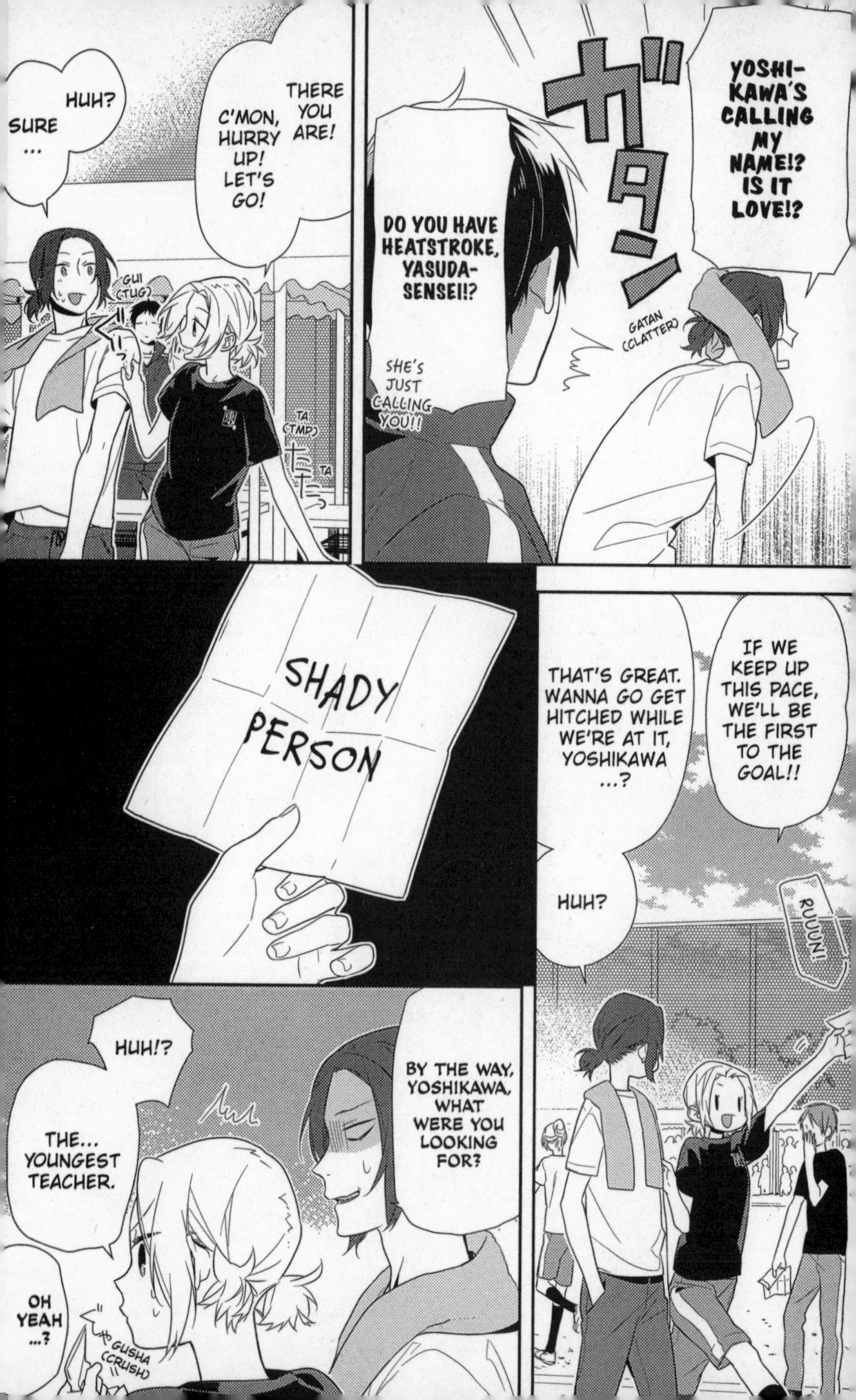
YOSHI-KAWA'S CALLING MY NAME!? IS IT LOVE!?
GATAN (CLATTER)
DO YOU HAVE HEATSTROKE, YASUDA-SENSEI!!?
SHE'S JUST CALLING YOU!!
THERE YOU ARE!
C'MON, HURRY UP! LET'S GO!
HUH? SURE...
GUI (TUG)
TA (TMP)
TA
IF WE KEEP UP THIS PACE, WE'LL BE THE FIRST TO THE GOAL!!
THAT'S GREAT. WANNA GO GET HITCHED WHILE WE'RE AT IT, YOSHIKAWA...?
HUH?
RUUUN!
SHADY PERSON
BY THE WAY, YOSHIKAWA, WHAT WERE YOU LOOKING FOR?
HUH!?
THE... YOUNGEST TEACHER.
OH YEAH...?
GUSHA (CRUSH)

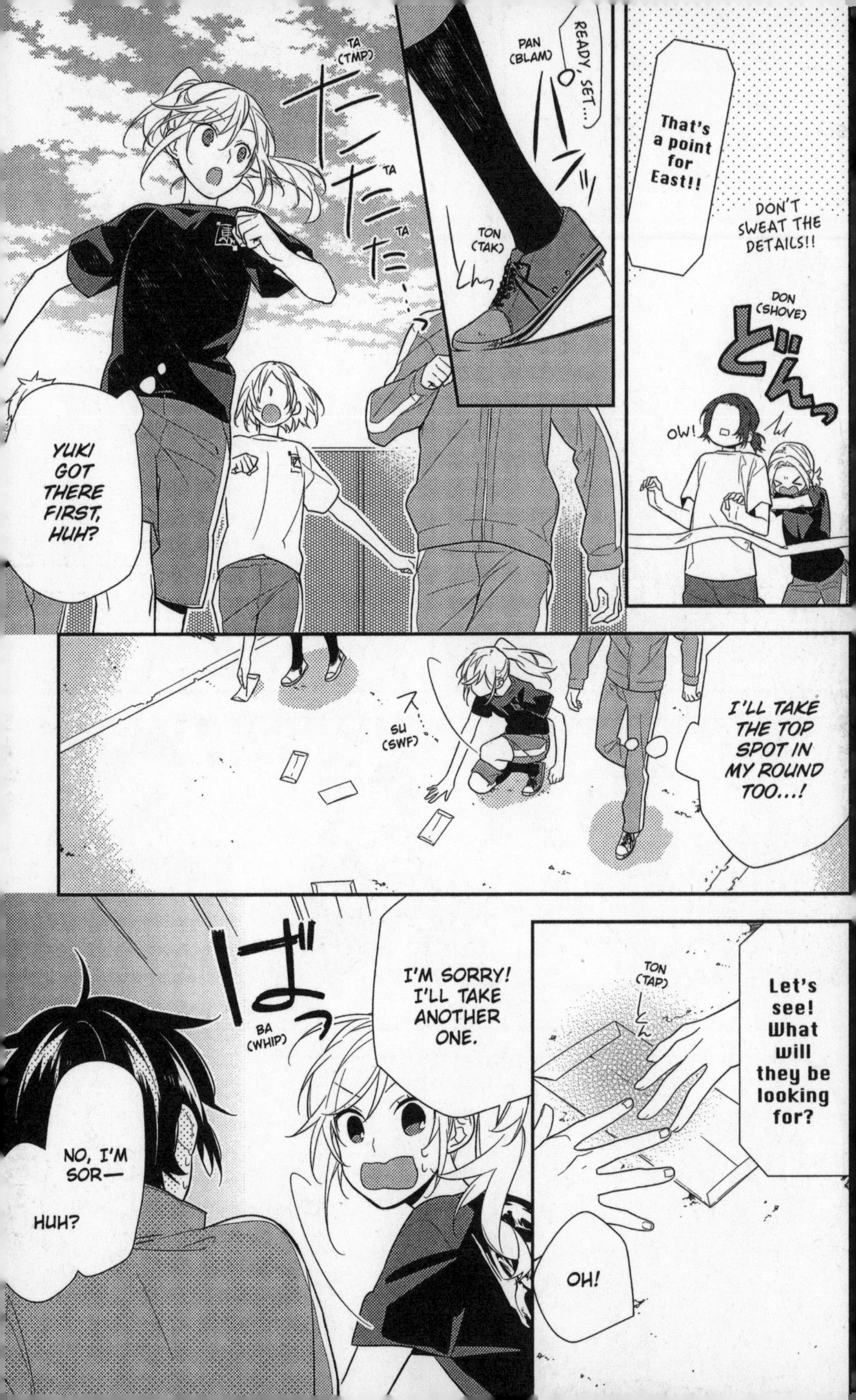
That's a point for East!!
DON'T SWEAT THE DETAILS!!
DON (SHOVE)
OW!
READY, SET...
PAN (BLAM)
TON (TAK)
TA (TMP)
TA
TA
YUKI GOT THERE FIRST, HUH?
I'LL TAKE THE TOP SPOT IN MY ROUND TOO...!
SU (SWF)
Let's see! What will they be looking for?
TON (TAP)
OH!
I'M SORRY! I'LL TAKE ANOTHER ONE.
BA (WHIP)
NO, I'M SOR—
HUH?

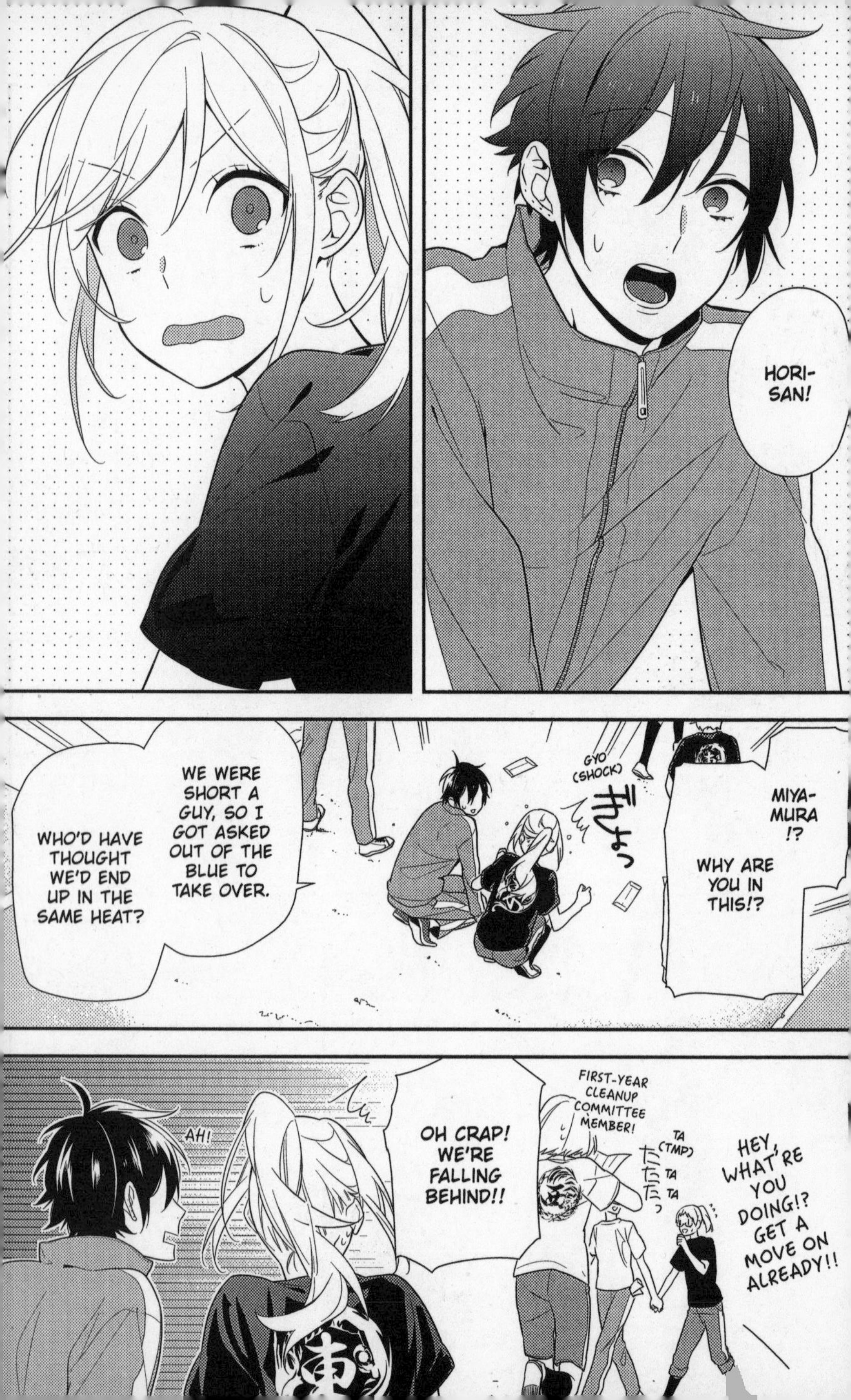
HORI-SAN!
MIYAMURA!?
WHY ARE YOU IN THIS!?
GYO (SHOCK)
ぎょっ
WE WERE SHORT A GUY, SO I GOT ASKED OUT OF THE BLUE TO TAKE OVER.
WHO'D HAVE THOUGHT WE'D END UP IN THE SAME HEAT?
HEY, WHAT'RE YOU DOING!? GET A MOVE ON ALREADY!!
TA (TMP) TA TA
たたたっ
FIRST-YEAR CLEANUP COMMITTEE MEMBER!
OH CRAP! WE'RE FALLING BEHIND!!
AH!

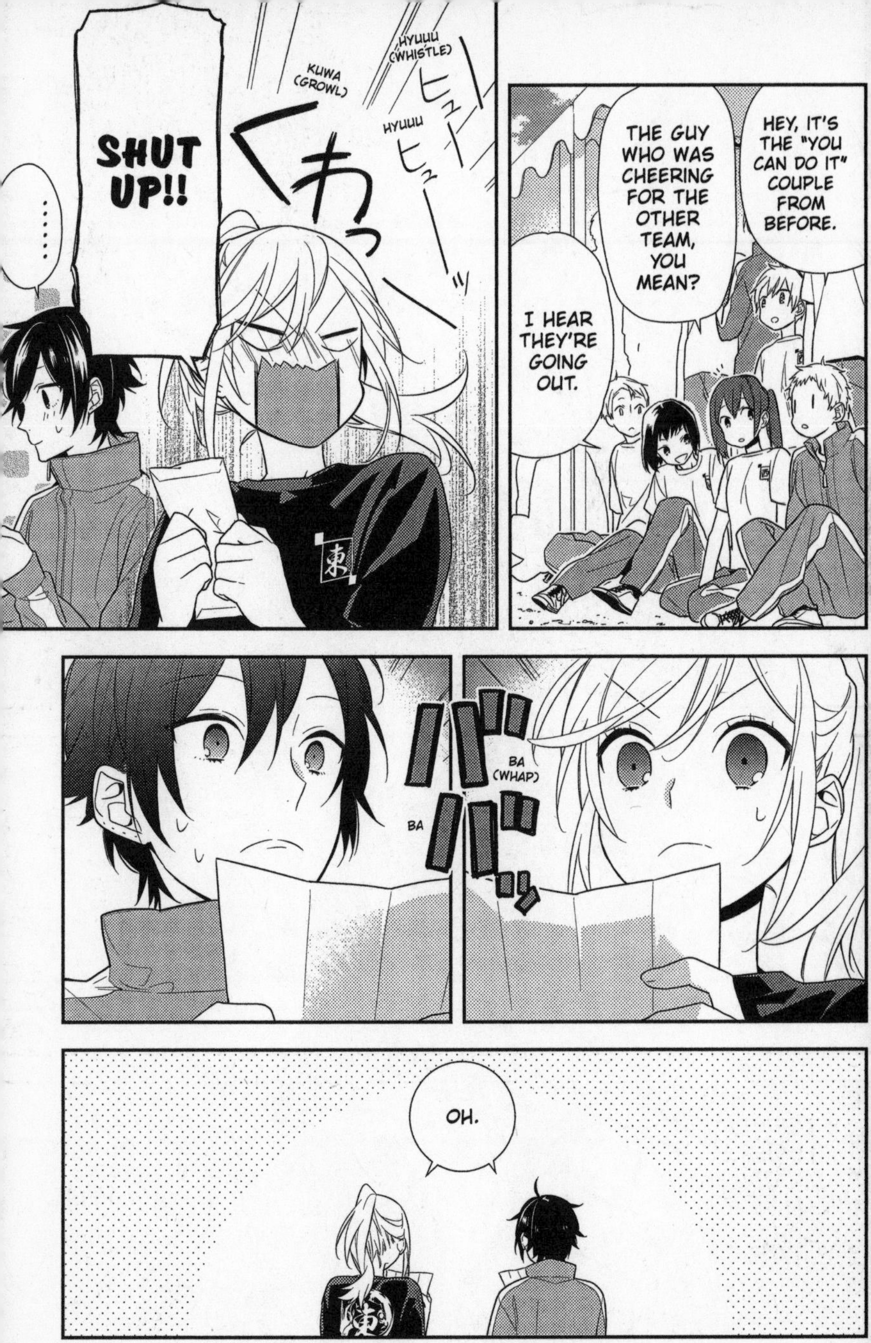
HEY, IT'S THE "YOU CAN DO IT" COUPLE FROM BEFORE.
THE GUY WHO WAS CHEERING FOR THE OTHER TEAM, YOU MEAN?
I HEAR THEY'RE GOING OUT.
HYUUU (WHISTLE)
HYUUU
KUWA (GROWL)
SHUT UP!!
......
BA (WHAP)
BA
OH.

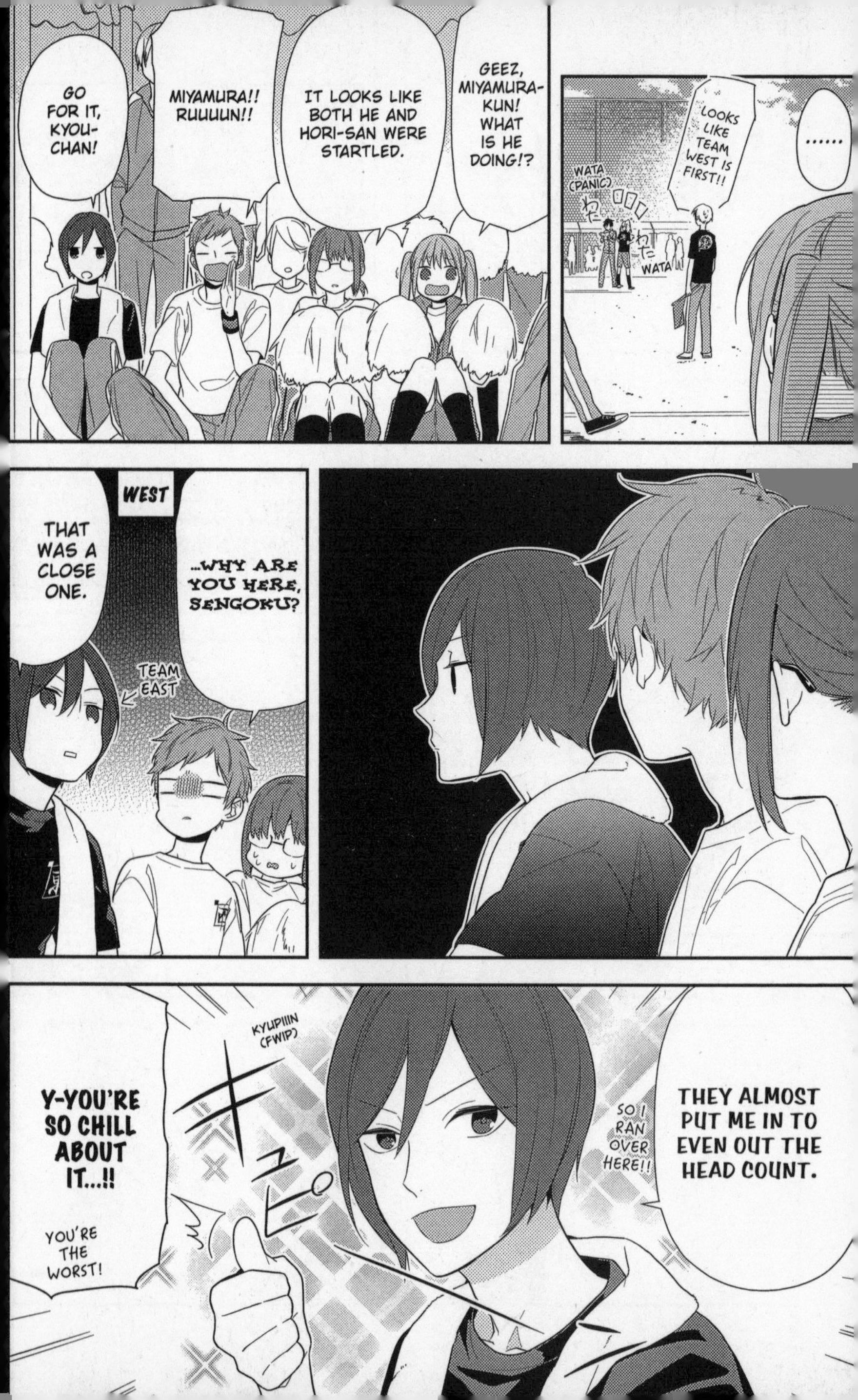
......
LOOKS LIKE TEAM WEST IS FIRST!!
WATA (PANIC)
WATA
GEEZ, MIYAMURA-KUN! WHAT IS HE DOING!?
IT LOOKS LIKE BOTH HE AND HORI-SAN WERE STARTLED.
MIYAMURA!! RUUUUN!!
GO FOR IT, KYOU-CHAN!
...WHY ARE YOU HERE, SENGOKU?
WEST
THAT WAS A CLOSE ONE.
TEAM EAST
THEY ALMOST PUT ME IN TO EVEN OUT THE HEAD COUNT.
SO I RAN OVER HERE!!
KYUPIIN (FWIP)
Y-YOU'RE SO CHILL ABOUT IT...!!
YOU'RE THE WORST!

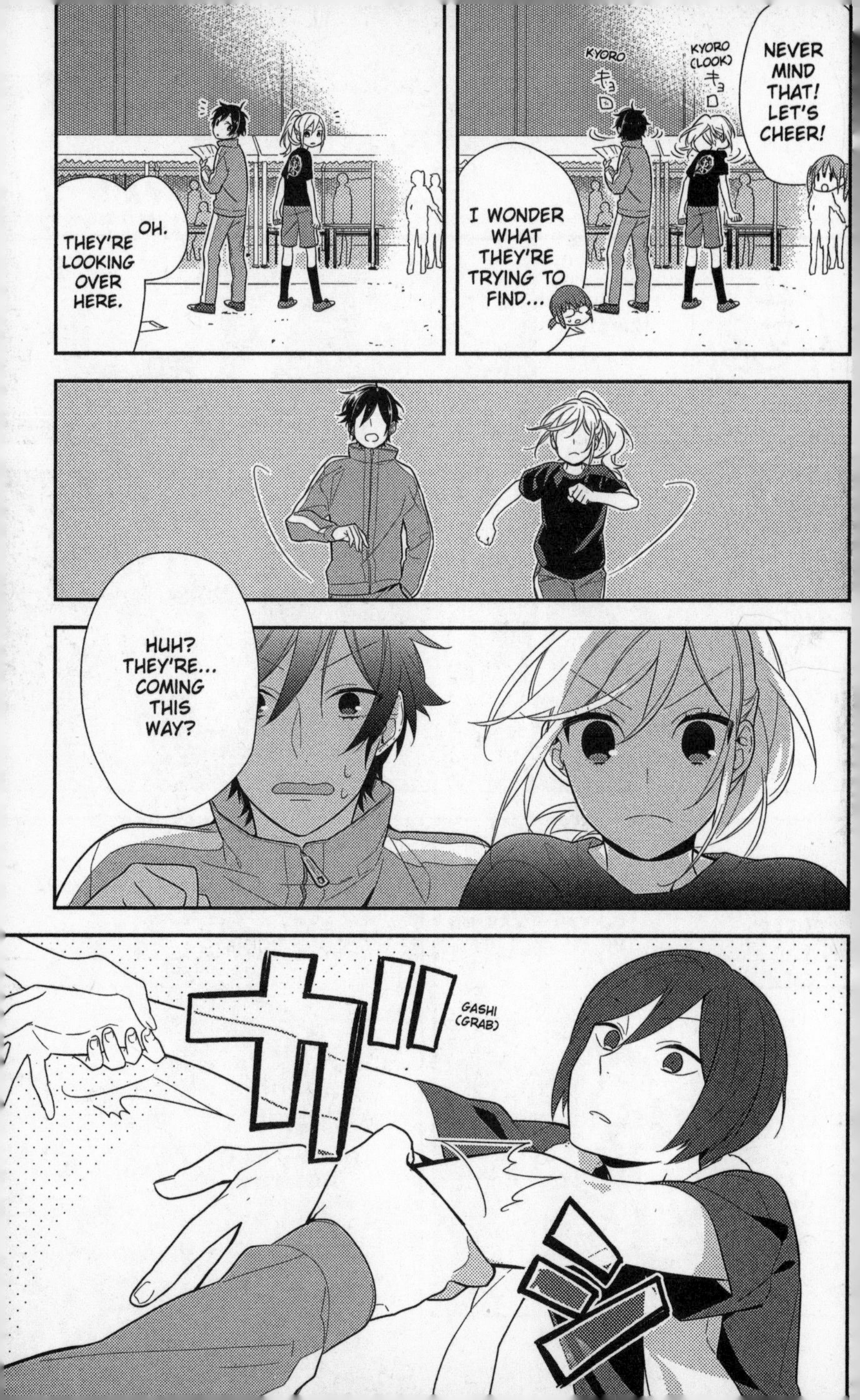
NEVER MIND THAT! LET'S CHEER!
KYORO (LOOK)
キョロ
KYORO
キョロ
I WONDER WHAT THEY'RE TRYING TO FIND...
OH.
THEY'RE LOOKING OVER HERE.
HUH? THEY'RE... COMING THIS WAY?
GASHI (GRAB)

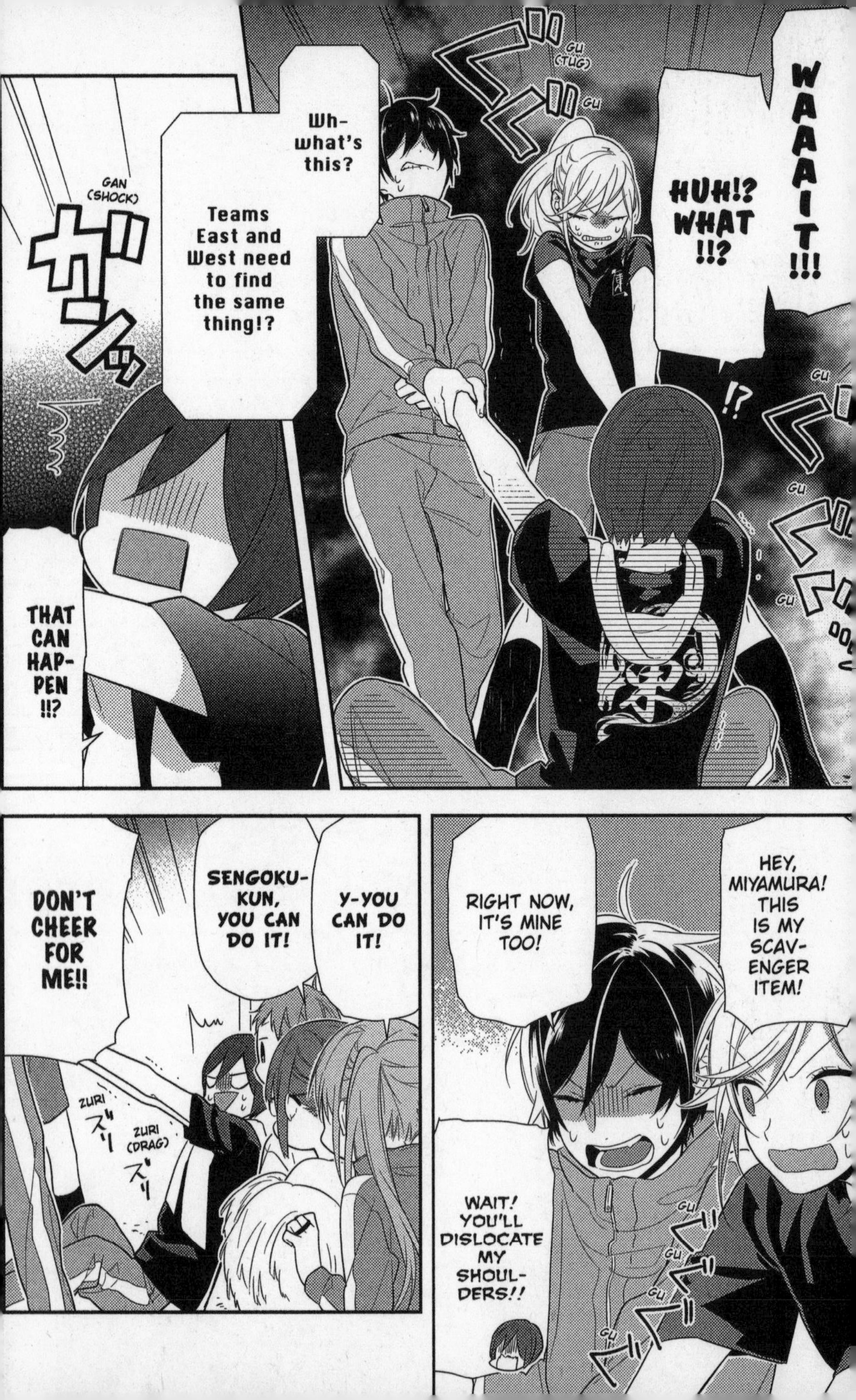
WAAAIT!!!
HUH!? WHAT!!?
GU (TUG)
GU
Wh-what's this?
Teams East and West need to find the same thing!?
!?
GU
GU
GU
GAN (SHOCK)
THAT CAN HAPPEN!!?
HEY, MIYAMURA! THIS IS MY SCAVENGER ITEM!
RIGHT NOW, IT'S MINE TOO!
WAIT! YOU'LL DISLOCATE MY SHOULDERS!!
GU
GU
GU
GU
Y-YOU CAN DO IT!
SENGOKU-KUN, YOU CAN DO IT!
DON'T CHEER FOR ME!!
ZURI
ZURI (DRAG)

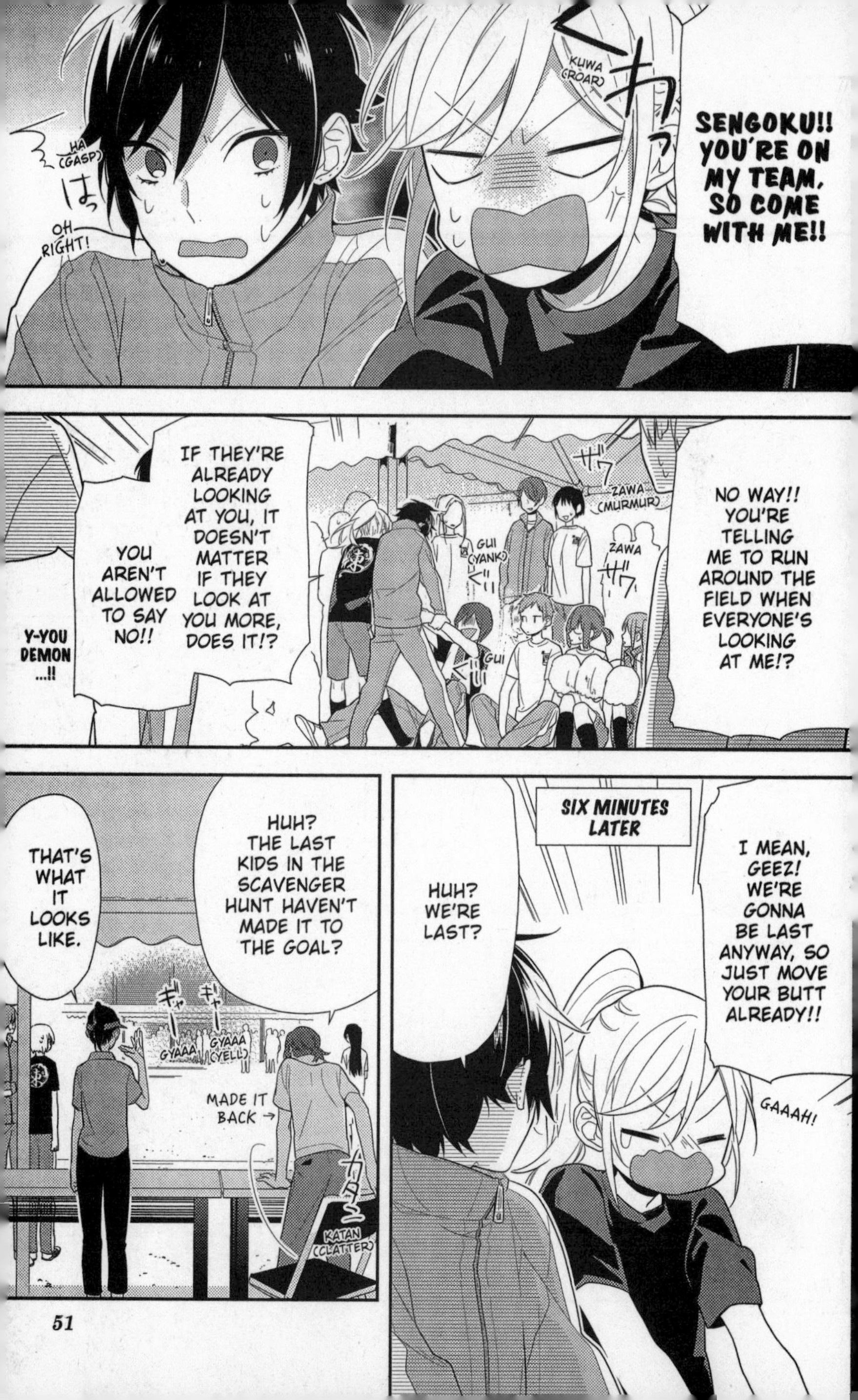
SENGOKU!! YOU'RE ON MY TEAM, SO COME WITH ME!!
KUWA (ROAR)
HA (GASP)
OH RIGHT!
NO WAY!! YOU'RE TELLING ME TO RUN AROUND THE FIELD WHEN EVERYONE'S LOOKING AT ME!?
ZAWA (MURMUR)
ZAWA
GUI (YANK)
GUI
IF THEY'RE ALREADY LOOKING AT YOU, IT DOESN'T MATTER IF THEY LOOK AT YOU MORE, DOES IT!?
YOU AREN'T ALLOWED TO SAY NO!!
Y-YOU DEMON ...!!
SIX MINUTES LATER
I MEAN, GEEZ! WE'RE GONNA BE LAST ANYWAY, SO JUST MOVE YOUR BUTT ALREADY!!
HUH? WE'RE LAST?
GAAAH!
HUH? THE LAST KIDS IN THE SCAVENGER HUNT HAVEN'T MADE IT TO THE GOAL?
THAT'S WHAT IT LOOKS LIKE.
GYAAA (YELL)
GYAAA
MADE IT BACK →
KATAN (CLATTER)

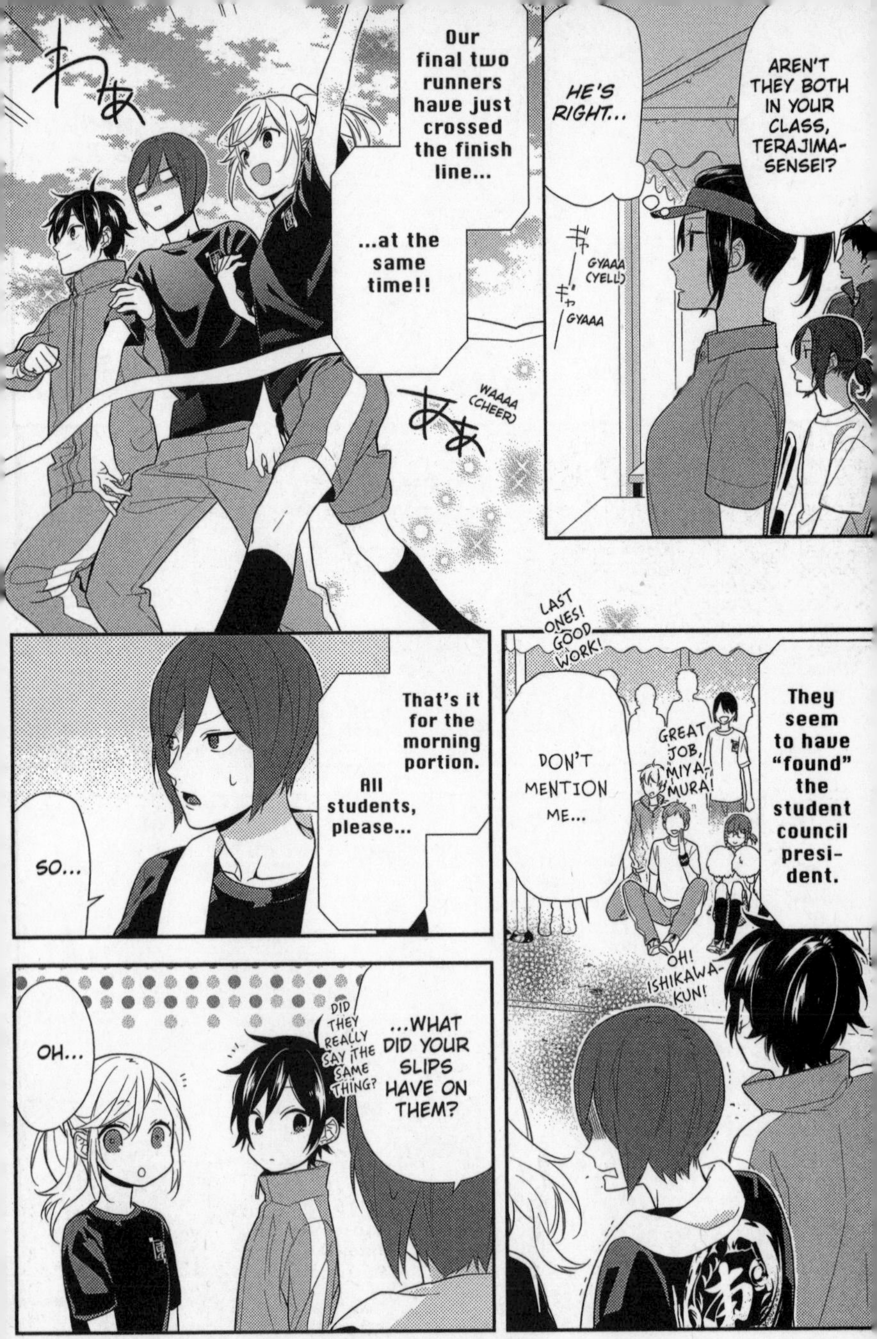
ARE'NT THEY BOTH IN YOUR CLASS, TERAJIMA-SENSEI?
HE'S RIGHT...
ギャ GYAAA (YELL)
ギャ GYAAA
わぁ
Our final two runners have just crossed the finish line...
...at the same time!!
ああ WAAAA (CHEER)
They seem to have "found" the student council president.
LAST ONES! GOOD WORK!
DON'T MENTION ME...
GREAT JOB, MIYA-MURA!
OH! ISHIKAWA-KUN!
That's it for the morning portion.
All students, please...
SO...
...WHAT DID YOUR SLIPS HAVE ON THEM?
DID THEY REALLY SAY THE SAME THING?
OH...

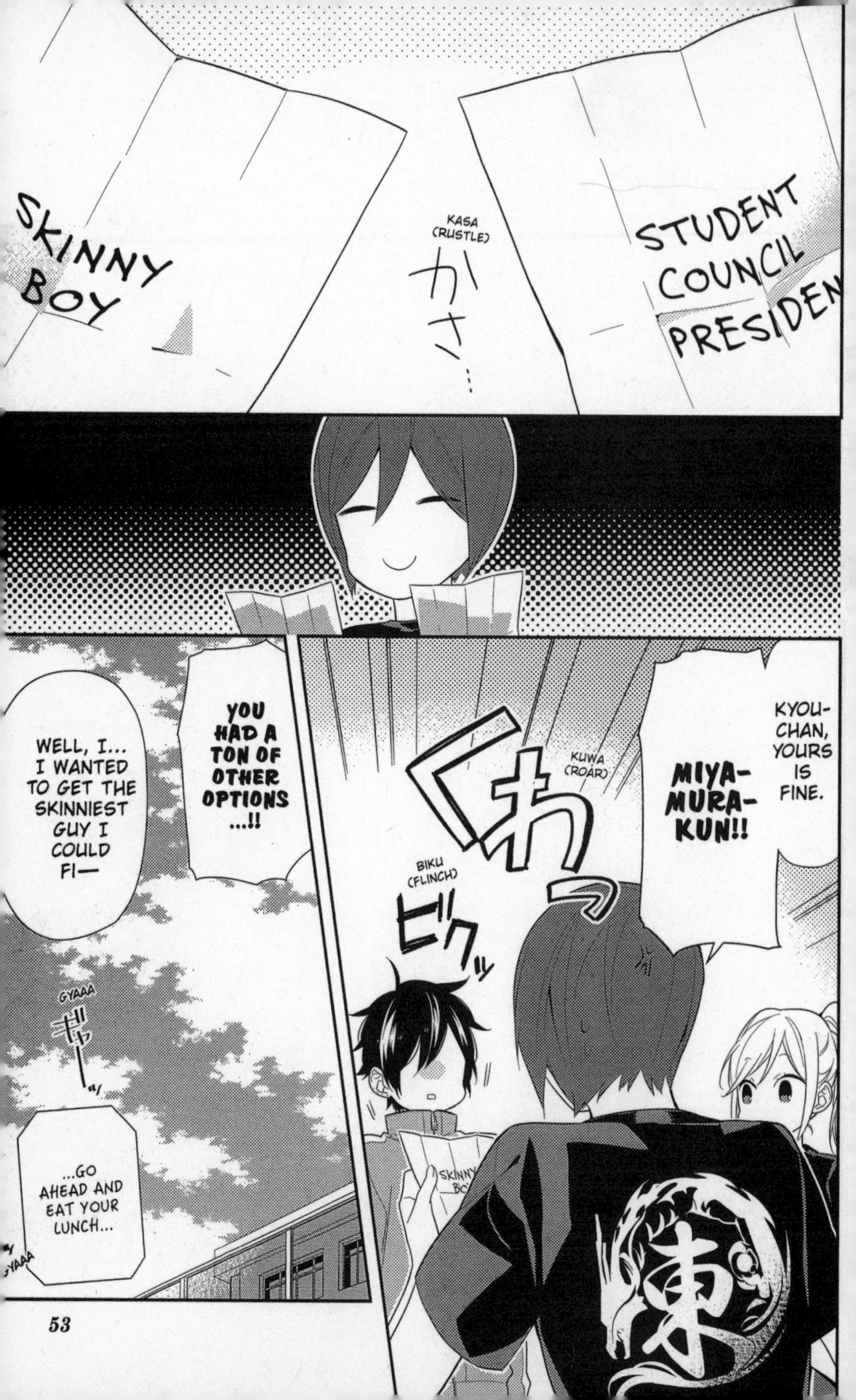
STUDENT COUNCIL PRESIDEN
KASA (RUSTLE)
かさ…
SKINNY BOY
KYOU-CHAN, YOURS IS FINE.
MIYA-MURA-KUN!!
KUWA (ROAR)
くわっ
BIKU (FLINCH)
ビクッ
SKINNY BOY
YOU HAD A TON OF OTHER OPTIONS...!!
WELL, I... I WANTED TO GET THE SKINNIEST GUY I COULD FI—
GYAAA
ぎゃー
...GO AHEAD AND EAT YOUR LUNCH...
GYAAA

HORIMIYA

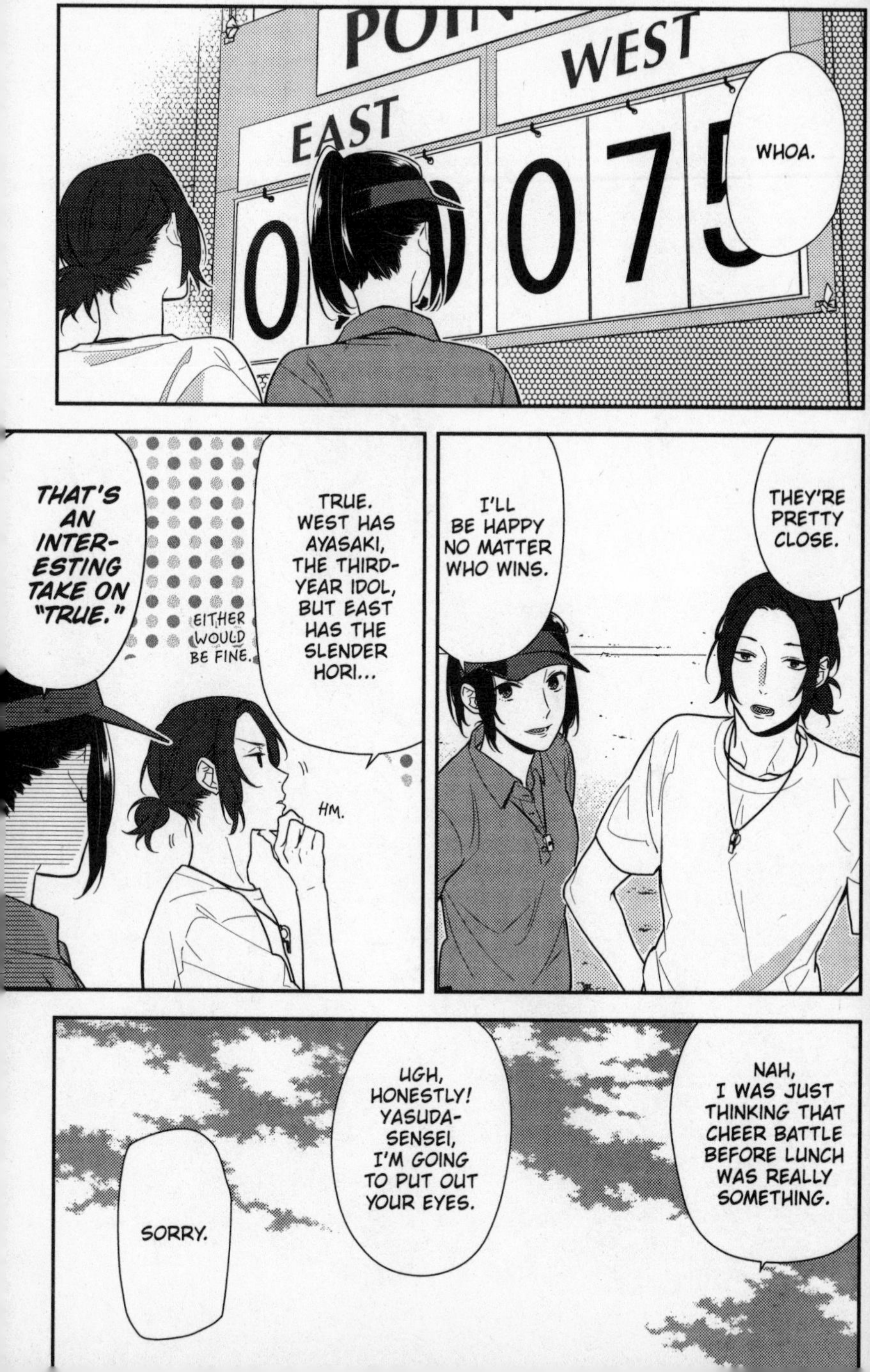
WEST
EAST
WHOA.
THEY'RE PRETTY CLOSE.
I'LL BE HAPPY NO MATTER WHO WINS.
TRUE. WEST HAS AYASAKI, THE THIRD-YEAR IDOL, BUT EAST HAS THE SLENDER HORI...
EITHER WOULD BE FINE.
HM.
THAT'S AN INTER-ESTING TAKE ON "TRUE."
NAH, I WAS JUST THINKING THAT CHEER BATTLE BEFORE LUNCH WAS REALLY SOMETHING.
UGH, HONESTLY! YASUDA-SENSEI, I'M GOING TO PUT OUT YOUR EYES.
SORRY.

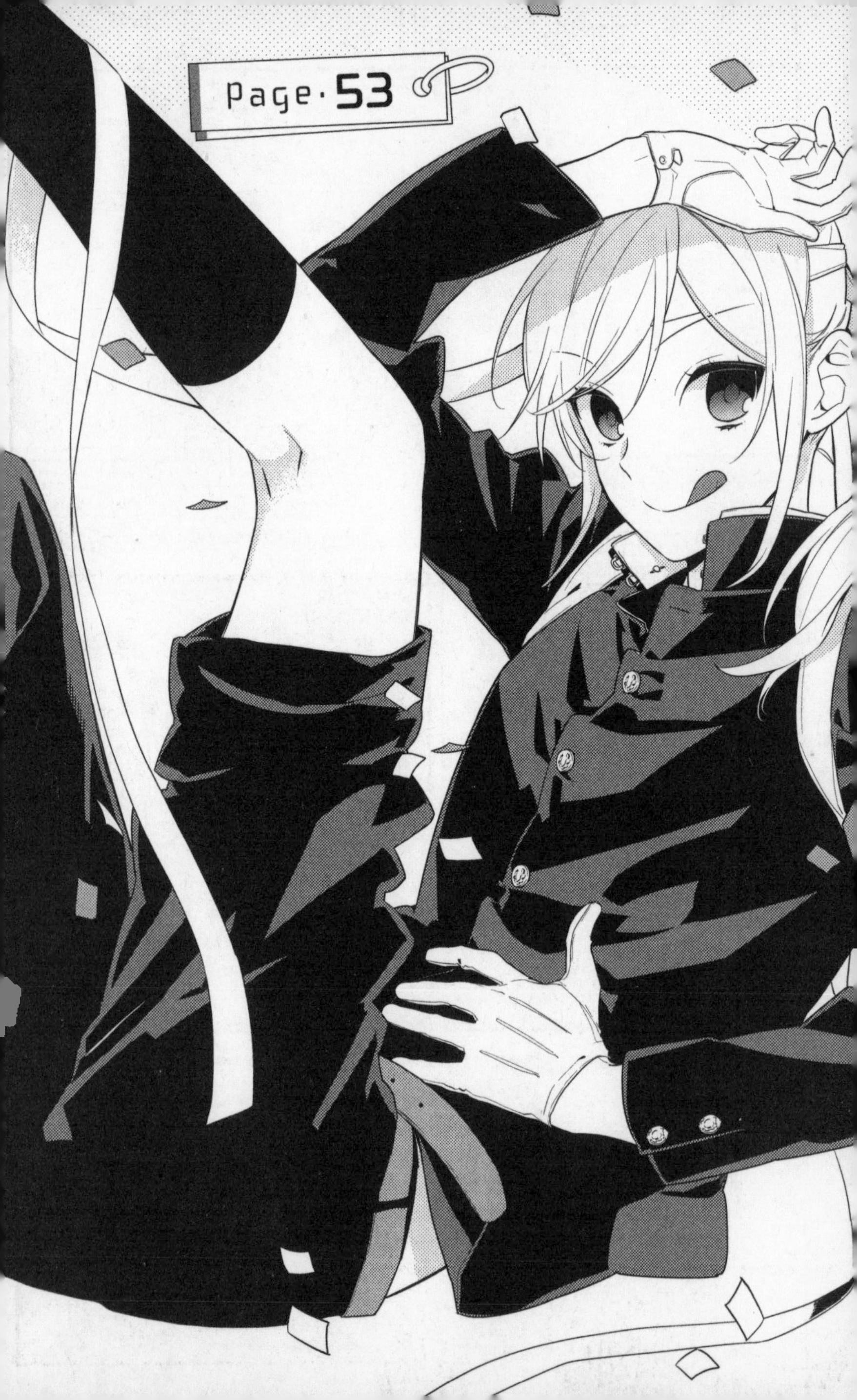
page.53

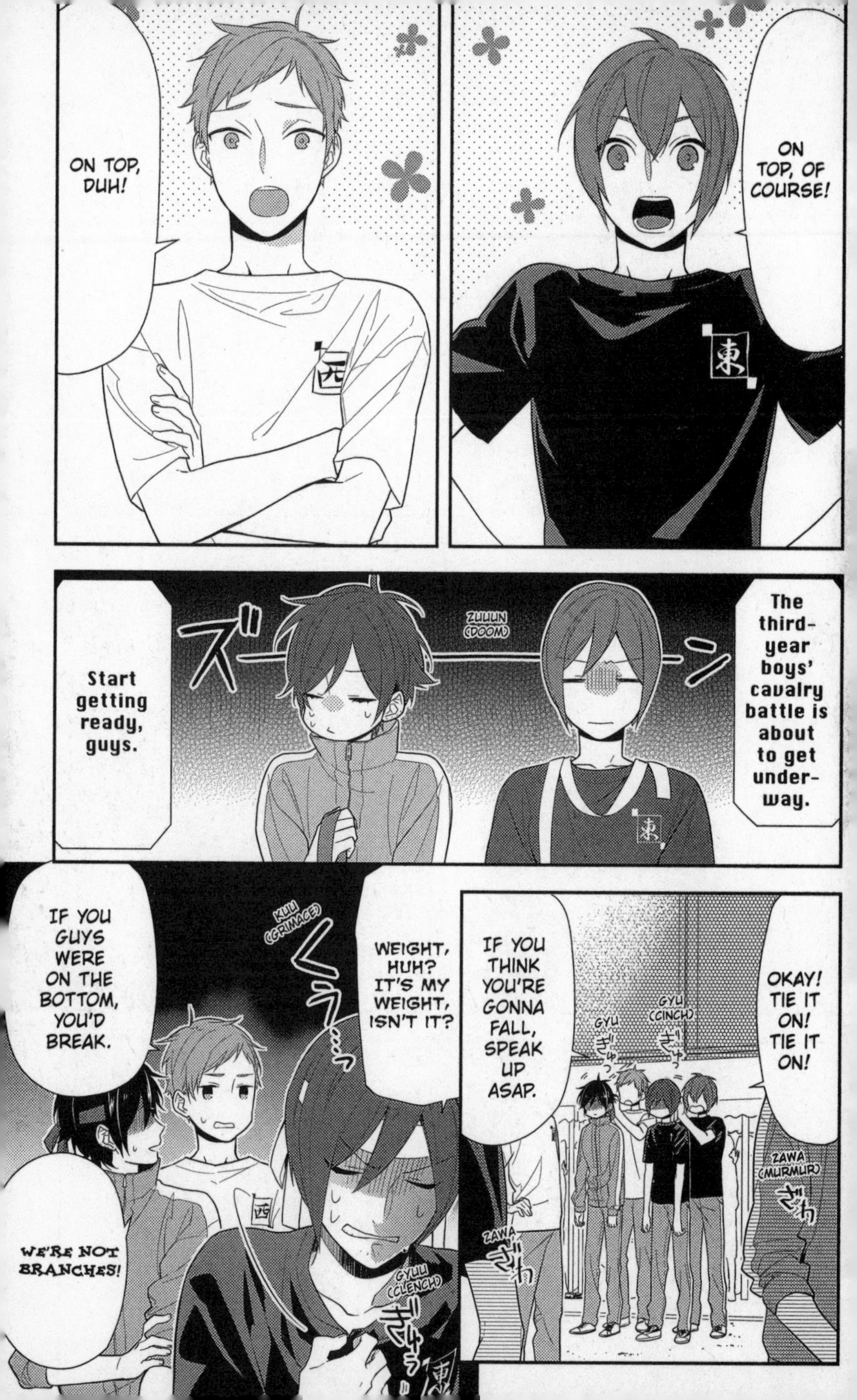

ON TOP, OF COURSE!
ON TOP, DUH!
The third-year boys' cavalry battle is about to get underway.
ZUUUN (DOOM)
Start getting ready, guys.
OKAY! TIE IT ON! TIE IT ON!
GYU (CINCH)
GYU
IF YOU THINK YOU'RE GONNA FALL, SPEAK UP ASAP.
ZAWA (MURMUR)
ZAWA
WEIGHT, HUH? IT'S MY WEIGHT, ISN'T IT?
KUU (GRIMACE)
IF YOU GUYS WERE ON THE BOTTOM, YOU'D BREAK.
WE'RE NOT BRANCHES!
GYUU (CLENCH)

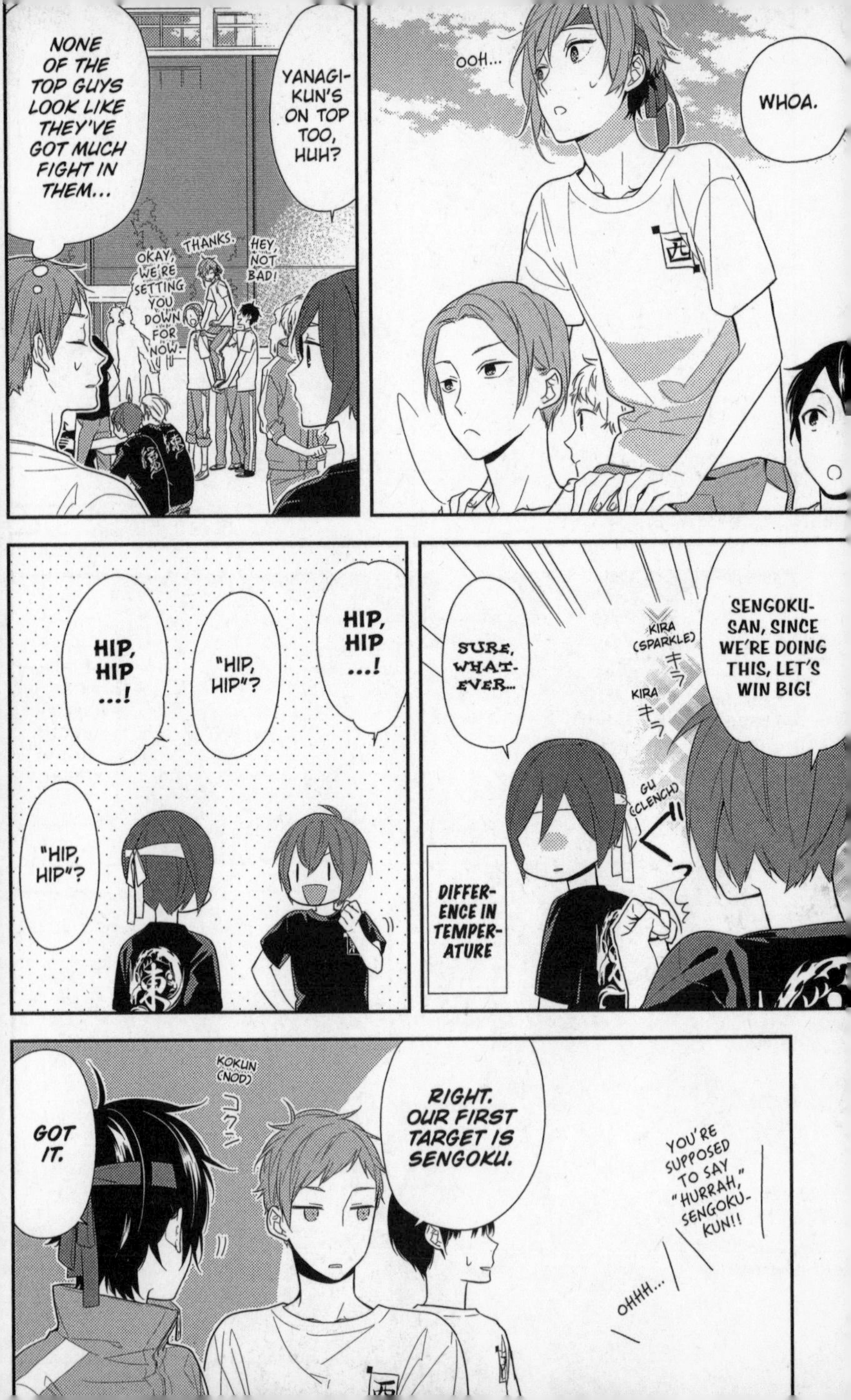
WHOA.
OOH...
YANAGI-KUN'S ON TOP TOO, HUH?
NONE OF THE TOP GUYS LOOK LIKE THEY'VE GOT MUCH FIGHT IN THEM...
HEY, NOT BAD!
THANKS.
OKAY, WE'RE SETTING YOU DOWN FOR NOW.
SENGOKU-SAN, SINCE WE'RE DOING THIS, LET'S WIN BIG!
KIRA (SPARKLE)
KIRA
SURE, WHATEVER...
GU (CLENCH)
DIFFERENCE IN TEMPERATURE
HIP, HIP ...!
"HIP, HIP"?
HIP, HIP ...!
"HIP, HIP"?
YOU'RE SUPPOSED TO SAY "HURRAH, SENGOKU-KUN!!"
RIGHT. OUR FIRST TARGET IS SENGOKU.
KOKUN (NOD)
GOT IT.
OHHH...

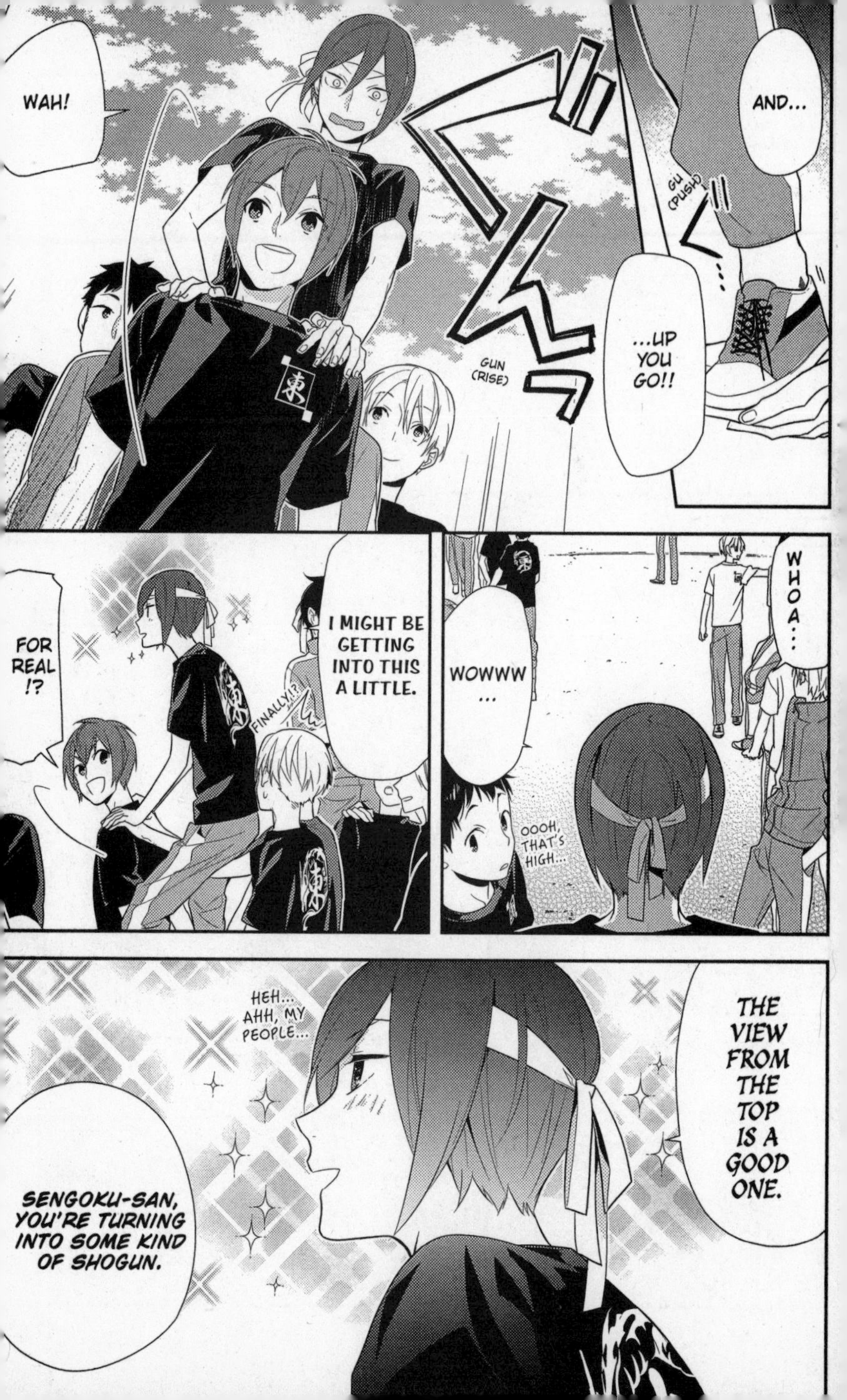
AND...
GU (PUSH)
...UP YOU GO!!
GUN (RISE)
WAH!
WHOA...
WOWWW...
OOOH, THAT'S HIGH...
I MIGHT BE GETTING INTO THIS A LITTLE.
FINALLY!?
FOR REAL!?
THE VIEW FROM THE TOP IS A GOOD ONE.
HEH... AHH, MY PEOPLE...
SENGOKU-SAN, YOU'RE TURNING INTO SOME KIND OF SHOGUN.

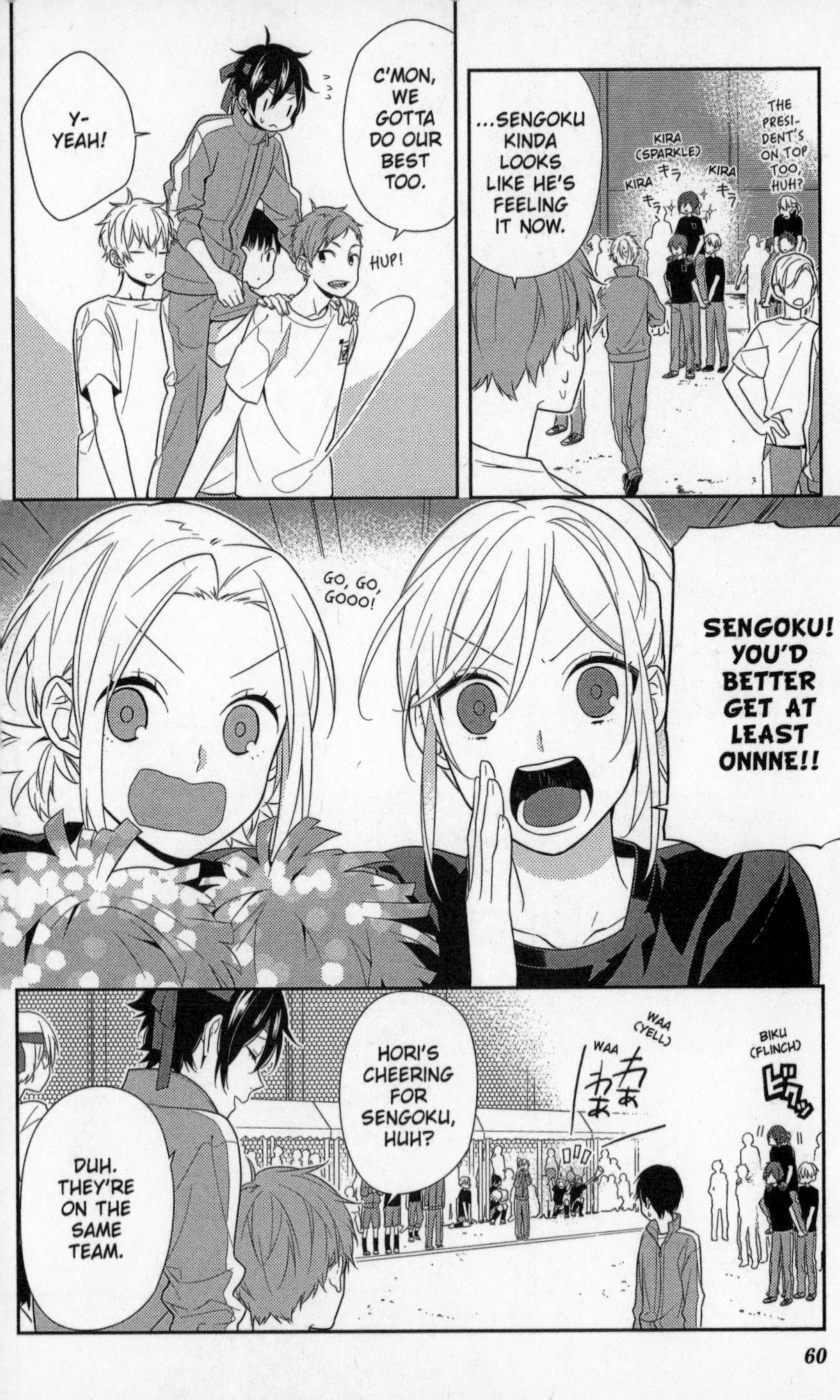
...SENGOKU KINDA LOOKS LIKE HE'S FEELING IT NOW.
KIRA (SPARKLE)
KIRA
KIRA
THE PRESIDENT'S ON TOP TOO, HUH?
C'MON, WE GOTTA DO OUR BEST TOO.
HUP!
Y-YEAH!
SENGOKU! YOU'D BETTER GET AT LEAST ONNNE!!
GO, GO, GOOO!
BIKU (FLINCH)
WAA (YELL)
WAA
HORI'S CHEERING FOR SENGOKU, HUH?
DUH. THEY'RE ON THE SAME TEAM.

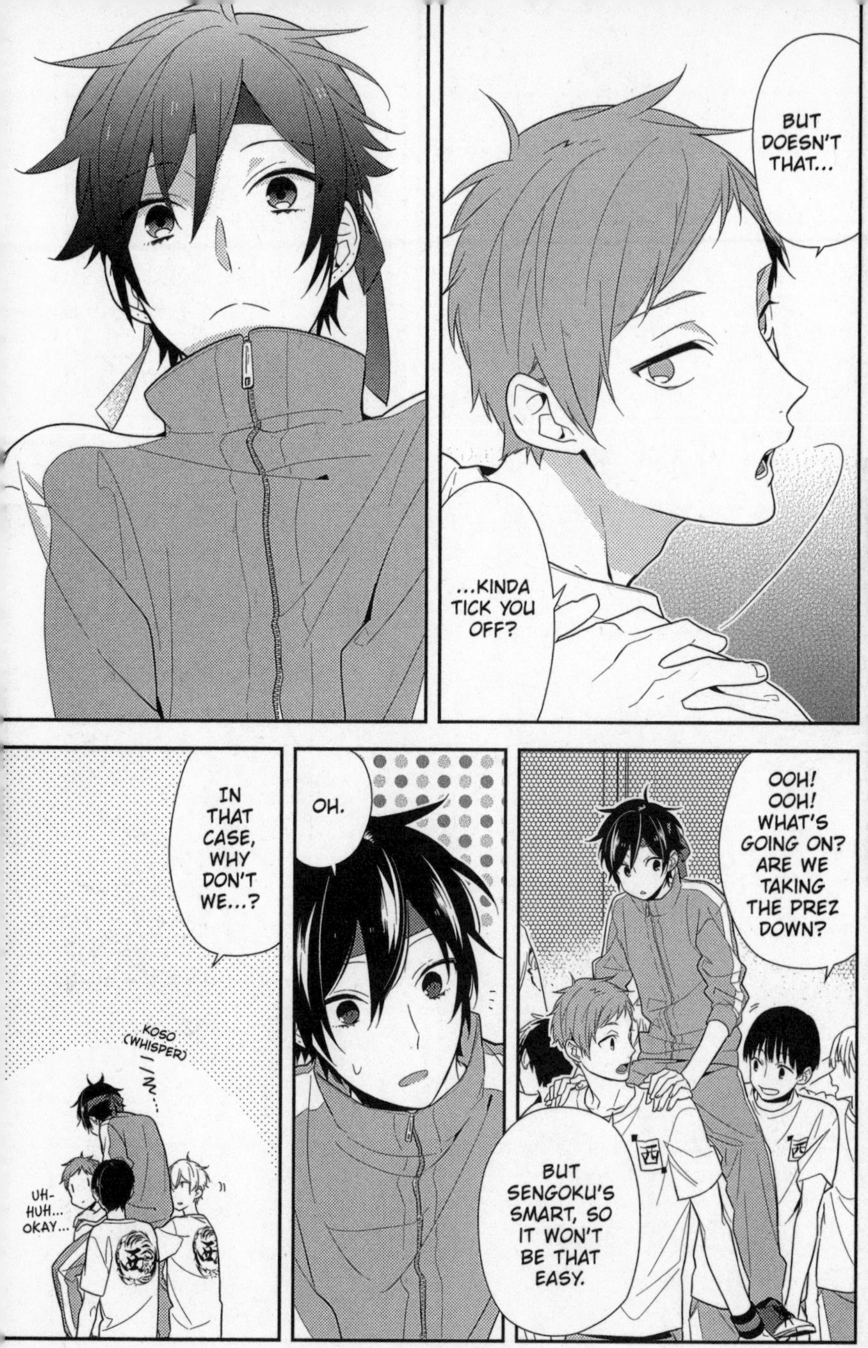
BUT DOESN'T THAT...
...KINDA TICK YOU OFF?
OOH! OOH! WHAT'S GOING ON? ARE WE TAKING THE PREZ DOWN?
BUT SENGOKU'S SMART, SO IT WON'T BE THAT EASY.
OH.
IN THAT CASE, WHY DON'T WE...?
KOSO (WHISPER)
UH-HUH... OKAY...

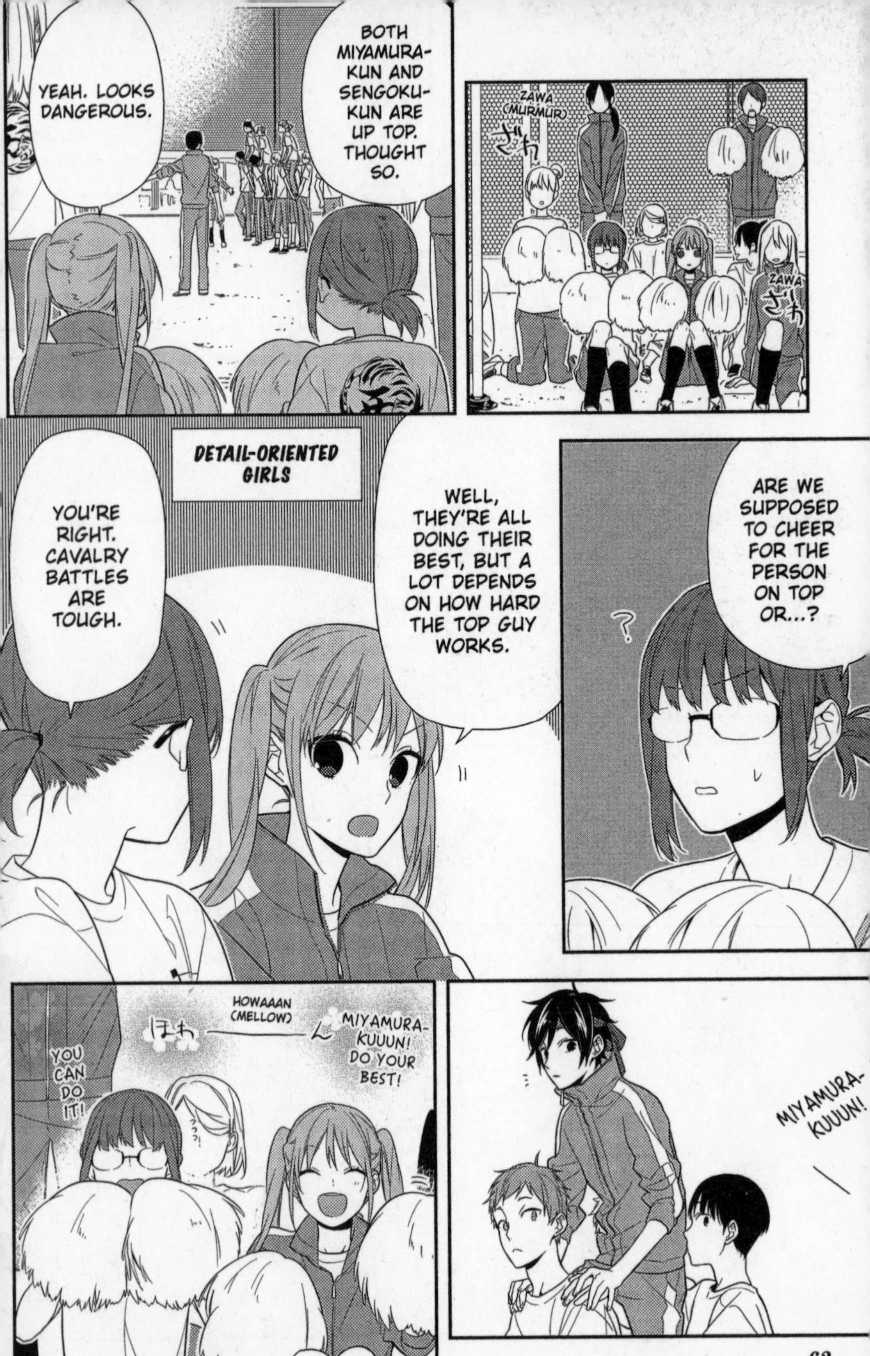
ZAWA (MURMUR)
ざわ
ZAWA
ざわ
BOTH MIYAMURA-KUN AND SENGOKU-KUN ARE UP TOP. THOUGHT SO.
YEAH. LOOKS DANGEROUS.
ARE WE SUPPOSED TO CHEER FOR THE PERSON ON TOP OR...?
?
DETAIL-ORIENTED GIRLS
WELL, THEY'RE ALL DOING THEIR BEST, BUT A LOT DEPENDS ON HOW HARD THE TOP GUY WORKS.
YOU'RE RIGHT. CAVALRY BATTLES ARE TOUGH.
MIYAMURA-KUUUN!
HOWAAAN (MELLOW)
ほわ——ん
MIYAMURA-KUUUN! DO YOUR BEST!
YOU CAN DO IT!

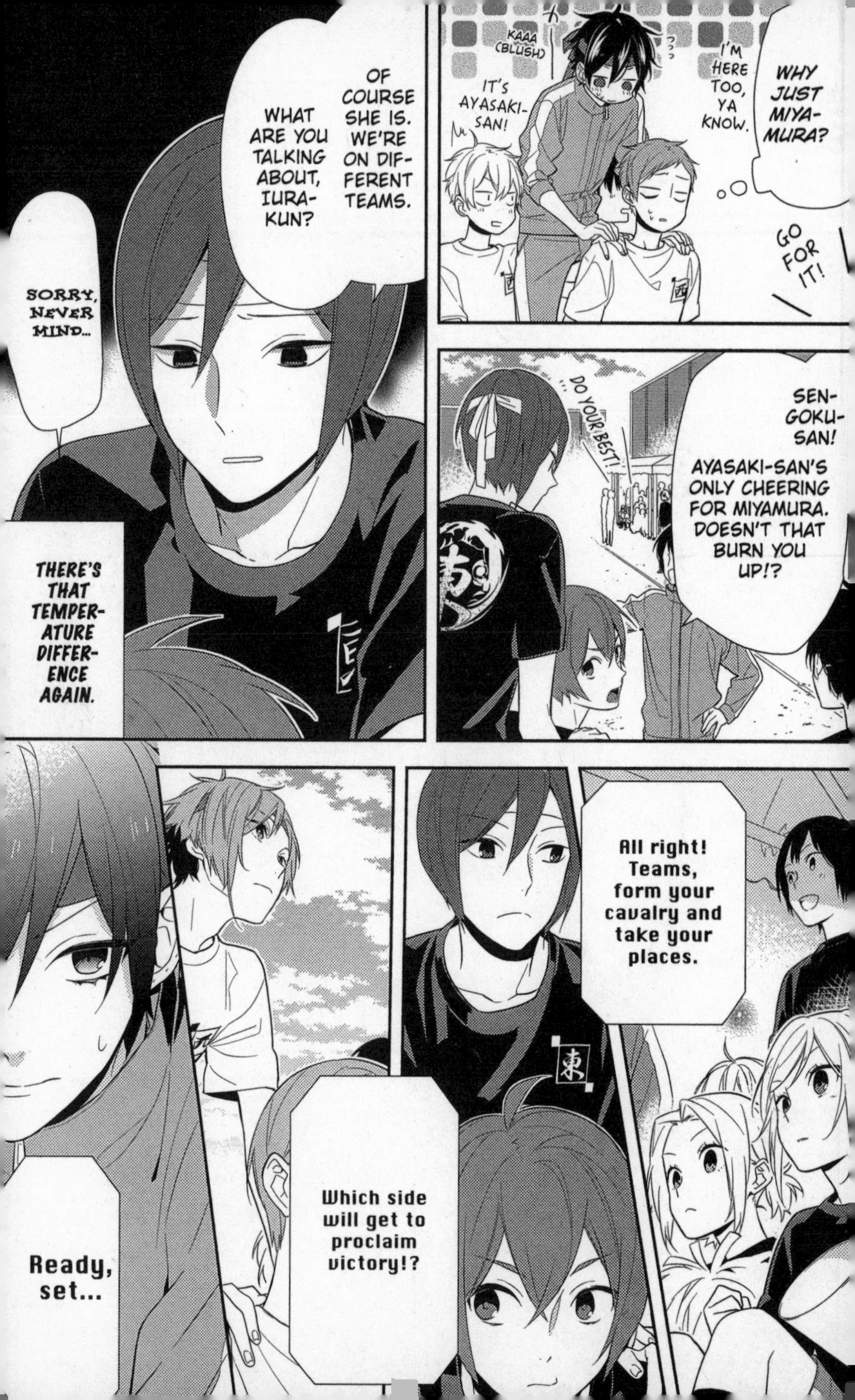
WHY JUST MIYAMURA?
I'M HERE TOO, YA KNOW.
KAAA (BLUSH)
IT'S AYASAKI-SAN!
GO FOR IT!
SEN-GOKU-SAN! AYASAKI-SAN'S ONLY CHEERING FOR MIYAMURA. DOESN'T THAT BURN YOU UP!?
DO YOUR BEST!
OF COURSE SHE IS. WE'RE ON DIF-FERENT TEAMS.
WHAT ARE YOU TALKING ABOUT, IURA-KUN?
SORRY, NEVER MIND...
THERE'S THAT TEMPER-ATURE DIFFER-ENCE AGAIN.
All right! Teams, form your cavalry and take your places.
Which side will get to proclaim victory!?
Ready, set...

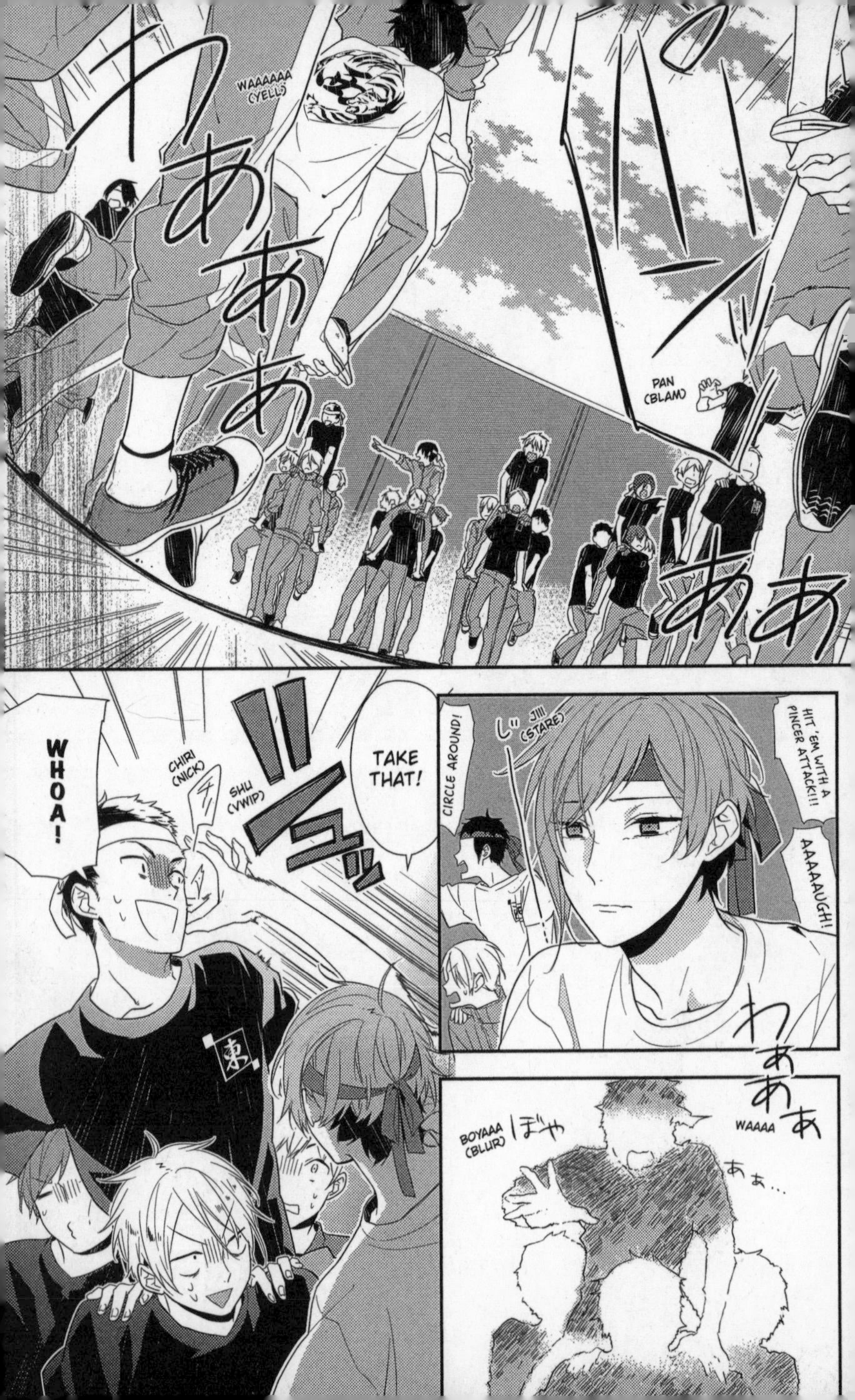
パーンッ
PAN (BLAM)
わああああ
WAAAAAA (YELL)
ああ
HIT 'EM WITH A PINCER ATTACK!!!
AAAAAUGH!
じ
JIII (STARE)
CIRCLE AROUND!
わあああ
WAAAA
ぼや
BOYAAA (BLUR)
あぁ…
TAKE THAT!
シュッ
SHU (VWIP)
チ
CHIRI (NICK)
WHOA!

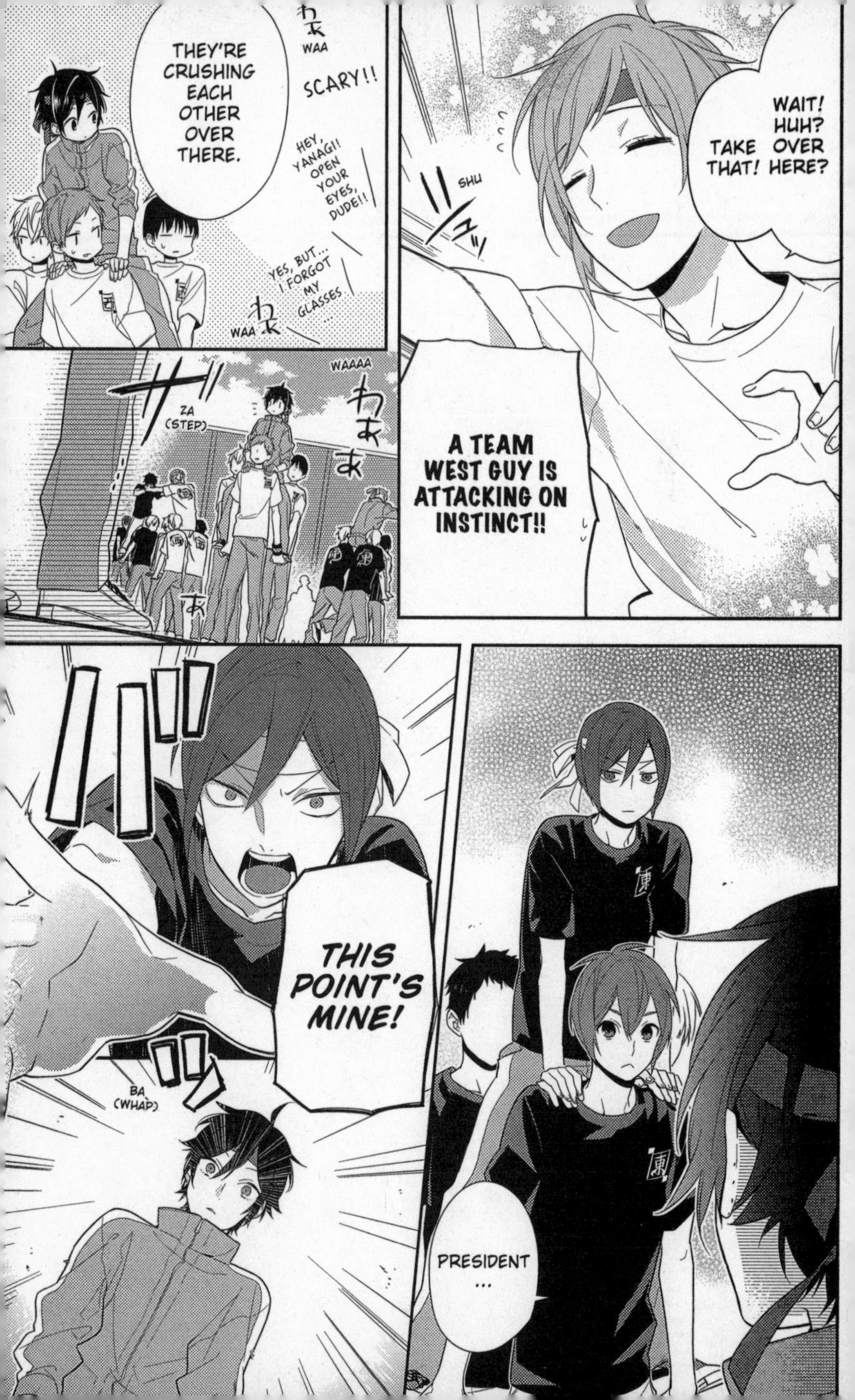
WAIT! HUH? OVER HERE?
TAKE THAT!
SHU
A TEAM WEST GUY IS ATTACKING ON INSTINCT!!
WAA
THEY'RE CRUSHING EACH OTHER OVER THERE.
SCARY!!
HEY, YANAGI!! OPEN YOUR EYES, DUDE!!
YES, BUT... I FORGOT MY GLASSES...
WAA
WAAAA
ZA (STEP)
PRESIDENT...
THIS POINT'S MINE!
BA (WHAP)

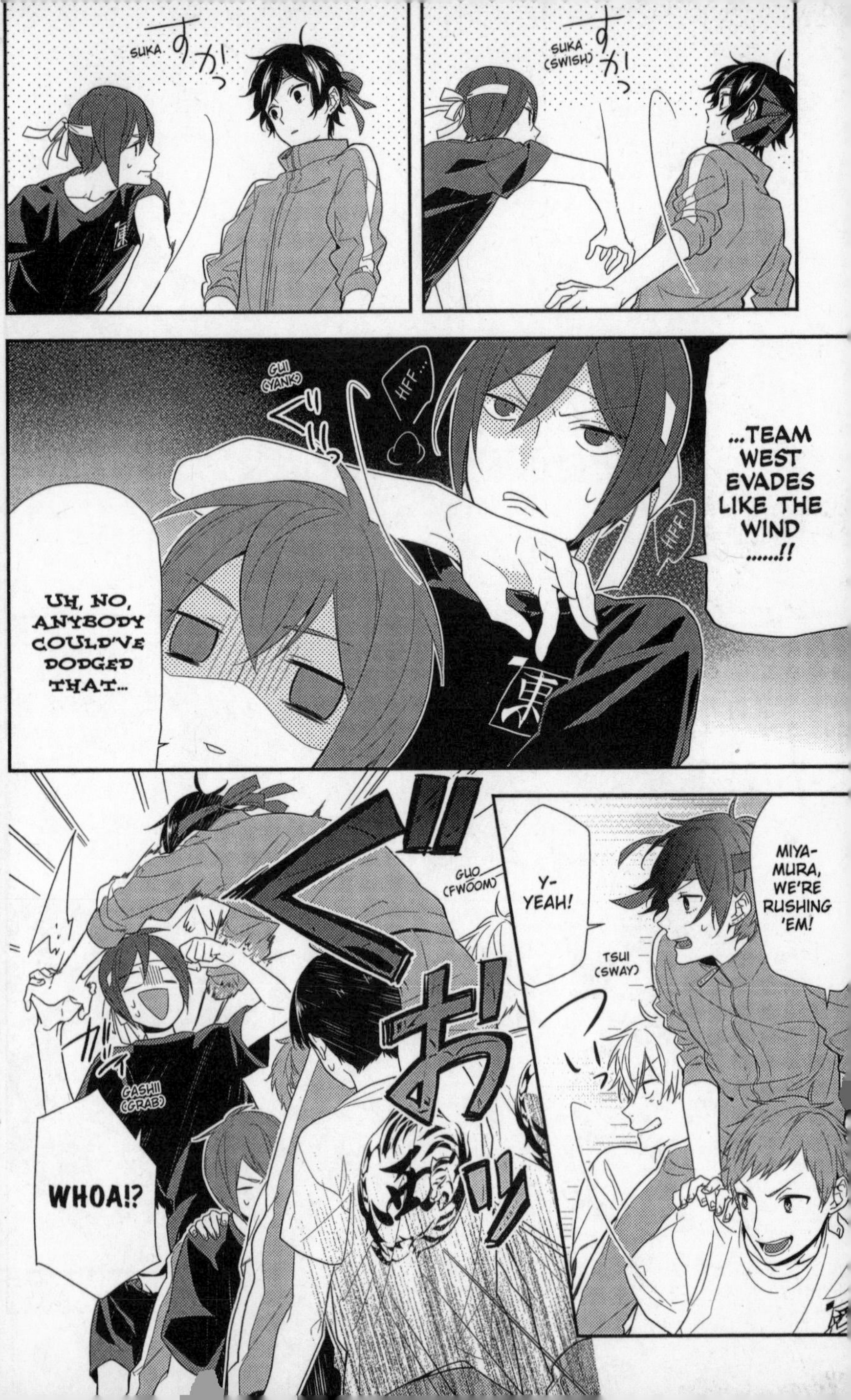

SUKA (SWISH)
すかっ
SUKA
すかっ
...TEAM WEST EVADES LIKE THE WIND ......!!
HFF!
GUI (YANK)
ぐいっ
HFF...
UH, NO, ANYBODY COULD'VE DODGED THAT...
MIYA-MURA, WE'RE RUSHING 'EM!
Y-YEAH!
GUO (FWOOM)
TSUI (SWAY)
ぐおっ
GASHI (GRAB)
WHOA!?

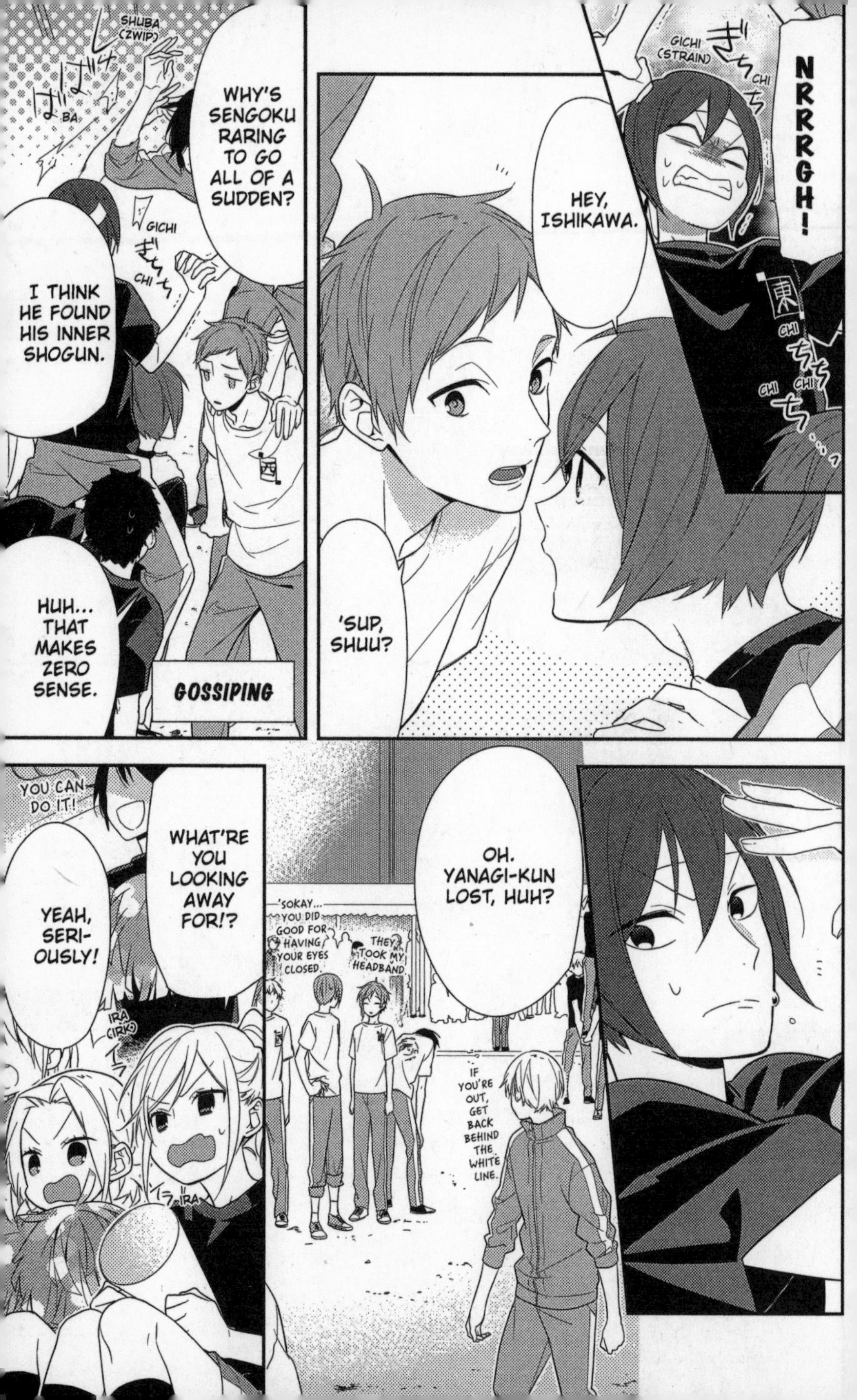
GICHI (STRAIN)
ぎち
CHI
NRRRGH!
東
CHI CHI CHI
HEY, ISHIKAWA.
'SUP, SHUU?
SHUBA (ZWIP)
BA
WHY'S SENGOKU RARING TO GO ALL OF A SUDDEN?
GICHI
ぎちち
CHI
I THINK HE FOUND HIS INNER SHOGUN.
HUH... THAT MAKES ZERO SENSE.
GOSSIPING
OH. YANAGI-KUN LOST, HUH?
'SOKAY... YOU DID GOOD FOR HAVING YOUR EYES CLOSED.
THEY TOOK MY HEADBAND.
IF YOU'RE OUT, GET BACK BEHIND THE WHITE LINE.
YOU CAN DO IT!
WHAT'RE YOU LOOKING AWAY FOR!?
YEAH, SERI-OUSLY!
IRA (IRK)
IRA IRA

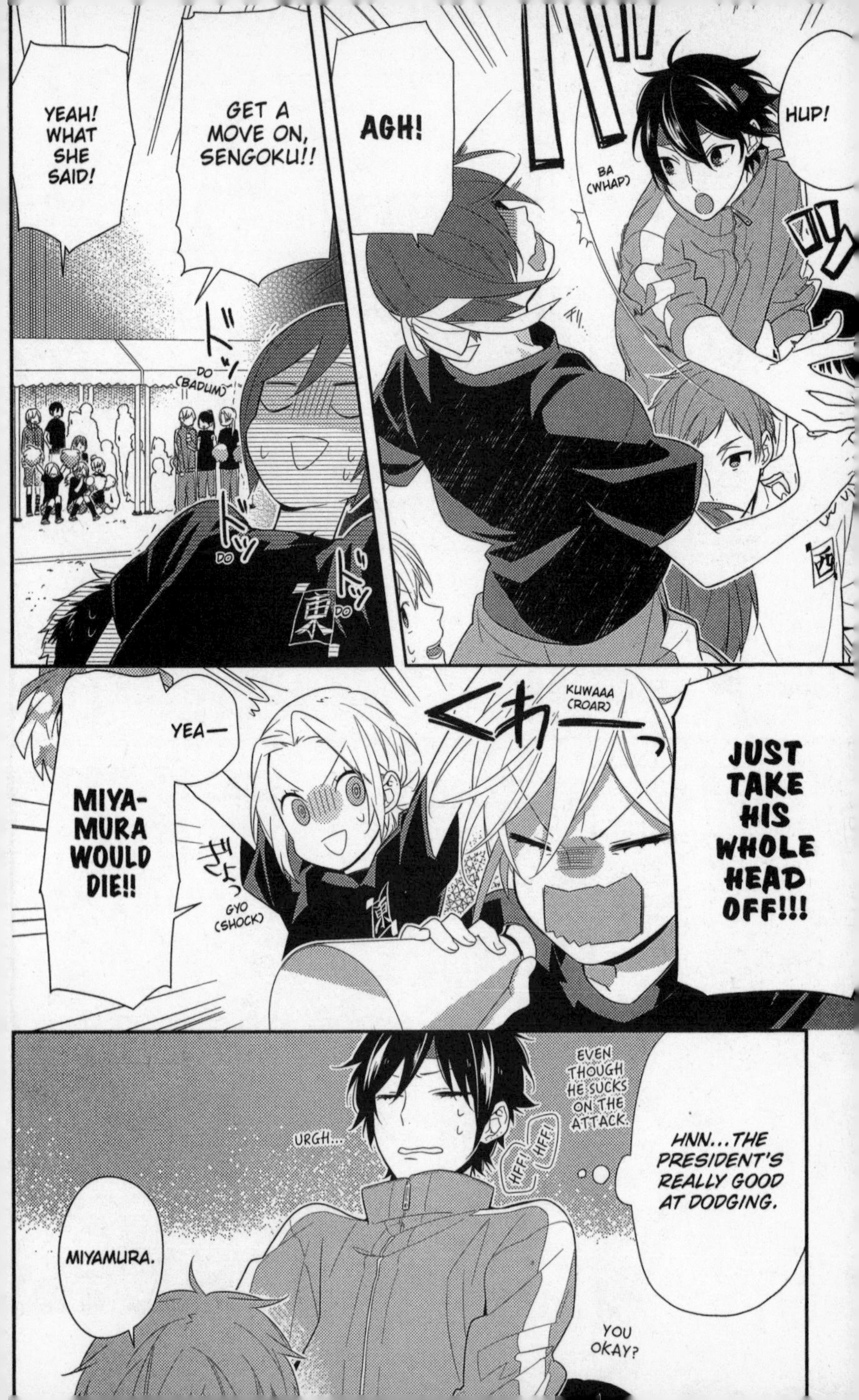
HUP!
BA (WHAP)
AGH!
GET A MOVE ON, SENGOKU!!
YEAH! WHAT SHE SAID!
DO (BADUM)
DO
DO
JUST TAKE HIS WHOLE HEAD OFF!!!
KUWAAA (ROAR)
YEA—
MIYA-MURA WOULD DIE!!
GYO (SHOCK)
HNN...THE PRESIDENT'S REALLY GOOD AT DODGING.
EVEN THOUGH HE SUCKS ON THE ATTACK.
HFF! HFF!
URGH...
YOU OKAY?
MIYAMURA.

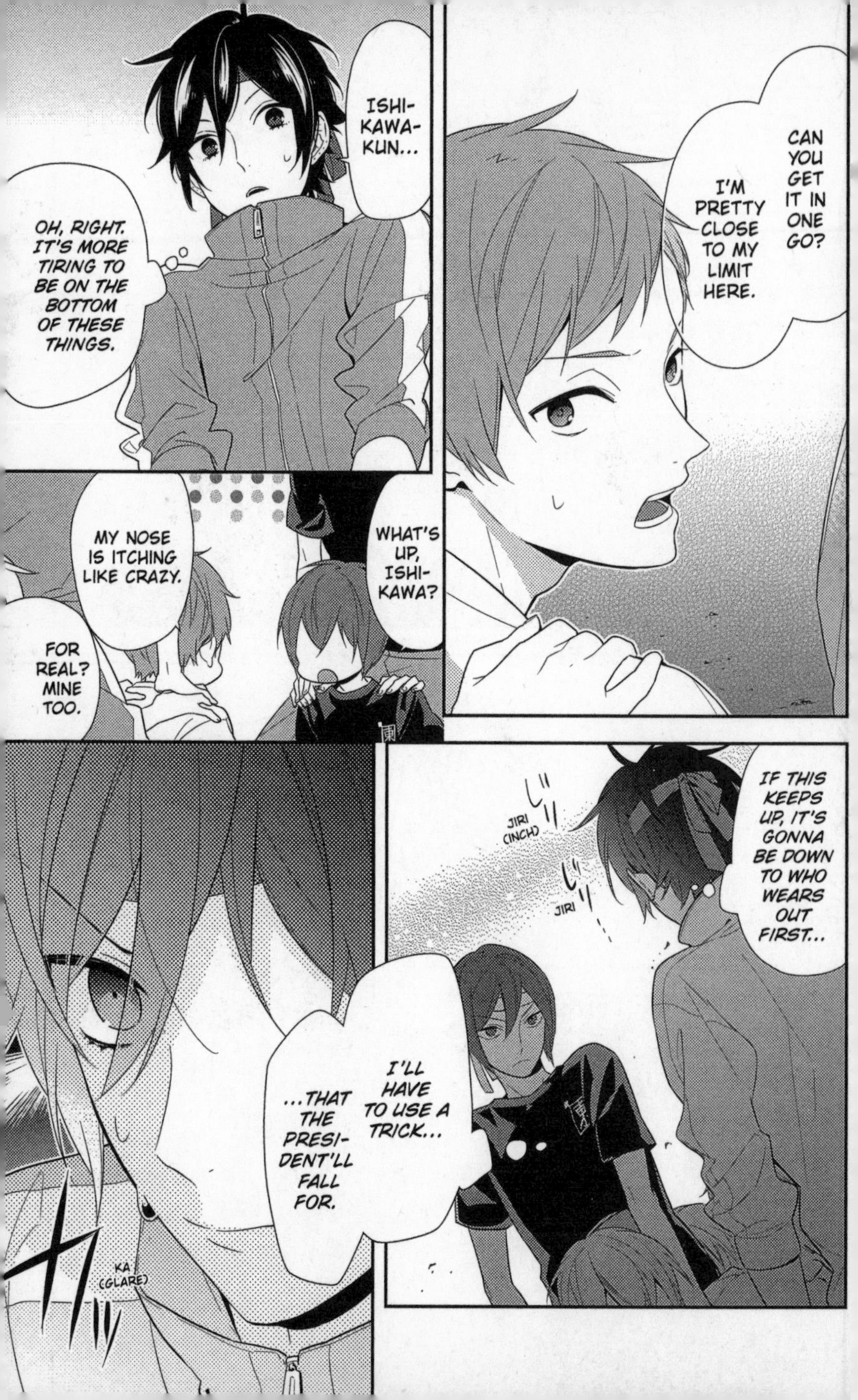
CAN YOU GET IT IN ONE GO?
I'M PRETTY CLOSE TO MY LIMIT HERE.
ISHI-KAWA-KUN...
OH, RIGHT. IT'S MORE TIRING TO BE ON THE BOTTOM OF THESE THINGS.
WHAT'S UP, ISHI-KAWA?
MY NOSE IS ITCHING LIKE CRAZY.
FOR REAL? MINE TOO.
IF THIS KEEPS UP, IT'S GONNA BE DOWN TO WHO WEARS OUT FIRST...
JIRI (INCH)
JIRI
I'LL HAVE TO USE A TRICK...
...THAT THE PRESI-DENT'LL FALL FOR.
KA (GLARE)

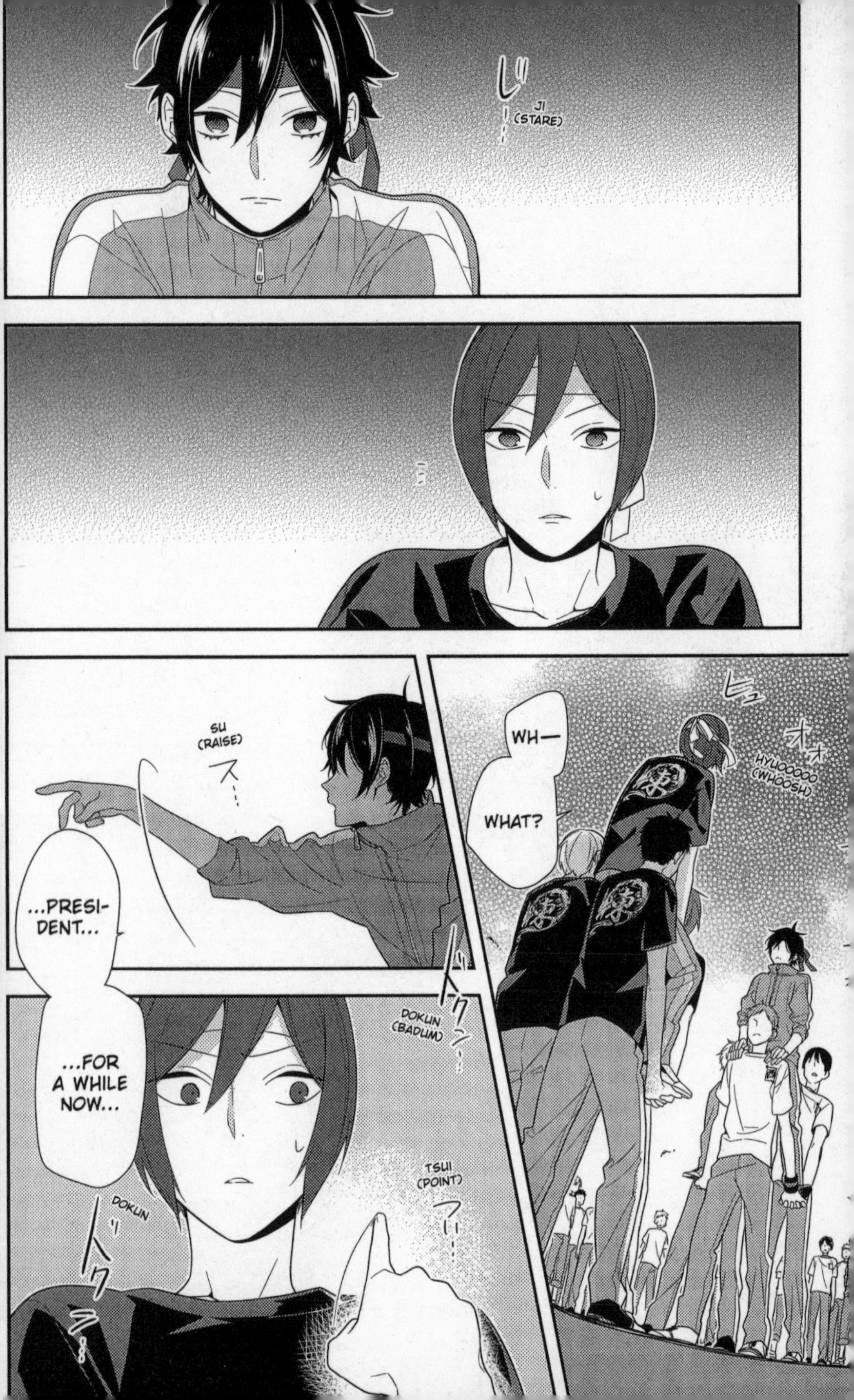

ジ
JI (STARE)
ヒュオオ
HYUOOOOO (WHOOSH)
WH— WHAT?
ス
SU (RAISE)
...PRESI-DENT...
...FOR A WHILE NOW...
ドクン
DOKUN (BADUM)
DOKUN
ドクン
TSUI (POINT)

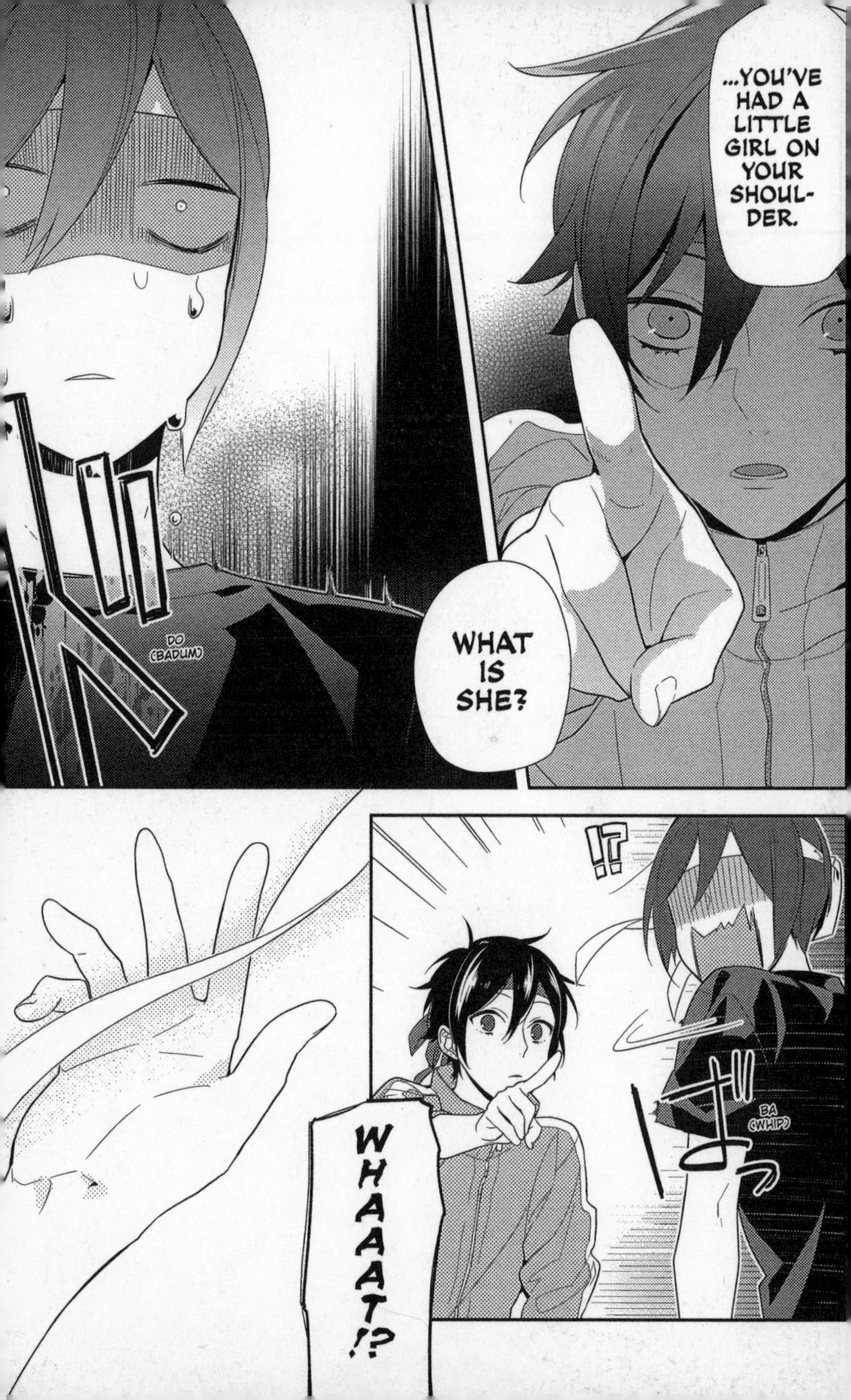
...YOU'VE HAD A LITTLE GIRL ON YOUR SHOUL-DER.
WHAT IS SHE?
DO (BADUM)
!?
BA (WHIP)
WHAAAT!?

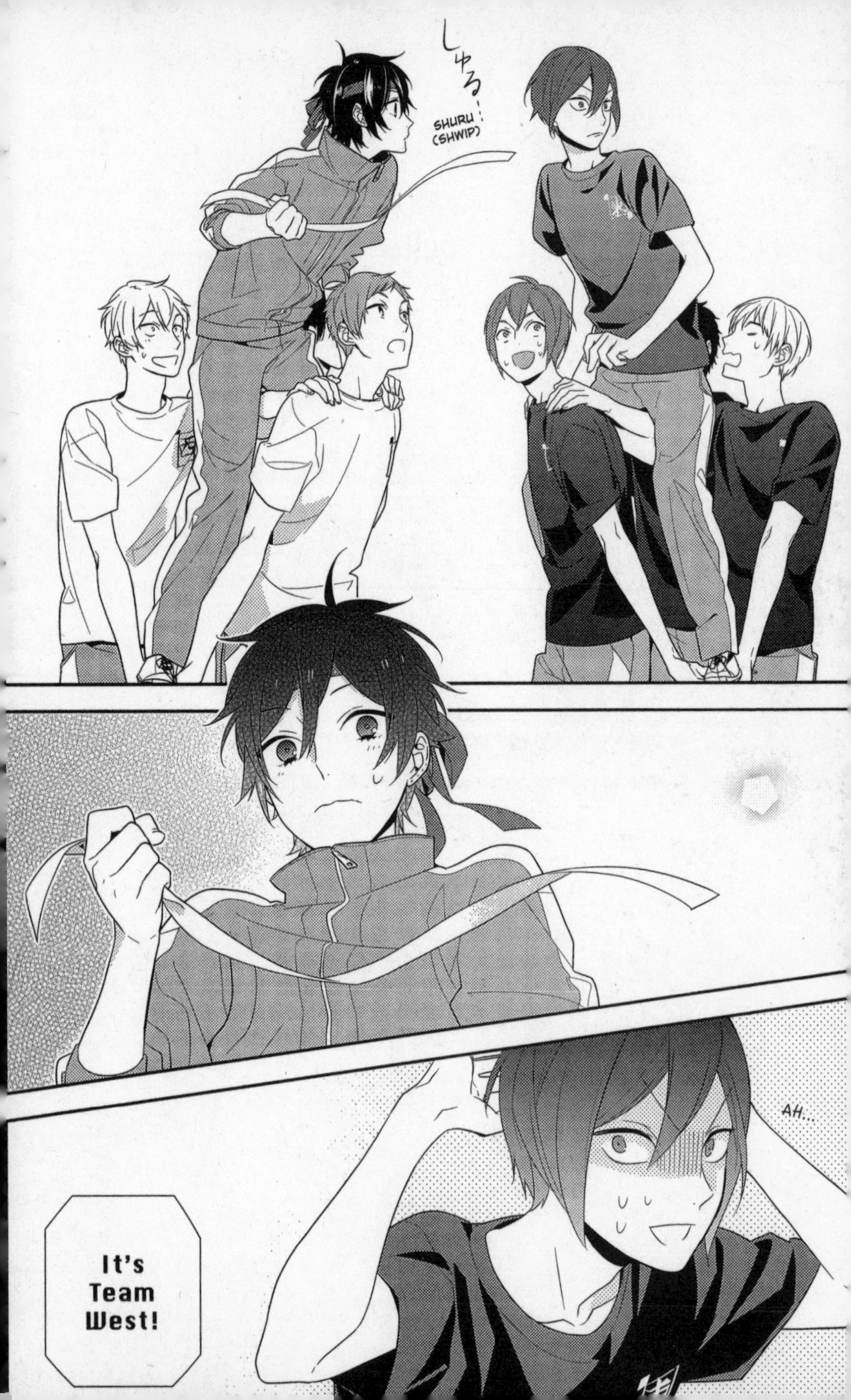
しゅる
SHURU (SHWIP)
AH...
It's Team West!

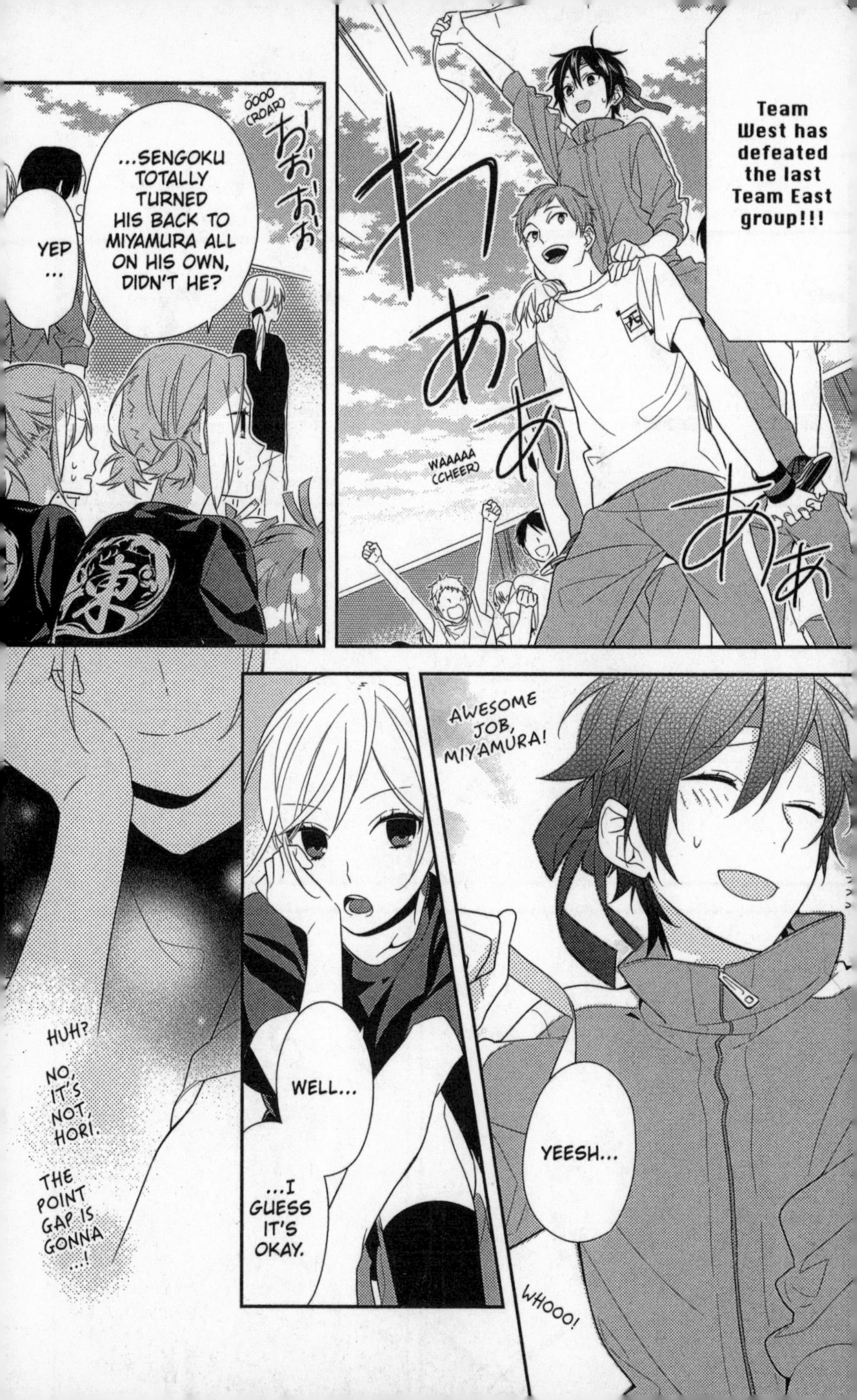

Team West has defeated the last Team East group!!!
わああ
ああ
WAAAAA (CHEER)
おおおお
OOOO (ROAR)
...SENGOKU TOTALLY TURNED HIS BACK TO MIYAMURA ALL ON HIS OWN, DIDN'T HE?
YEP ...
AWESOME JOB, MIYAMURA!
YEESH...
WHOOO!
WELL...
...I GUESS IT'S OKAY.
HUH?
NO, IT'S NOT, HORI.
THE POINT GAP IS GONNA ...!

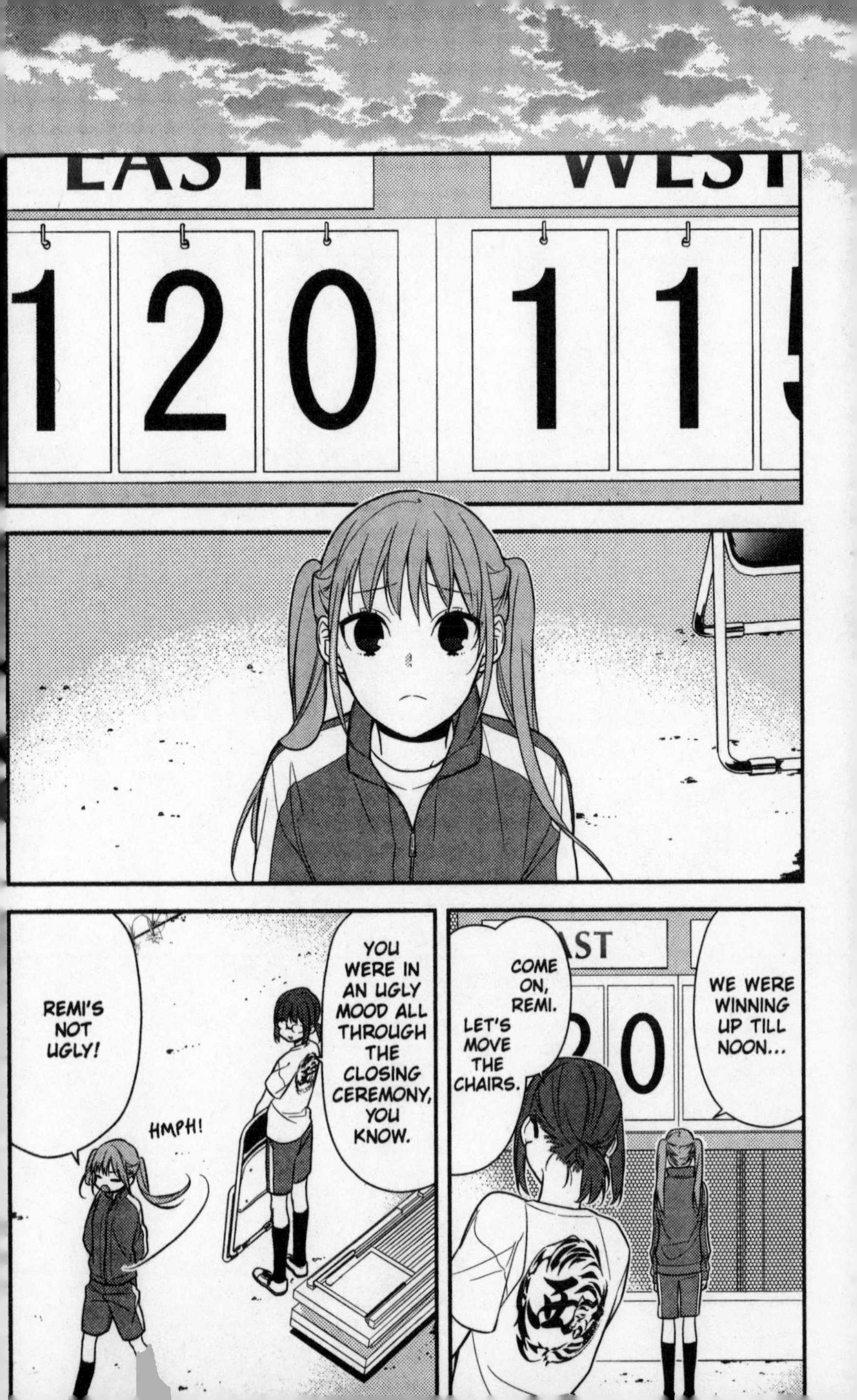
EAST
WEST
120
11
WE WERE WINNING UP TILL NOON...
COME ON, REMI.
LET'S MOVE THE CHAIRS.
YOU WERE IN AN UGLY MOOD ALL THROUGH THE CLOSING CEREMONY, YOU KNOW.
REMI'S NOT UGLY!
HMPH!

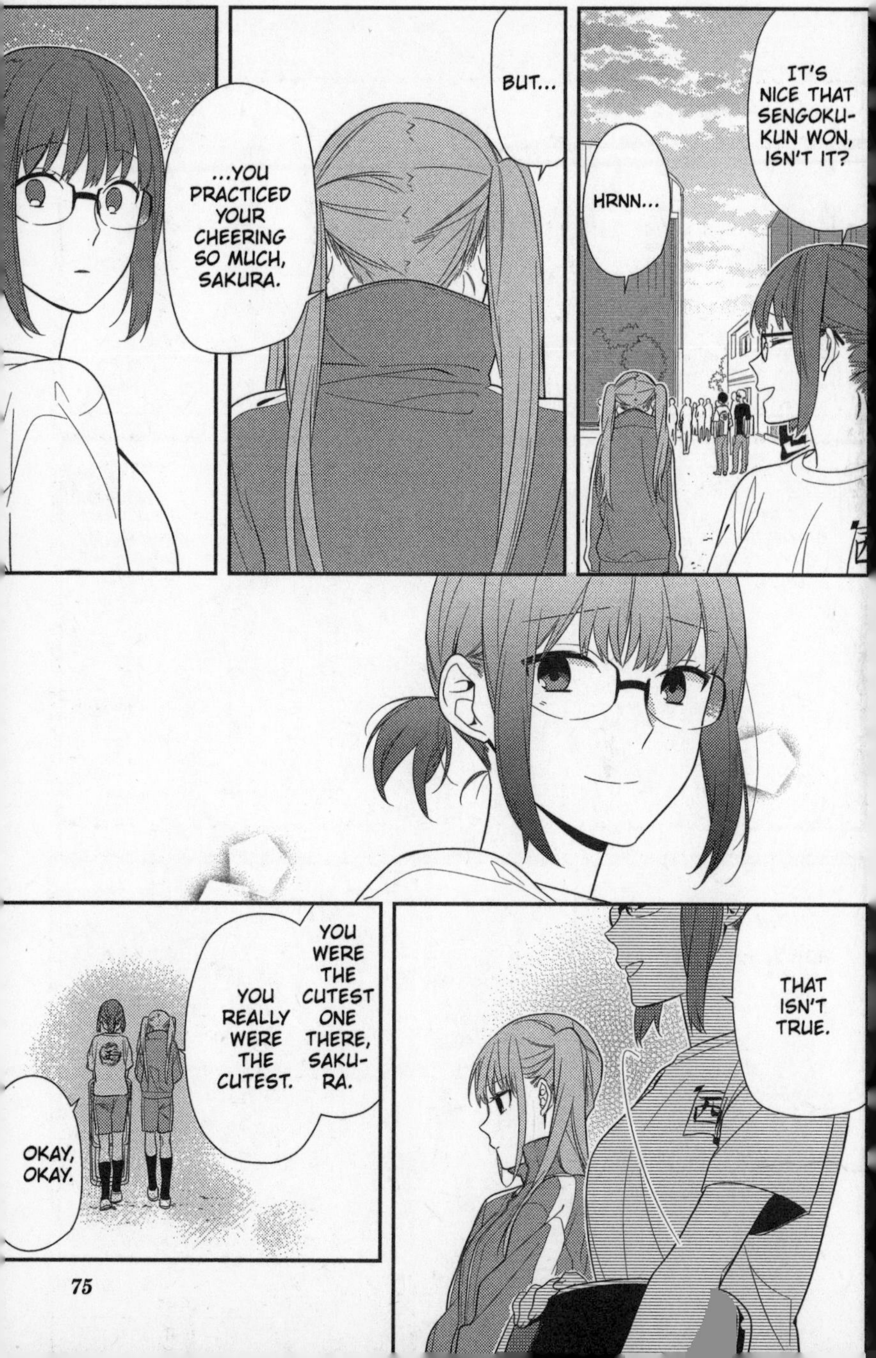
IT'S NICE THAT SENGOKU-KUN WON, ISN'T IT?
HRNN...
BUT...
...YOU PRACTICED YOUR CHEERING SO MUCH, SAKURA.
THAT ISN'T TRUE.
YOU WERE THE CUTEST ONE THERE, SAKURA.
YOU REALLY WERE THE CUTEST.
OKAY, OKAY.

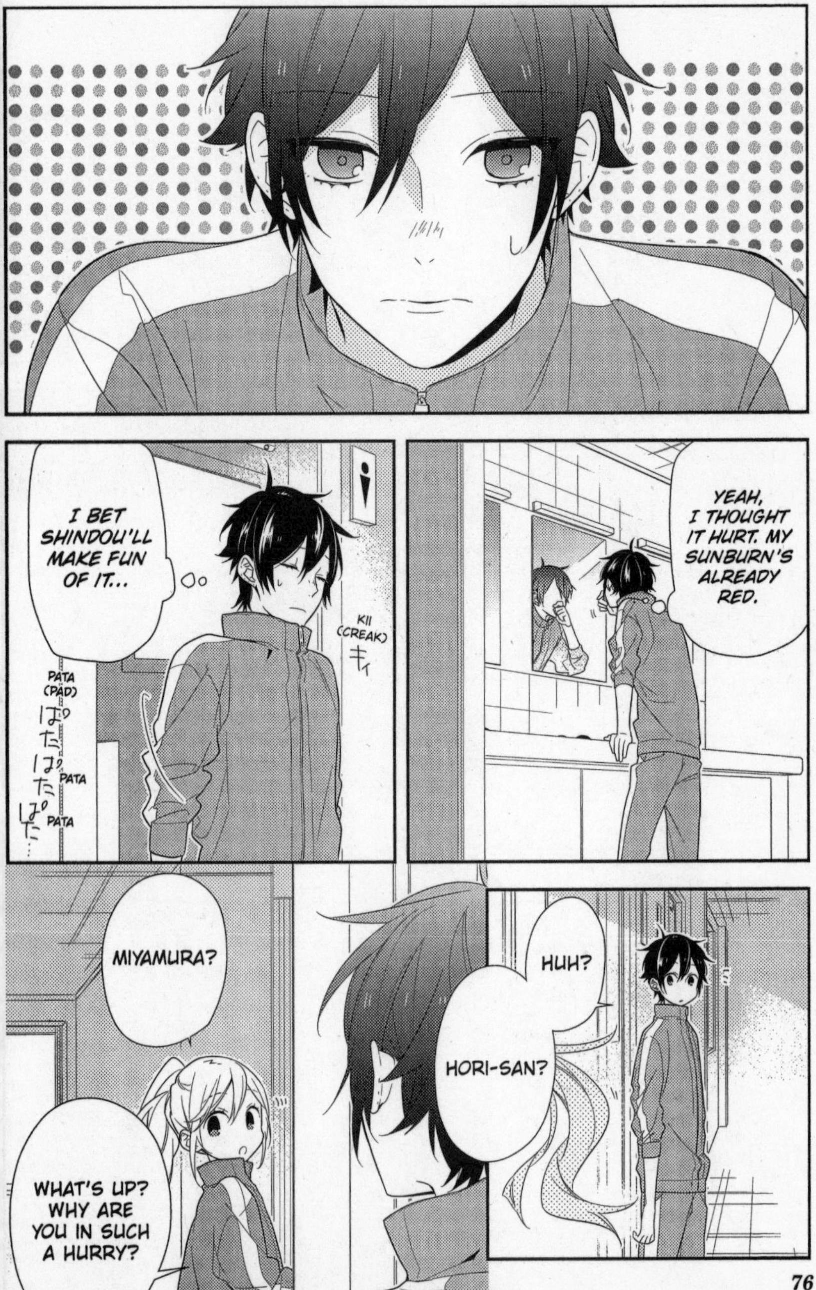
YEAH, I THOUGHT IT HURT. MY SUNBURN'S ALREADY RED.
I BET SHINDOU'LL MAKE FUN OF IT...
KII (CREAK)
キィ
PATA (PÄD)
ぱたぱたぱた…
PATA
PATA
HUH?
MIYAMURA?
HORI-SAN?
WHAT'S UP? WHY ARE YOU IN SUCH A HURRY?

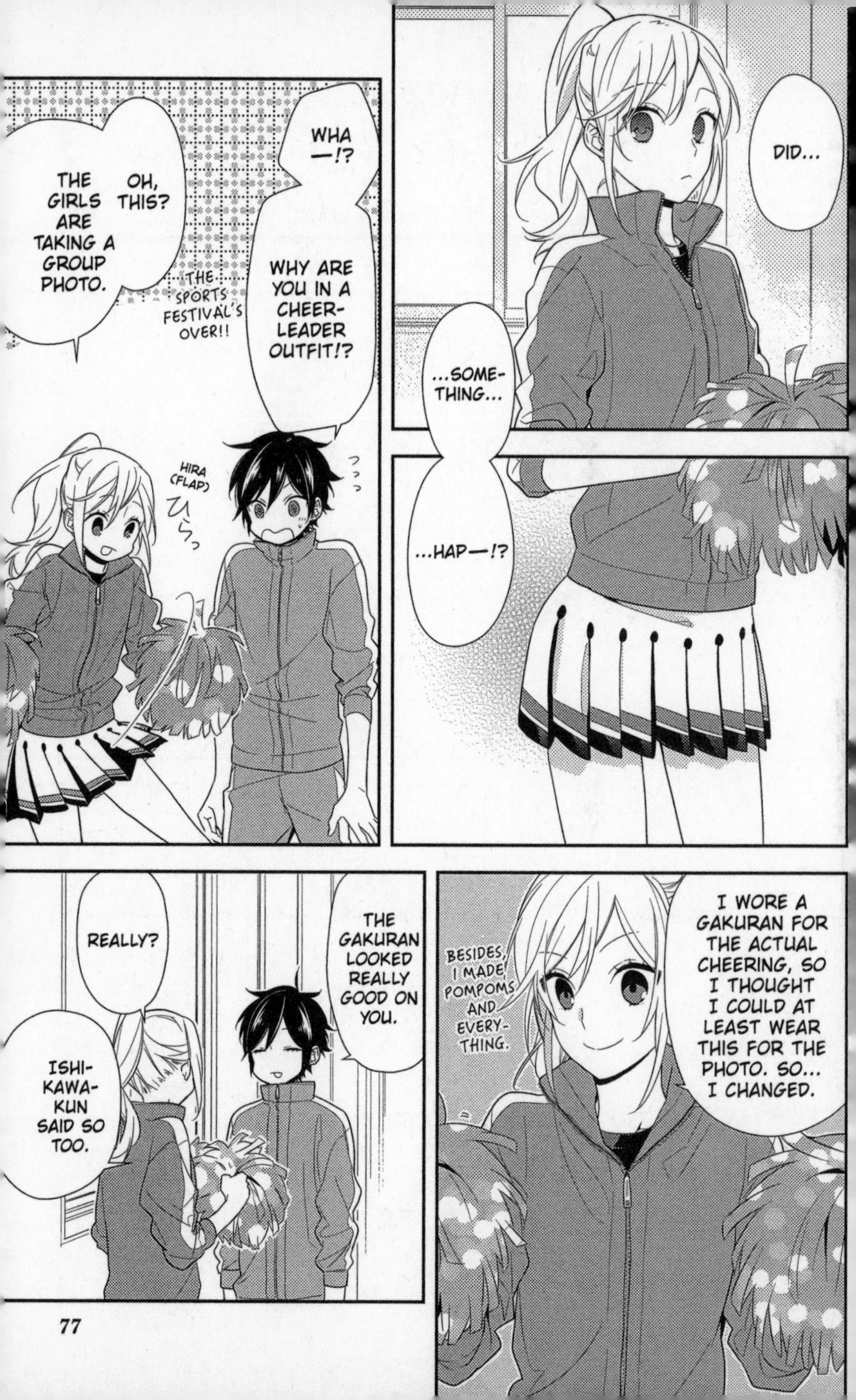
DID...
...SOME-THING...
...HAP—!?
WHA—!?
WHY ARE YOU IN A CHEER-LEADER OUTFIT!?
THE SPORTS FESTIVAL'S OVER!!
OH, THIS?
THE GIRLS ARE TAKING A GROUP PHOTO.
HIRA (FLAP)
I WORE A GAKURAN FOR THE ACTUAL CHEERING, SO I THOUGHT I COULD AT LEAST WEAR THIS FOR THE PHOTO. SO... I CHANGED.
BESIDES, I MADE POMPOMS AND EVERY-THING.
THE GAKURAN LOOKED REALLY GOOD ON YOU.
REALLY?
ISHI-KAWA-KUN SAID SO TOO.

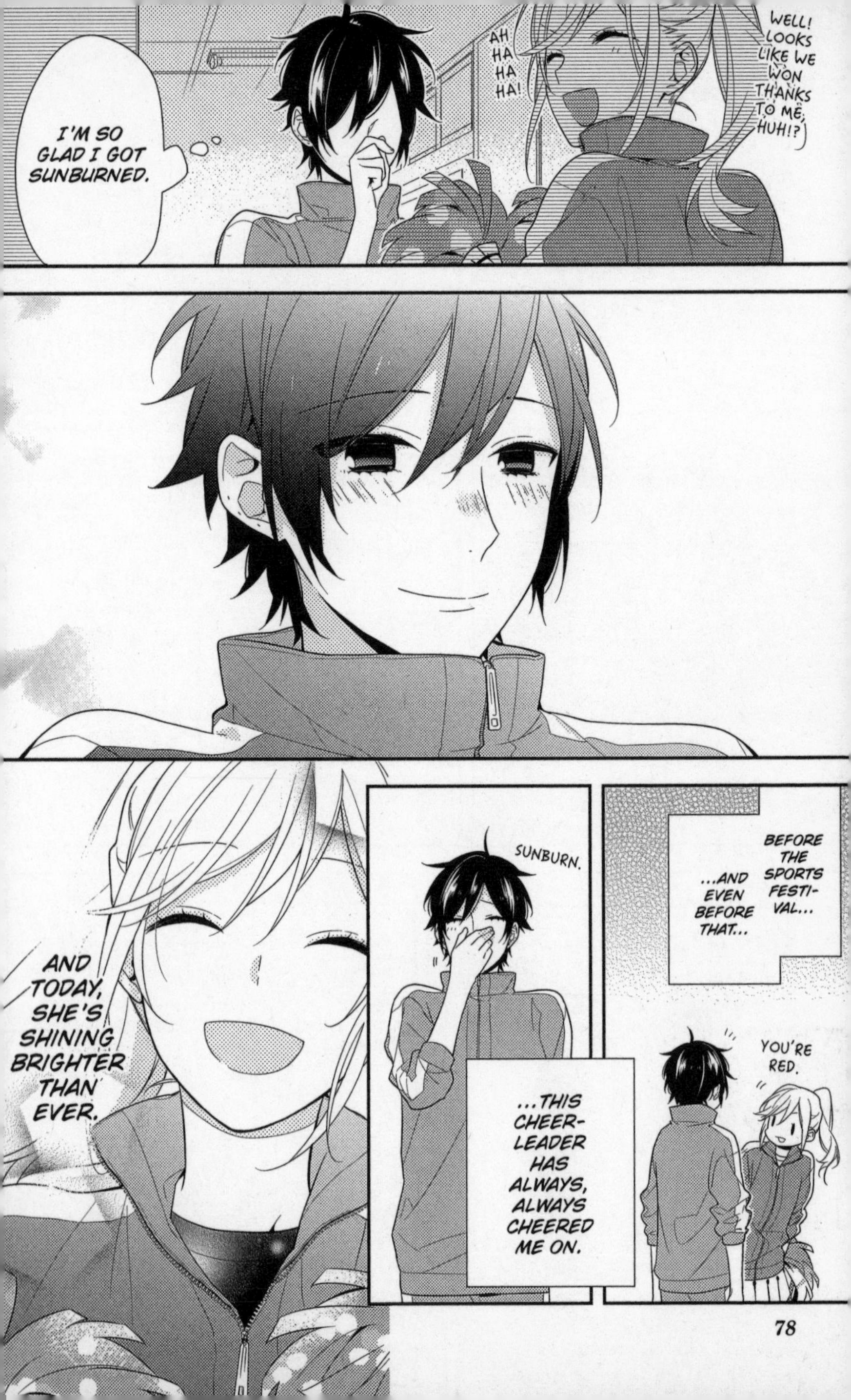
WELL! LOOKS LIKE WE WON THANKS TO ME, HUH!?
AH HA HA HA!
I'M SO GLAD I GOT SUNBURNED.
BEFORE THE SPORTS FESTI-VAL...
...AND EVEN BEFORE THAT...
YOU'RE RED.
SUNBURN.
...THIS CHEER-LEADER HAS ALWAYS, ALWAYS CHEERED ME ON.
AND TODAY, SHE'S SHINING BRIGHTER THAN EVER.

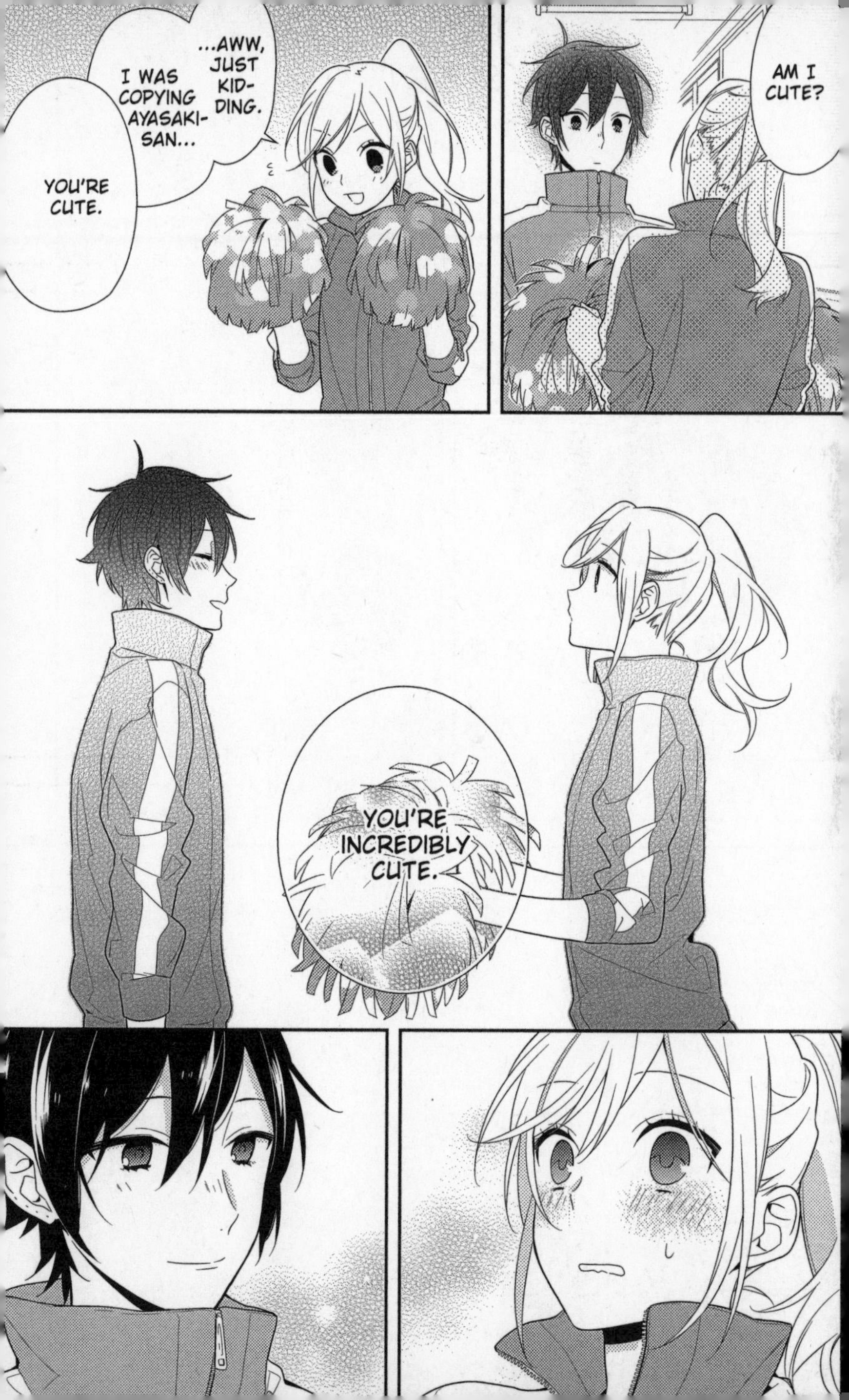
AM I CUTE?
...AWW, JUST KID-DING.
I WAS COPYING AYASAKI-SAN...
YOU'RE CUTE.
YOU'RE INCREDIBLY CUTE.

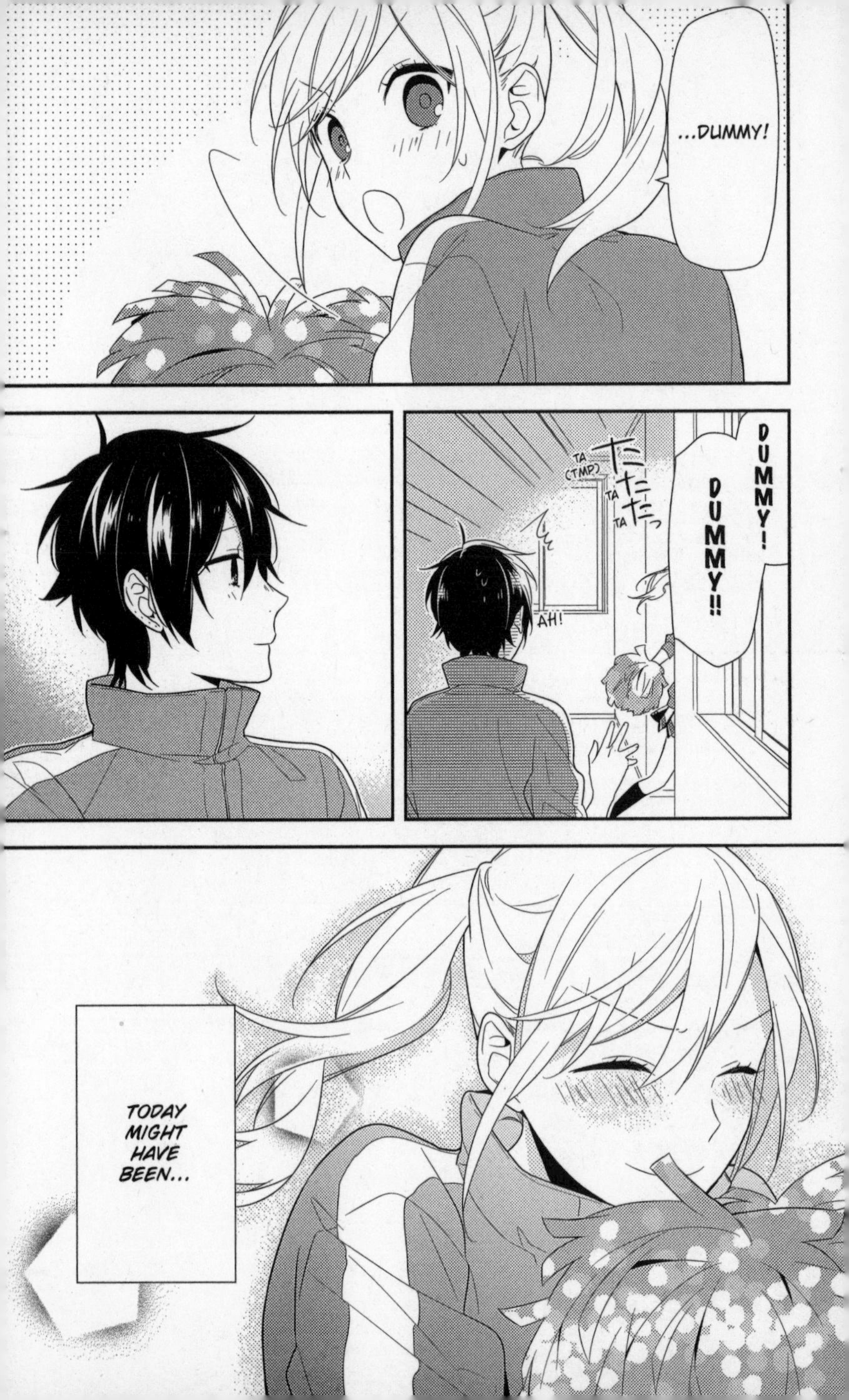
...DUMMY!
DUMMY! DUMMY!!
TA (TMP)
TA
TA
AH!
TODAY MIGHT HAVE BEEN...

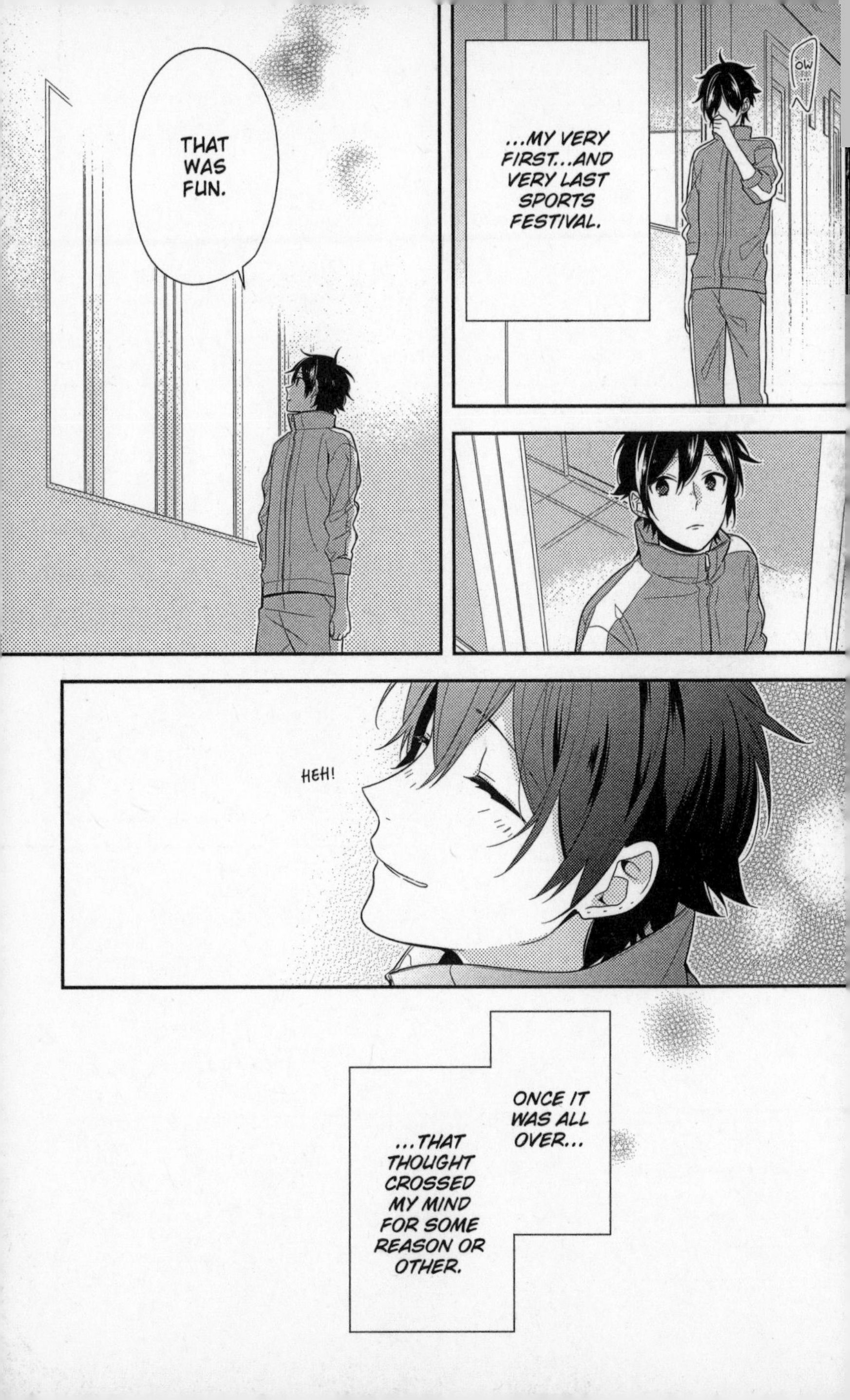
OW
...MY VERY FIRST...AND VERY LAST SPORTS FESTIVAL.
THAT WAS FUN.
HEH!
ONCE IT WAS ALL OVER...
...THAT THOUGHT CROSSED MY MIND FOR SOME REASON OR OTHER.

HORIMIYA

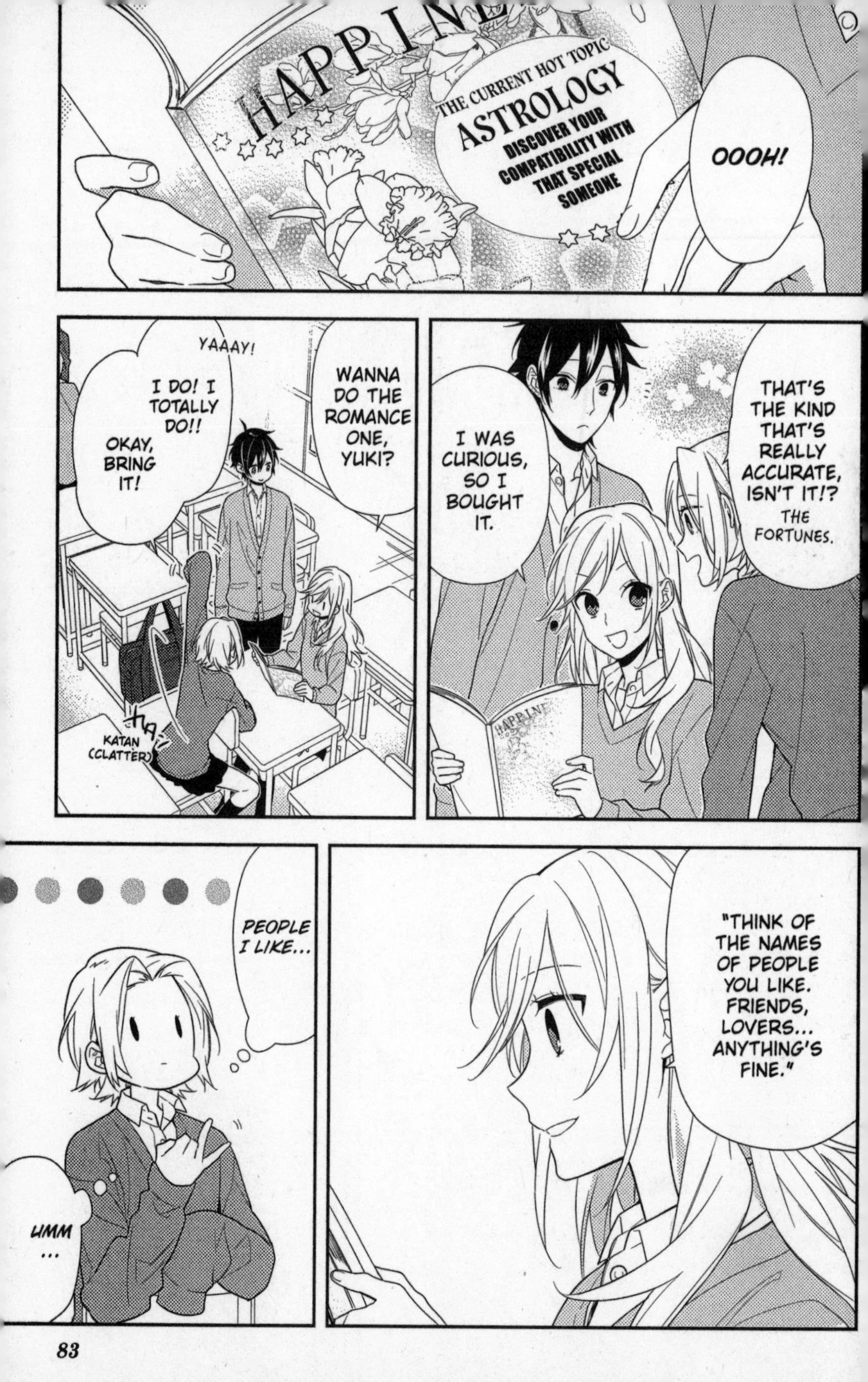
THE CURRENT HOT TOPIC
ASTROLOGY
DISCOVER YOUR COMPATIBILITY WITH THAT SPECIAL SOMEONE
OOOH!
THAT'S THE KIND THAT'S REALLY ACCURATE, ISN'T IT!? THE FORTUNES.
I WAS CURIOUS, SO I BOUGHT IT.
WANNA DO THE ROMANCE ONE, YUKI?
YAAAY!
I DO! I TOTALLY DO!!
OKAY, BRING IT!
KATAN (CLATTER)
"THINK OF THE NAMES OF PEOPLE YOU LIKE. FRIENDS, LOVERS... ANYTHING'S FINE."
PEOPLE I LIKE...
UMM ...

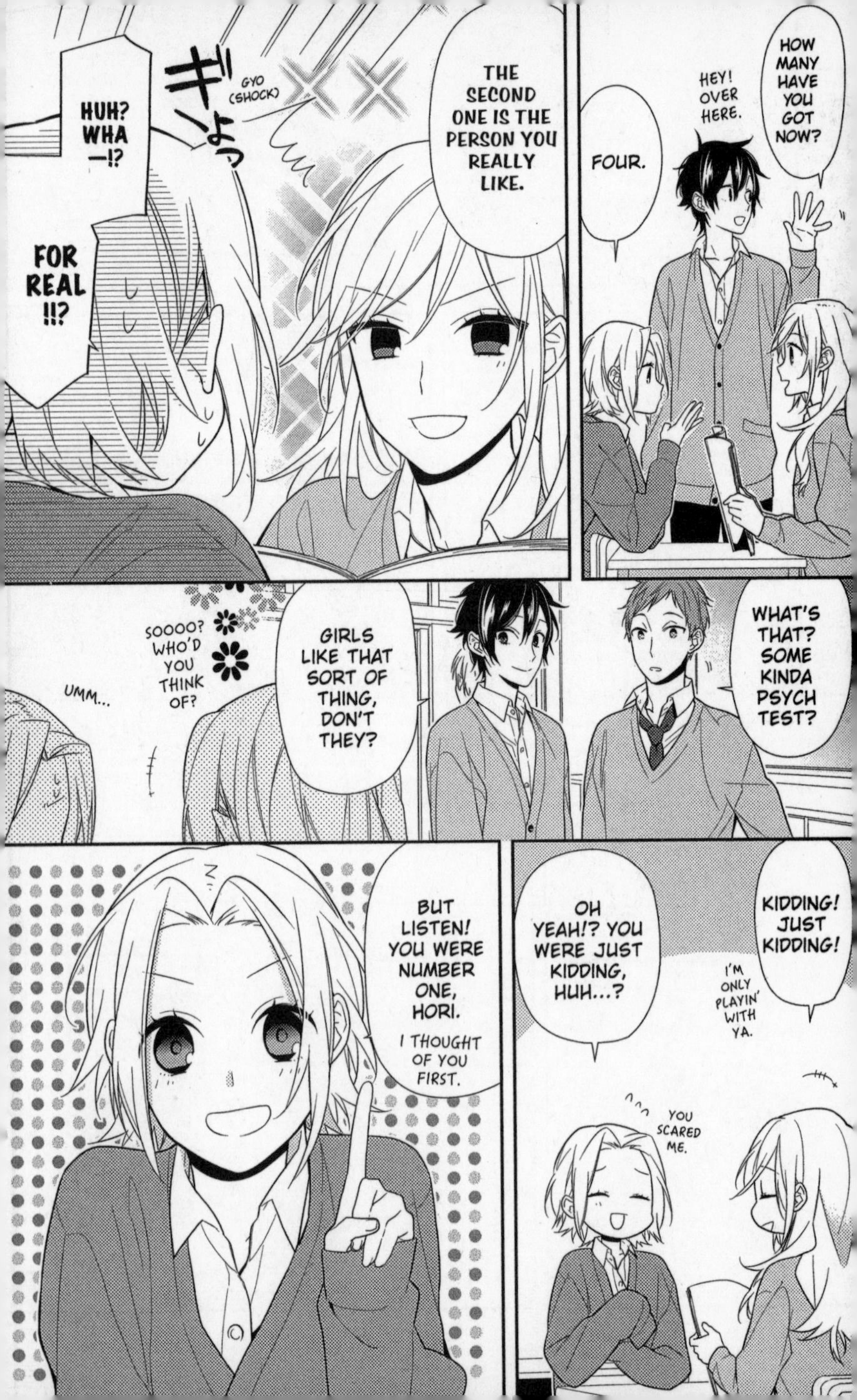
HOW MANY HAVE YOU GOT NOW?
HEY! OVER HERE.
FOUR.
THE SECOND ONE IS THE PERSON YOU REALLY LIKE.
ギょっ
GYO (SHOCK)
HUH? WHA—!?
FOR REAL!!?
WHAT'S THAT? SOME KINDA PSYCH TEST?
GIRLS LIKE THAT SORT OF THING, DON'T THEY?
SOOOO? WHO'D YOU THINK OF?
UMM...
KIDDING! JUST KIDDING!
I'M ONLY PLAYIN' WITH YA.
OH YEAH!? YOU WERE JUST KIDDING, HUH...?
YOU SCARED ME.
BUT LISTEN! YOU WERE NUMBER ONE, HORI.
I THOUGHT OF YOU FIRST.

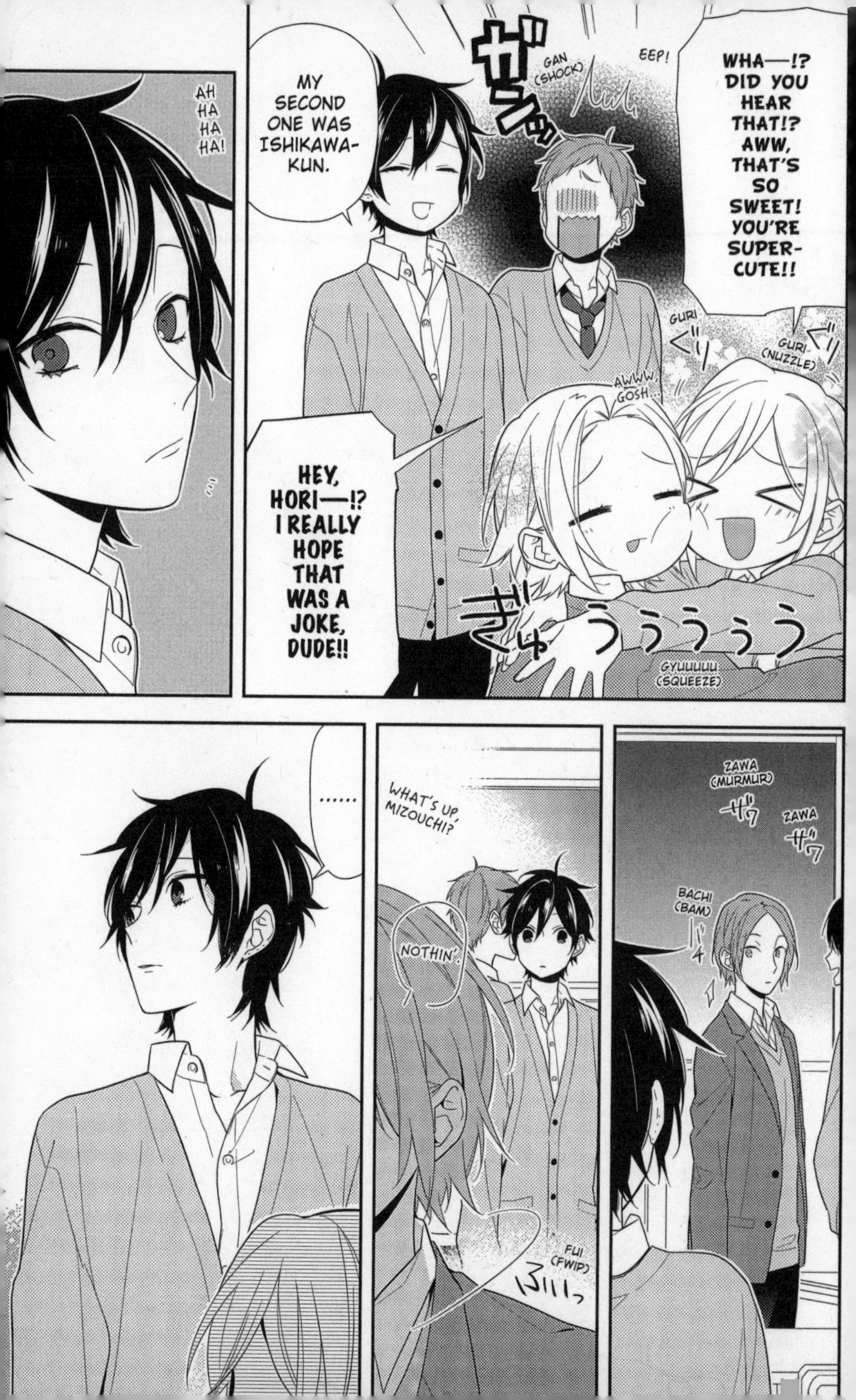
WHA—!? DID YOU HEAR THAT!? AWW, THAT'S SO SWEET! YOU'RE SUPER-CUTE!!
EEP!
GAN (SHOCK)
MY SECOND ONE WAS ISHIKAWA-KUN.
GURI (NUZZLE)
GURI
AWWW, GOSH...
HEY, HORI—!? I REALLY HOPE THAT WAS A JOKE, DUDE!!
GYUUUUU (SQUEEZE)
AH HA HA HA!
ZAWA (MURMUR)
ZAWA
BACHI (BAM)
WHAT'S UP, MIZOUCHI?
NOTHIN'.
FUI (FWIP)
......

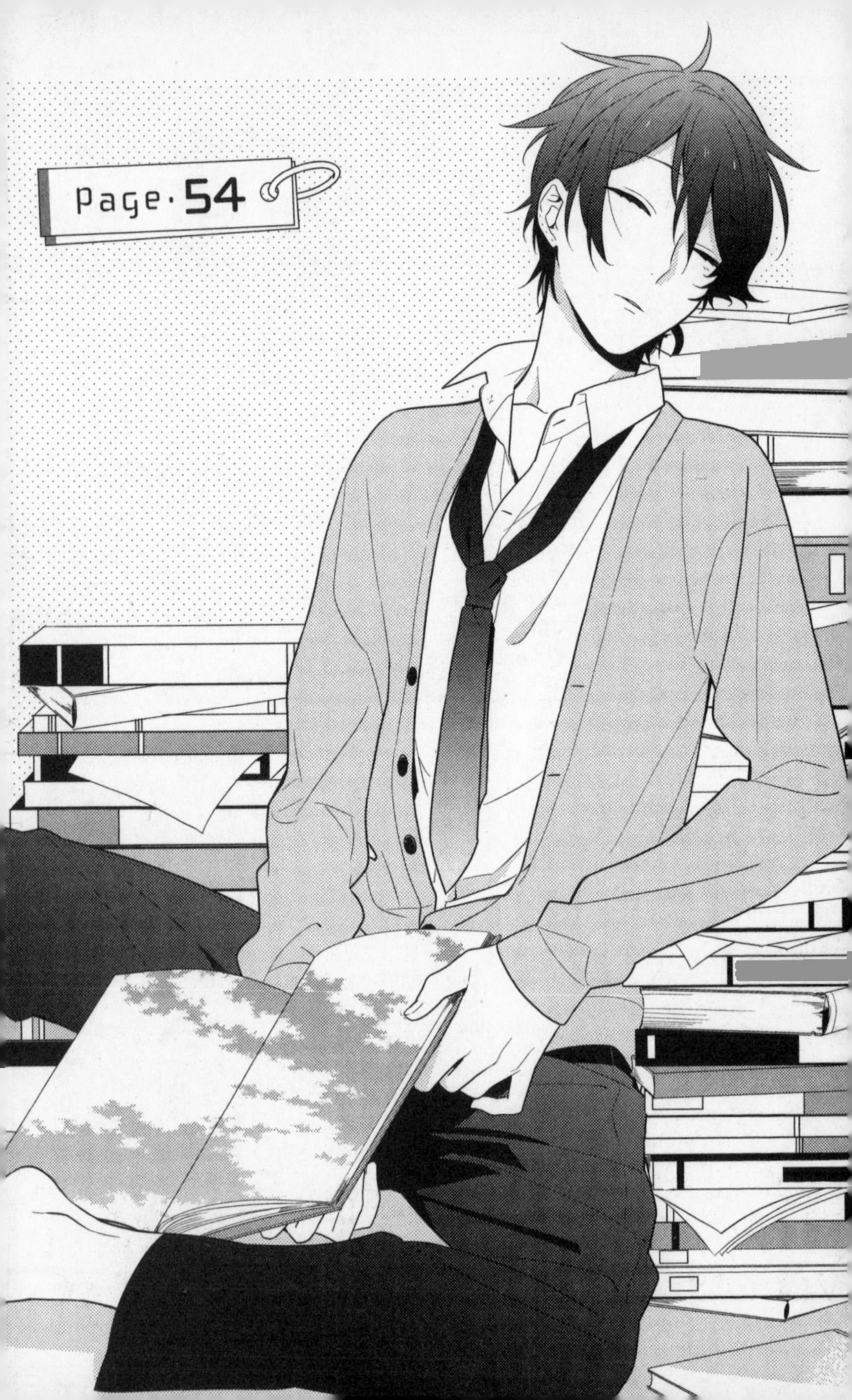
Page·54

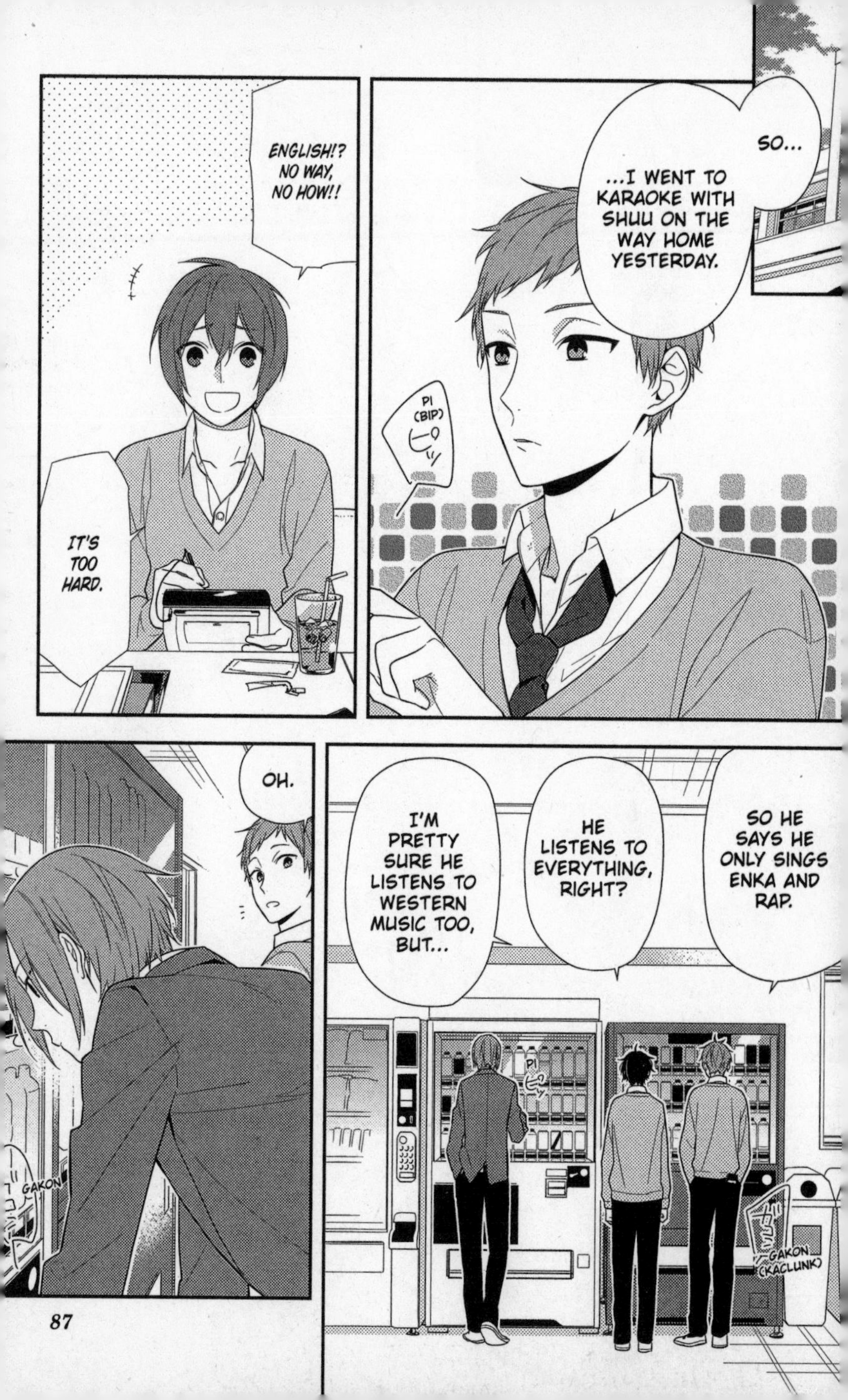
SO...
...I WENT TO KARAOKE WITH SHUU ON THE WAY HOME YESTERDAY.
PI (BIP)
ENGLISH!? NO WAY, NO HOW!!
IT'S TOO HARD.
SO HE SAYS HE ONLY SINGS ENKA AND RAP.
HE LISTENS TO EVERYTHING, RIGHT?
I'M PRETTY SURE HE LISTENS TO WESTERN MUSIC TOO, BUT...
PI
GAKON (KACLUNK)
OH.
GAKON

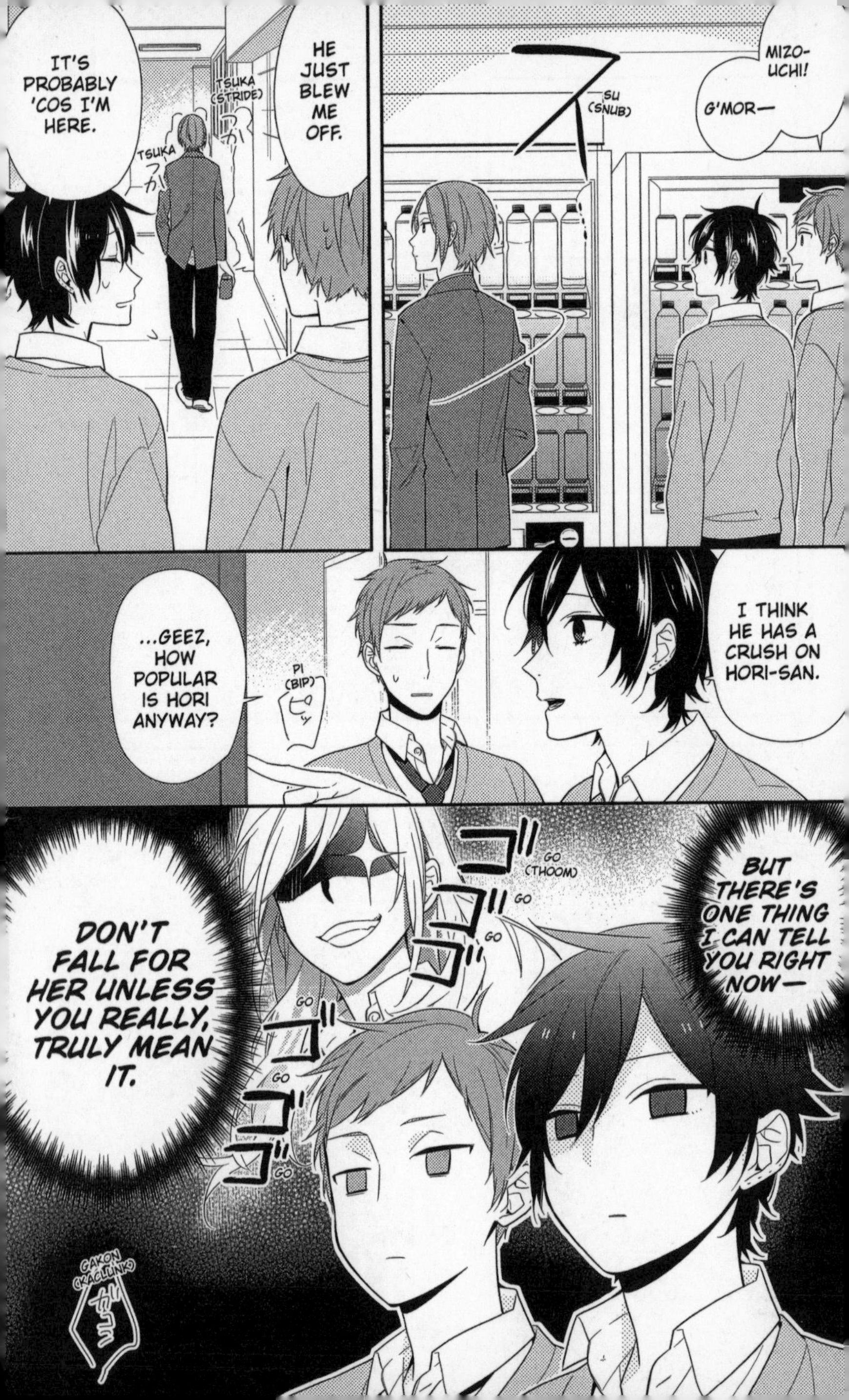
MIZO-UCHI!
G'MOR—
SU (SNUB)
HE JUST BLEW ME OFF.
TSUKA (STRIDE)
TSUKA
IT'S PROBABLY 'COS I'M HERE.
I THINK HE HAS A CRUSH ON HORI-SAN.
PI (BIP)
...GEEZ, HOW POPULAR IS HORI ANYWAY?
BUT THERE'S ONE THING I CAN TELL YOU RIGHT NOW—
GO (THOOM)
GO
GO
DON'T FALL FOR HER UNLESS YOU REALLY, TRULY MEAN IT.
GO
GO
GO
GAKON (KACLUNK)

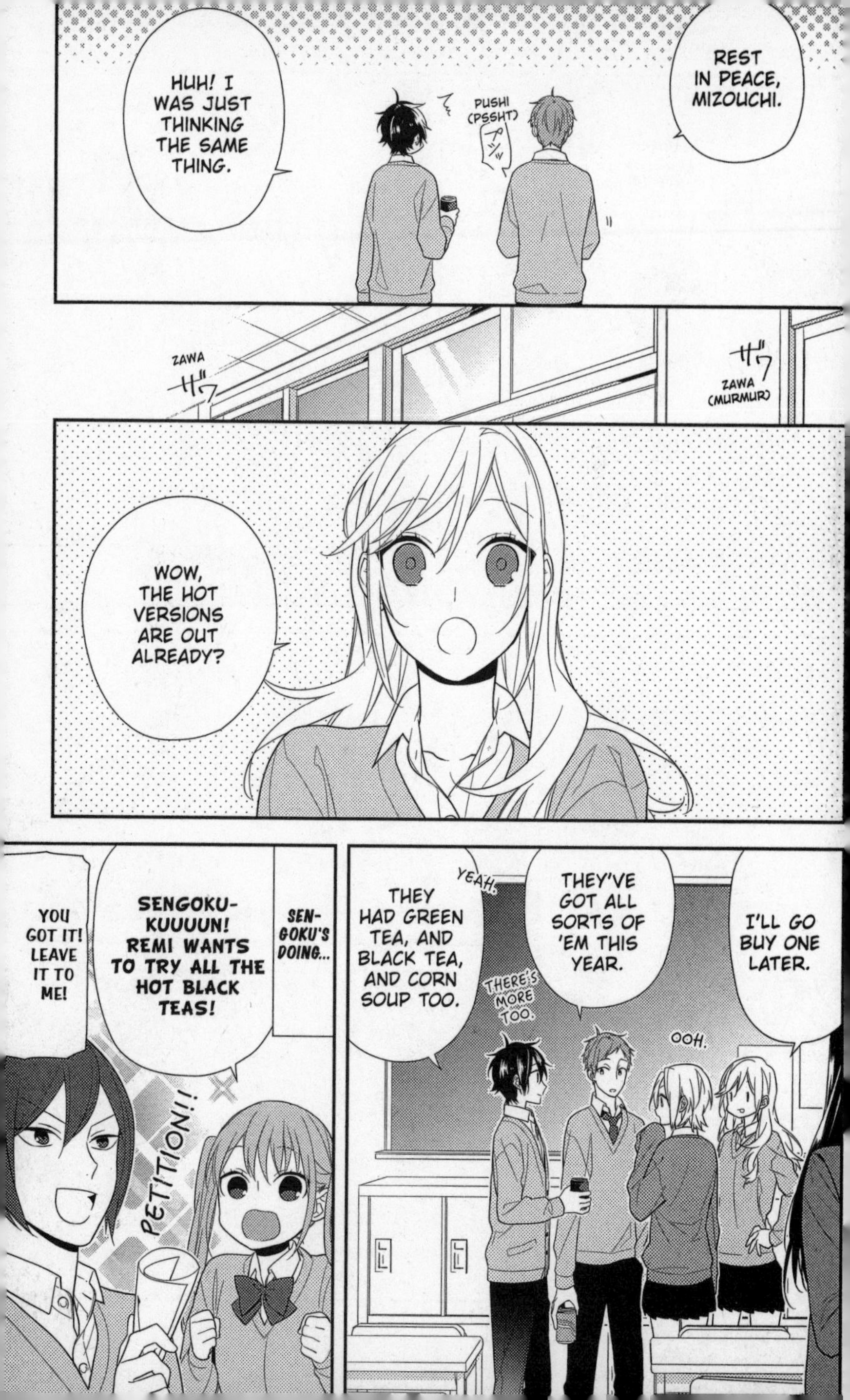
REST IN PEACE, MIZOUCHI.
PUSHI (PSSHT)
プシッ
HUH! I WAS JUST THINKING THE SAME THING.
ザワ
ZAWA (MURMUR)
ZAWA
ザワ
WOW, THE HOT VERSIONS ARE OUT ALREADY?
I'LL GO BUY ONE LATER.
OOH.
THEY'VE GOT ALL SORTS OF 'EM THIS YEAR.
THERE'S MORE TOO.
YEAH.
THEY HAD GREEN TEA, AND BLACK TEA, AND CORN SOUP TOO.
SEN-GOKU'S DOING...
SENGOKU-KUUUUN! REMI WANTS TO TRY ALL THE HOT BLACK TEAS!
PETITION!!
YOU GOT IT! LEAVE IT TO ME!

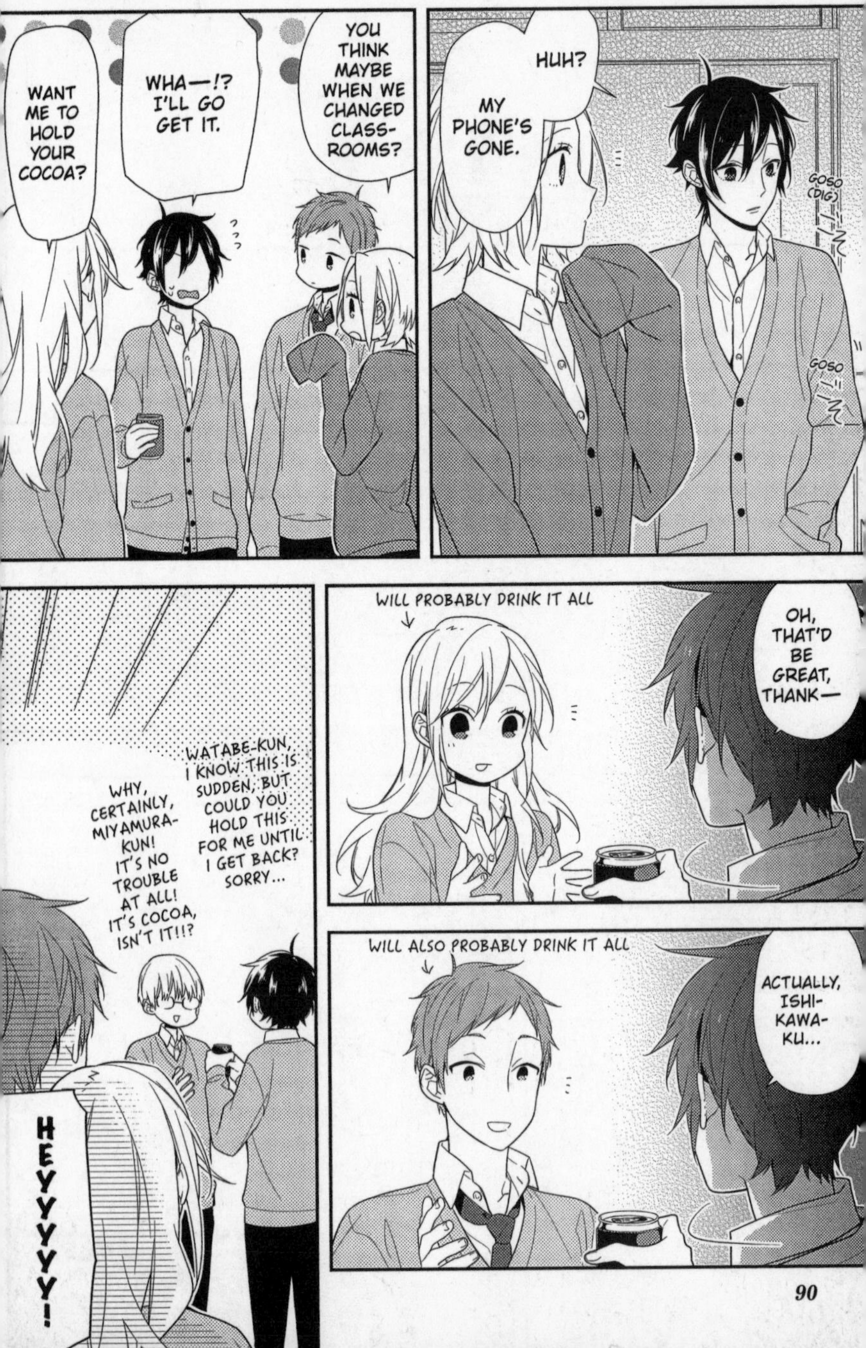
HUH?
MY PHONE'S GONE.
GOSO (DIG)
GOSO
YOU THINK MAYBE WHEN WE CHANGED CLASS-ROOMS?
WHA—!? I'LL GO GET IT.
WANT ME TO HOLD YOUR COCOA?
OH, THAT'D BE GREAT, THANK—
WILL PROBABLY DRINK IT ALL
ACTUALLY, ISHI-KAWA-KU...
WILL ALSO PROBABLY DRINK IT ALL
WATABE-KUN, I KNOW THIS IS SUDDEN, BUT COULD YOU HOLD THIS FOR ME UNTIL I GET BACK? SORRY...
WHY, CERTAINLY, MIYAMURA-KUN! IT'S NO TROUBLE AT ALL! IT'S COCOA, ISN'T IT!!?
HEYYYYY!

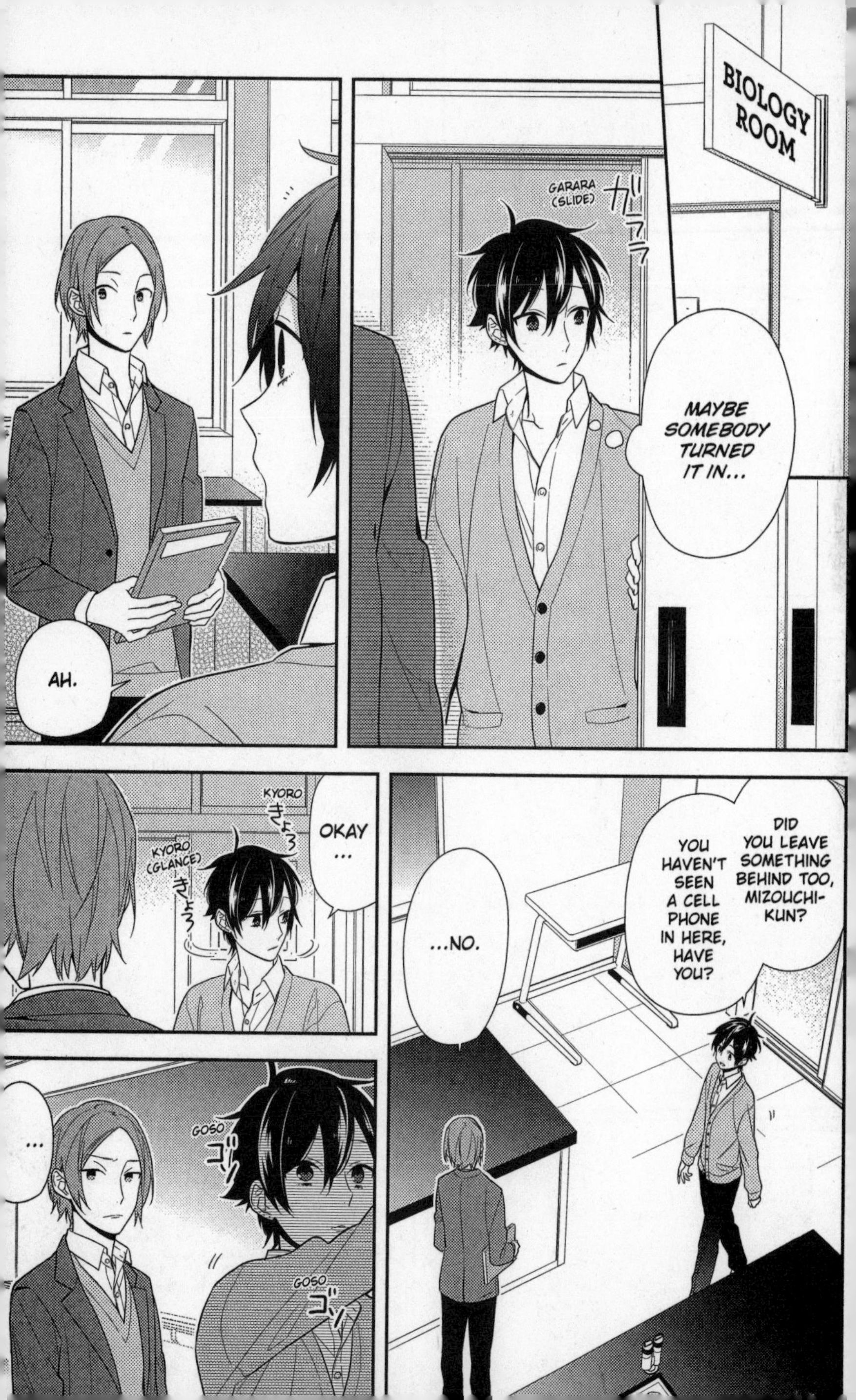

BIOLOGY ROOM
GARARA (SLIDE)
MAYBE SOMEBODY TURNED IT IN...
AH.
DID YOU LEAVE SOMETHING BEHIND TOO, MIZOUCHI-KUN?
YOU HAVEN'T SEEN A CELL PHONE IN HERE, HAVE YOU?
...NO.
KYORO
KYORO (GLANCE)
OKAY...
...
GOSO
GOSO

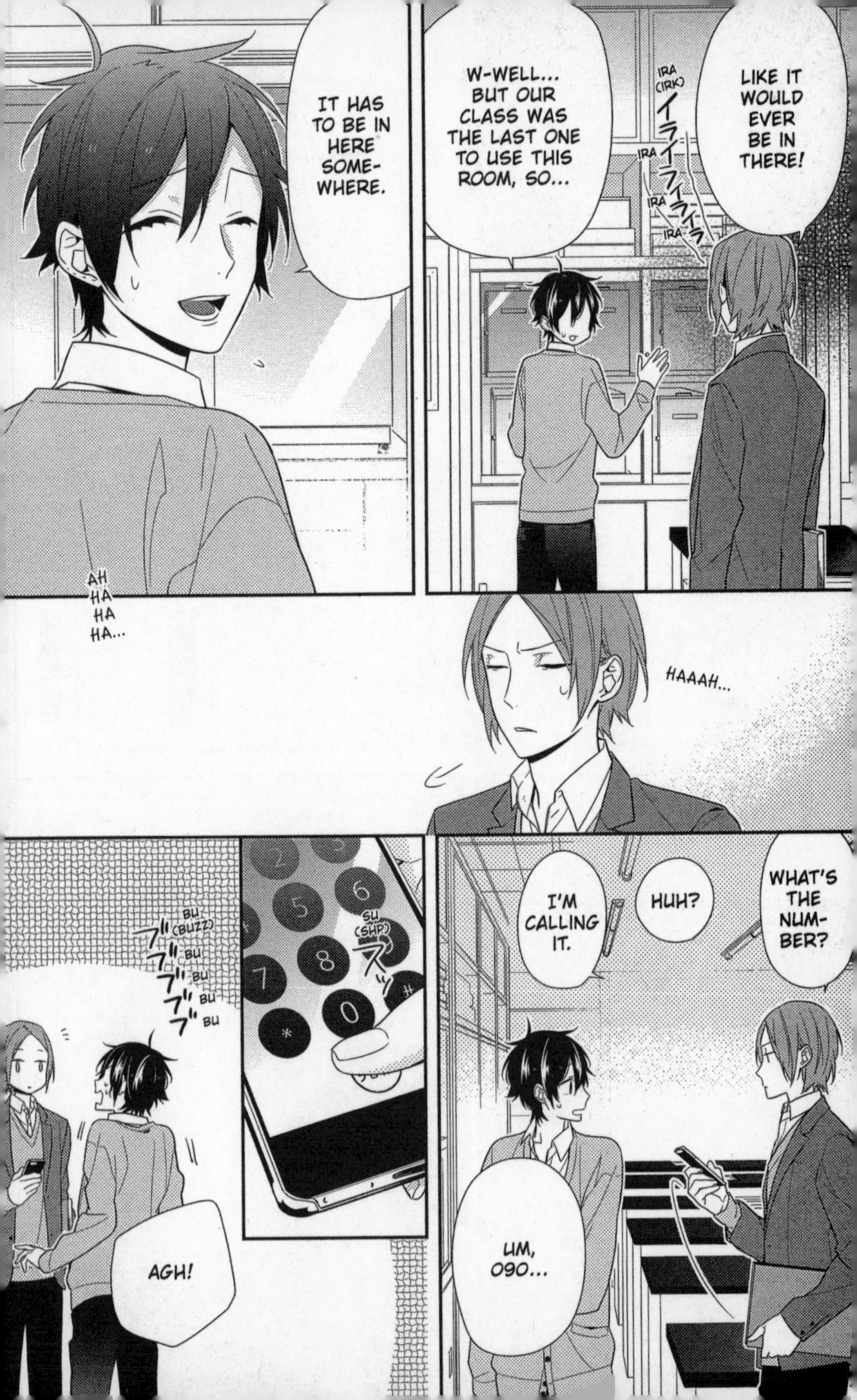
LIKE IT WOULD EVER BE IN THERE!
IRA (IRK) IRA IRA IRA
イライライラ
W-WELL... BUT OUR CLASS WAS THE LAST ONE TO USE THIS ROOM, SO...
IT HAS TO BE IN HERE SOME-WHERE.
AH HA HA HA...
HAAAH...
WHAT'S THE NUM-BER?
HUH?
I'M CALLING IT.
UM, 090...
SU (SHP)
ス
BU (BUZZ) BU BU BU BU
ブブブブブ
AGH!

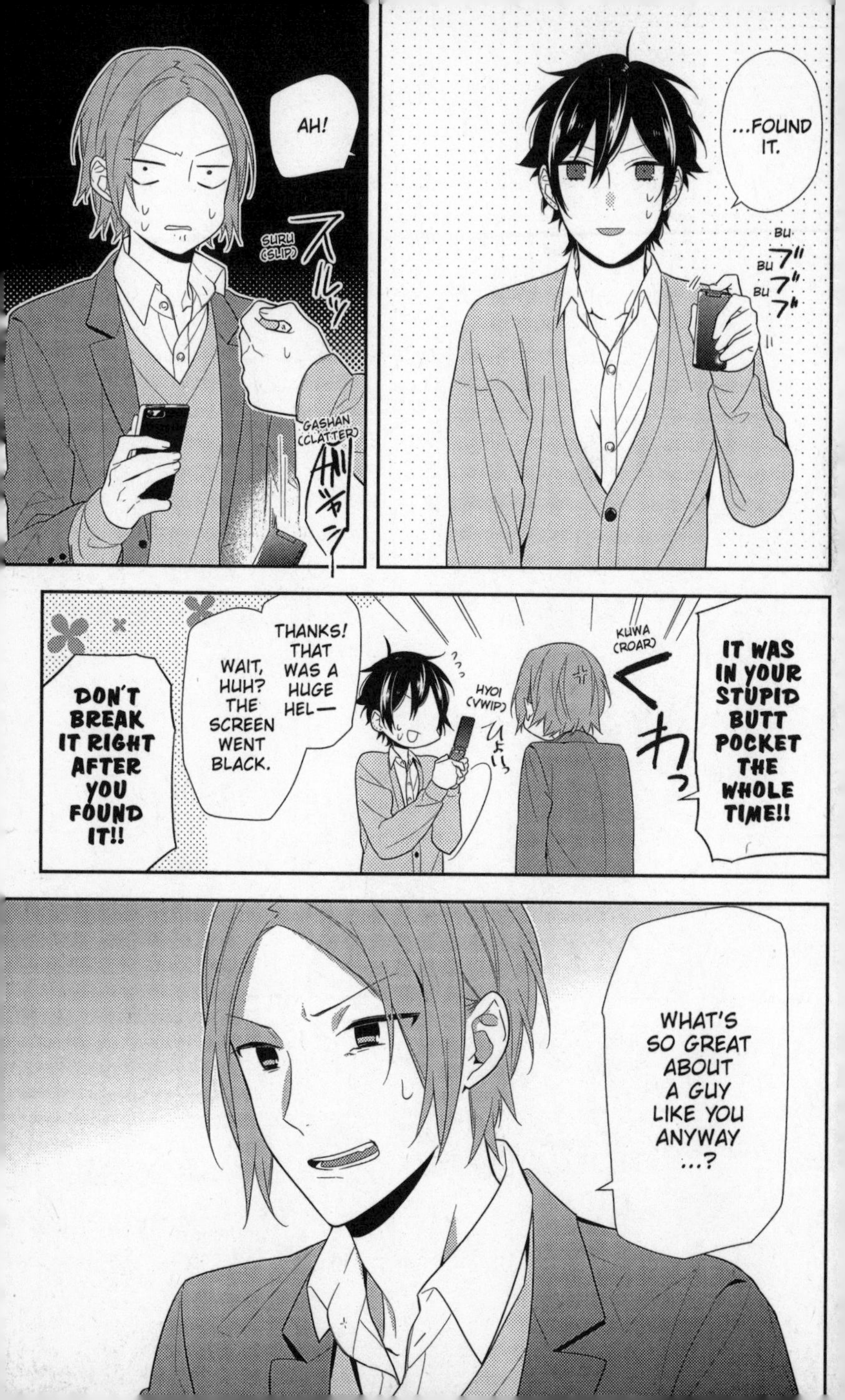
...FOUND IT.
BU BU BU
AH!
SURU (SLIP)
GASHAN (CLATTER)
IT WAS IN YOUR STUPID BUTT POCKET THE WHOLE TIME!!
KUWA (ROAR)
HYOI (VWIP)
THANKS! THAT WAS A HUGE HEL—
WAIT, HUH? THE SCREEN WENT BLACK.
DON'T BREAK IT RIGHT AFTER YOU FOUND IT!!
WHAT'S SO GREAT ABOUT A GUY LIKE YOU ANYWAY ...?

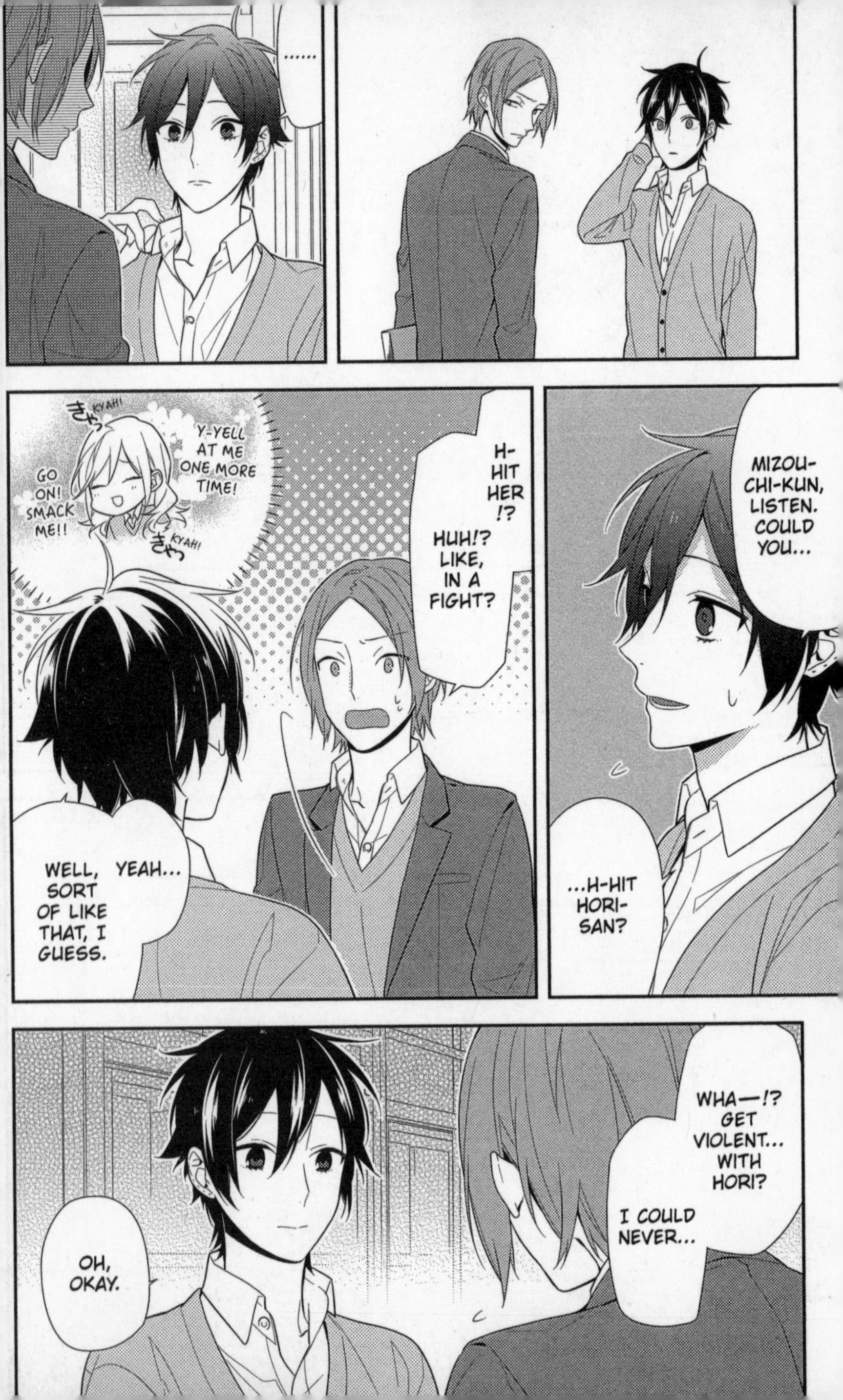
......
MIZOU-CHI-KUN, LISTEN. COULD YOU...
...H-HIT HORI-SAN?
H-HIT HER!?
HUH!? LIKE, IN A FIGHT?
Y-YELL AT ME ONE MORE TIME!
GO ON! SMACK ME!!
きゃっ KYAH!
きゃっ KYAH!
WELL, YEAH... SORT OF LIKE THAT, I GUESS.
WHA—!? GET VIOLENT... WITH HORI?
I COULD NEVER...
OH, OKAY.

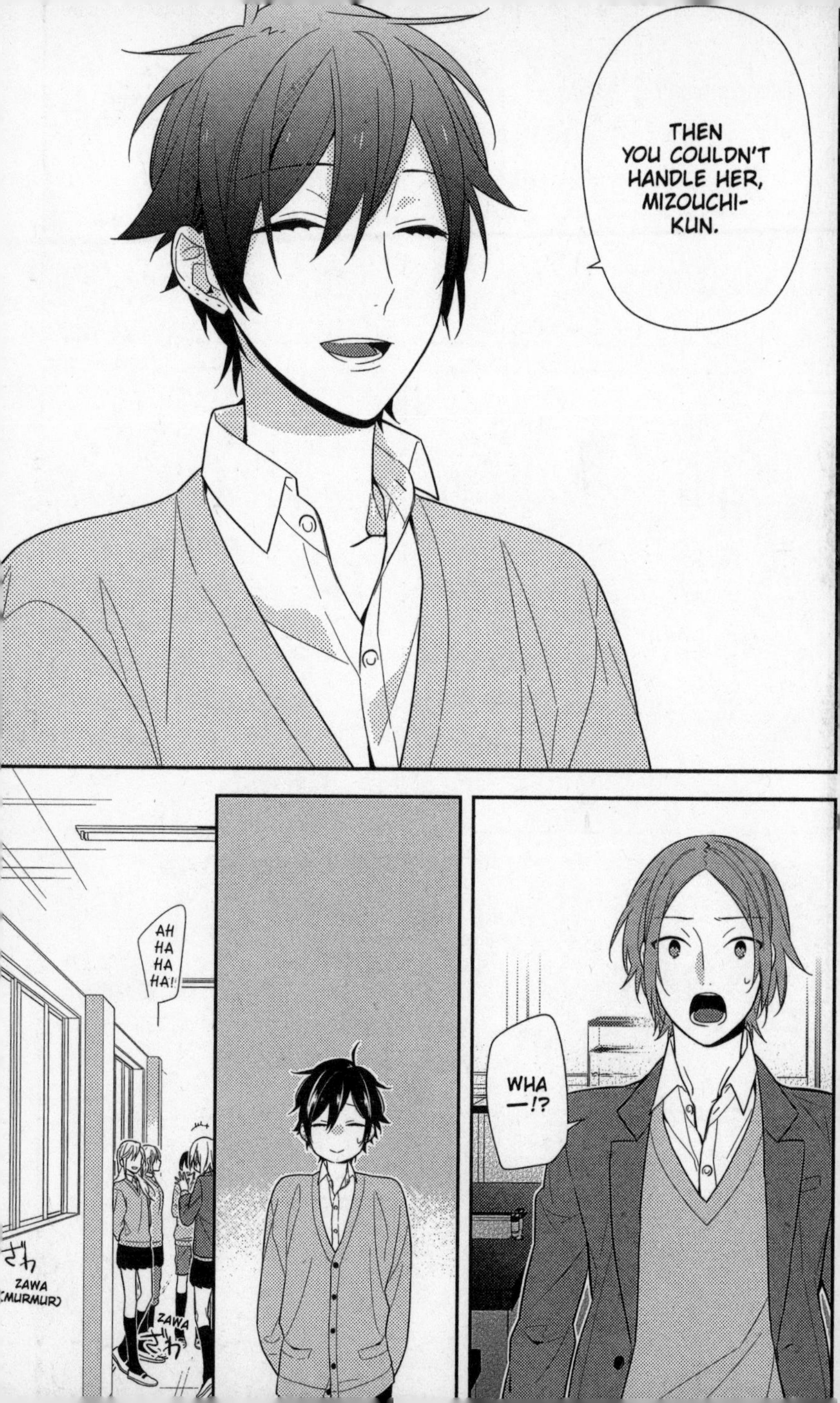
THEN YOU COULDN'T HANDLE HER, MIZOUCHI-KUN.
WHA—!?
AH HA HA HA!
ざわ
ZAWA (MURMUR)
ZAWA
ざわ

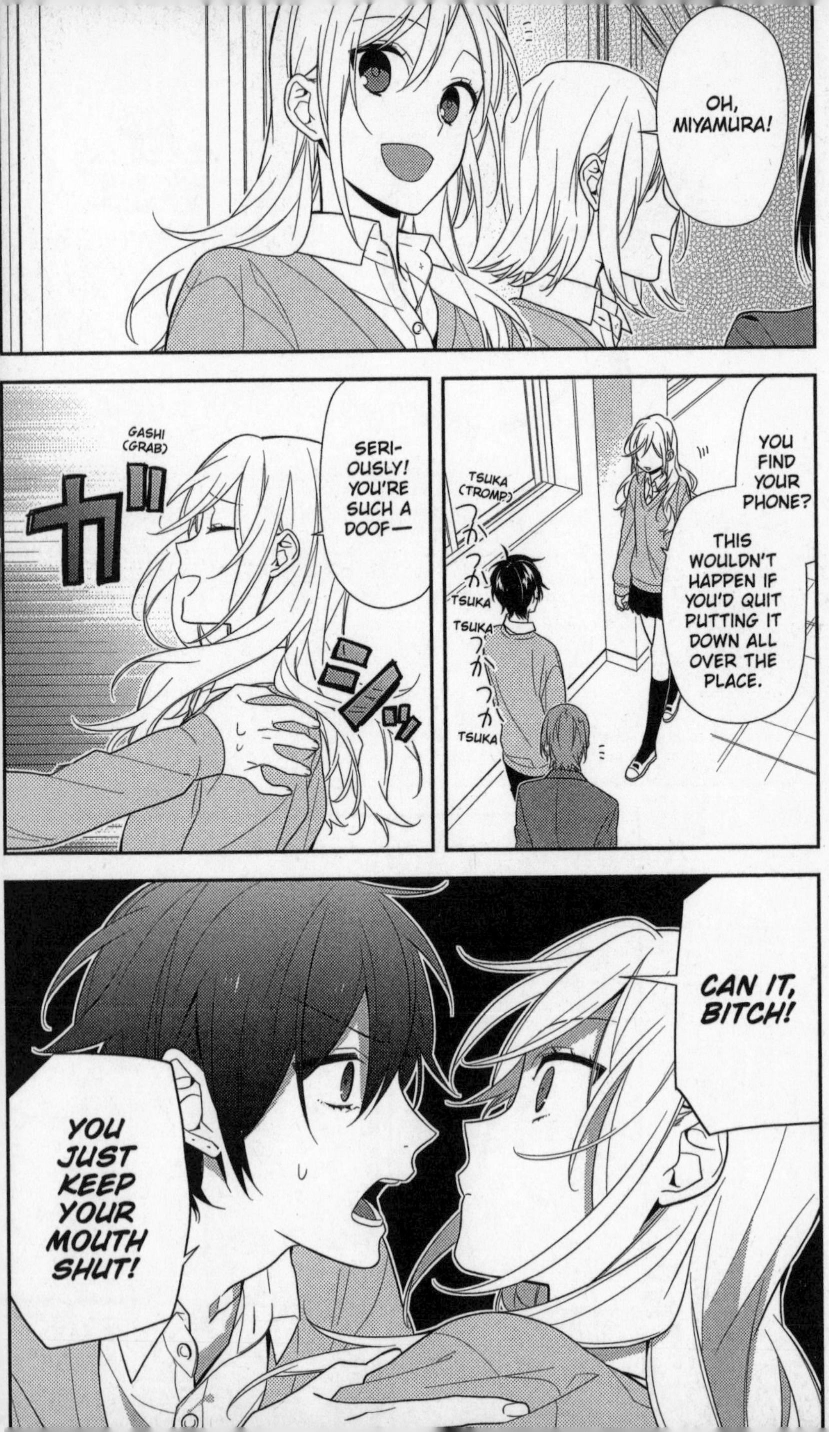

OH, MIYAMURA!
YOU FIND YOUR PHONE?
THIS WOULDN'T HAPPEN IF YOU'D QUIT PUTTING IT DOWN ALL OVER THE PLACE.
TSUKA (TROMP)
TSUKA
TSUKA
TSUKA
SERI-OUSLY! YOU'RE SUCH A DOOF—
GASHI (GRAB)
CAN IT, BITCH!
YOU JUST KEEP YOUR MOUTH SHUT!

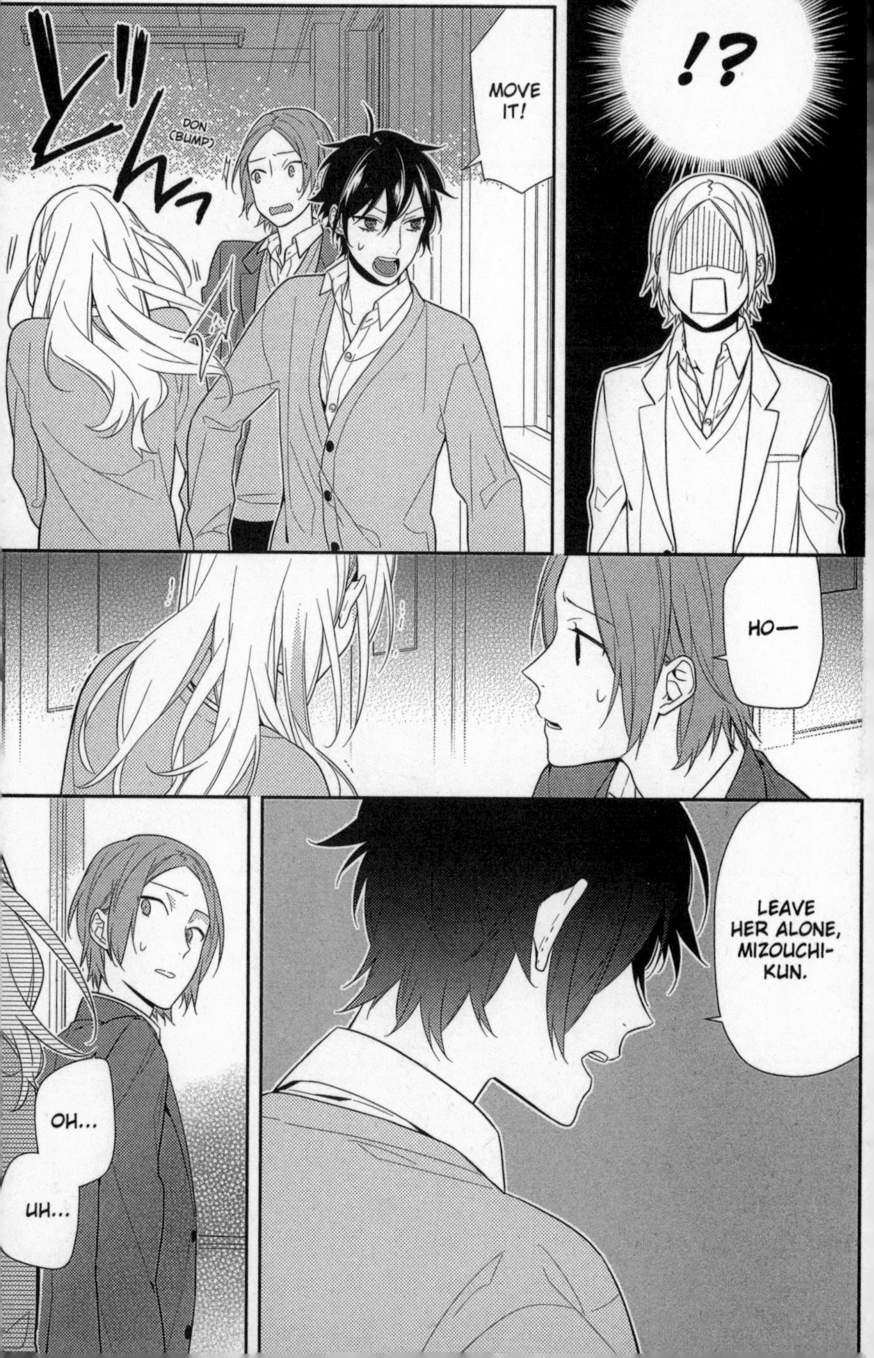
!?
MOVE IT!
DON (BUMP)
HO—
LEAVE HER ALONE, MIZOUCHI-KUN.
OH...
UH...

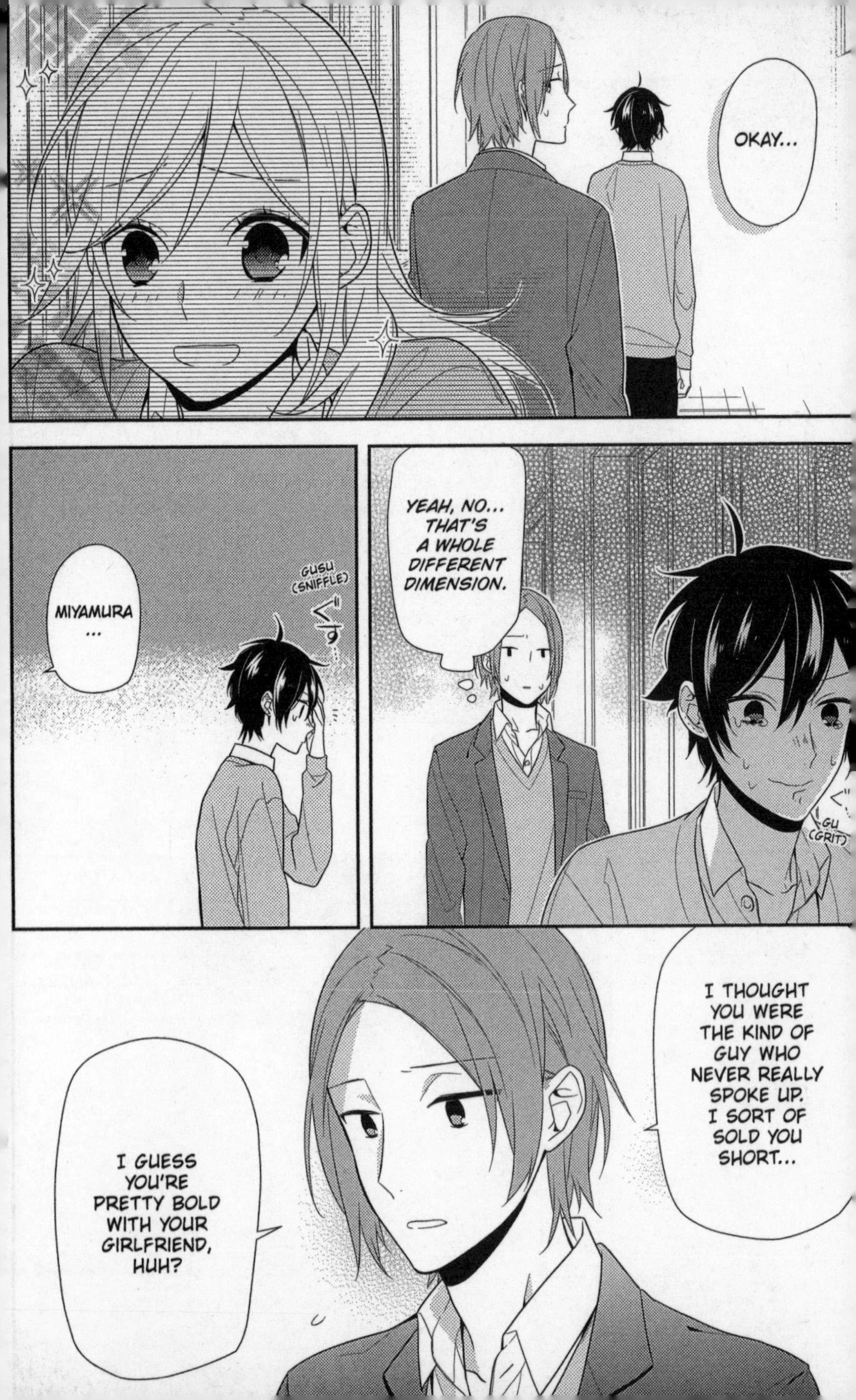
OKAY...
YEAH, NO... THAT'S A WHOLE DIFFERENT DIMENSION.
ぐ…
GU (GRIT)
ぐす…
GUSU (SNIFFLE)
MIYAMURA ...
I THOUGHT YOU WERE THE KIND OF GUY WHO NEVER REALLY SPOKE UP. I SORT OF SOLD YOU SHORT...
I GUESS YOU'RE PRETTY BOLD WITH YOUR GIRLFRIEND, HUH?

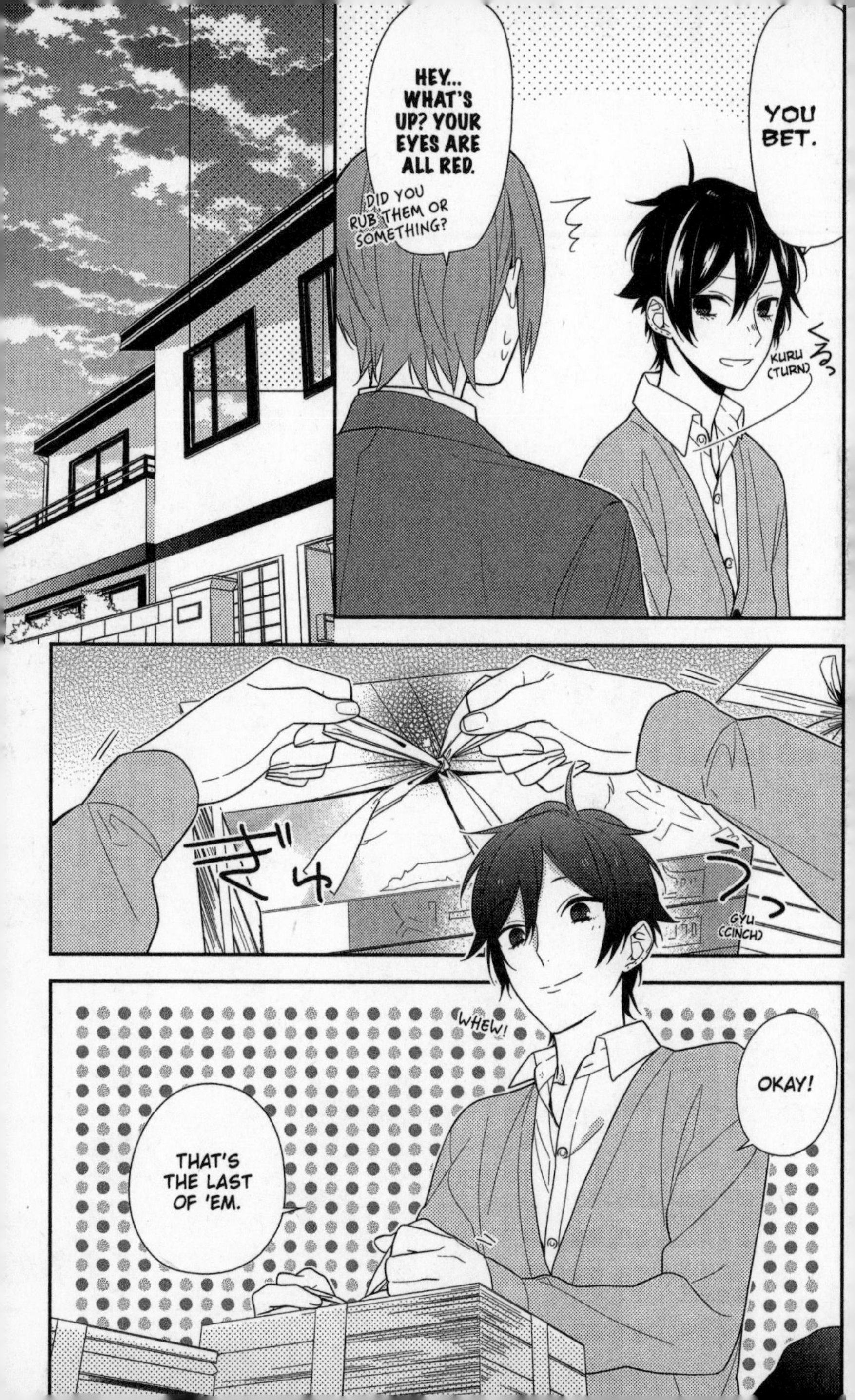
YOU BET.
HEY... WHAT'S UP? YOUR EYES ARE ALL RED.
DID YOU RUB THEM OR SOMETHING?
KURU (TURN)
GYU (CINCH)
OKAY!
WHEW!
THAT'S THE LAST OF 'EM.

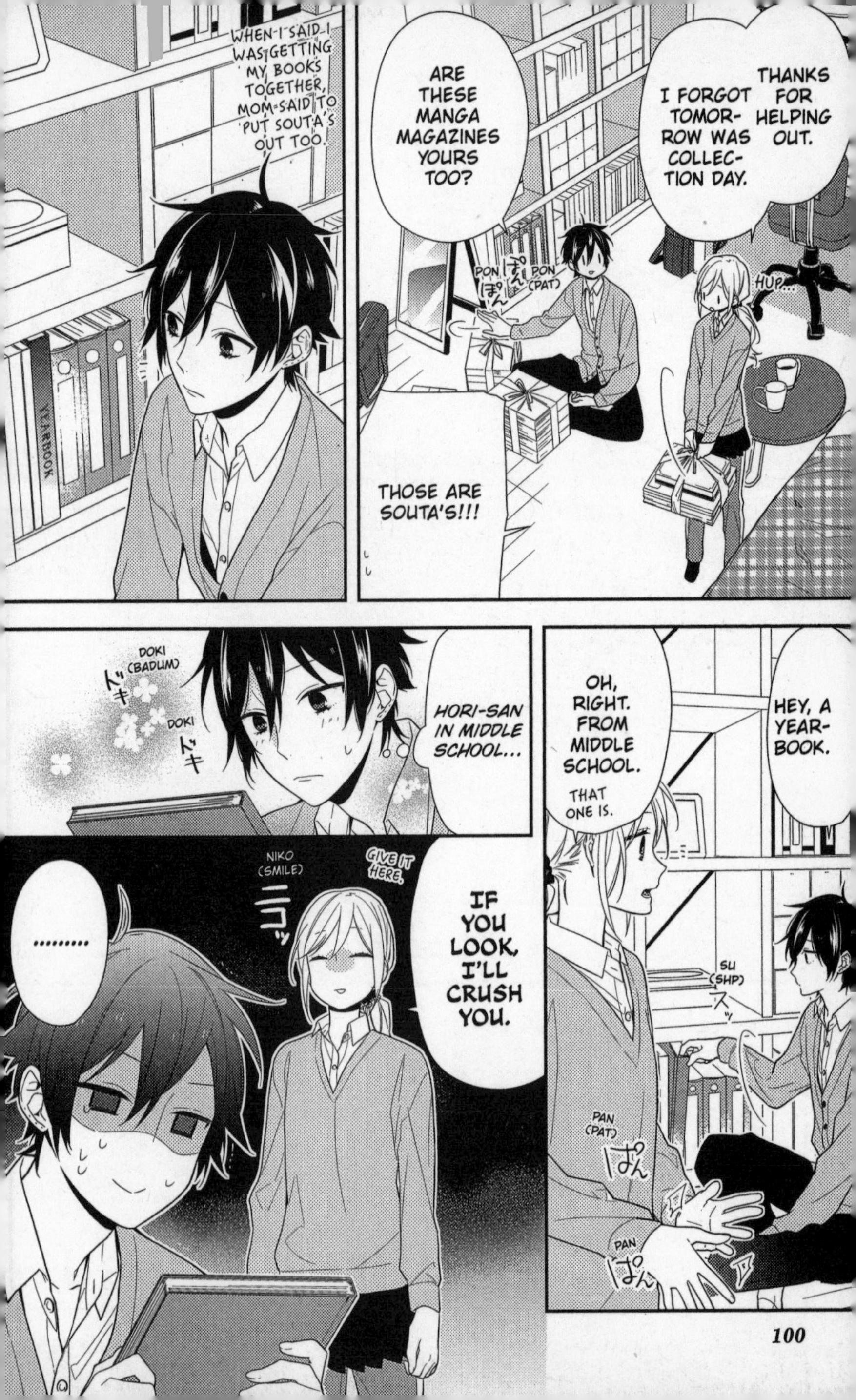
THANKS FOR HELPING OUT.
I FORGOT TOMORROW WAS COLLECTION DAY.
HUP...
ARE THESE MANGA MAGAZINES YOURS TOO?
PON PON (PAT)
THOSE ARE SOUTA'S!!!
WHEN I SAID I WAS GETTING MY BOOKS TOGETHER, MOM SAID TO PUT SOUTA'S OUT TOO.
YEARBOOK
HEY, A YEARBOOK.
OH, RIGHT. FROM MIDDLE SCHOOL.
THAT ONE IS.
SU (SHP)
PAN (PAT)
PAN
HORI-SAN IN MIDDLE SCHOOL...
DOKI (BADUM)
DOKI
IF YOU LOOK, I'LL CRUSH YOU.
GIVE IT HERE.
NIKO (SMILE)
.........

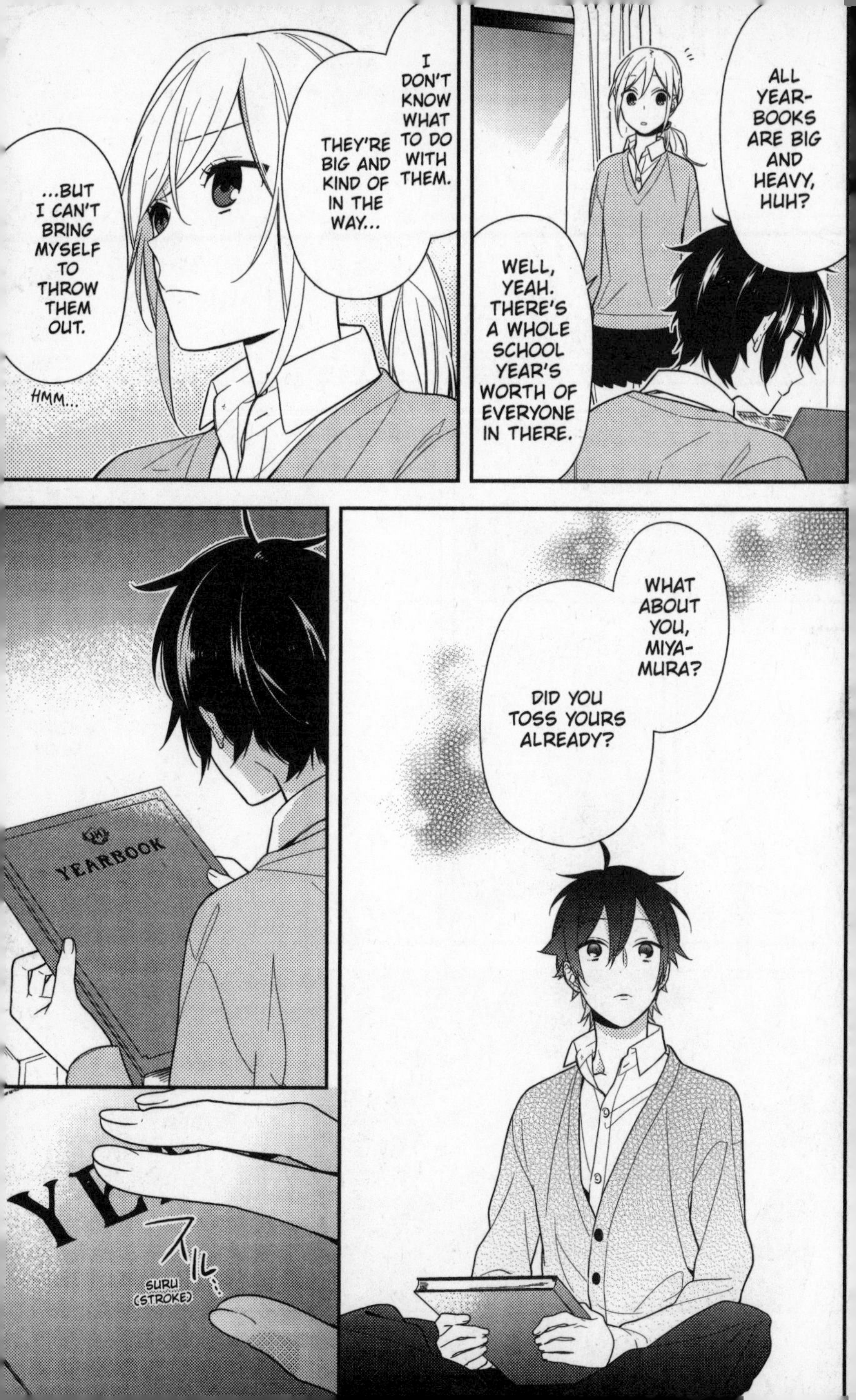
ALL YEAR-BOOKS ARE BIG AND HEAVY, HUH?
WELL, YEAH. THERE'S A WHOLE SCHOOL YEAR'S WORTH OF EVERYONE IN THERE.
I DON'T KNOW WHAT TO DO WITH THEM.
THEY'RE BIG AND KIND OF IN THE WAY...
...BUT I CAN'T BRING MYSELF TO THROW THEM OUT.
HMM...
WHAT ABOUT YOU, MIYA-MURA?
DID YOU TOSS YOURS ALREADY?
YEARBOOK
スル…
SURU (STROKE)

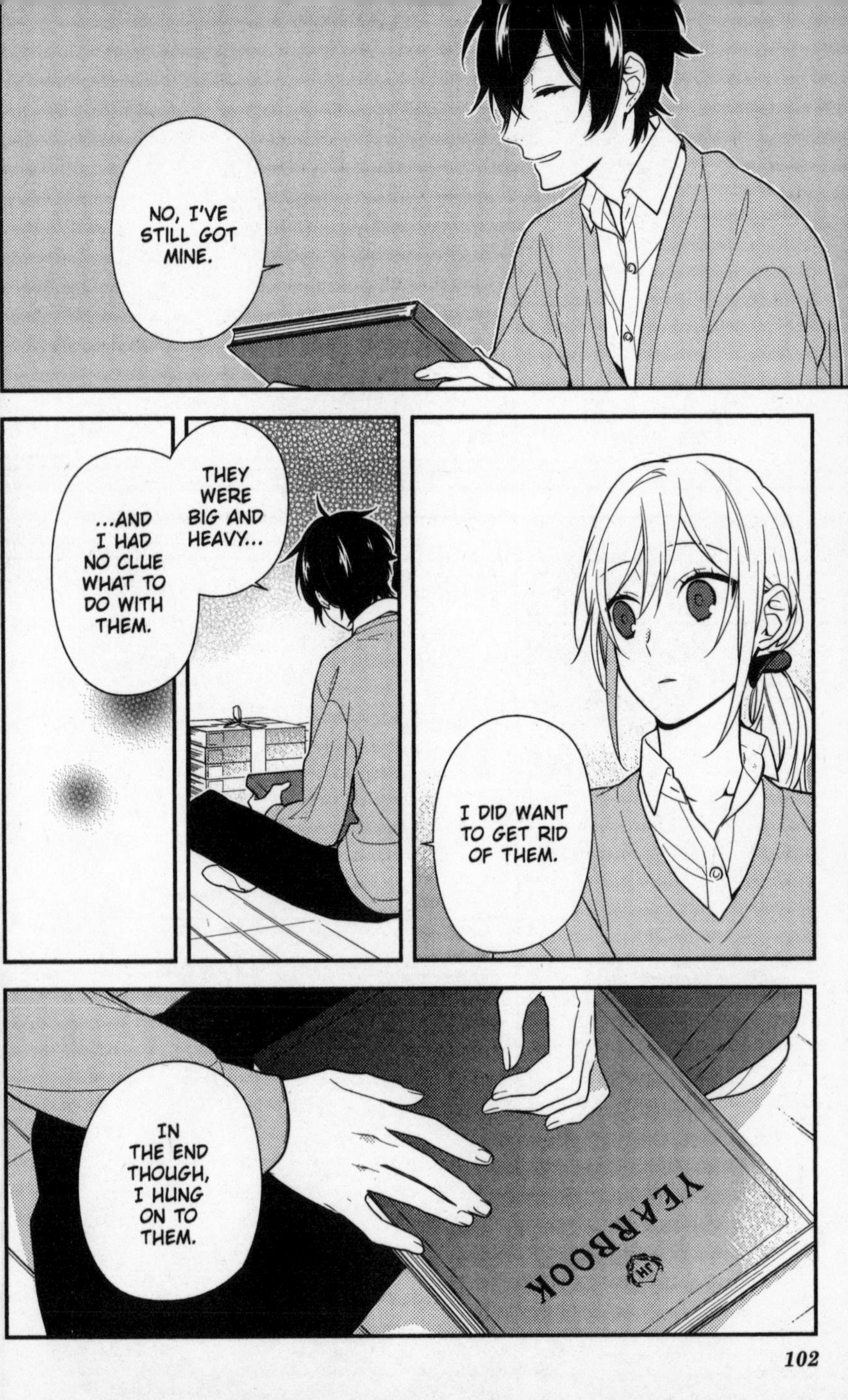
NO, I'VE STILL GOT MINE.
I DID WANT TO GET RID OF THEM.
THEY WERE BIG AND HEAVY...
...AND I HAD NO CLUE WHAT TO DO WITH THEM.
IN THE END THOUGH, I HUNG ON TO THEM.
YEARBOOK

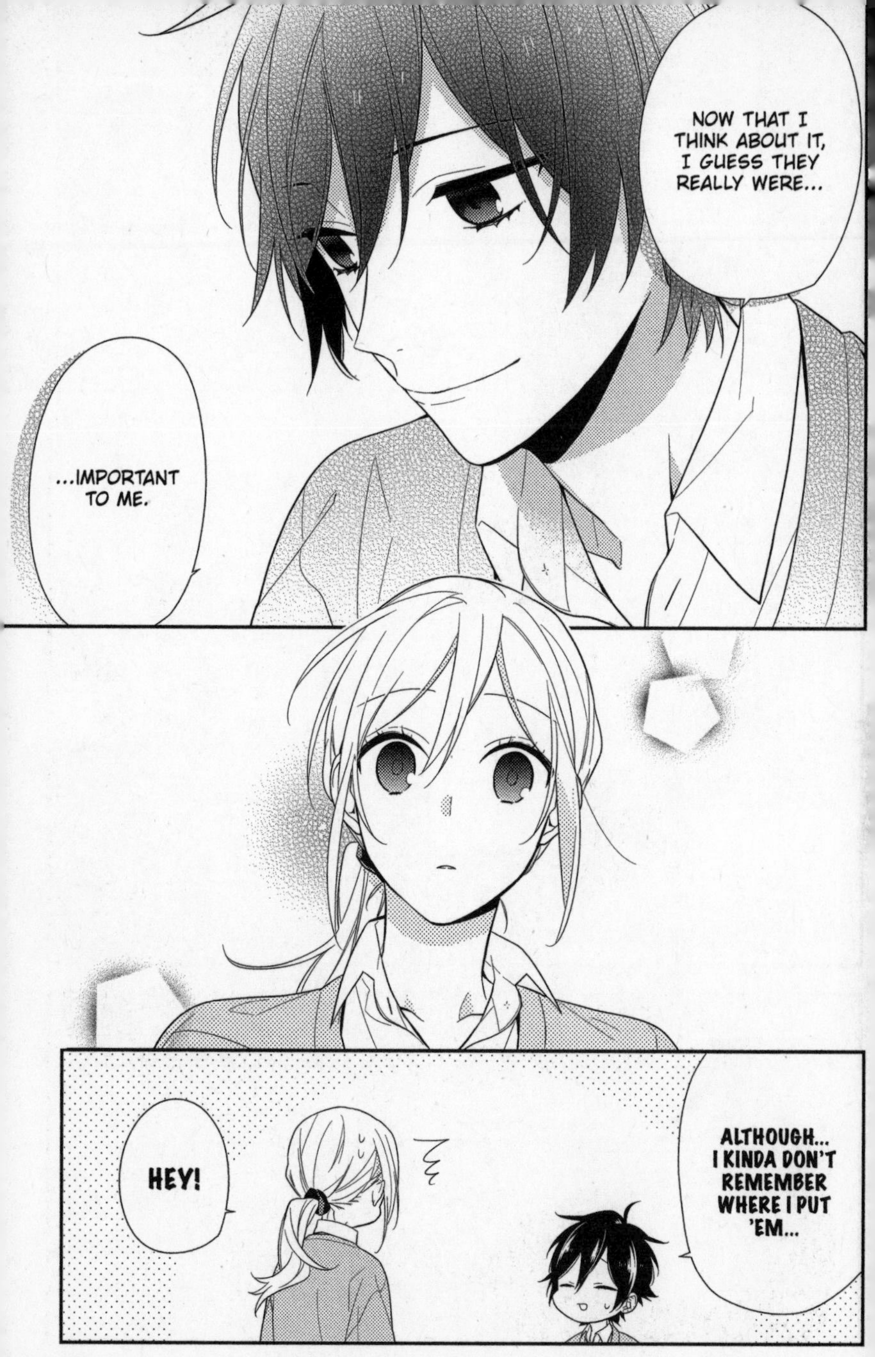
NOW THAT I THINK ABOUT IT, I GUESS THEY REALLY WERE...
...IMPORTANT TO ME.
ALTHOUGH... I KINDA DON'T REMEMBER WHERE I PUT 'EM...
HEY!

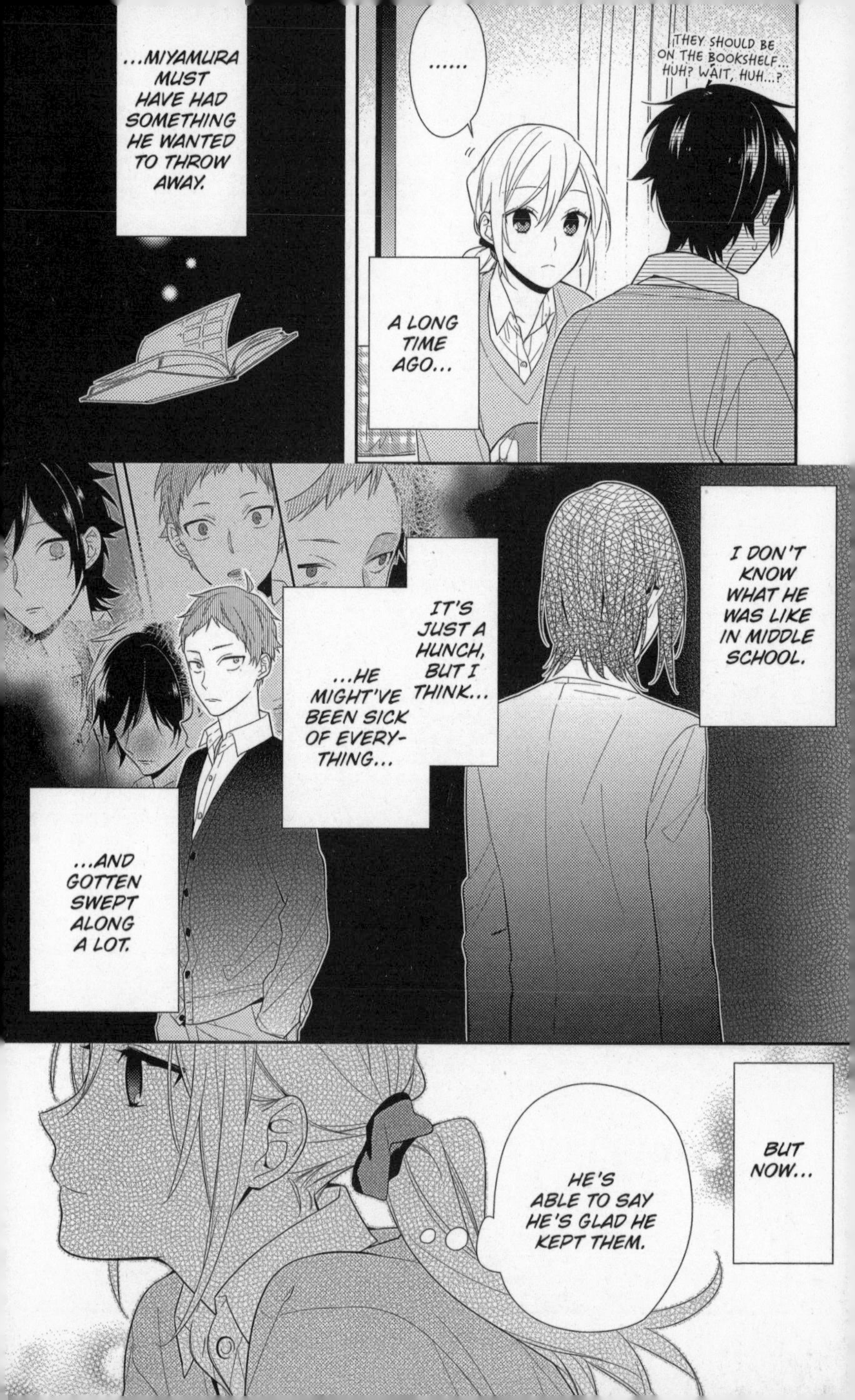
THEY SHOULD BE ON THE BOOKSHELF... HUH? WAIT, HUH...?
......
A LONG TIME AGO...
...MIYAMURA MUST HAVE HAD SOMETHING HE WANTED TO THROW AWAY.
I DON'T KNOW WHAT HE WAS LIKE IN MIDDLE SCHOOL.
IT'S JUST A HUNCH, BUT I THINK...
...HE MIGHT'VE BEEN SICK OF EVERYTHING...
...AND GOTTEN SWEPT ALONG A LOT.
BUT NOW...
HE'S ABLE TO SAY HE'S GLAD HE KEPT THEM.

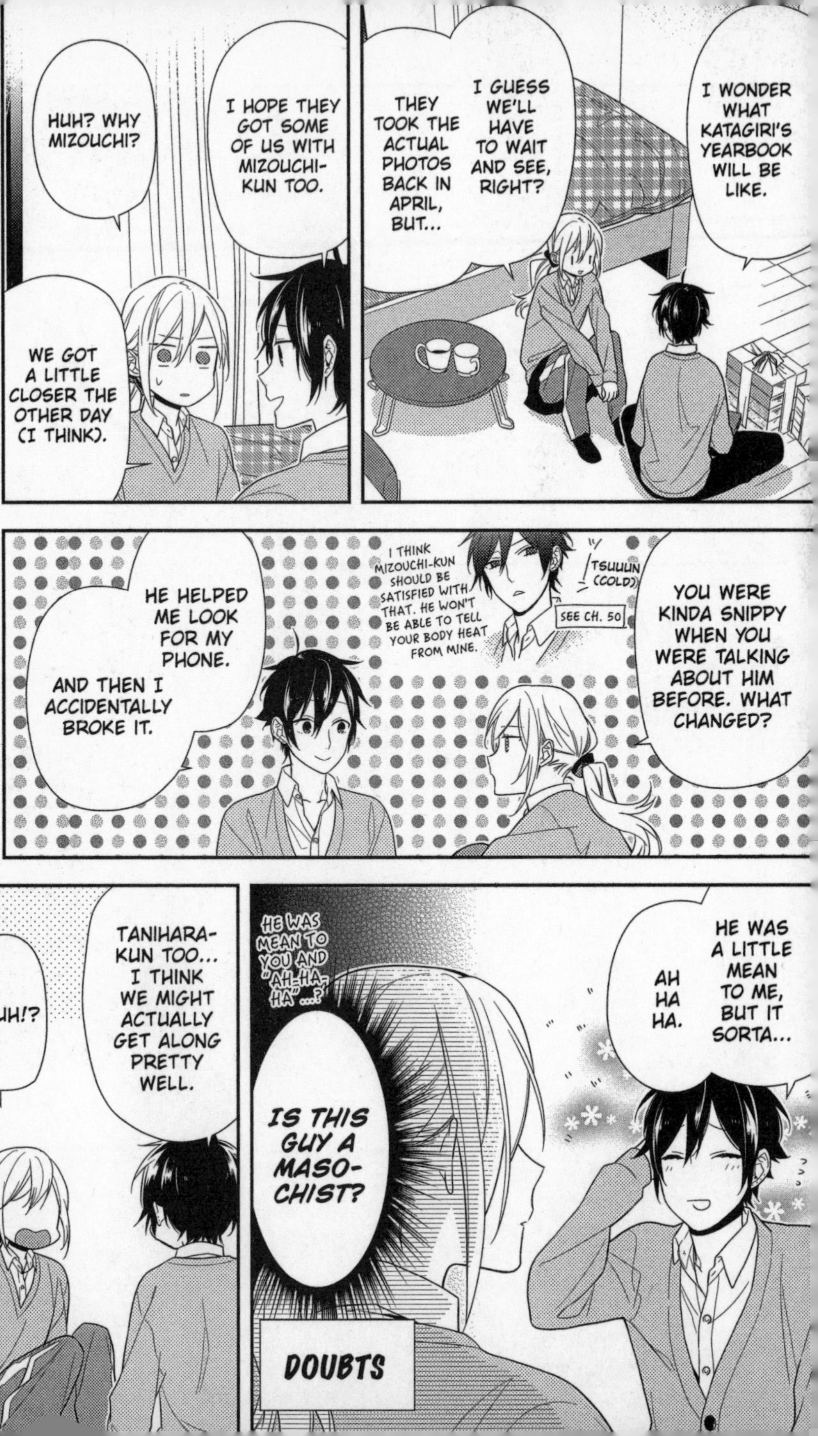
I WONDER WHAT KATAGIRI'S YEARBOOK WILL BE LIKE.
I GUESS WE'LL HAVE TO WAIT AND SEE, RIGHT?
THEY TOOK THE ACTUAL PHOTOS BACK IN APRIL, BUT...
I HOPE THEY GOT SOME OF US WITH MIZOUCHI-KUN TOO.
HUH? WHY MIZOUCHI?
WE GOT A LITTLE CLOSER THE OTHER DAY (I THINK).
YOU WERE KINDA SNIPPY WHEN YOU WERE TALKING ABOUT HIM BEFORE. WHAT CHANGED?
TSUUUN (COLD)
SEE CH. 50
I THINK MIZOUCHI-KUN SHOULD BE SATISFIED WITH THAT. HE WON'T BE ABLE TO TELL YOUR BODY HEAT FROM MINE.
HE HELPED ME LOOK FOR MY PHONE.
AND THEN I ACCIDENTALLY BROKE IT.
HE WAS A LITTLE MEAN TO ME, BUT IT SORTA...
AH HA HA.
HE WAS MEAN TO YOU AND "AH-HA-HA"...?
IS THIS GUY A MASOCHIST?
DOUBTS
TANIHARA-KUN TOO... I THINK WE MIGHT ACTUALLY GET ALONG PRETTY WELL.
HUH!?

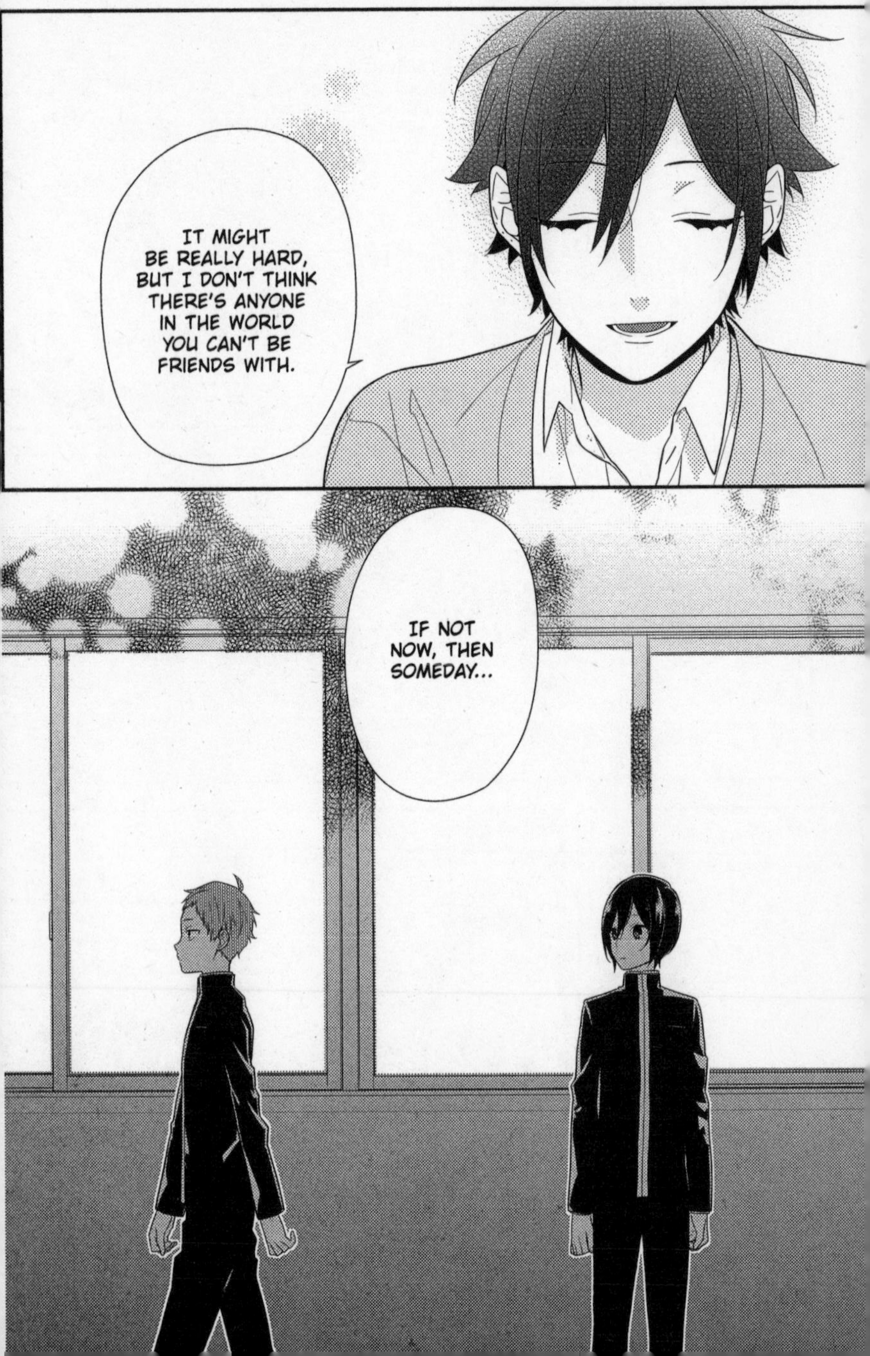
IT MIGHT BE REALLY HARD, BUT I DON'T THINK THERE'S ANYONE IN THE WORLD YOU CAN'T BE FRIENDS WITH.
IF NOT NOW, THEN SOMEDAY...

HORIMIYA

HORIMIYA

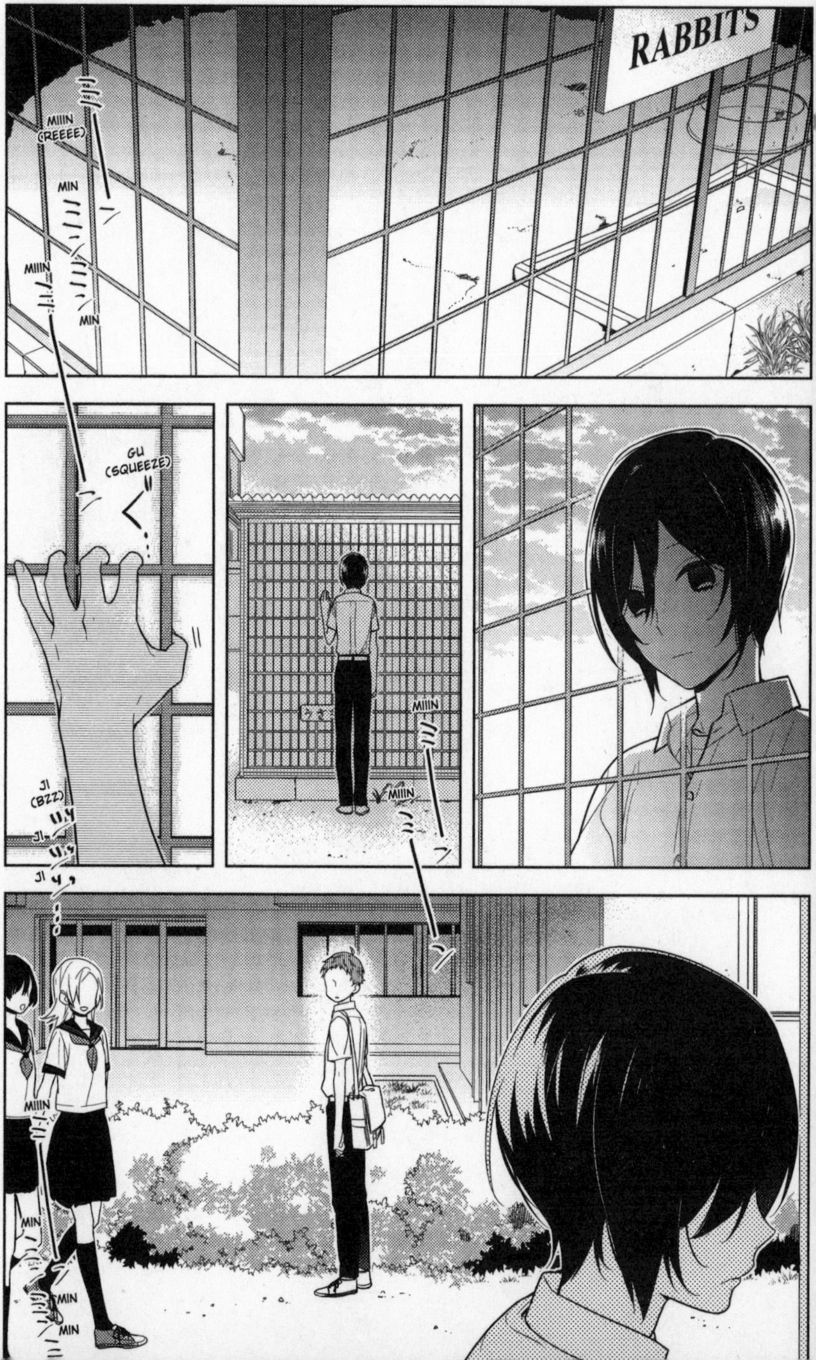
RABBITS
MIIIN (REEEE)
MIN
MIIIN
MIN
MIIIN
MIIIN
GU (SQUEEZE)
JI (BZZ)
JI
JI
MIIIN
MIN
MIN
MIN

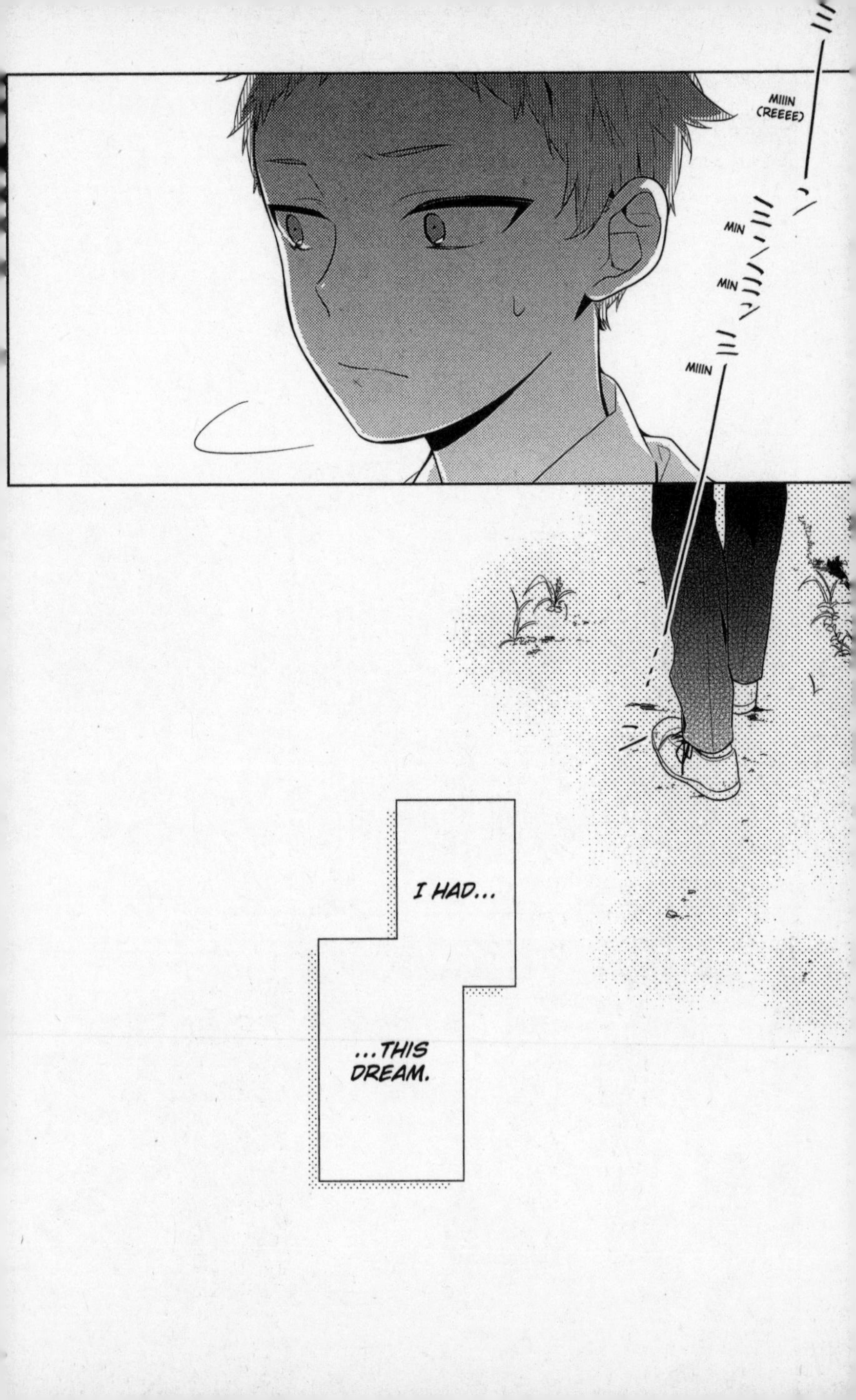
ミーーン
MIIIN (REEEE)
ミンミンミンミ
MIN
MIN
MIIIN
I HAD...
...THIS DREAM.

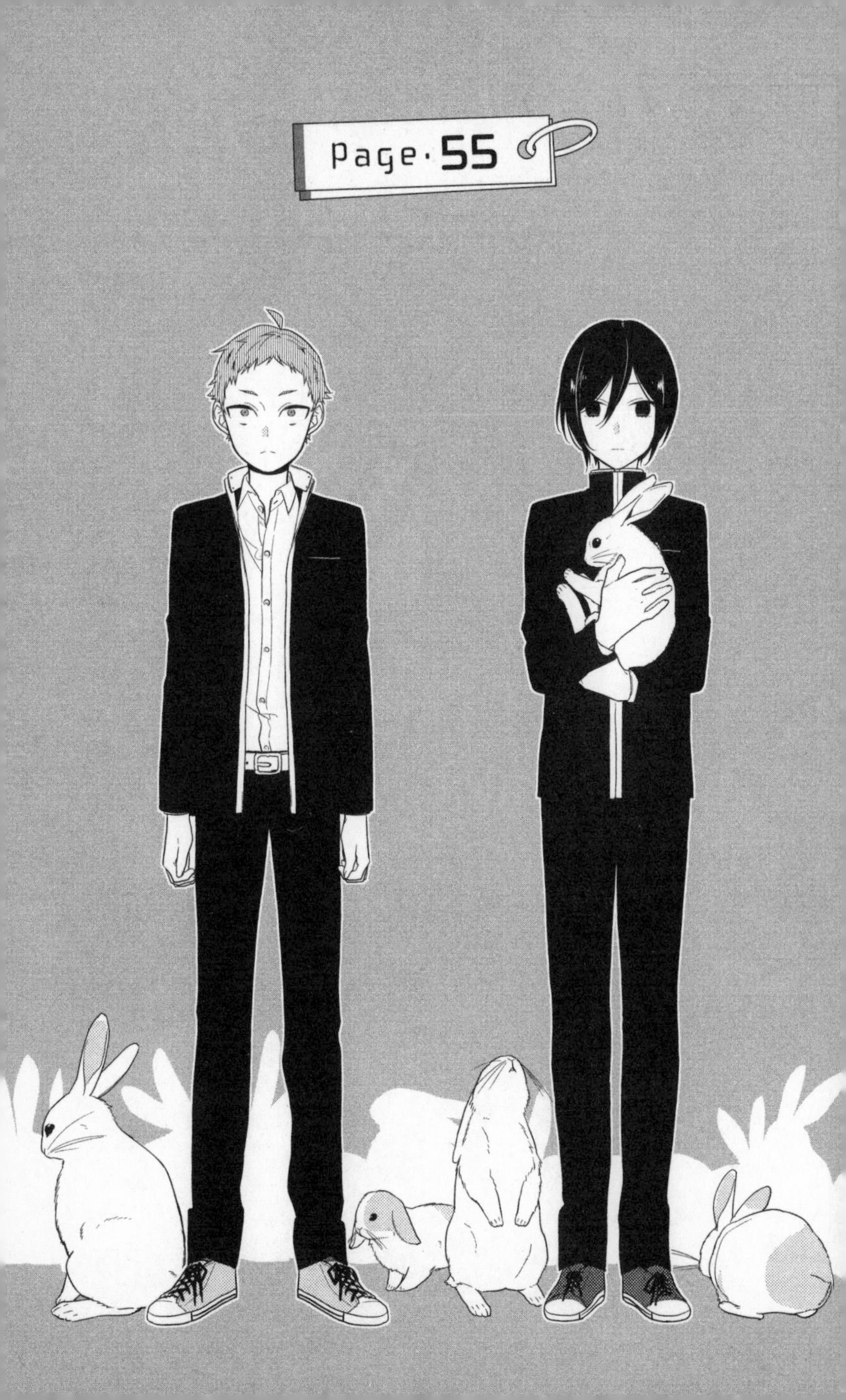
Page · 55

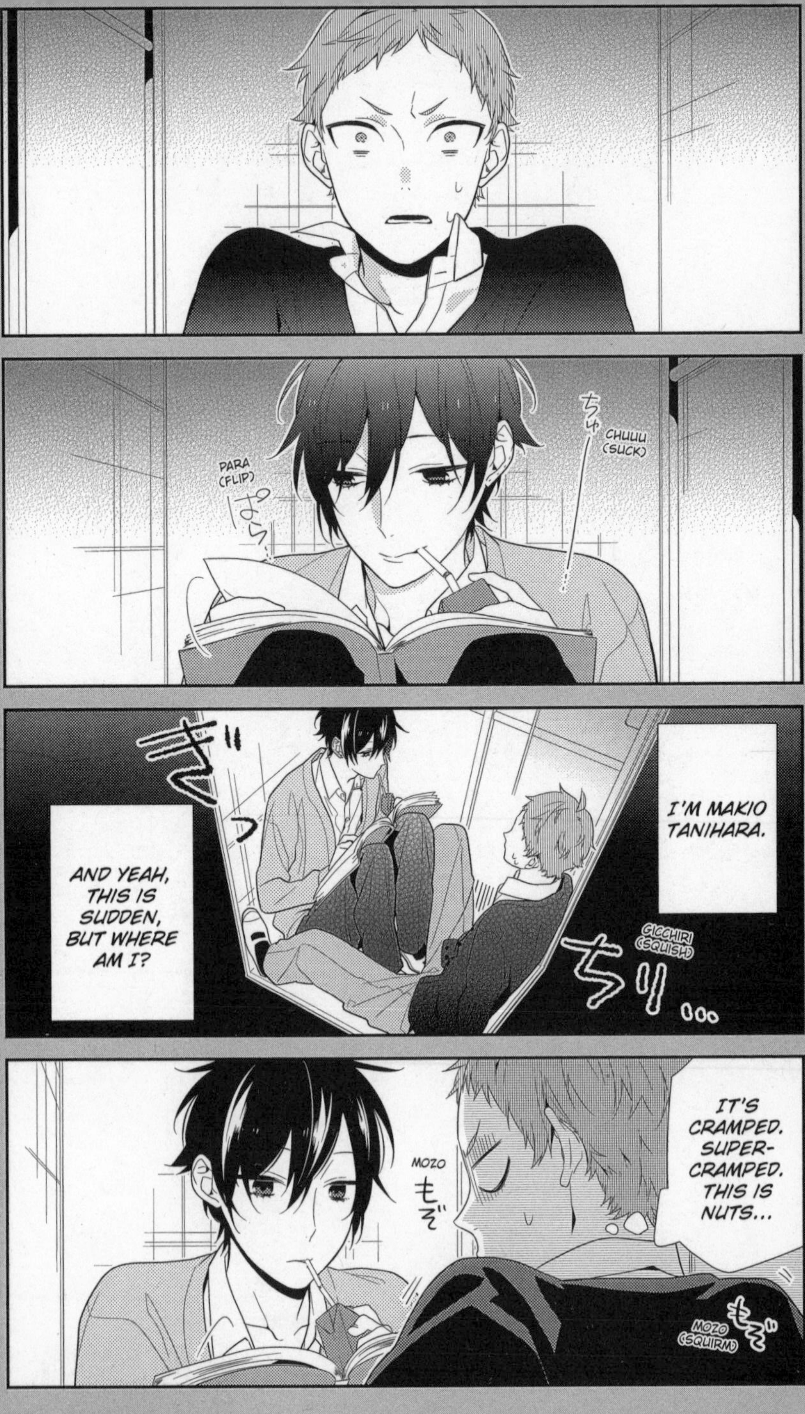
ちゅー
CHUUU (SUCK)
PARA (FLIP)
ぱら…
I'M MAKIO TANIHARA.
ぎっ
GICCHIRI (SQUISH)
ちり…
AND YEAH, THIS IS SUDDEN, BUT WHERE AM I?
IT'S CRAMPED. SUPER-CRAMPED. THIS IS NUTS…
もぞ
MOZO (SQUIRM)
MOZO
もぞ

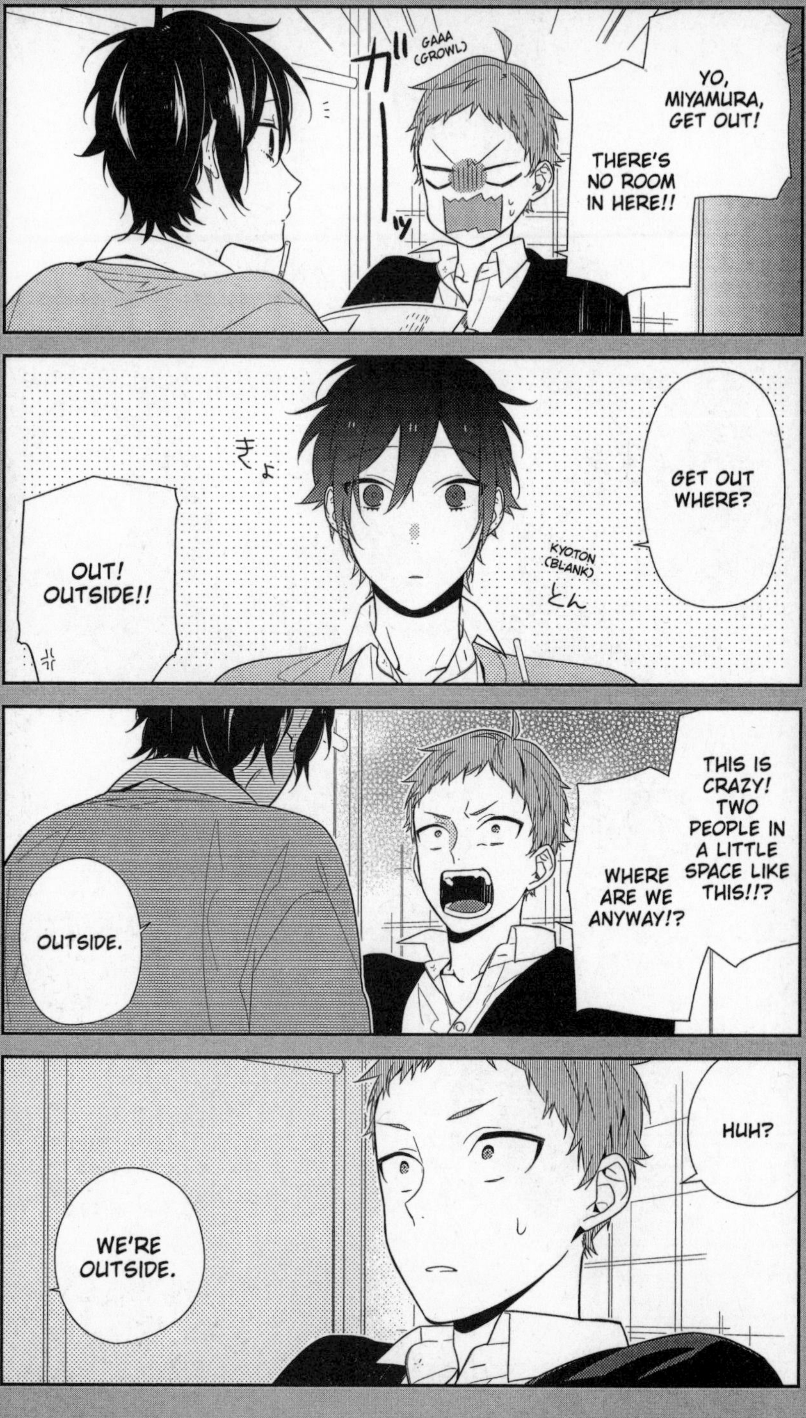
YO, MIYAMURA, GET OUT!
THERE'S NO ROOM IN HERE!!
ガーッ
GAAA (GROWL)
GET OUT WHERE?
きょとん
KYOTON (BLANK)
OUT! OUTSIDE!!
THIS IS CRAZY! TWO PEOPLE IN A LITTLE SPACE LIKE THIS!!?
WHERE ARE WE ANYWAY!?
OUTSIDE.
HUH?
WE'RE OUTSIDE.

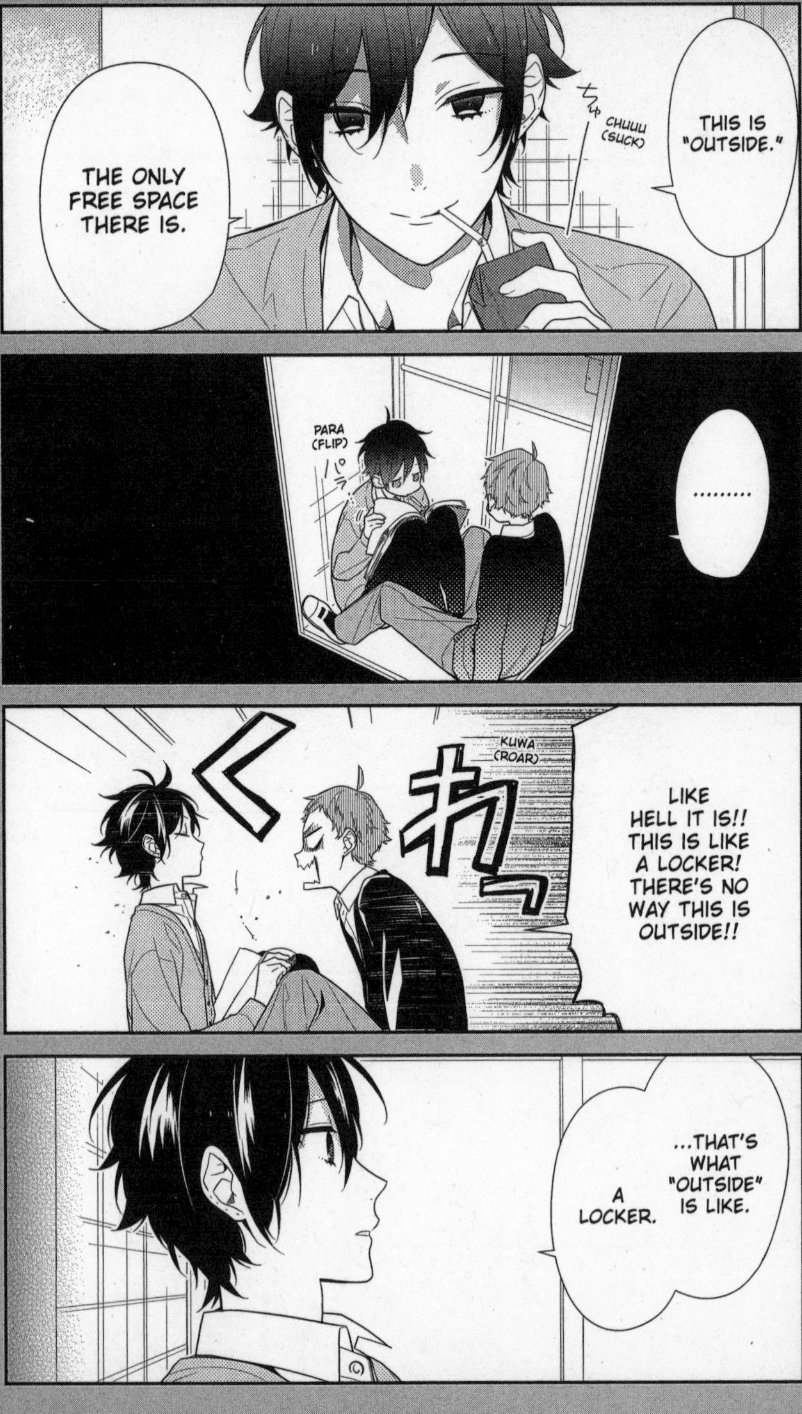
THIS IS "OUTSIDE."
CHUUU (SUCK)
THE ONLY FREE SPACE THERE IS.
.........
PARA (FLIP)
LIKE HELL IT IS!! THIS IS LIKE A LOCKER! THERE'S NO WAY THIS IS OUTSIDE!!
KUWA (ROAR)
...THAT'S WHAT "OUTSIDE" IS LIKE.
A LOCKER.

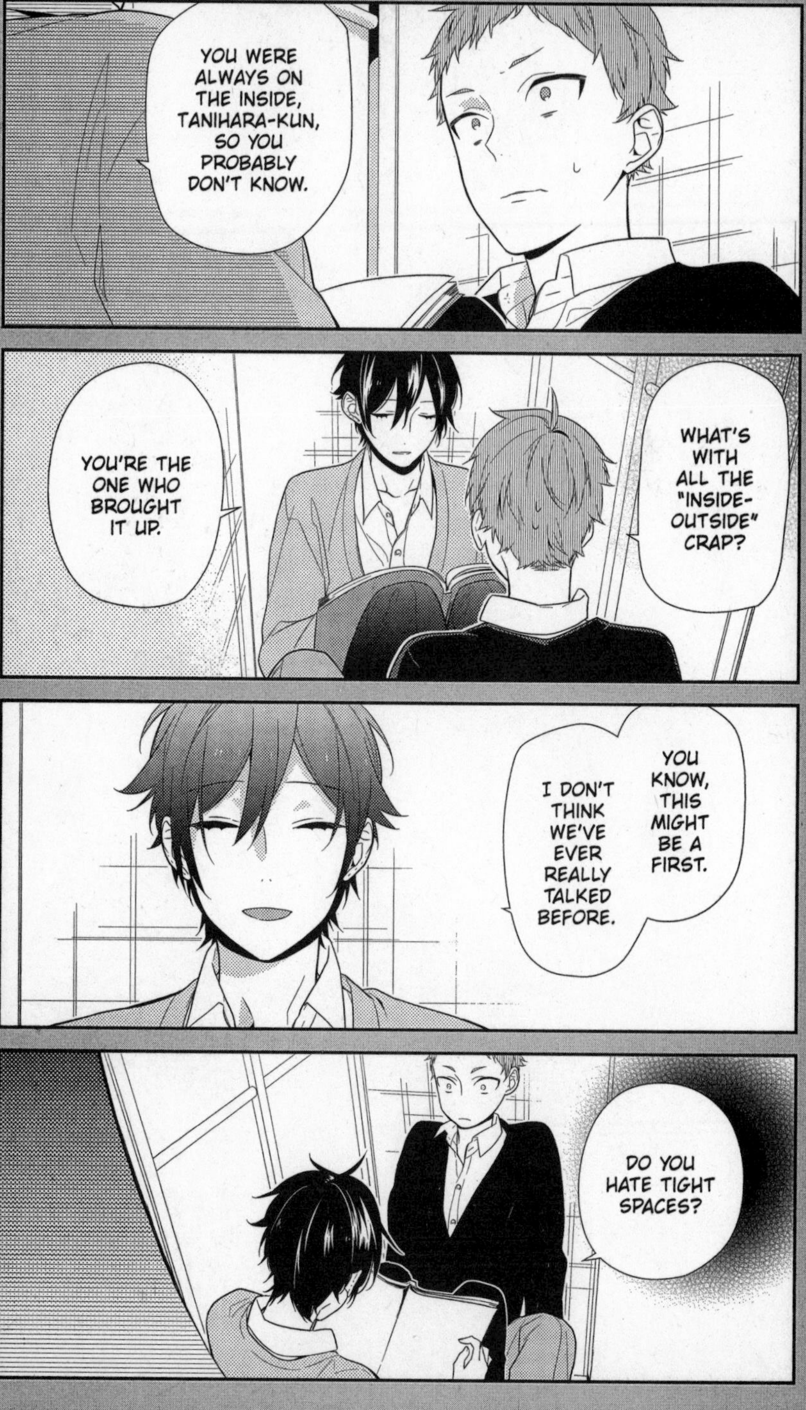
YOU WERE ALWAYS ON THE INSIDE, TANIHARA-KUN, SO YOU PROBABLY DON'T KNOW.
WHAT'S WITH ALL THE "INSIDE-OUTSIDE" CRAP?
YOU'RE THE ONE WHO BROUGHT IT UP.
YOU KNOW, THIS MIGHT BE A FIRST.
I DON'T THINK WE'VE EVER REALLY TALKED BEFORE.
DO YOU HATE TIGHT SPACES?

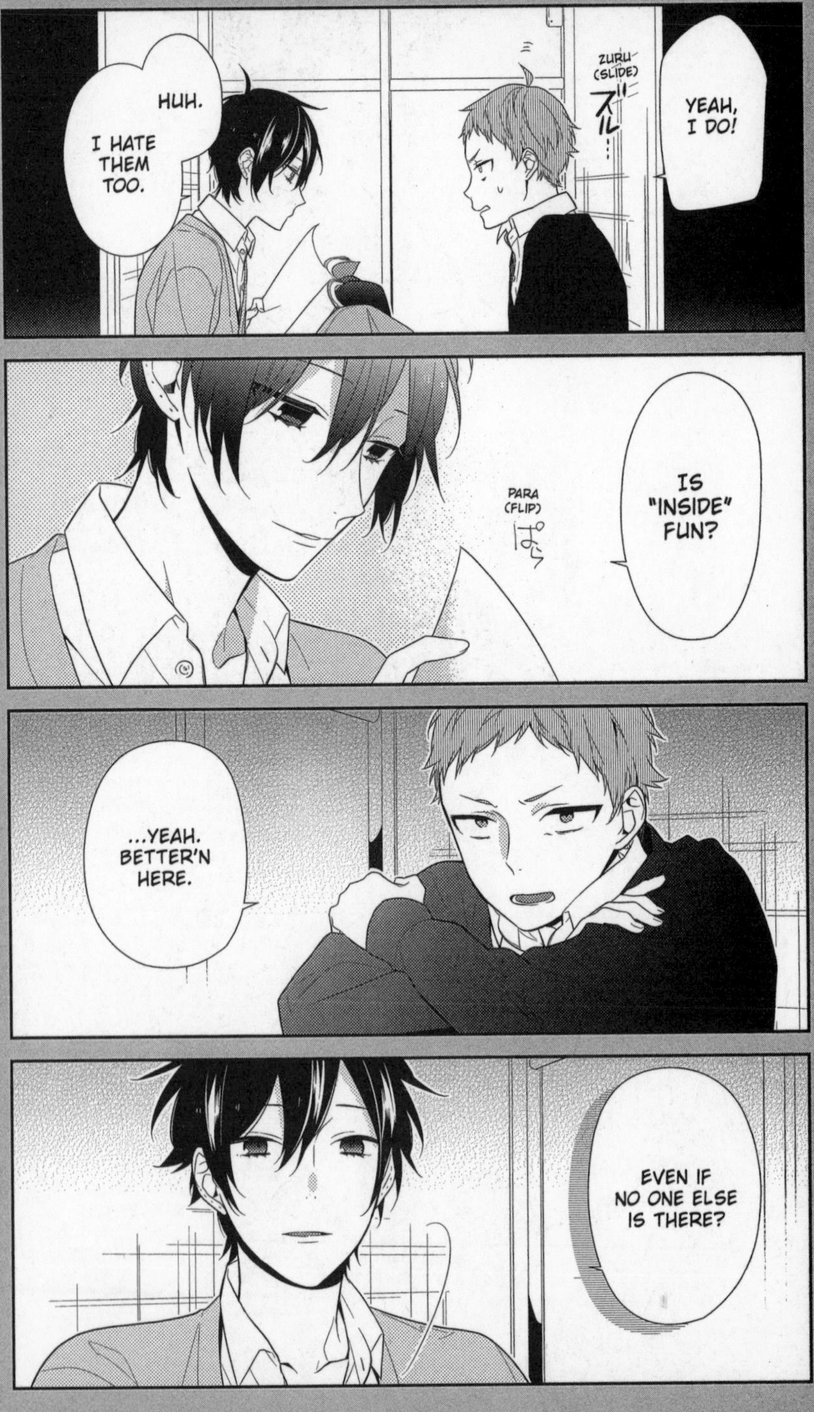
YEAH, I DO!
ZURU (SLIDE)
ズル…
HUH.
I HATE THEM TOO.
IS "INSIDE" FUN?
PARA (FLIP)
ぱら
...YEAH. BETTER'N HERE.
EVEN IF NO ONE ELSE IS THERE?

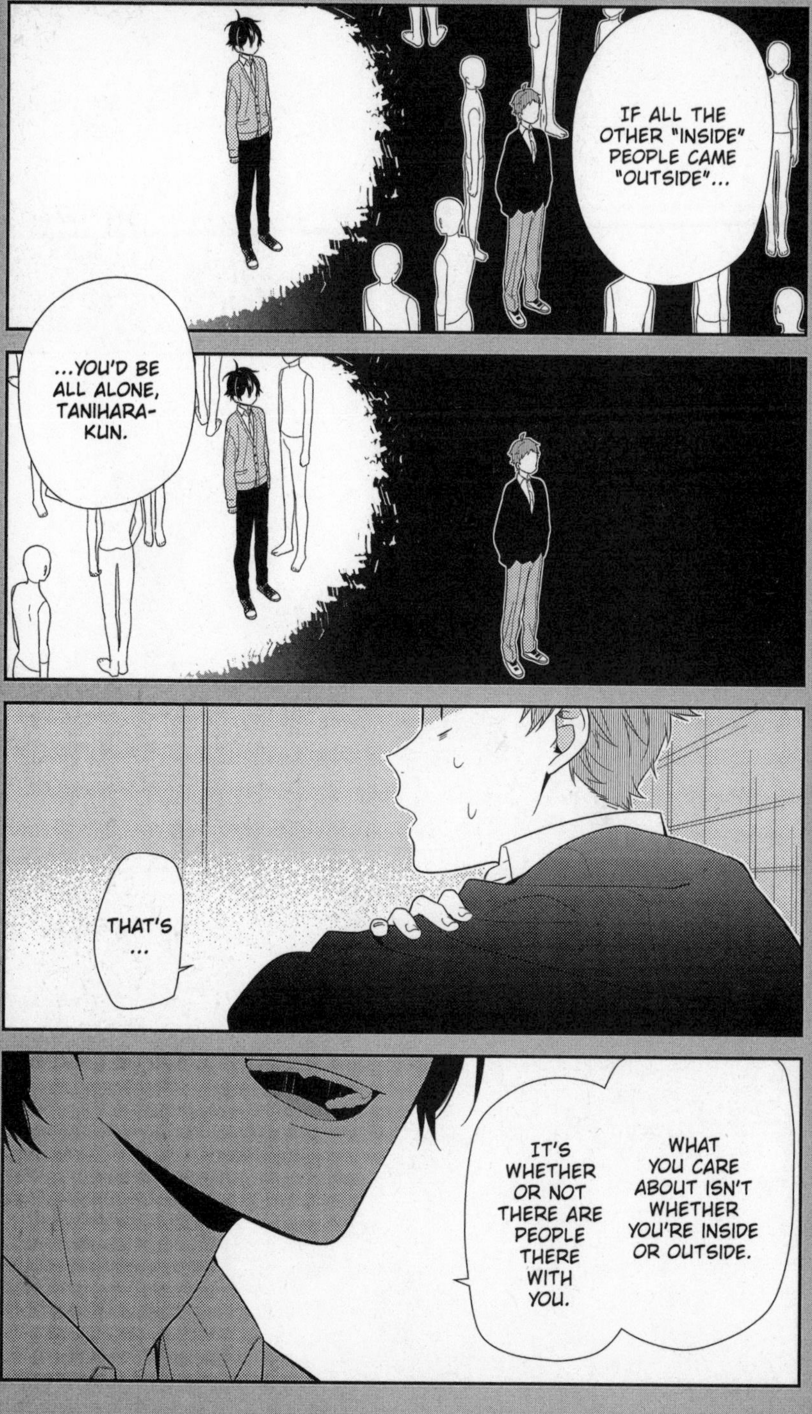
IF ALL THE OTHER "INSIDE" PEOPLE CAME "OUTSIDE"...
...YOU'D BE ALL ALONE, TANIHARA-KUN.
THAT'S ...
WHAT YOU CARE ABOUT ISN'T WHETHER YOU'RE INSIDE OR OUTSIDE.
IT'S WHETHER OR NOT THERE ARE PEOPLE THERE WITH YOU.

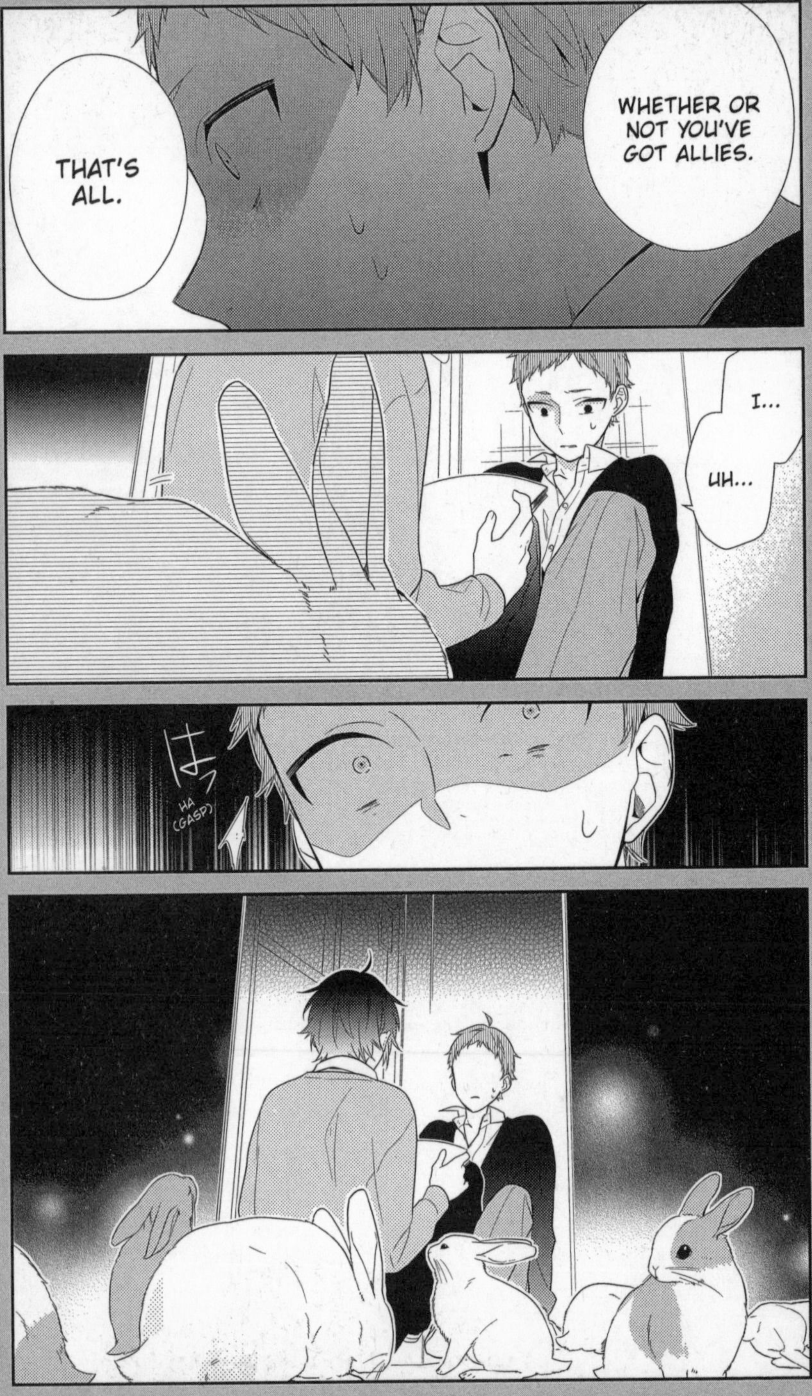
WHETHER OR NOT YOU'VE GOT ALLIES.
THAT'S ALL.
I...
UH...
はっ
HA (GASP)

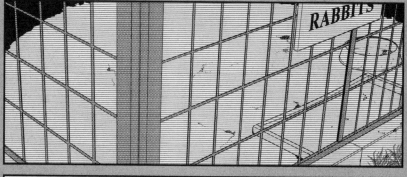

I FORGOT... TO FEED ...EVEN THEM... THOUGH I WAS IN CHARGE.

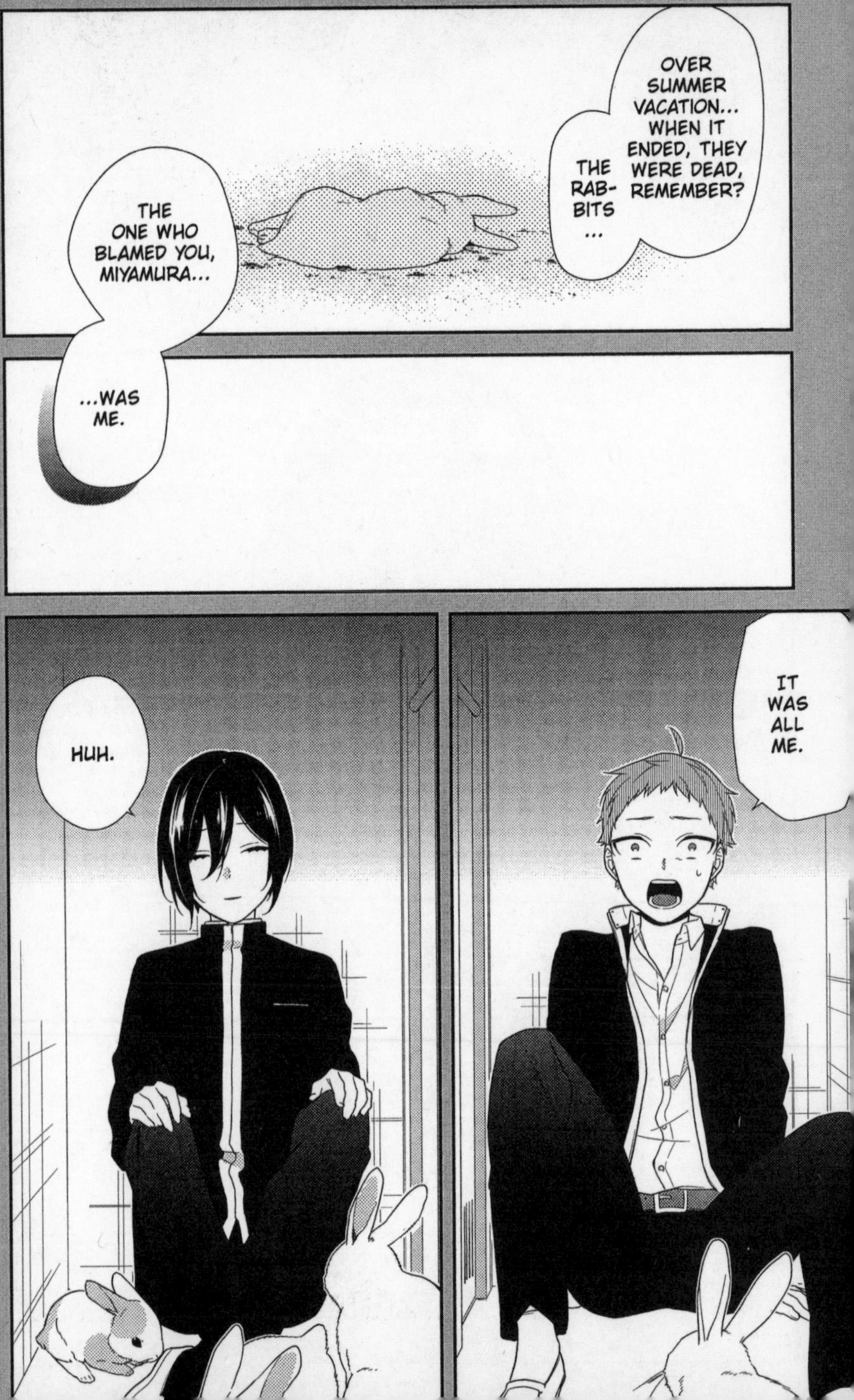
OVER SUMMER VACATION... WHEN IT ENDED, THEY WERE DEAD, REMEMBER?
THE RAB-BITS ...
THE ONE WHO BLAMED YOU, MIYAMURA...
...WAS ME.
IT WAS ALL ME.
HUH.

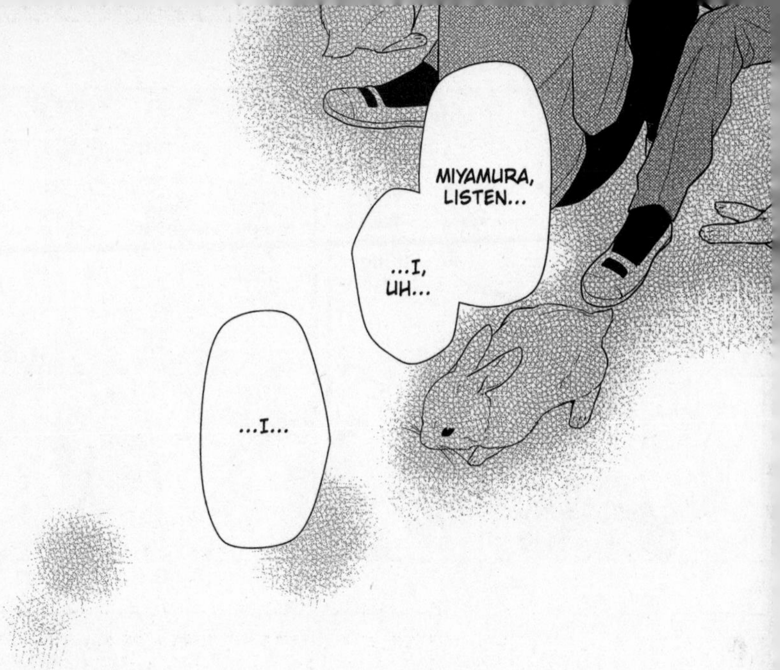
MIYAMURA, LISTEN...
...I, UH...
...I...

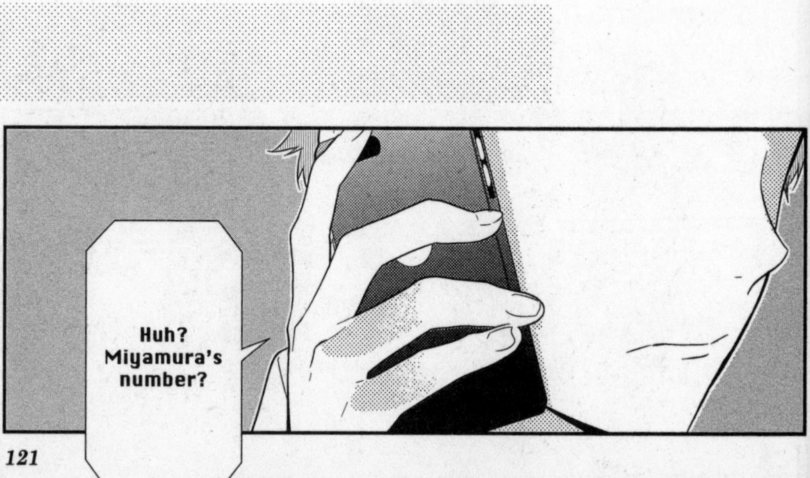
Huh? Miyamura's number?

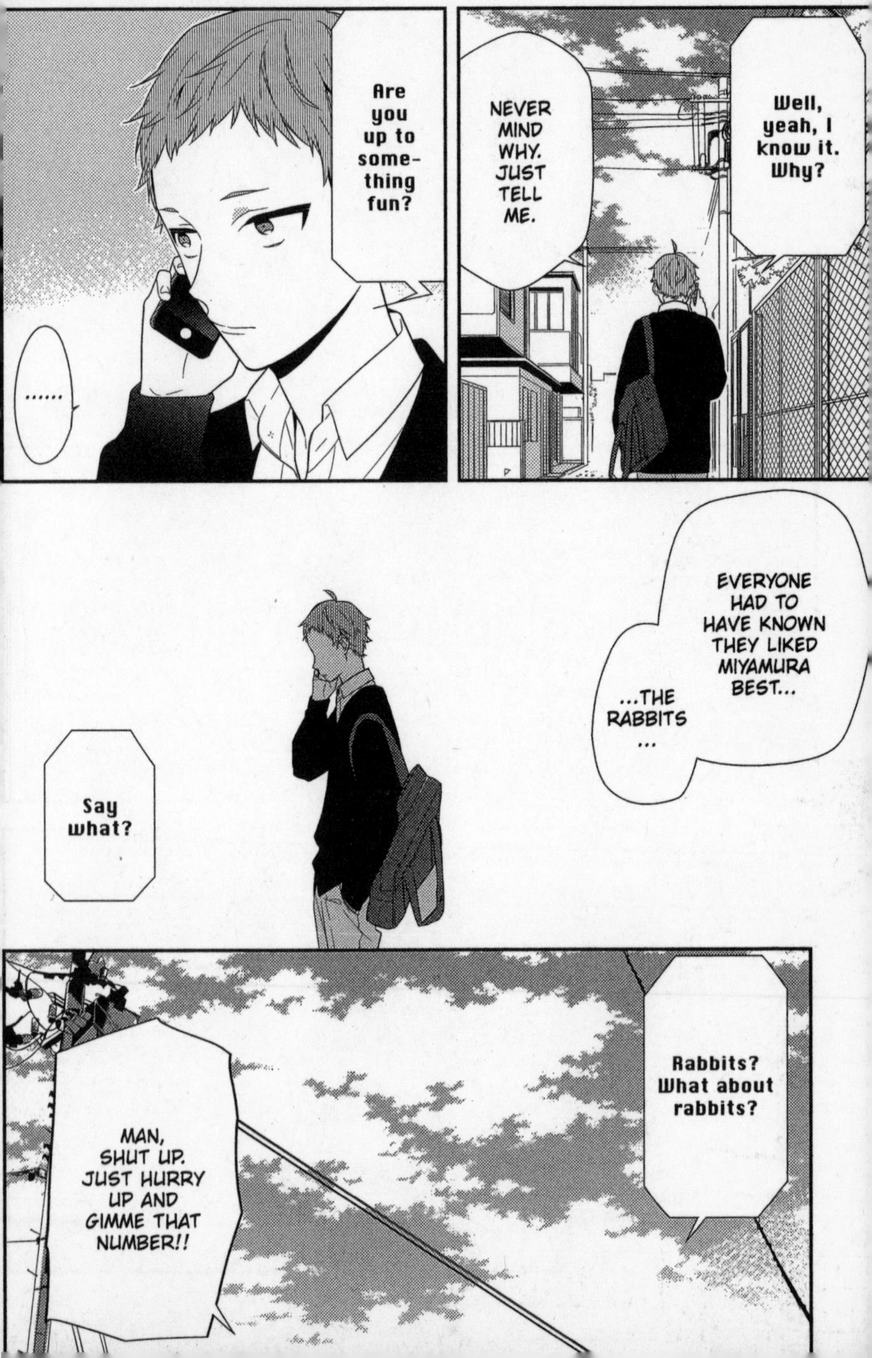
Well, yeah, I know it. Why?
NEVER MIND WHY. JUST TELL ME.
Are you up to some-thing fun?
......
EVERYONE HAD TO HAVE KNOWN THEY LIKED MIYAMURA BEST...
...THE RABBITS...
Say what?
Rabbits? What about rabbits?
MAN, SHUT UP. JUST HURRY UP AND GIMME THAT NUMBER!!

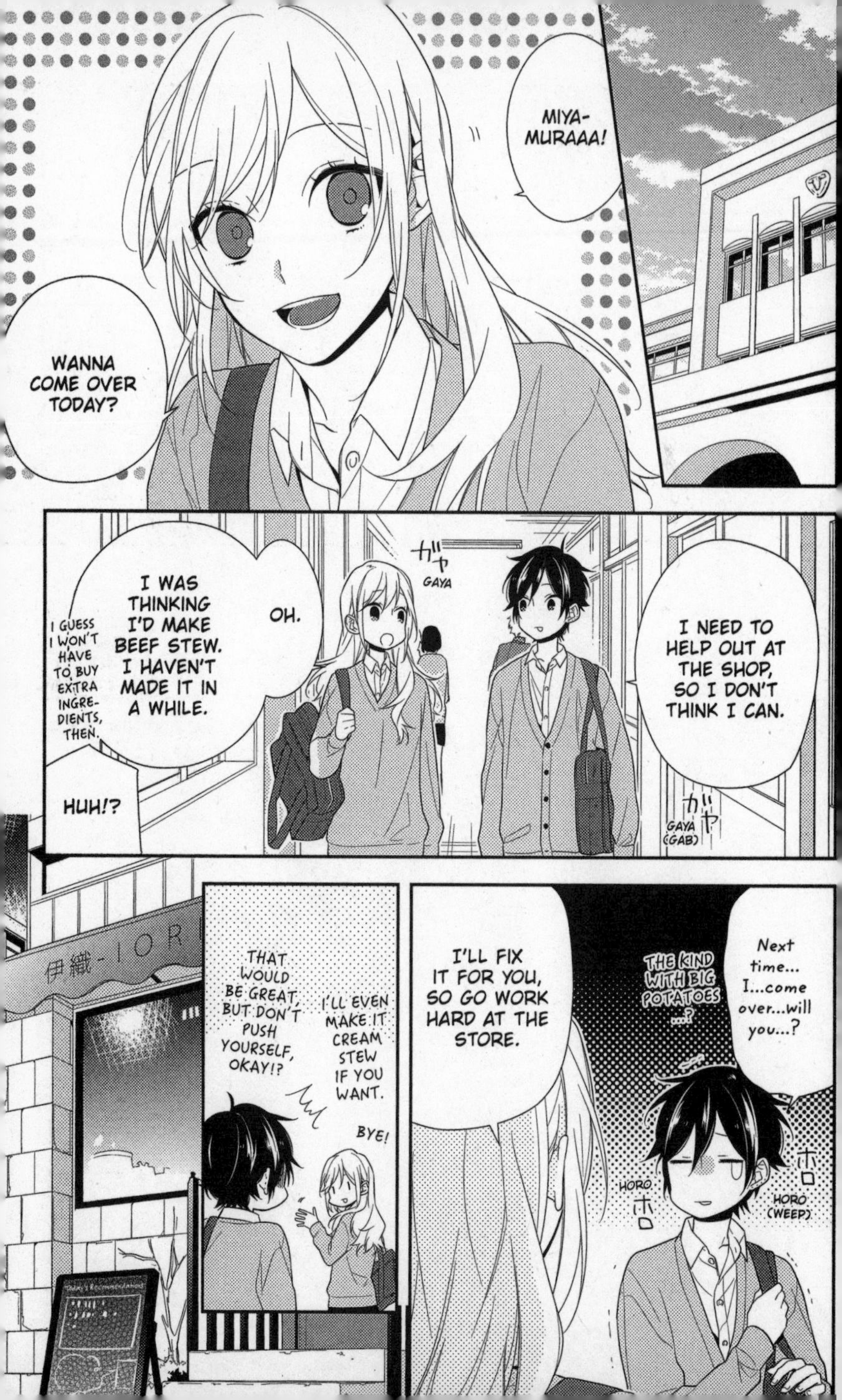
MIYA-MURAAA!
WANNA COME OVER TODAY?
I NEED TO HELP OUT AT THE SHOP, SO I DON'T THINK I CAN.
ガヤ GAYA (GAB)
ガヤ GAYA
OH.
I WAS THINKING I'D MAKE BEEF STEW. I HAVEN'T MADE IT IN A WHILE.
I GUESS I WON'T HAVE TO BUY EXTRA INGREDIENTS, THEN.
HUH!?
Next time... I...come over...will you...?
THE KIND WITH BIG POTATOES ...?
I'LL FIX IT FOR YOU, SO GO WORK HARD AT THE STORE.
ホロ HORO (WEEP)
ホロ HORO
I'LL EVEN MAKE IT CREAM STEW IF YOU WANT.
THAT WOULD BE GREAT, BUT DON'T PUSH YOURSELF, OKAY!?
BYE!
伊織-IOR

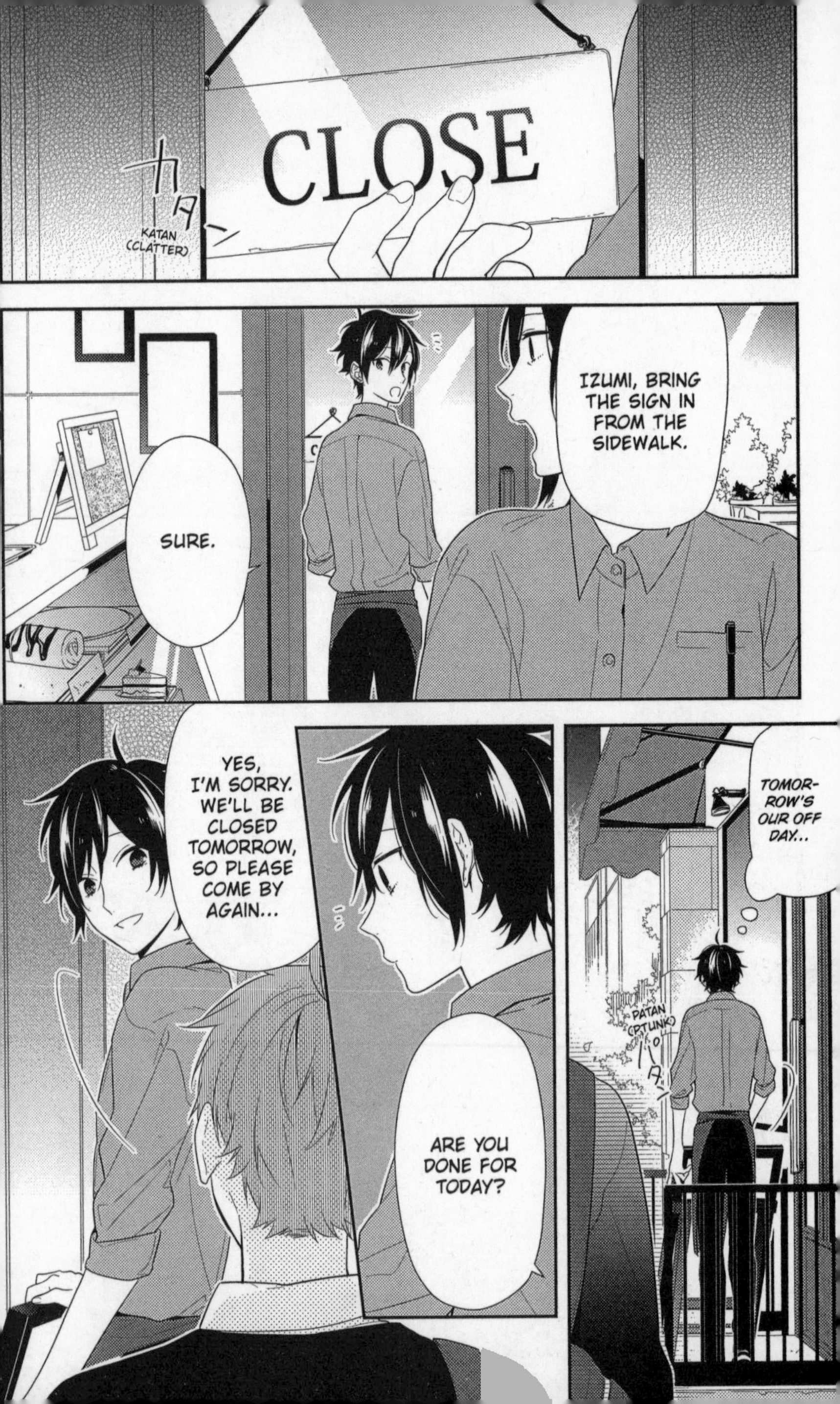
CLOSE
KATAN (CLATTER)
IZUMI, BRING THE SIGN IN FROM THE SIDEWALK.
SURE.
TOMORROW'S OUR OFF DAY...
PATAN (PTUNK)
ARE YOU DONE FOR TODAY?
YES, I'M SORRY. WE'LL BE CLOSED TOMORROW, SO PLEASE COME BY AGAIN...

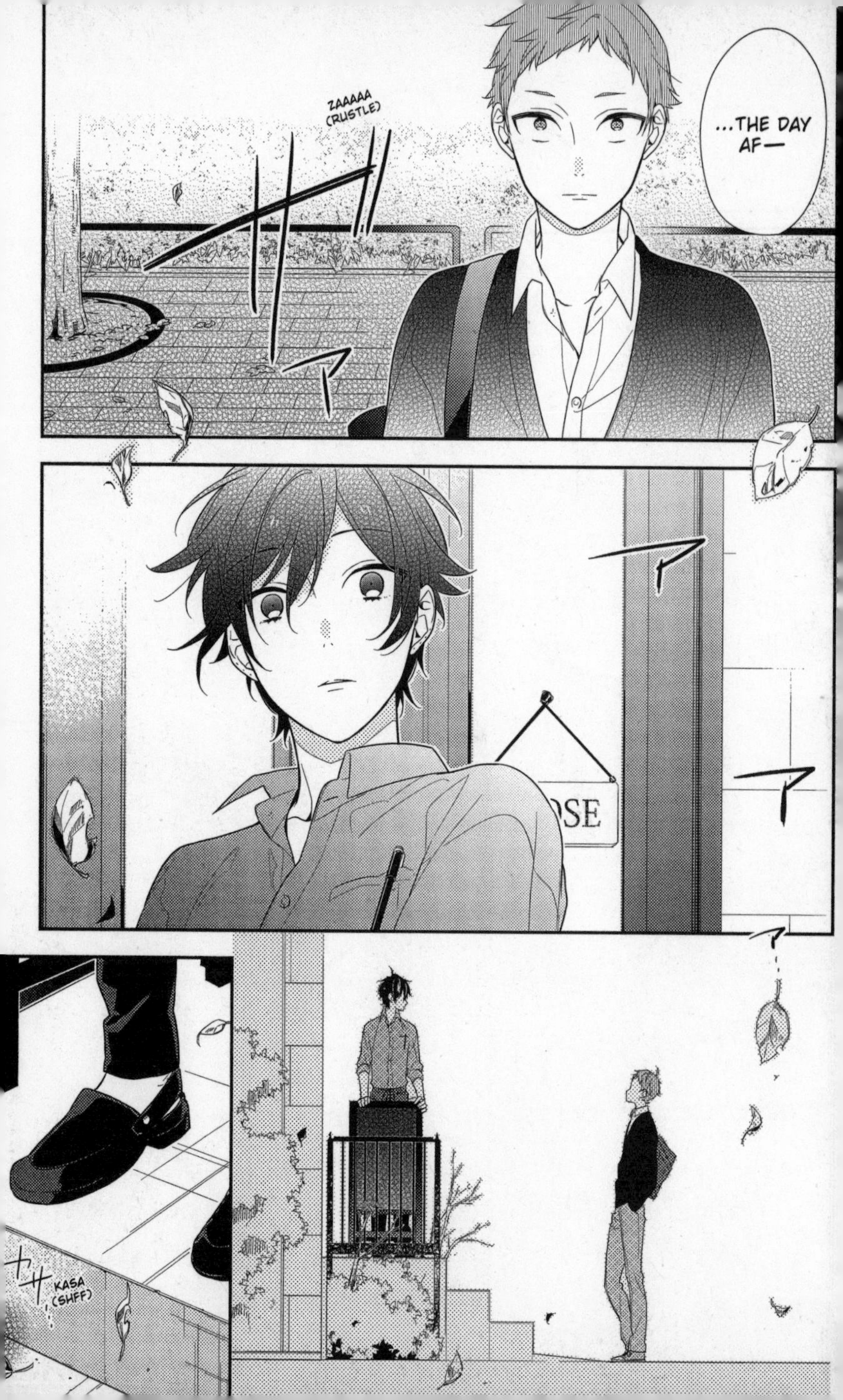
...THE DAY AF—
ZAAAAA (RUSTLE)
OSE
KASA (SHFF)

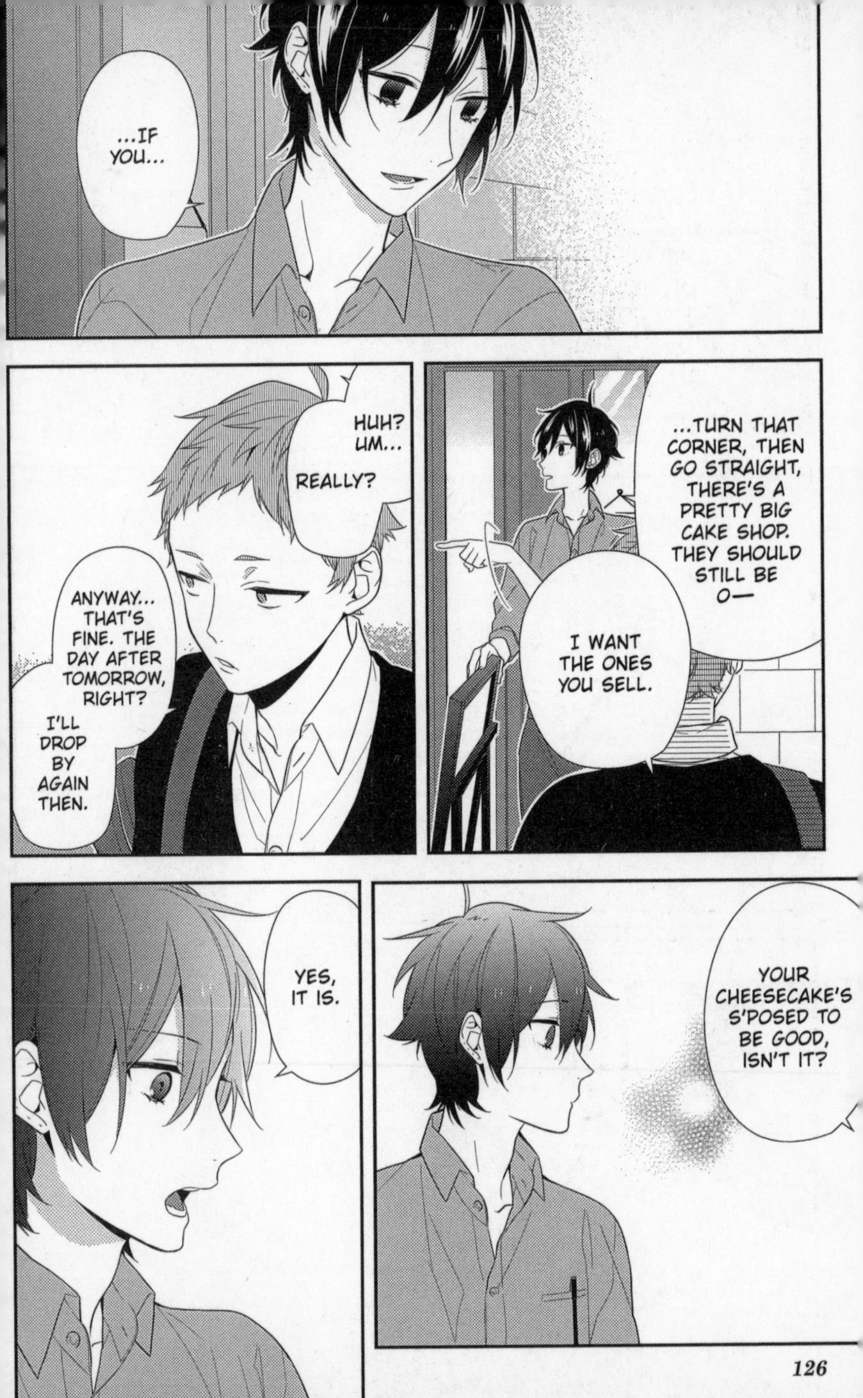
...IF YOU...
...TURN THAT CORNER, THEN GO STRAIGHT, THERE'S A PRETTY BIG CAKE SHOP. THEY SHOULD STILL BE O—
I WANT THE ONES YOU SELL.
HUH? UM...
REALLY?
ANYWAY... THAT'S FINE. THE DAY AFTER TOMORROW, RIGHT?
I'LL DROP BY AGAIN THEN.
YOUR CHEESECAKE'S S'POSED TO BE GOOD, ISN'T IT?
YES, IT IS.

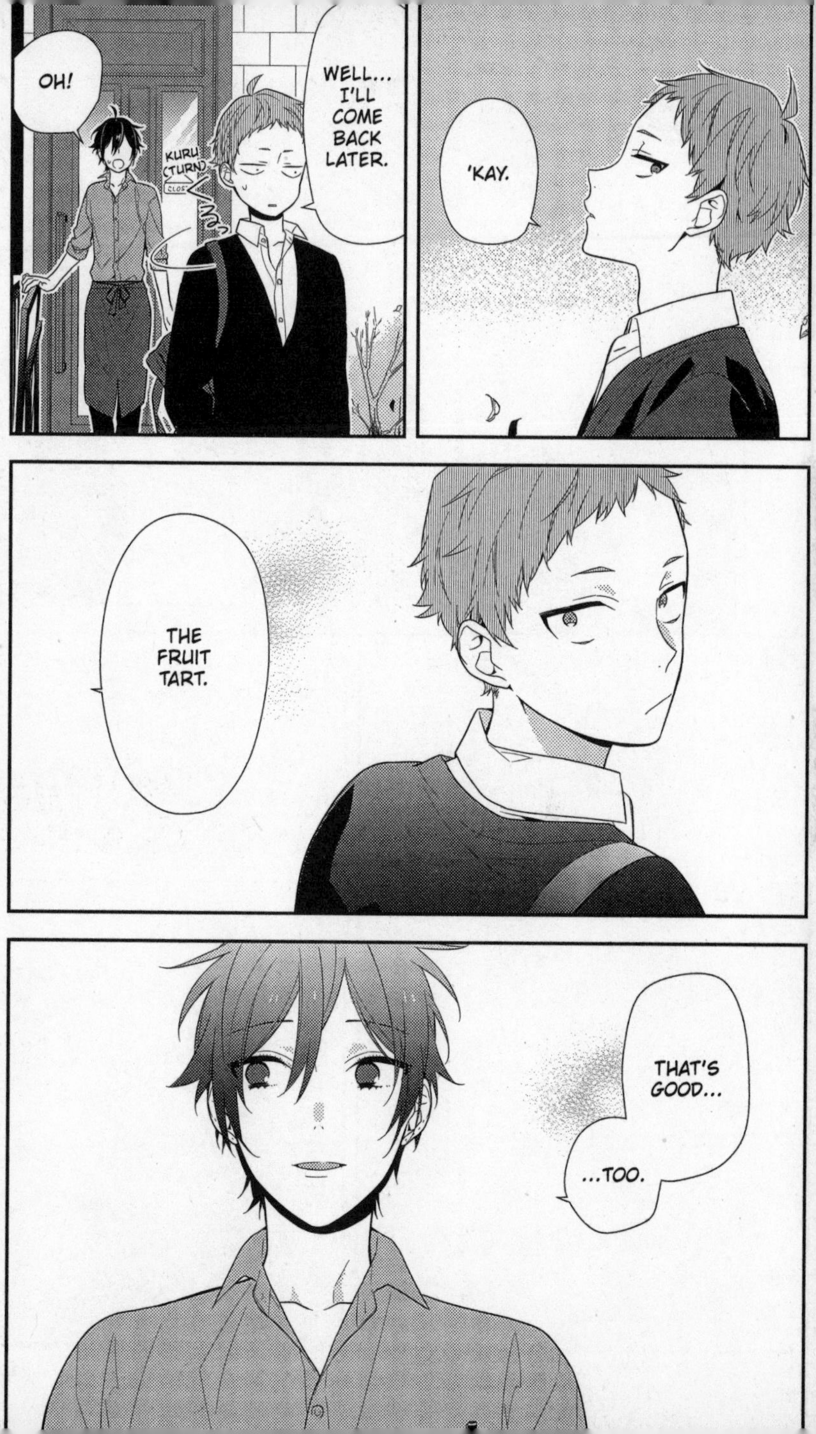
'KAY.
WELL... I'LL COME BACK LATER.
KURU (TURN)
OH!
THE FRUIT TART.
THAT'S GOOD...
...TOO.

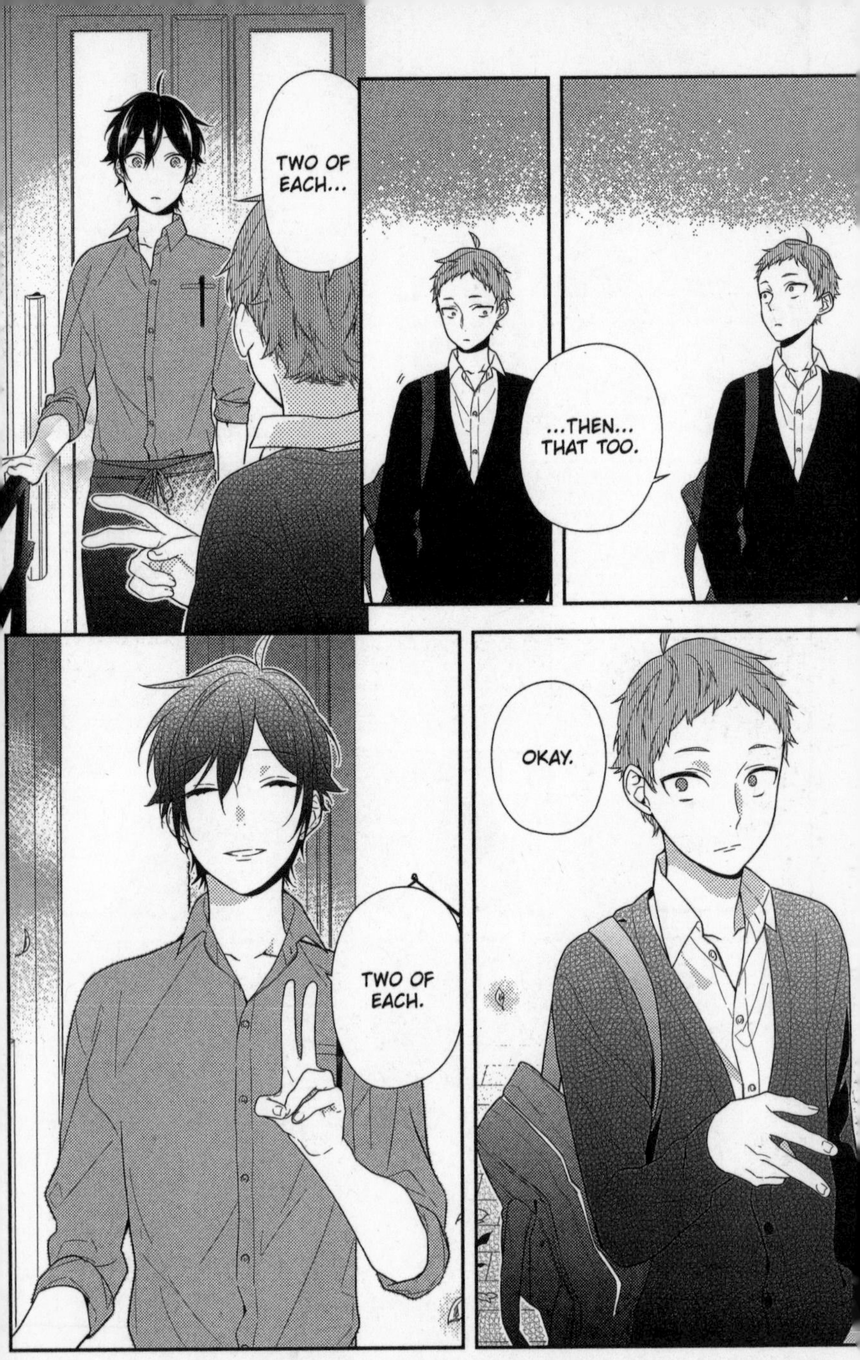
...THEN... THAT TOO.
TWO OF EACH...
OKAY.
TWO OF EACH.

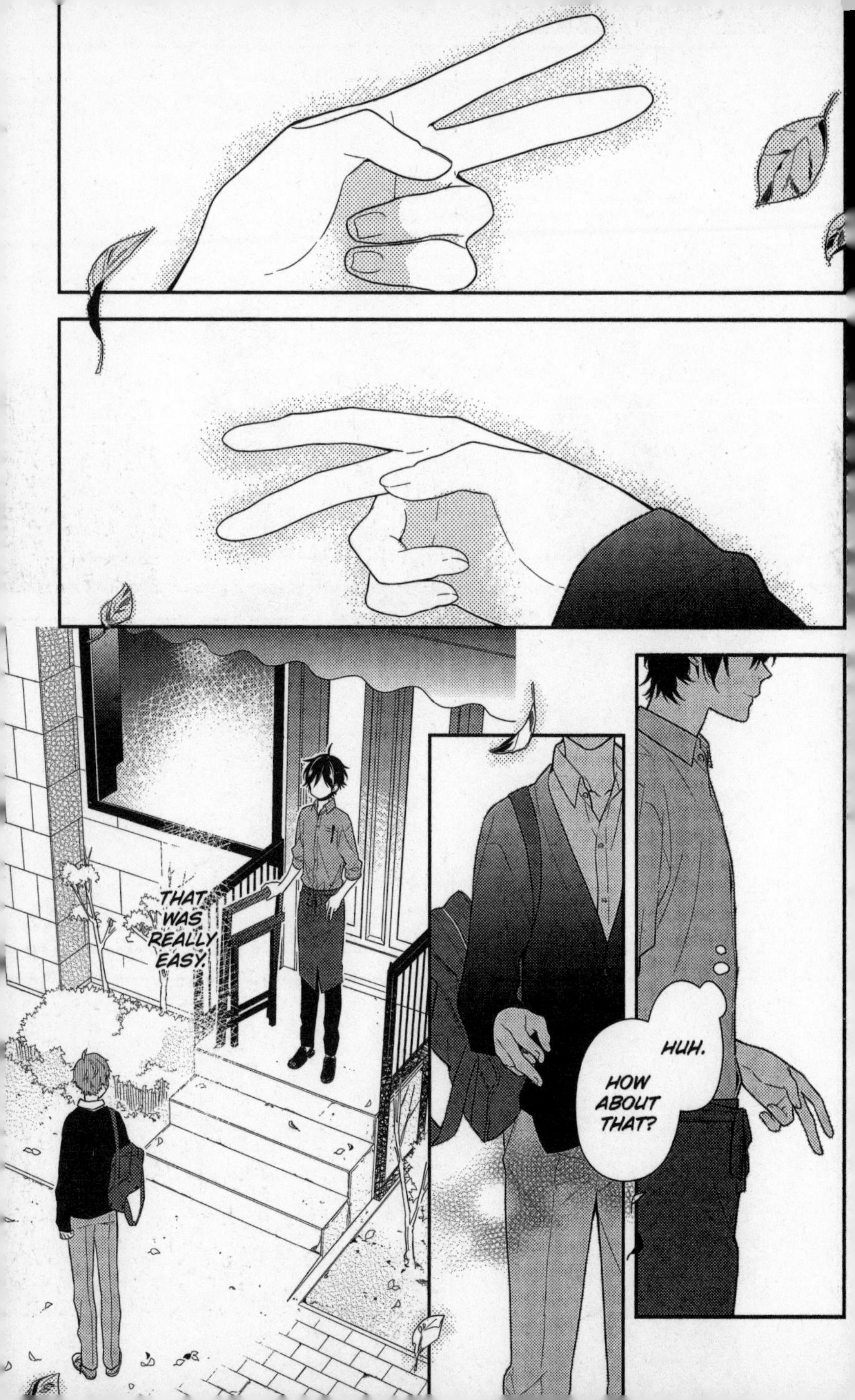
HUH.
HOW ABOUT THAT?
THAT WAS REALLY EASY.

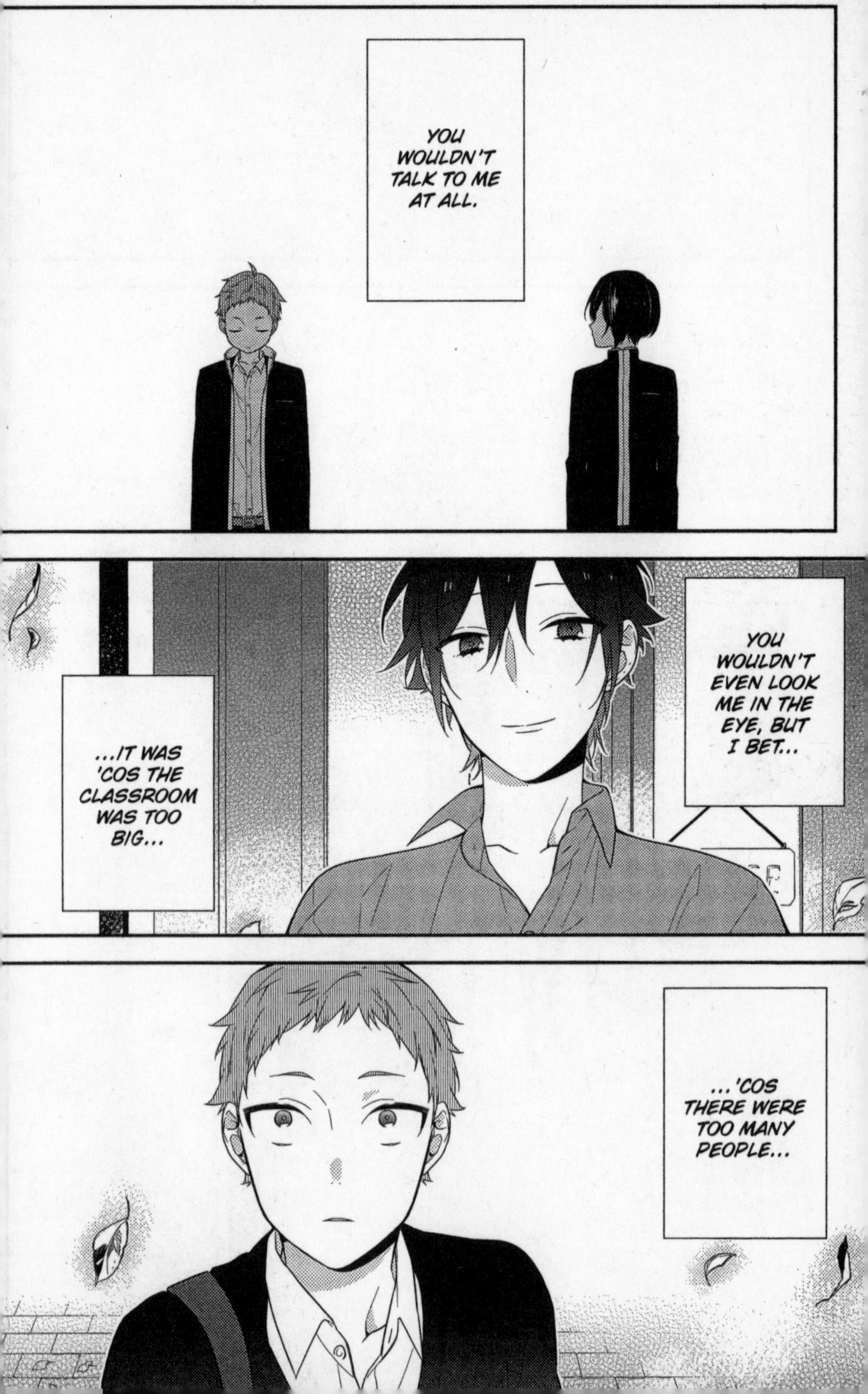
YOU WOULDN'T TALK TO ME AT ALL.
YOU WOULDN'T EVEN LOOK ME IN THE EYE, BUT I BET...
...IT WAS 'COS THE CLASSROOM WAS TOO BIG...
...'COS THERE WERE TOO MANY PEOPLE...

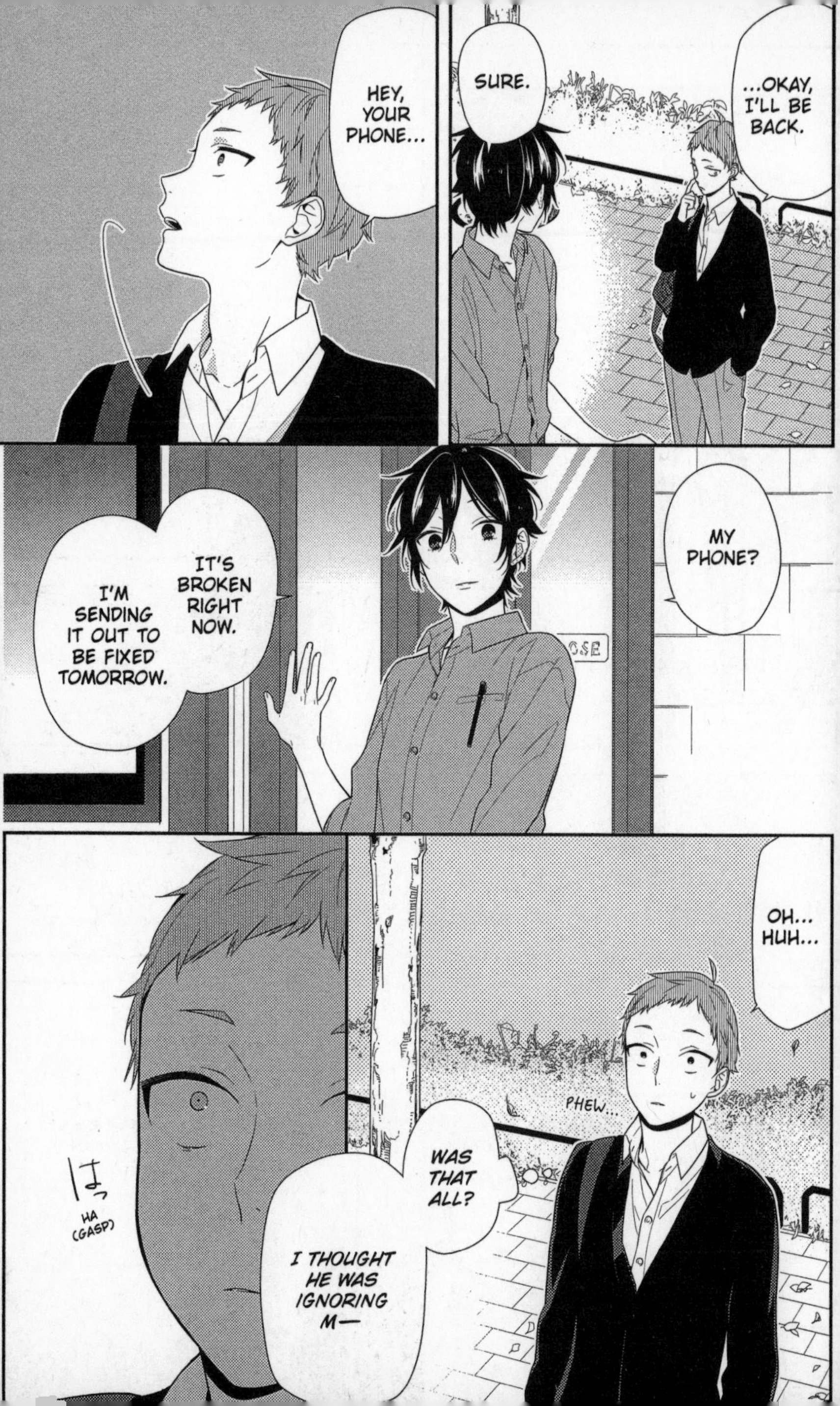
...OKAY, I'LL BE BACK.
SURE.
HEY, YOUR PHONE...
MY PHONE?
IT'S BROKEN RIGHT NOW.
I'M SENDING IT OUT TO BE FIXED TOMORROW.
OH... HUH...
PHEW...
WAS THAT ALL?
I THOUGHT HE WAS IGNORING M—
はっ
HA (GASP)

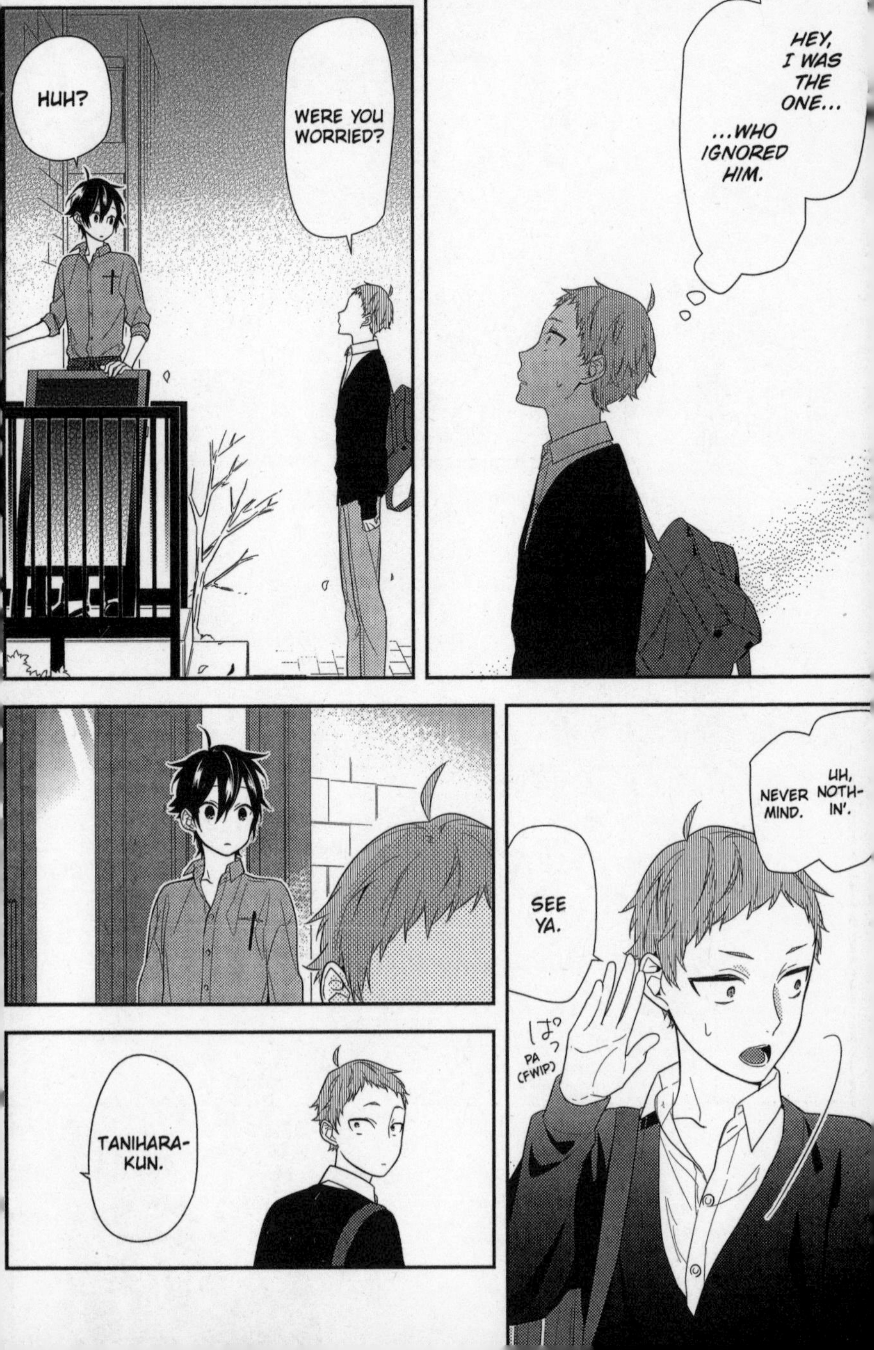
HEY, I WAS THE ONE...
...WHO IGNORED HIM.
WERE YOU WORRIED?
HUH?
UH, NOTHIN'.
NEVER MIND.
SEE YA.
ぱっ
PA (FWIP)
TANIHARA-KUN.

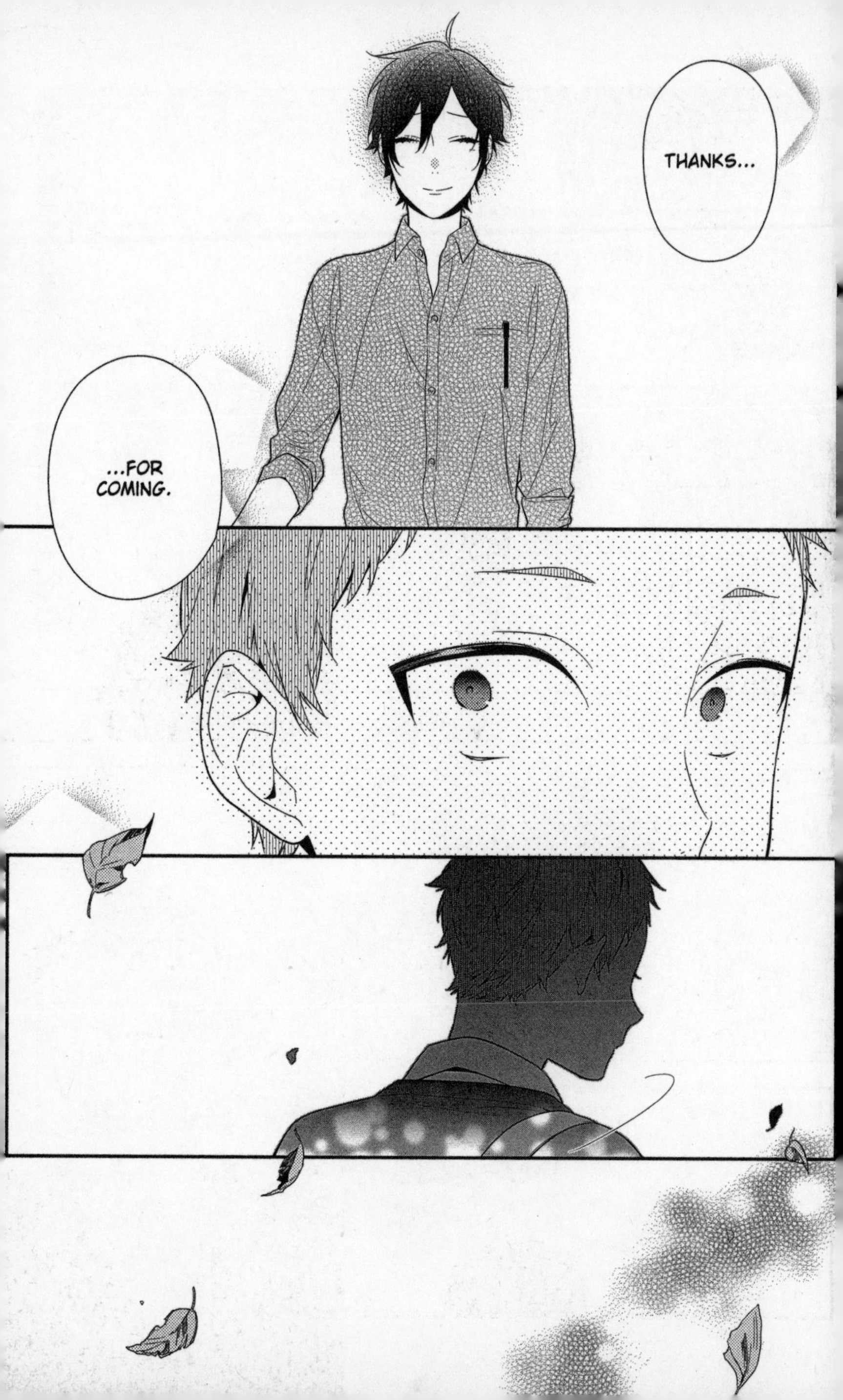
THANKS...
...FOR COMING.

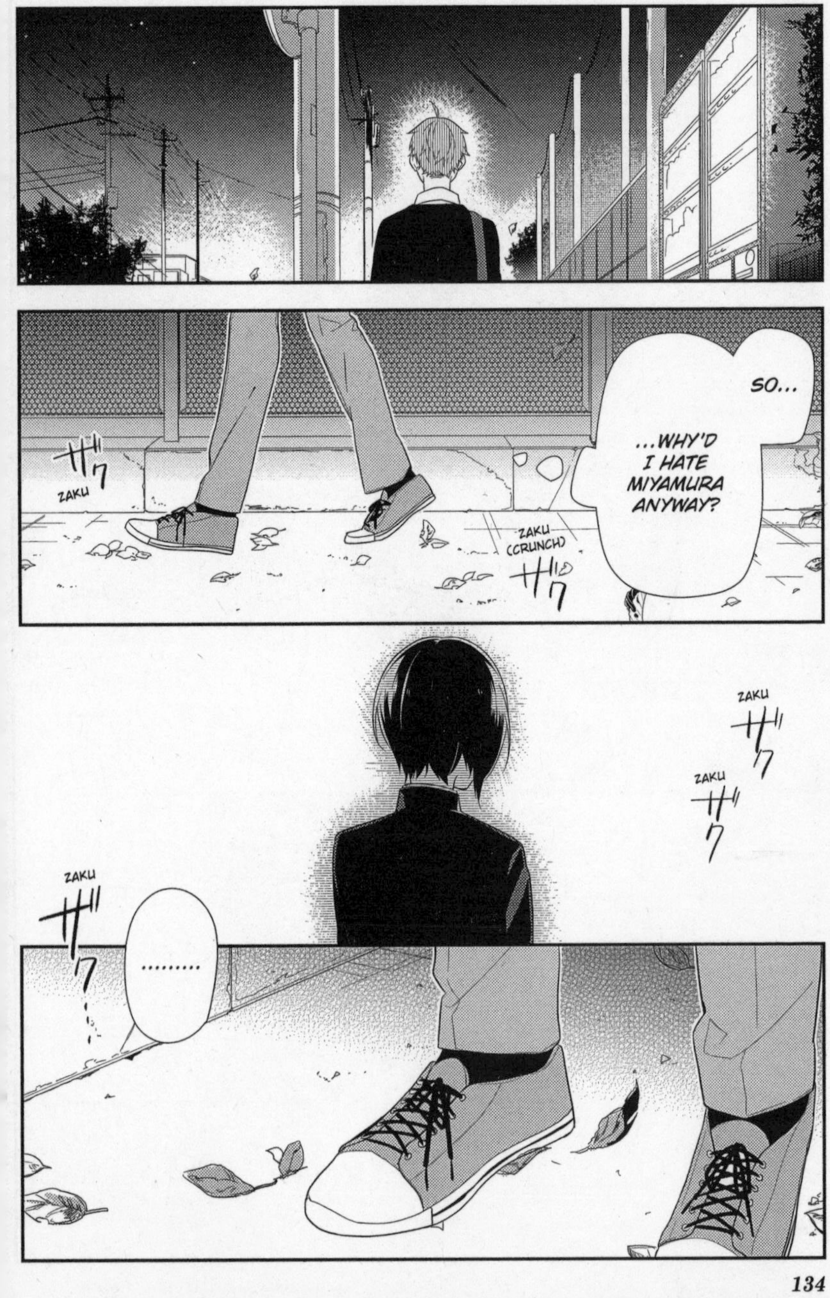
SO...
...WHY'D I HATE MIYAMURA ANYWAY?
ZAKU (CRUNCH)
ZAKU
ZAKU
ZAKU
ZAKU
.........

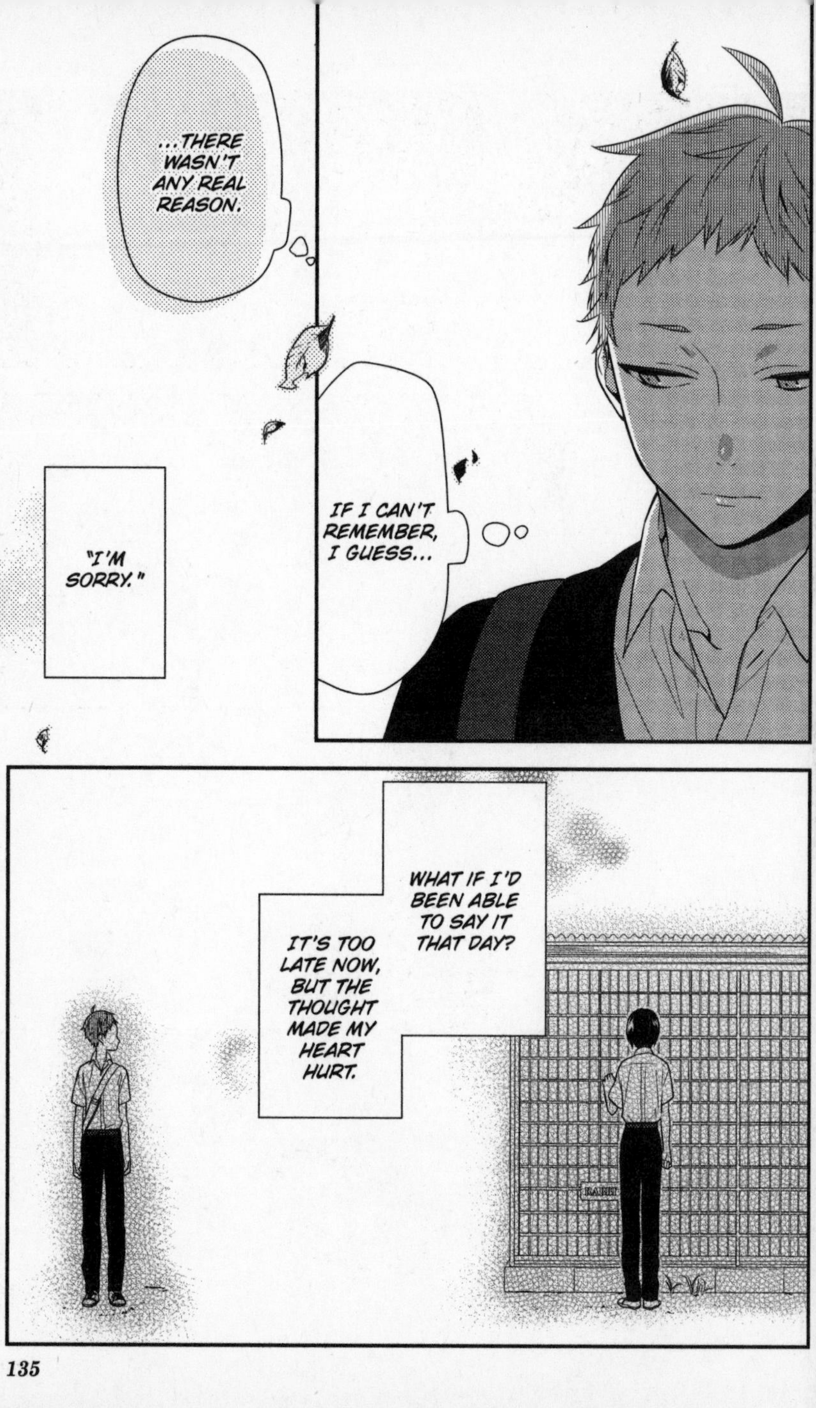
IF I CAN'T REMEMBER, I GUESS...
...THERE WASN'T ANY REAL REASON.
"I'M SORRY."
WHAT IF I'D BEEN ABLE TO SAY IT THAT DAY?
IT'S TOO LATE NOW, BUT THE THOUGHT MADE MY HEART HURT.

HORIMIYA

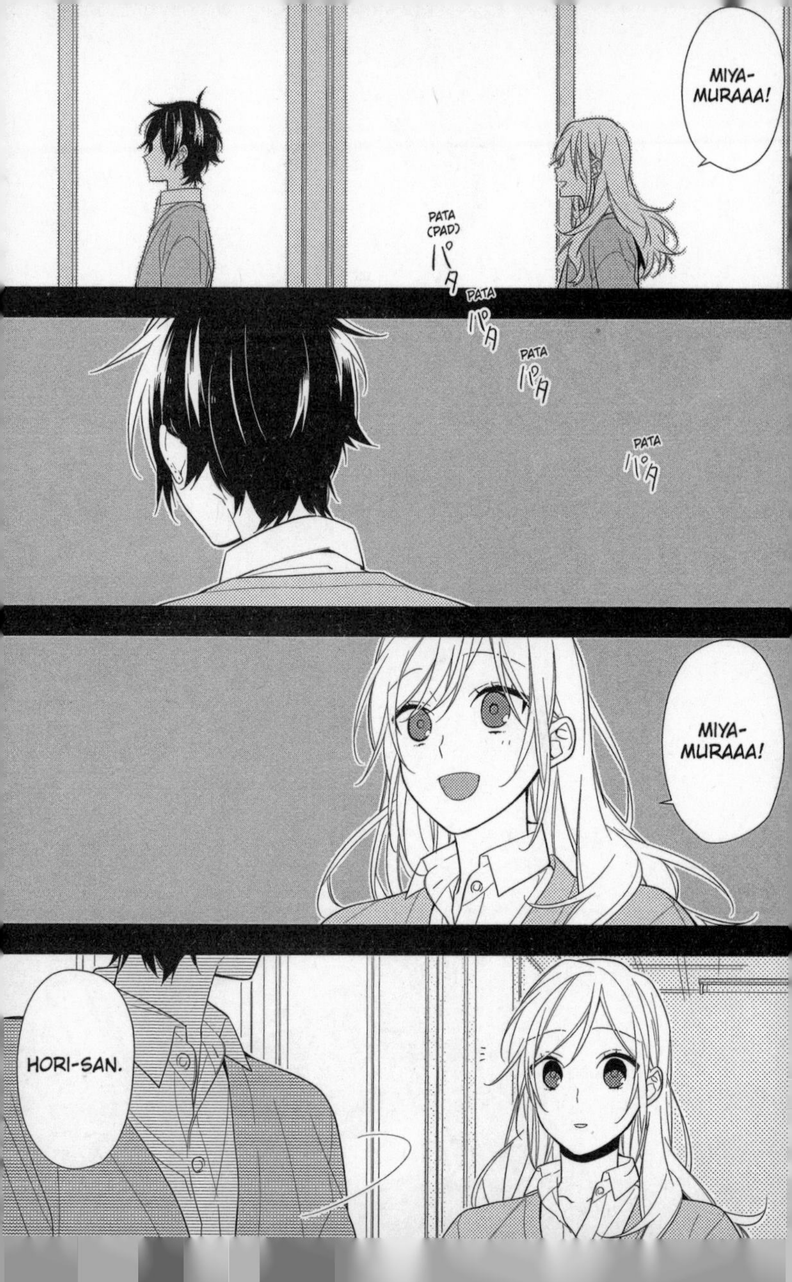
MIYA-MURAAA!
PATA (PAD) パタ
PATA パタ
PATA パタ
PATA パタ
MIYA-MURAAA!
HORI-SAN.

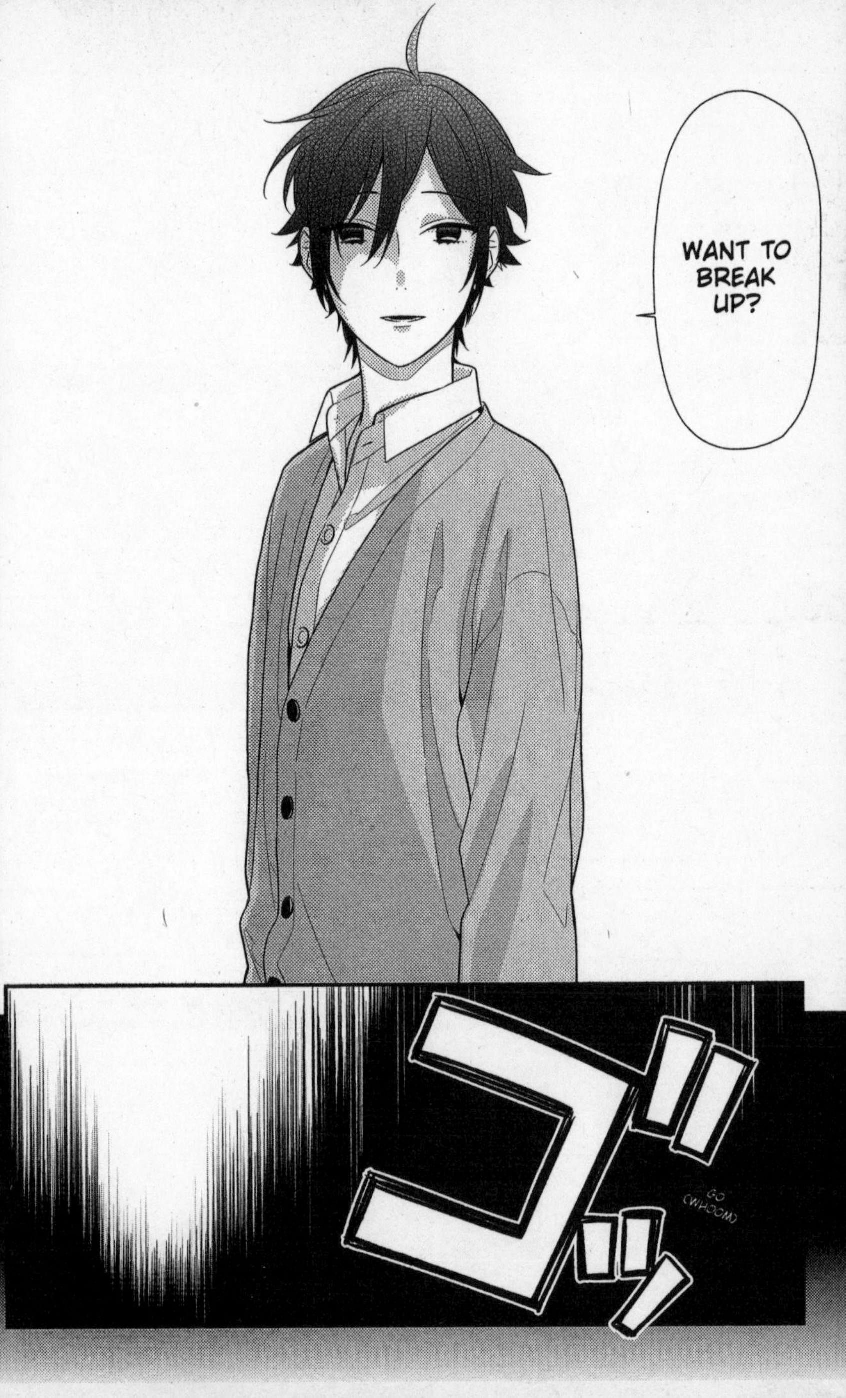
WANT TO BREAK UP?
ゴッ
GO (WHOOM)

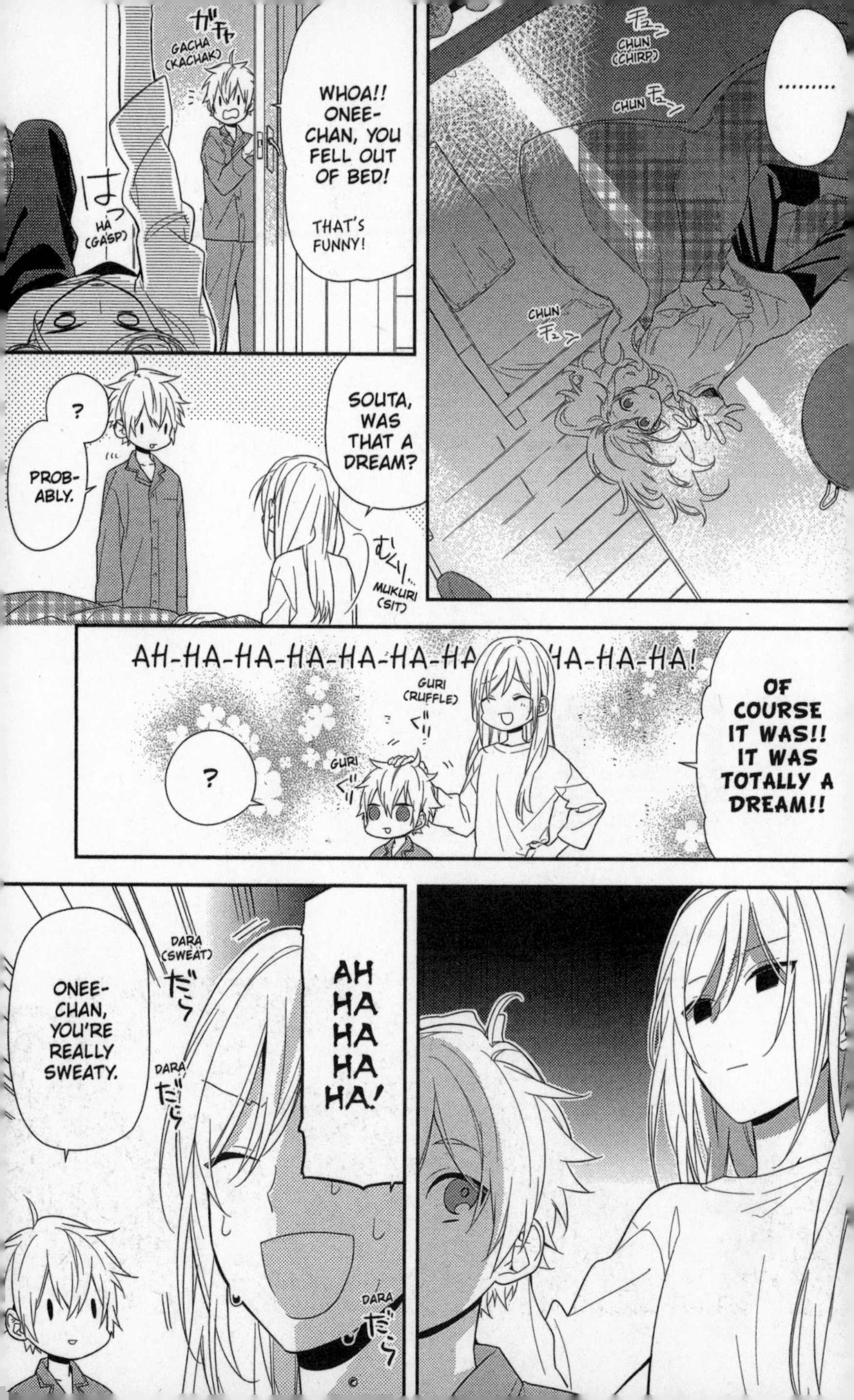
........
CHUN (CHIRP)
CHUN
CHUN
GACHA (KACHAK)
WHOA!! ONEE-CHAN, YOU FELL OUT OF BED!
THAT'S FUNNY!
HA (GASP)
SOUTA, WAS THAT A DREAM?
?
PROBABLY.
MUKURI (SIT)
OF COURSE IT WAS!! IT WAS TOTALLY A DREAM!!
AH-HA-HA-HA-HA-HA-HA HA-HA-HA!
GURI (RUFFLE)
GURI
?
AH HA HA HA HA HA!
DARA (SWEAT)
DARA
DARA
ONEE-CHAN, YOU'RE REALLY SWEATY.

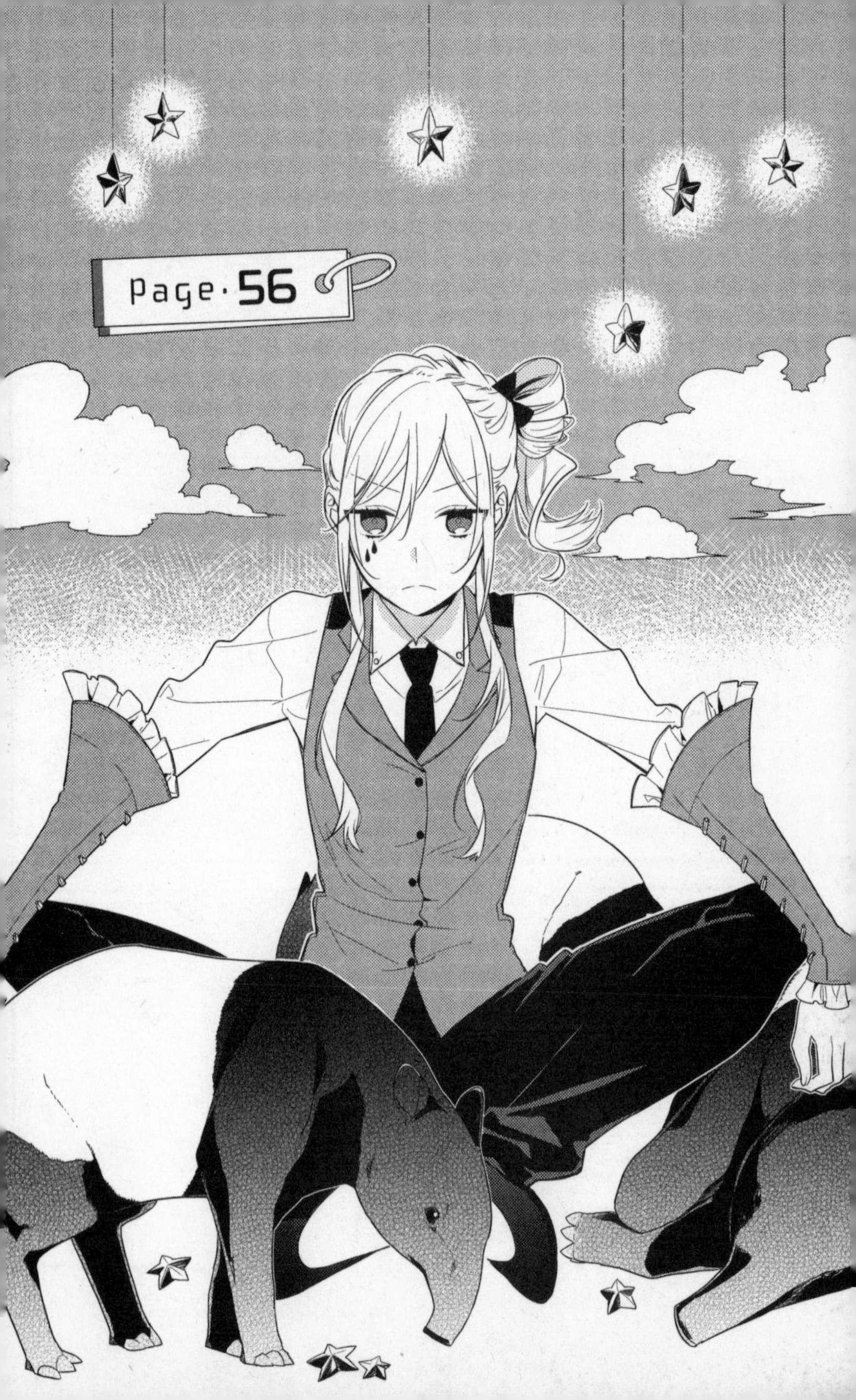
page.56

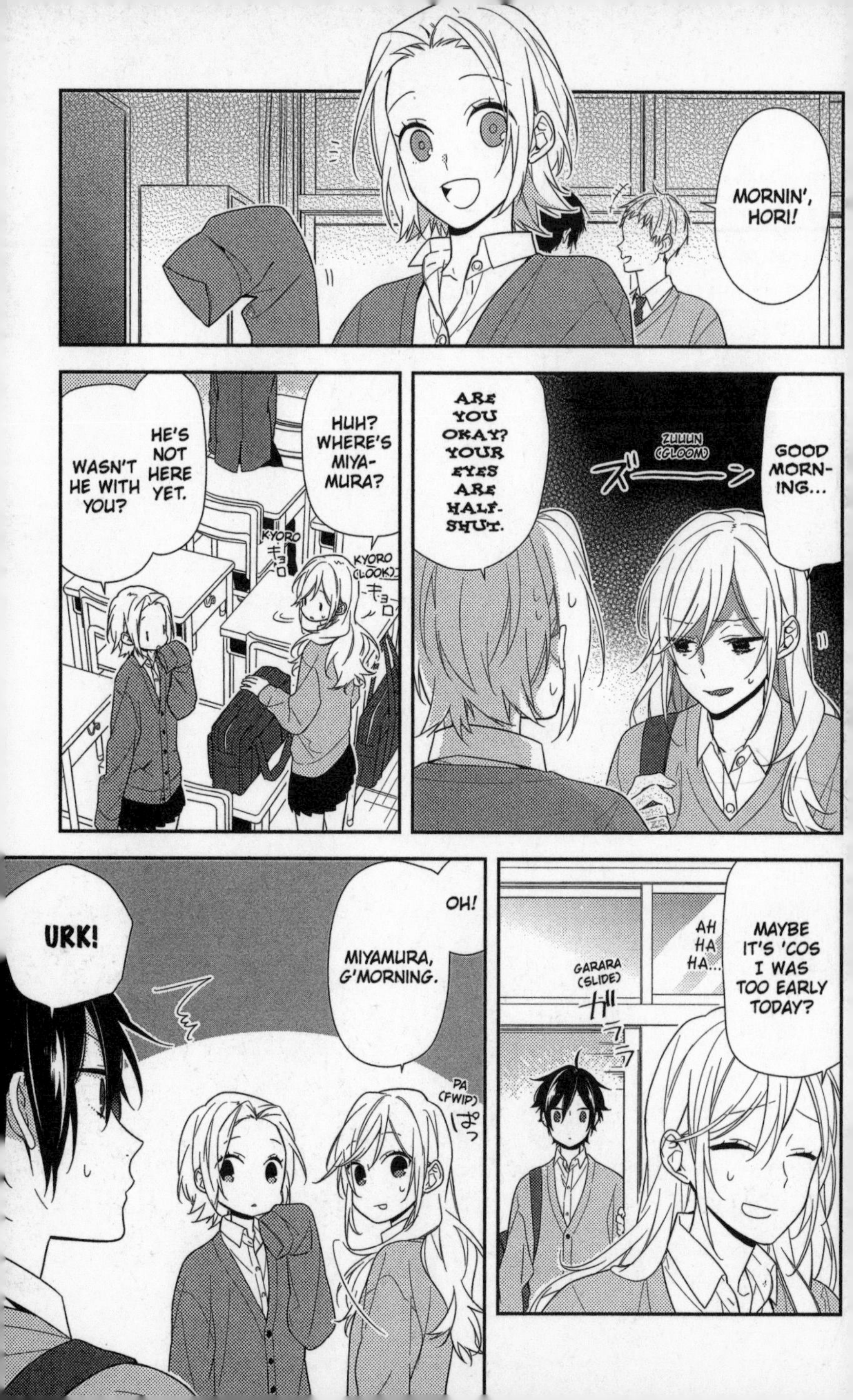
MORNIN', HORI!
GOOD MORNING...
ZUUUN (GLOOM)
ARE YOU OKAY? YOUR EYES ARE HALF-SHUT.
HUH? WHERE'S MIYAMURA?
KYORO (LOOK)
KYORO
HE'S NOT HERE YET.
WASN'T HE WITH YOU?
MAYBE IT'S 'COS I WAS TOO EARLY TODAY?
AH HA HA...
GARARA (SLIDE)
OH!
MIYAMURA, G'MORNING.
PA (FWIP)
URK!

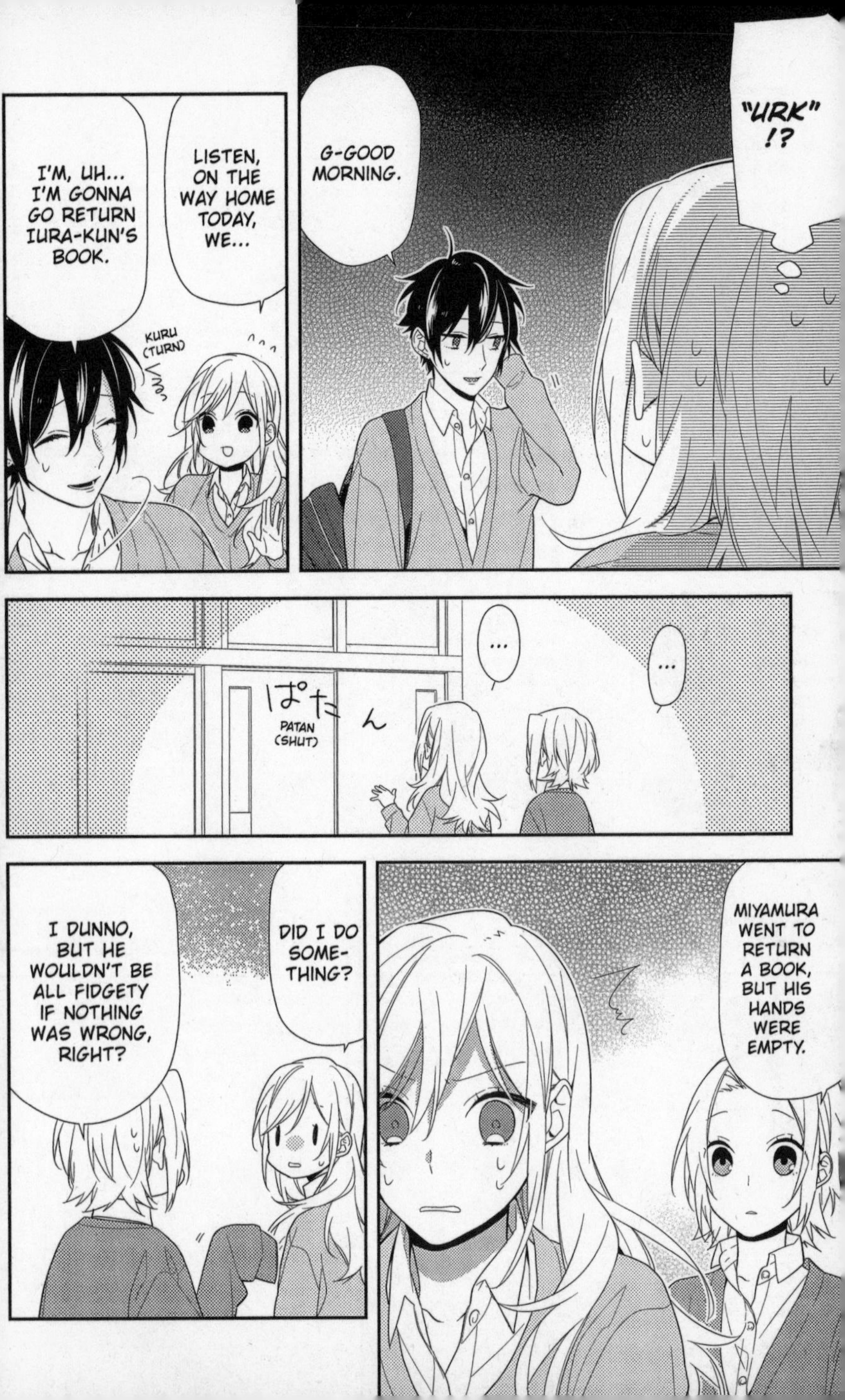
"URK" !?
G-GOOD MORNING.
LISTEN, ON THE WAY HOME TODAY, WE...
I'M, UH... I'M GONNA GO RETURN IURA-KUN'S BOOK.
KURU (TURN)
...
...
ぱたん
PATAN (SHUT)
MIYAMURA WENT TO RETURN A BOOK, BUT HIS HANDS WERE EMPTY.
DID I DO SOMETHING?
I DUNNO, BUT HE WOULDN'T BE ALL FIDGETY IF NOTHING WAS WRONG, RIGHT?

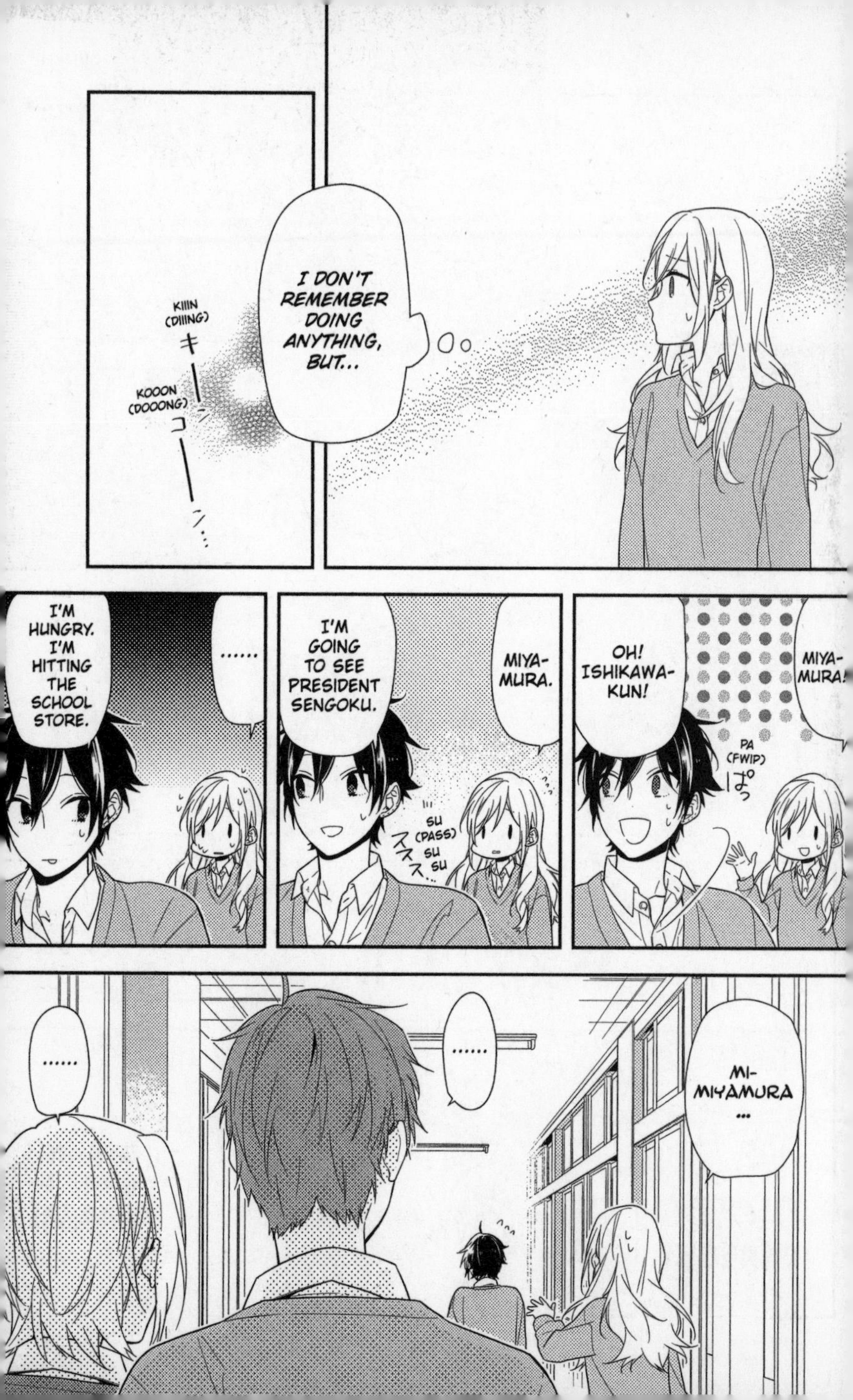
I DON'T REMEMBER DOING ANYTHING, BUT...
KIIIN (DIIING)
キーン
KOOON (DOOONG)
コーン...
MIYA-MURA!
OH! ISHIKAWA-KUN!
PA (FWIP)
ぱっ
MIYA-MURA.
I'M GOING TO SEE PRESIDENT SENGOKU.
SU (PASS) SU SU
ススス...
......
I'M HUNGRY. I'M HITTING THE SCHOOL STORE.
MI-MIYAMURA...
......
......

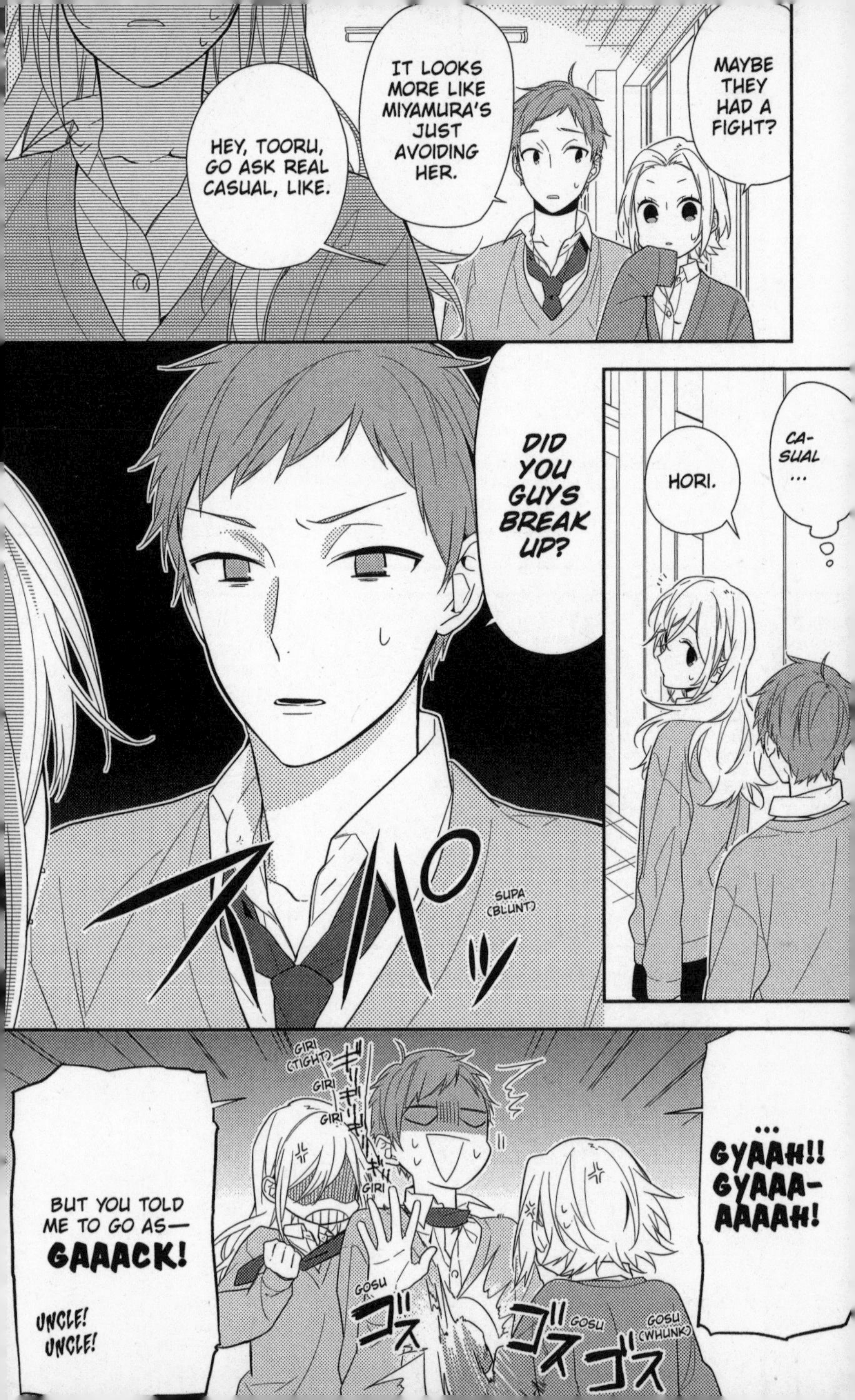
MAYBE THEY HAD A FIGHT?
IT LOOKS MORE LIKE MIYAMURA'S JUST AVOIDING HER.
HEY, TOORU, GO ASK REAL CASUAL, LIKE.
CA-SUAL ...
HORI.
DID YOU GUYS BREAK UP?
SUPA (BLUNT)
... GYAAH!! GYAAA-AAAAH!
GIRI (TIGHT)
GIRI
GIRI
GIRI
GOSU (WHUNK)
GOSU
GOSU
BUT YOU TOLD ME TO GO AS— GAAACK!
UNCLE! UNCLE!

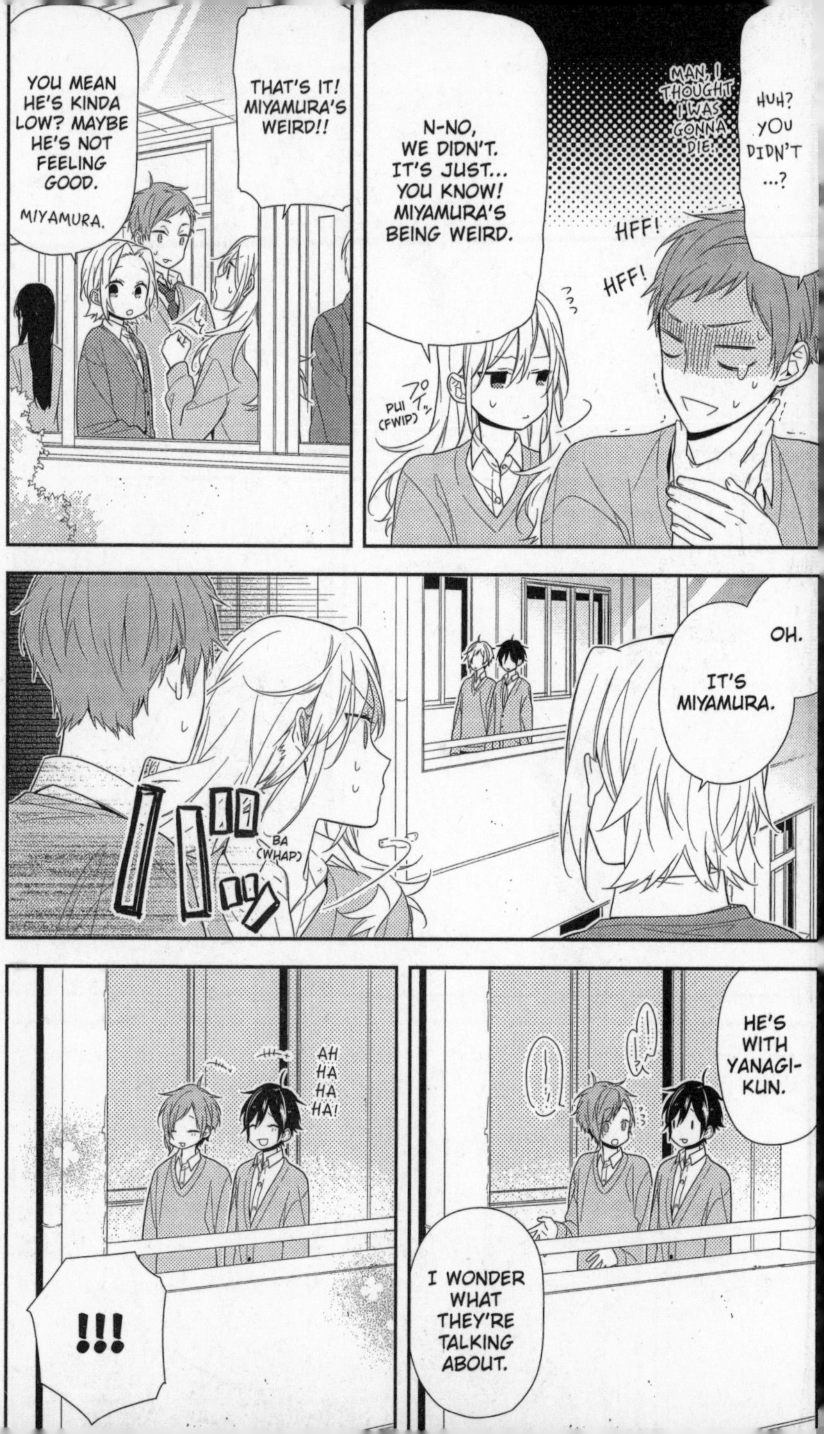
HUH? YOU DIDN'T ...?
MAN, I THOUGHT I WAS GONNA DIE.
HFF!
HFF!
N-NO, WE DIDN'T. IT'S JUST... YOU KNOW! MIYAMURA'S BEING WEIRD.
PUI (FWIP)
THAT'S IT! MIYAMURA'S WEIRD!!
YOU MEAN HE'S KINDA LOW? MAYBE HE'S NOT FEELING GOOD.
MIYAMURA.
OH.
IT'S MIYAMURA.
BA (WHAP)
HE'S WITH YANAGI-KUN.
I WONDER WHAT THEY'RE TALKING ABOUT.
AH HA HA HA!
!!!

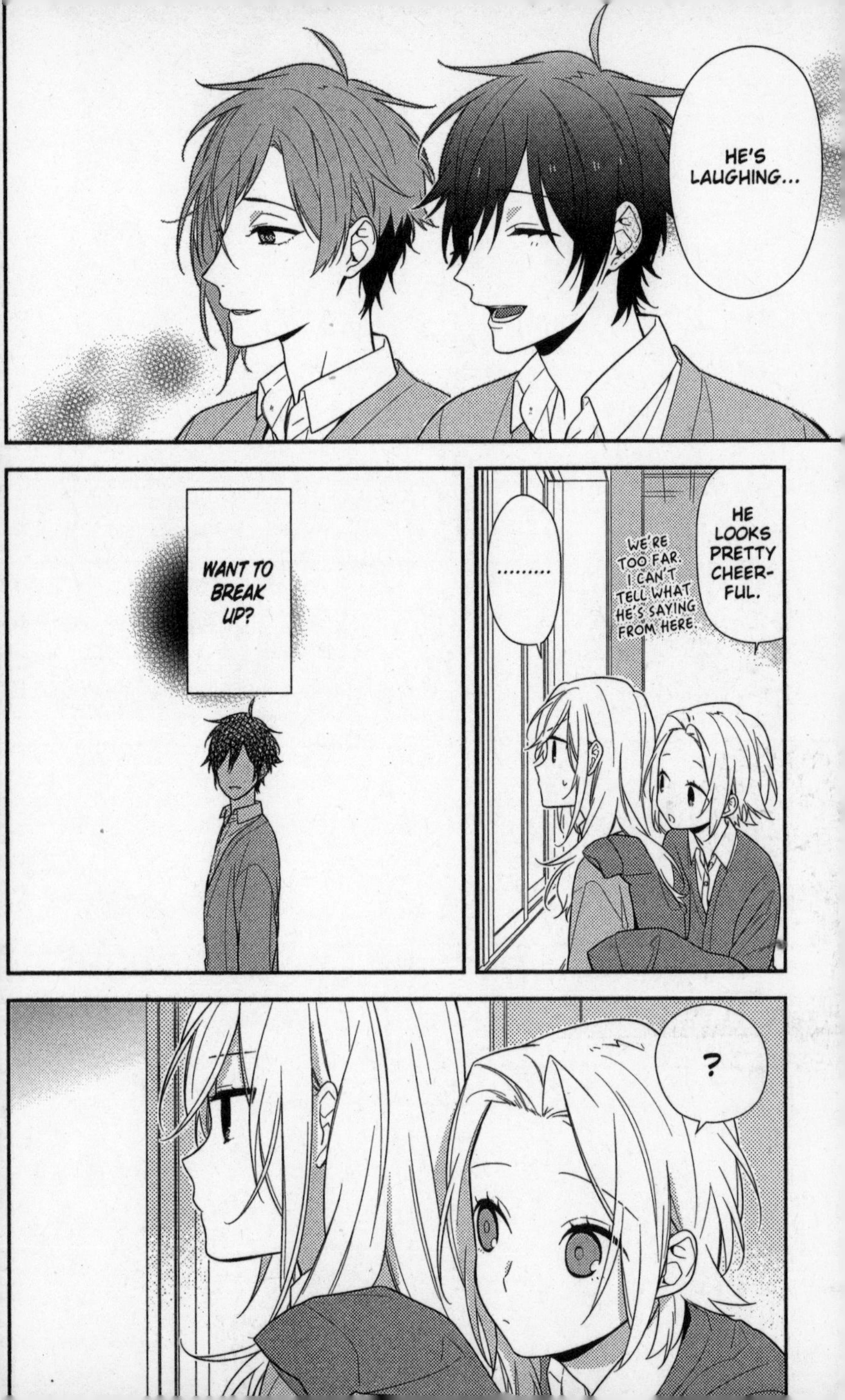
HE'S LAUGHING...
HE LOOKS PRETTY CHEER-FUL.
WE'RE TOO FAR. I CAN'T TELL WHAT HE'S SAYING FROM HERE.
.........
WANT TO BREAK UP?
?

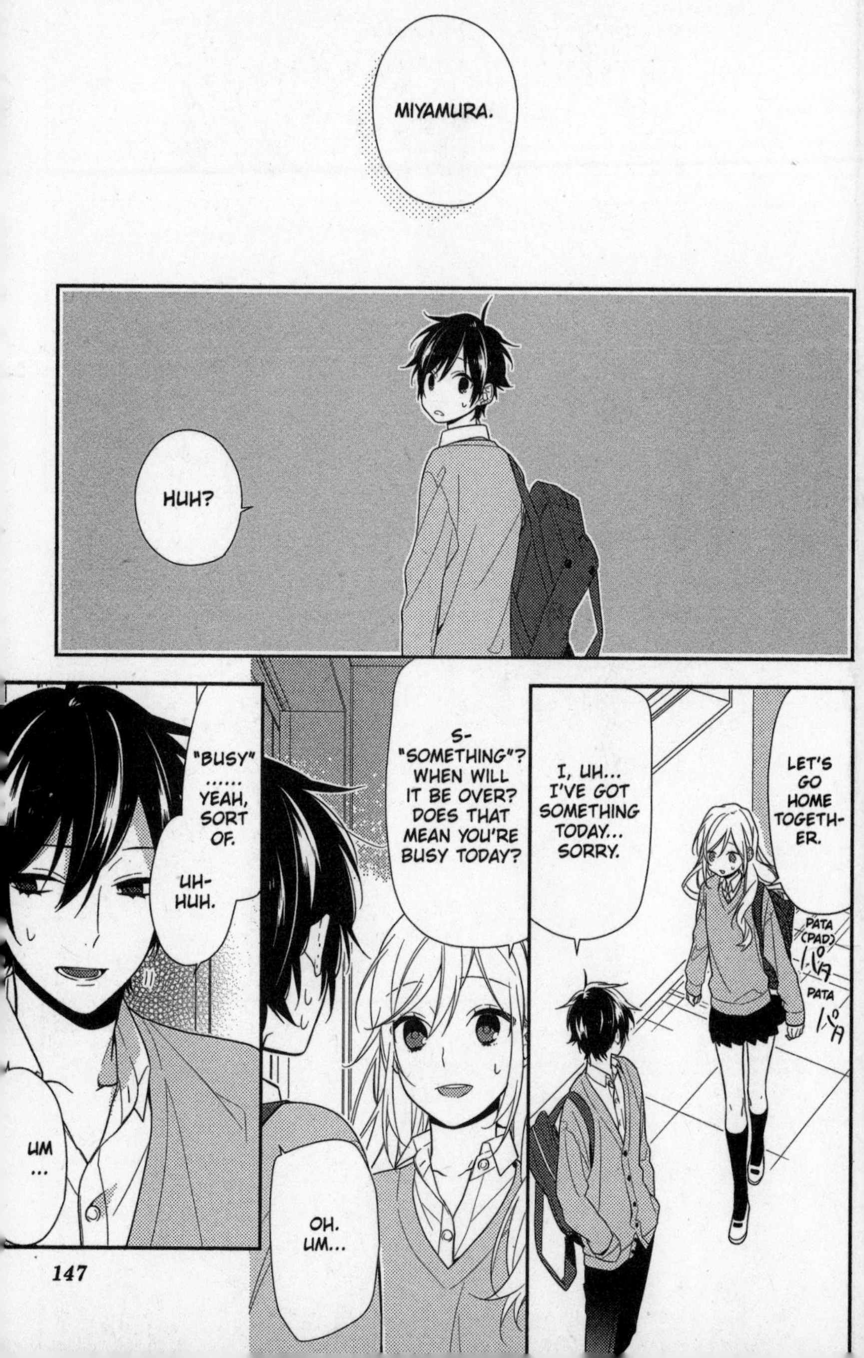
MIYAMURA.
HUH?
LET'S GO HOME TOGETH-ER.
PATA (PAD) パタ
PATA パタ
I, UH... I'VE GOT SOMETHING TODAY... SORRY.
S- "SOMETHING"? WHEN WILL IT BE OVER? DOES THAT MEAN YOU'RE BUSY TODAY?
OH. UM...
"BUSY" ...... YEAH, SORT OF.
UH-HUH.
UM ...

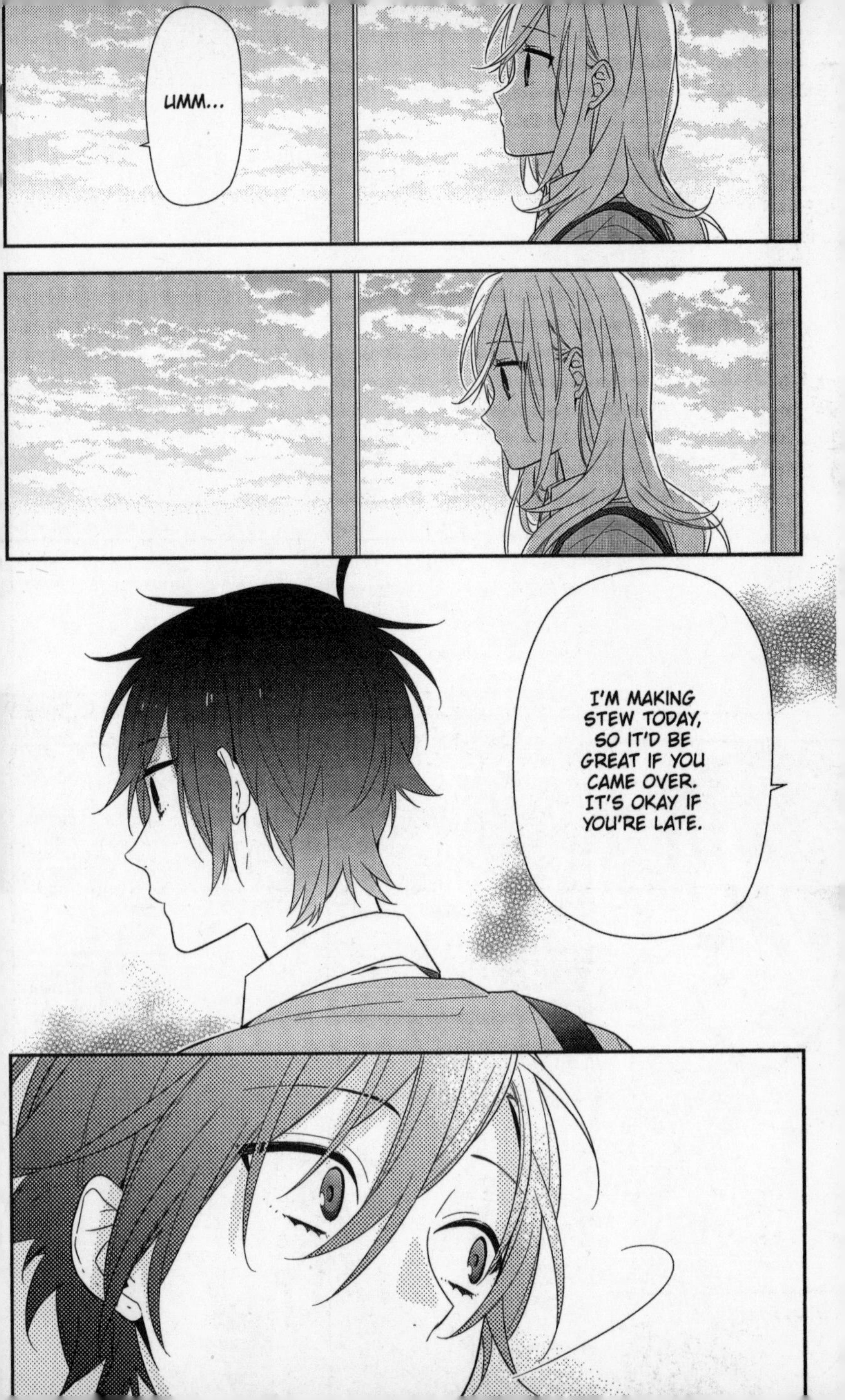
UMM...
I'M MAKING STEW TODAY, SO IT'D BE GREAT IF YOU CAME OVER. IT'S OKAY IF YOU'RE LATE.

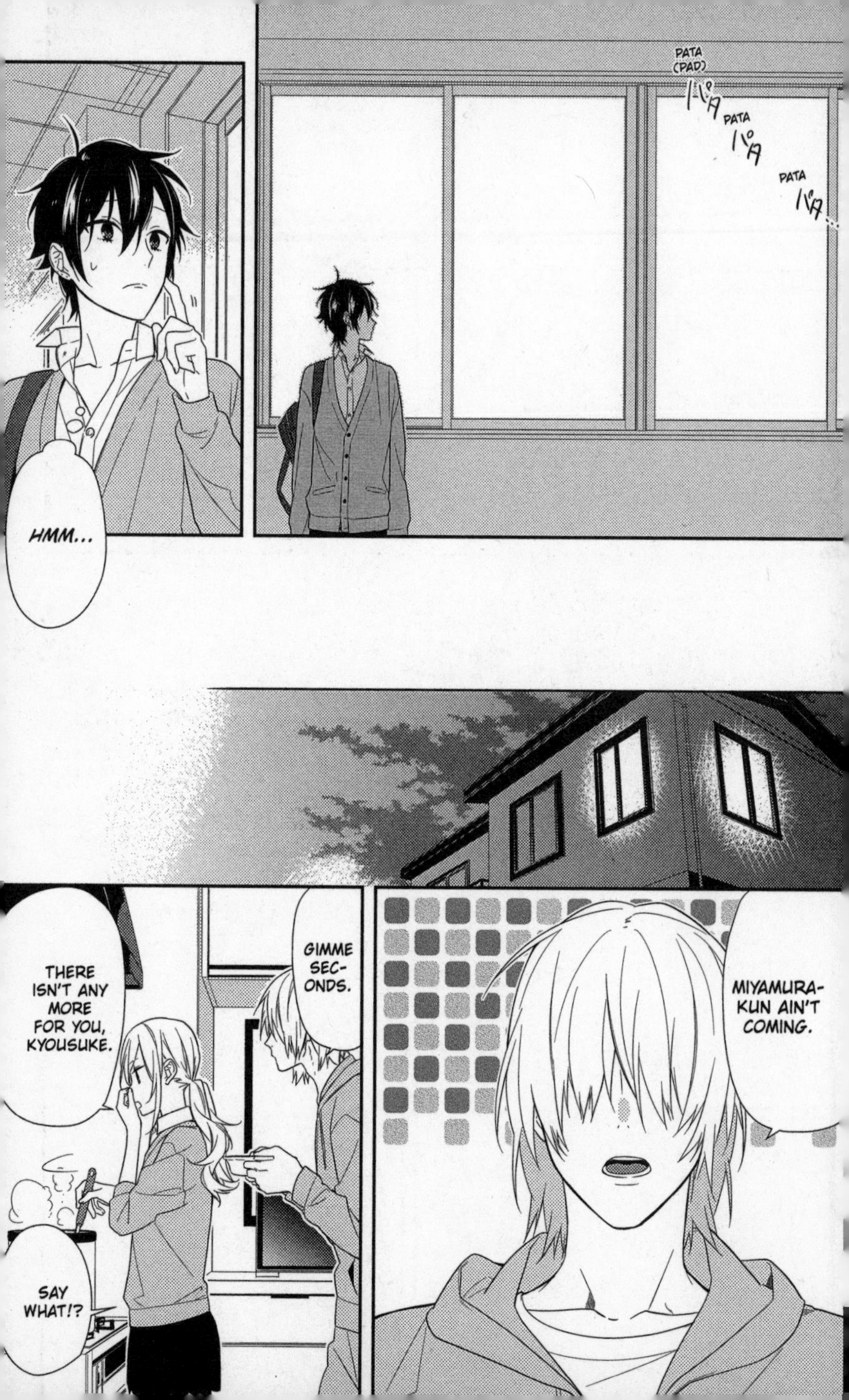

PATA (PAD)
パタ
PATA
パタ
PATA
パタ…
HMM...
MIYAMURA-KUN AIN'T COMING.
GIMME SECONDS.
THERE ISN'T ANY MORE FOR YOU, KYOUSUKE.
SAY WHAT!?

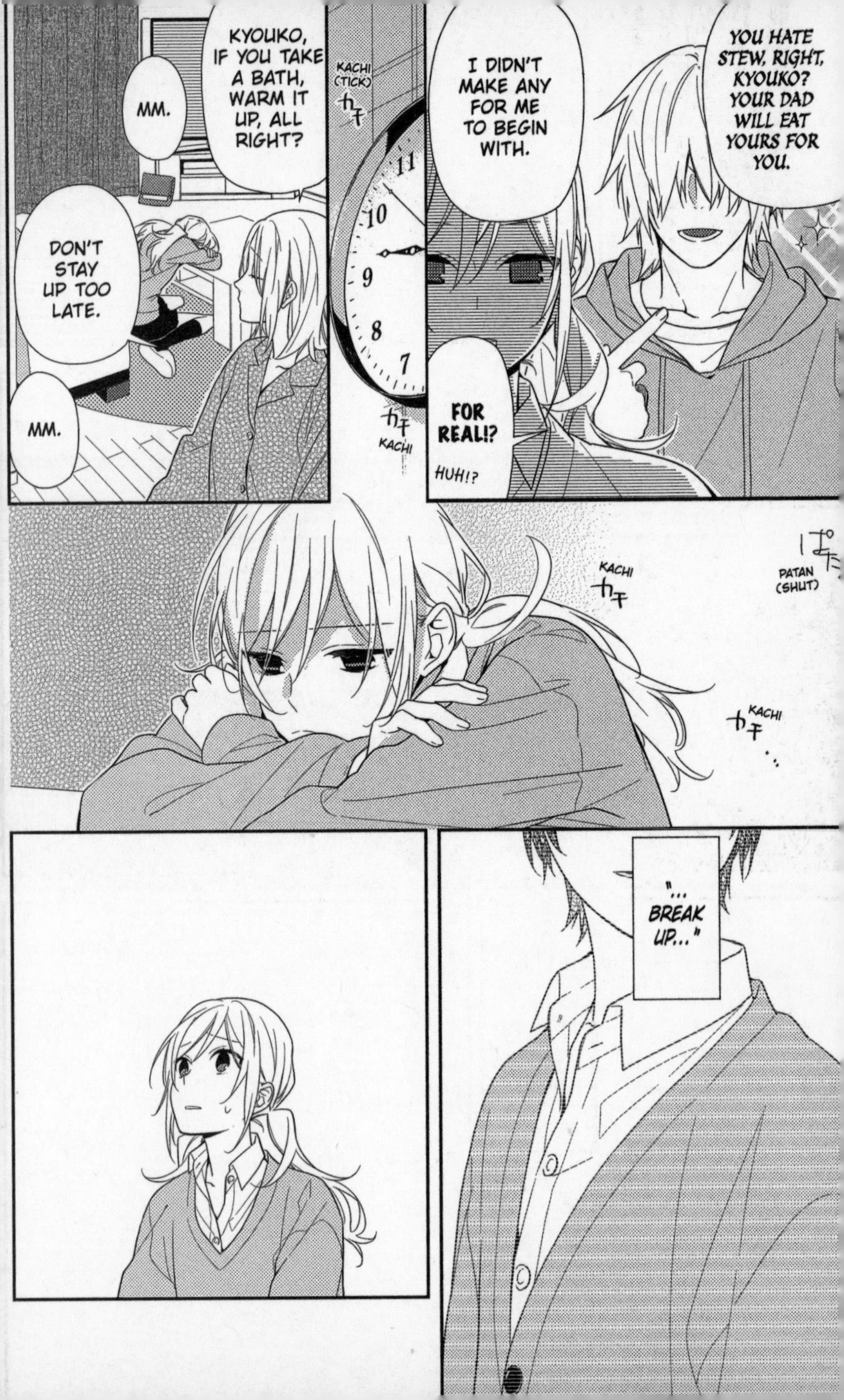

YOU HATE STEW, RIGHT, KYOUKO? YOUR DAD WILL EAT YOURS FOR YOU.
I DIDN'T MAKE ANY FOR ME TO BEGIN WITH.
FOR REAL!?
HUH!?
カチ
KACHI (TICK)
カチ
KACHI
KYOUKO, IF YOU TAKE A BATH, WARM IT UP, ALL RIGHT?
MM.
DON'T STAY UP TOO LATE.
MM.
ぱた
PATAN (SHUT)
カチ
KACHI
カチ
KACHI
"... BREAK UP..."

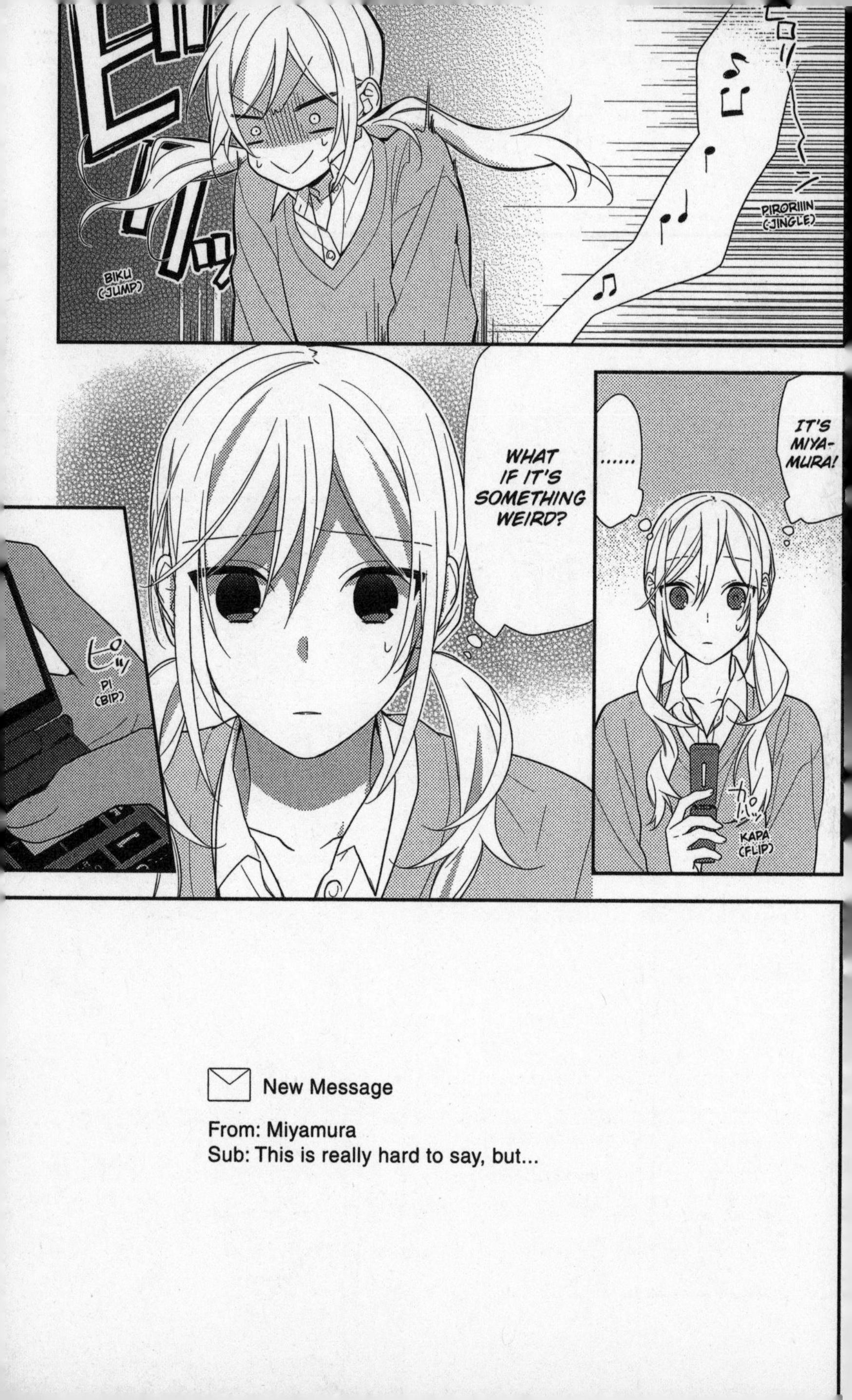
PIRORIIIN (JINGLE)
BIKU (JUMP)
IT'S MIYAMURA!
......
KAPA (FLIP)
WHAT IF IT'S SOMETHING WEIRD?
PI (BIP)
New Message
From: Miyamura
Sub: This is really hard to say, but...

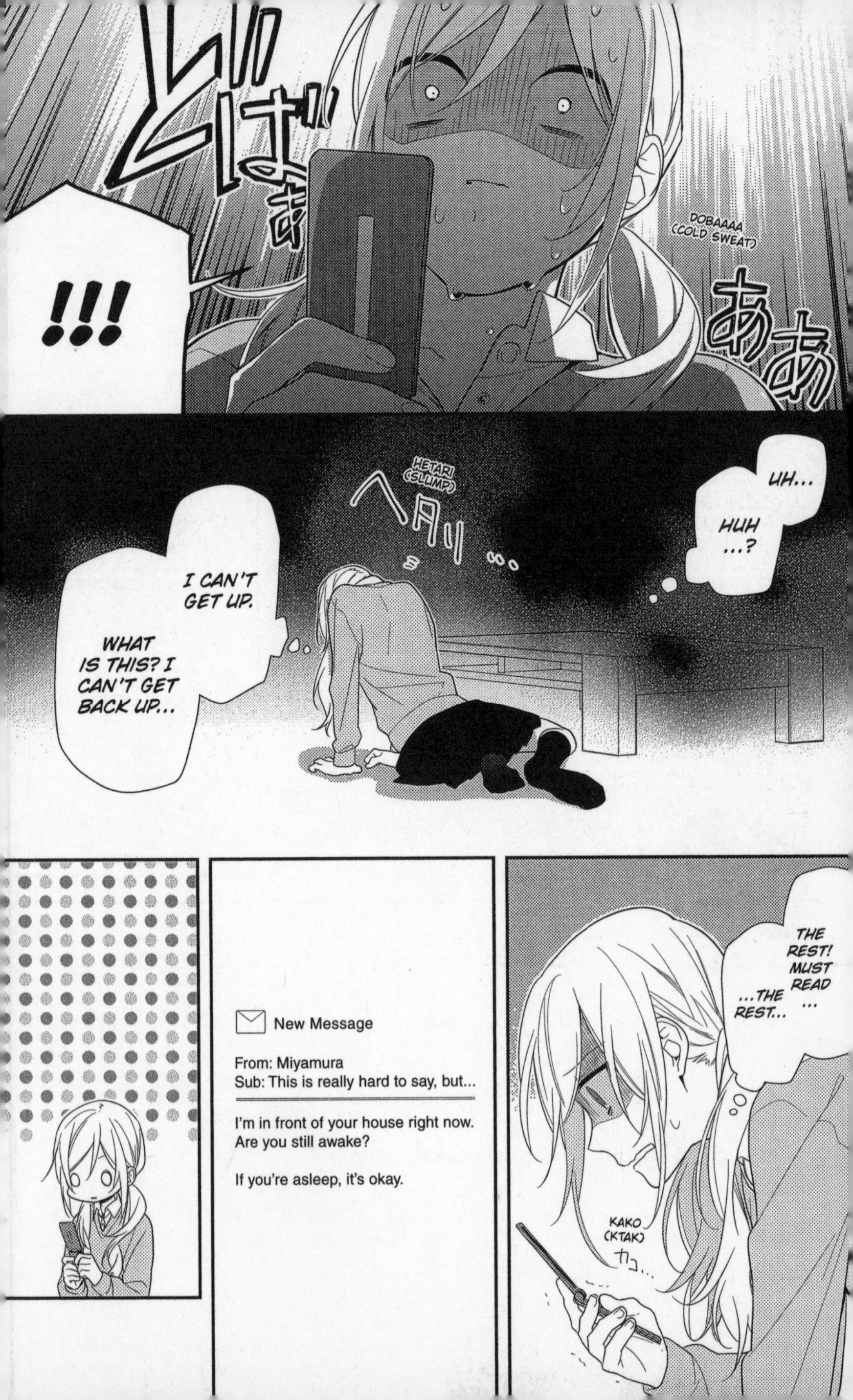
DOBAAAA (COLD SWEAT)
ああ
!!!
UH... HUH...?
HETARI (SLUMP)
ヘタリ...
I CAN'T GET UP.
WHAT IS THIS? I CAN'T GET BACK UP...
THE REST! MUST READ...
...THE REST...
KAKO (KTAK)
カコ...
New Message
From: Miyamura
Sub: This is really hard to say, but...
I'm in front of your house right now. Are you still awake?
If you're asleep, it's okay.

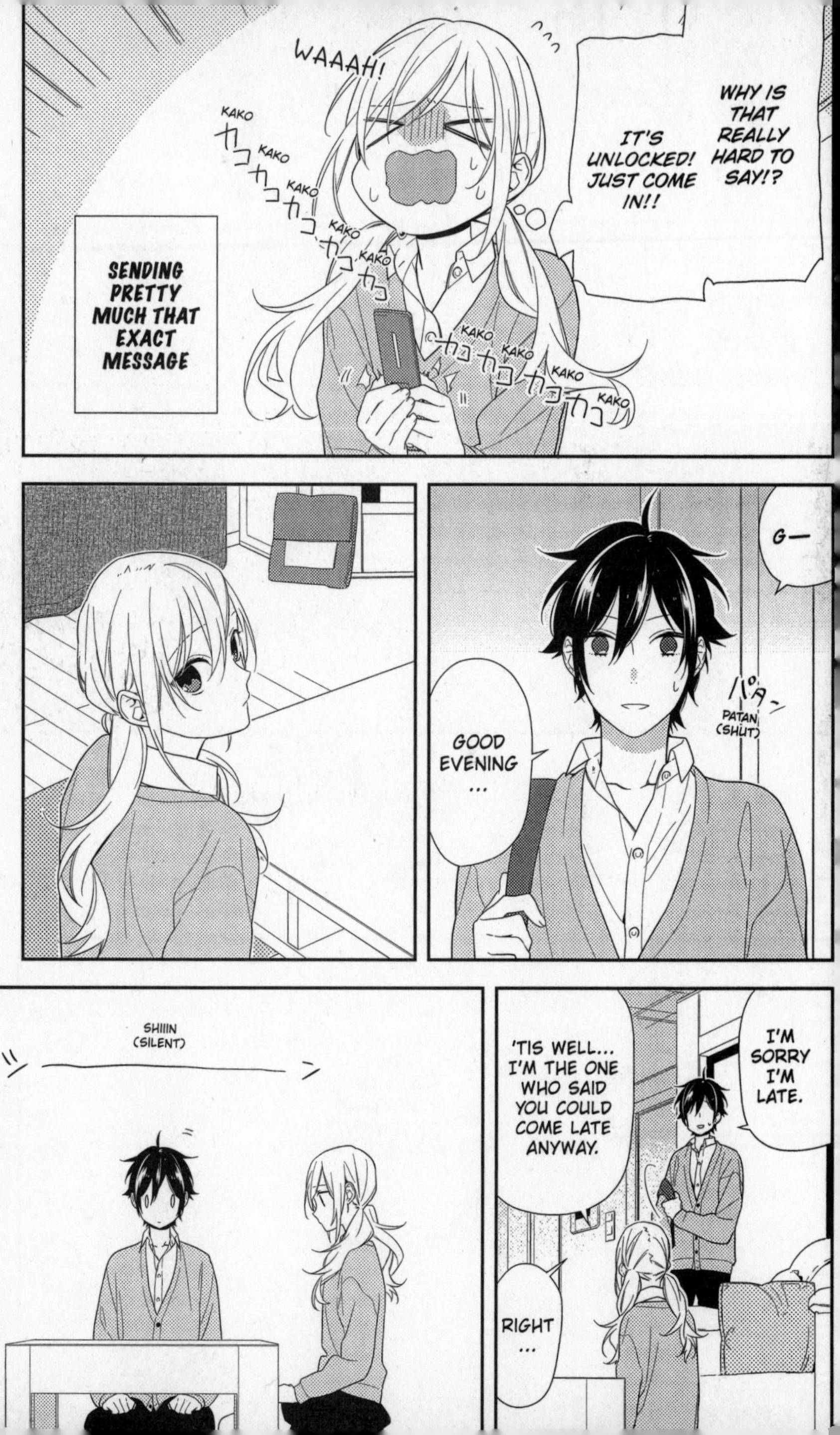
WHY IS THAT REALLY HARD TO SAY!?
IT'S UNLOCKED! JUST COME IN!!
WAAAH!
KAKO カコ KAKO カコ KAKO カコ KAKO カコ KAKO カコ
KAKO カコ KAKO カコ KAKO カコ KAKO カコ
SENDING PRETTY MUCH THAT EXACT MESSAGE
G—
パタン
PATAN (SHUT)
GOOD EVENING ...
I'M SORRY I'M LATE.
'TIS WELL... I'M THE ONE WHO SAID YOU COULD COME LATE ANYWAY.
RIGHT ...
SHIIIN (SILENT)

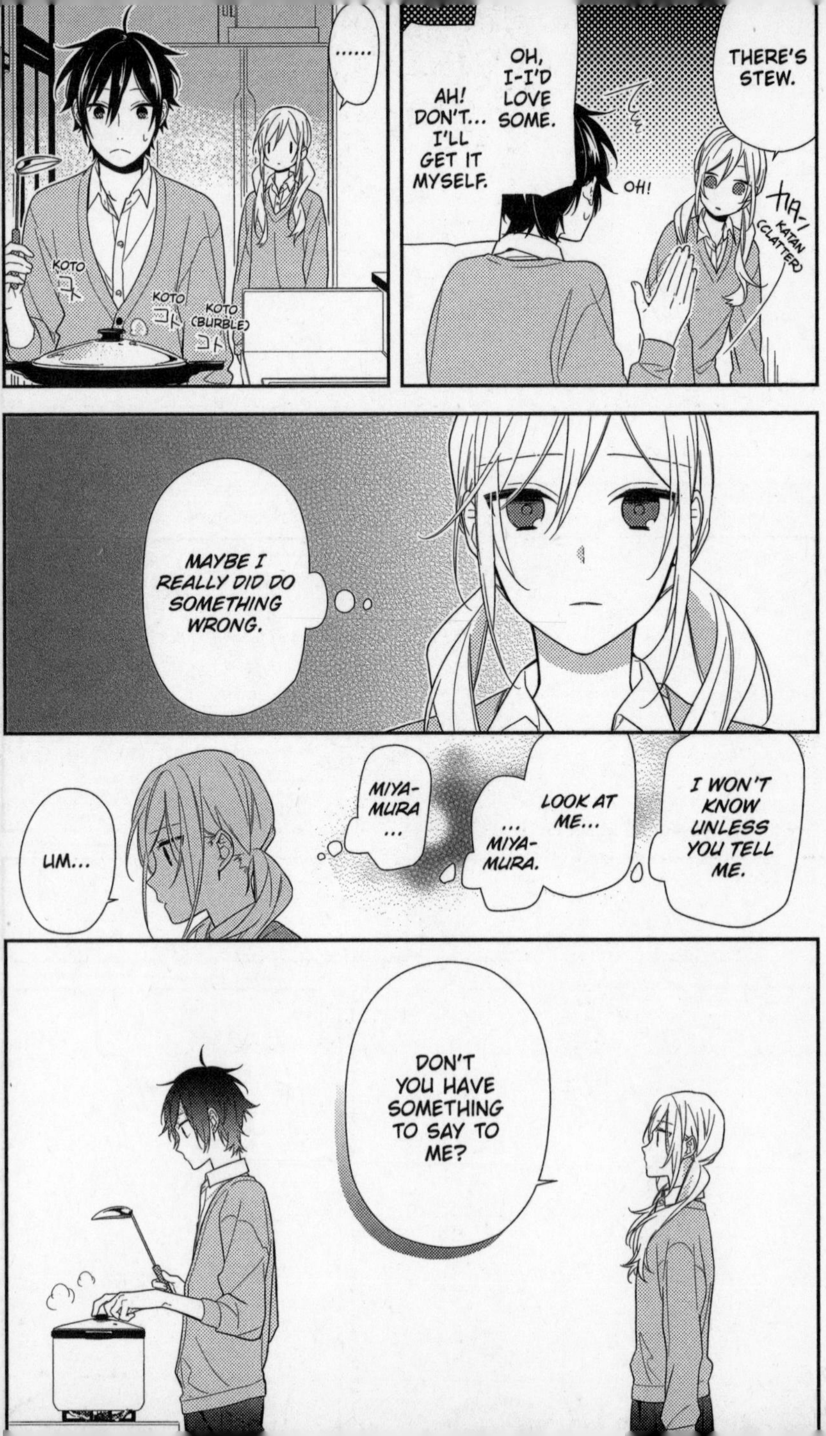
THERE'S STEW.
OH!
KATAN (CLATTER)
OH, I-I'D LOVE SOME.
AH! DON'T... I'LL GET IT MYSELF.
......
KOTO
KOTO
KOTO (BURBLE)
MAYBE I REALLY DID DO SOMETHING WRONG.
I WON'T KNOW UNLESS YOU TELL ME.
LOOK AT ME...
...MIYAMURA.
MIYAMURA...
UM...
DON'T YOU HAVE SOMETHING TO SAY TO ME?

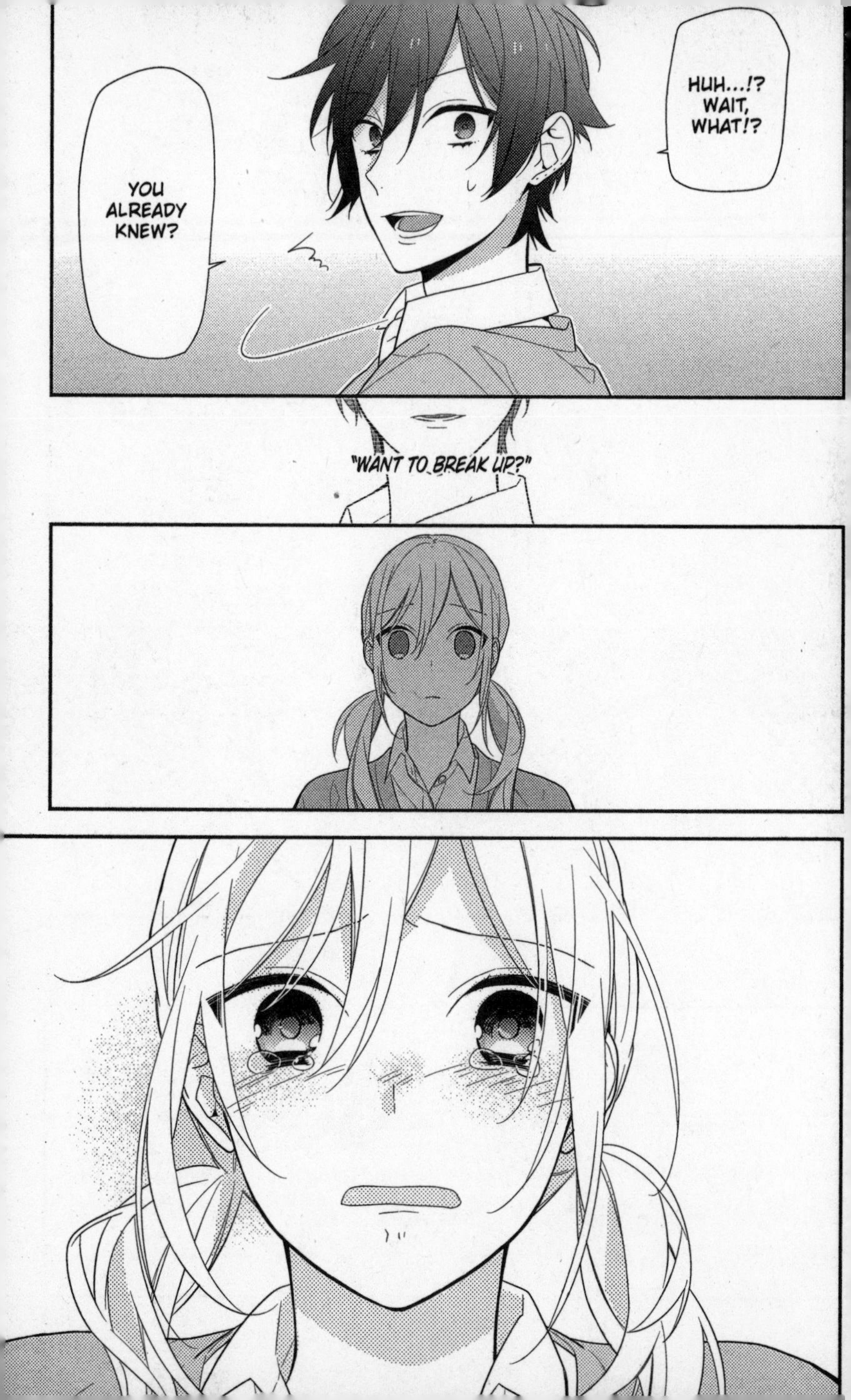
HUH...!? WAIT, WHAT!?
YOU ALREADY KNEW?
"WANT TO BREAK UP?"

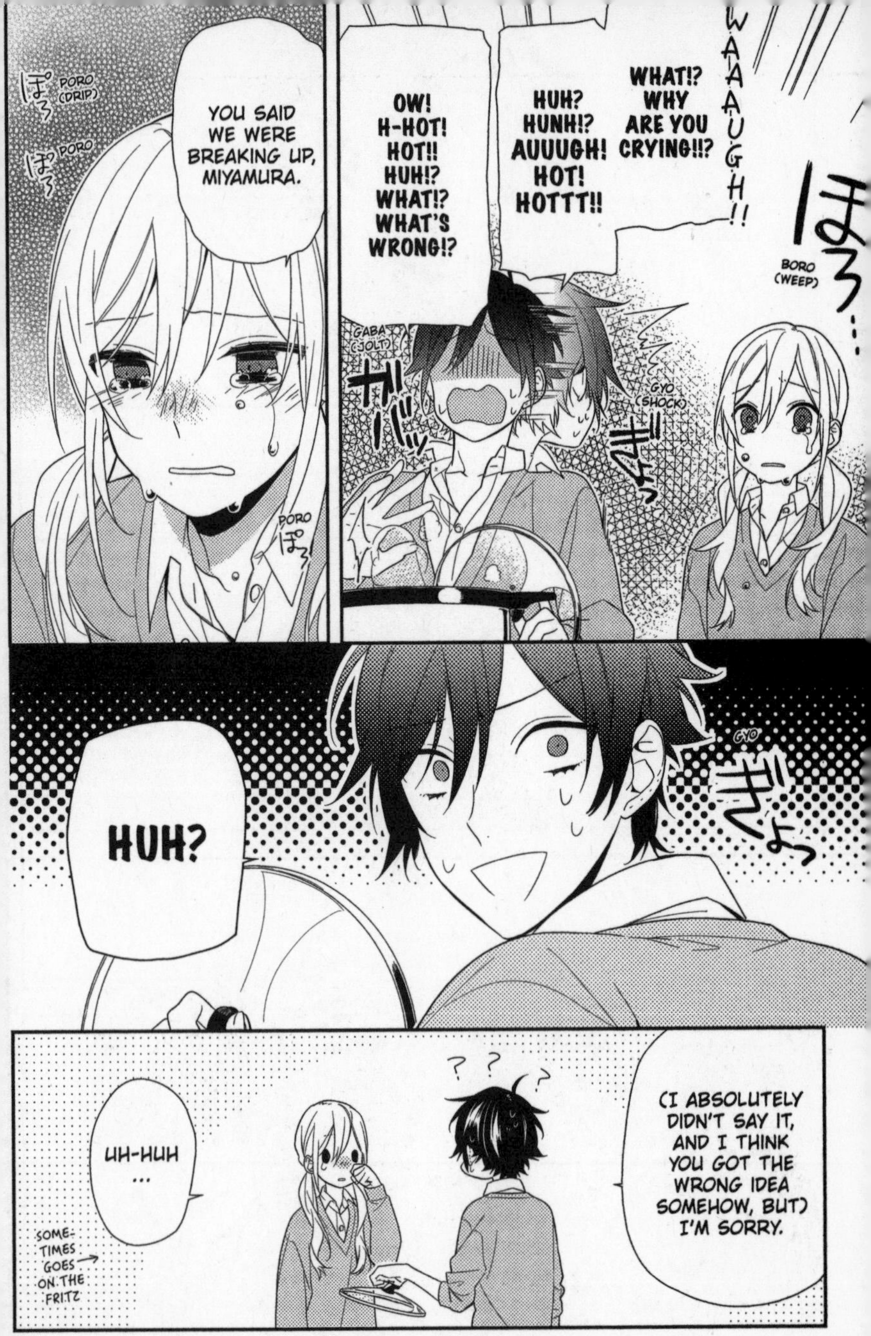
WAAAUGH!!
WHAT!? WHY ARE YOU CRYING!!?
HUH? HUNH!? AUUUGH! HOT! HOTTT!!
OW! H-HOT! HOT!! HUH!? WHAT!? WHAT'S WRONG!?
BORO (WEEP)
GYO (SHOCK)
GABA (JOLT)
YOU SAID WE WERE BREAKING UP, MIYAMURA.
PORO (DRIP)
PORO
PORO
GYO
HUH?
(I ABSOLUTELY DIDN'T SAY IT, AND I THINK YOU GOT THE WRONG IDEA SOMEHOW, BUT) I'M SORRY.
UH-HUH ...
SOME-TIMES GOES ON THE FRITZ

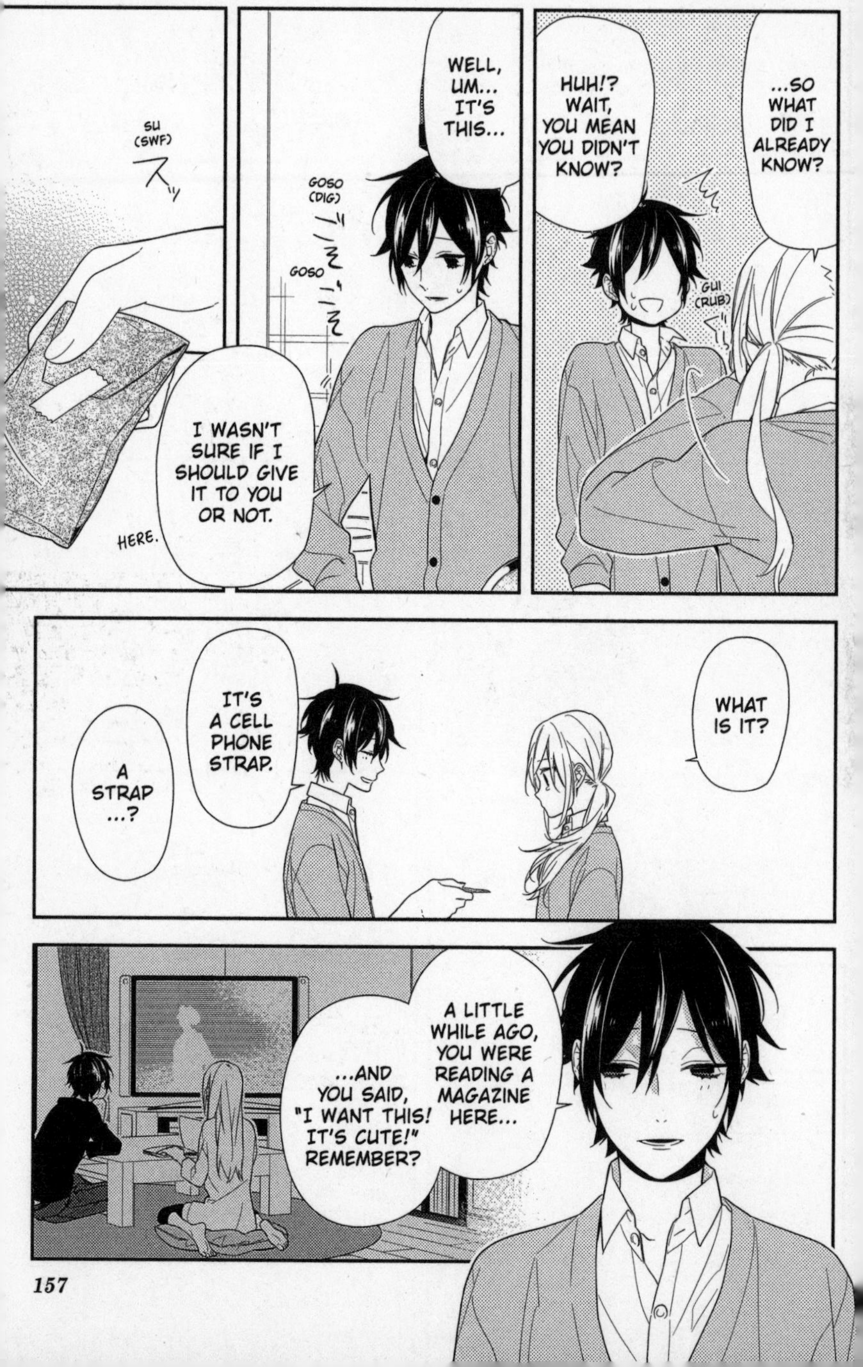
...SO WHAT DID I ALREADY KNOW?
HUH!? WAIT, YOU MEAN YOU DIDN'T KNOW?
GUI (RUB)
WELL, UM... IT'S THIS...
GOSO (DIG)
GOSO
I WASN'T SURE IF I SHOULD GIVE IT TO YOU OR NOT.
SU (SWF)
HERE.
WHAT IS IT?
IT'S A CELL PHONE STRAP.
A STRAP ...?
A LITTLE WHILE AGO, YOU WERE READING A MAGAZINE HERE...
...AND YOU SAID, "I WANT THIS! IT'S CUTE!" REMEMBER?

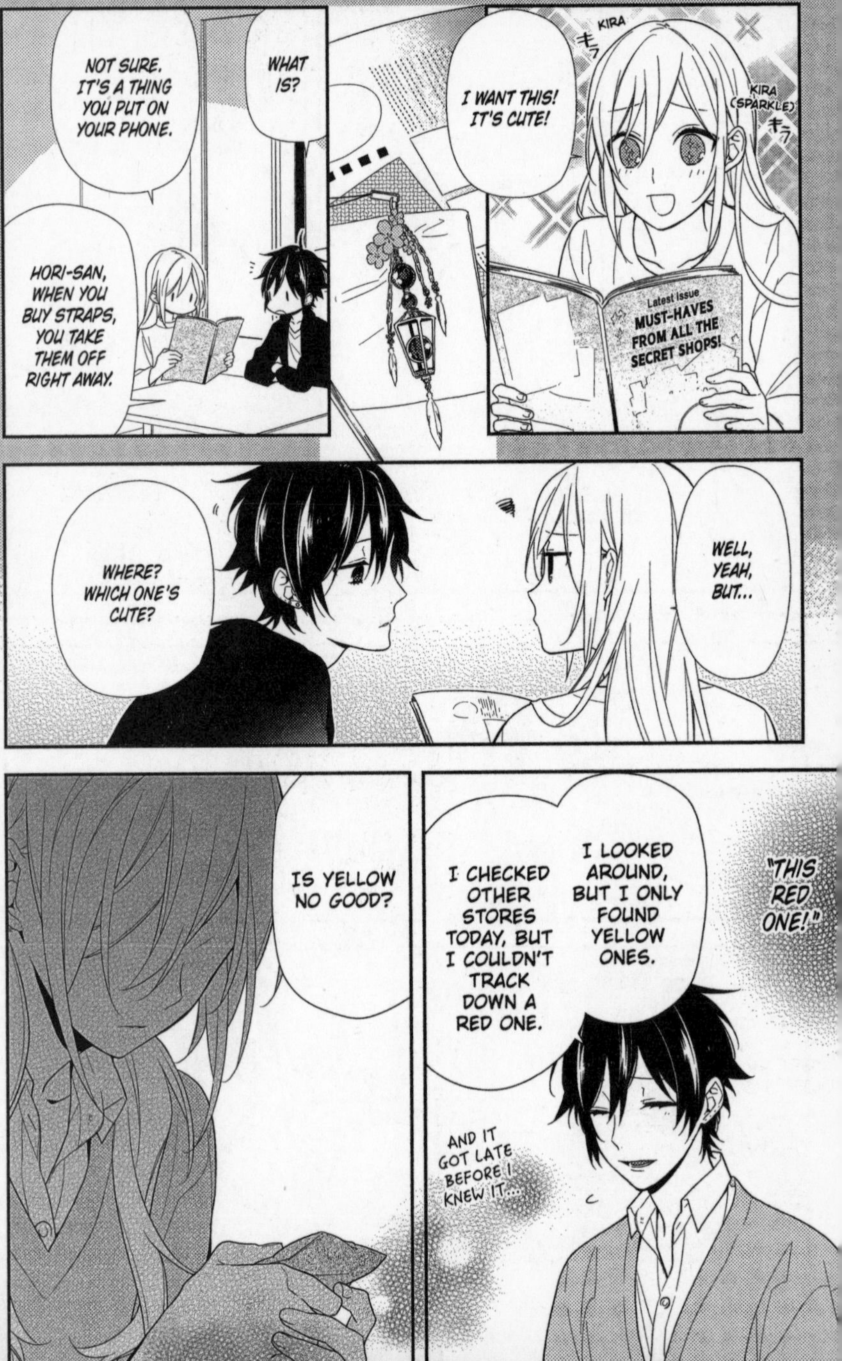
KIRA
キラ
I WANT THIS! IT'S CUTE!
KIRA (SPARKLE)
キラ
Latest Issue
MUST-HAVES FROM ALL THE SECRET SHOPS!
WHAT IS?
NOT SURE. IT'S A THING YOU PUT ON YOUR PHONE.
HORI-SAN, WHEN YOU BUY STRAPS, YOU TAKE THEM OFF RIGHT AWAY.
WELL, YEAH, BUT...
WHERE? WHICH ONE'S CUTE?
"THIS RED ONE!"
I LOOKED AROUND, BUT I ONLY FOUND YELLOW ONES.
I CHECKED OTHER STORES TODAY, BUT I COULDN'T TRACK DOWN A RED ONE.
AND IT GOT LATE BEFORE I KNEW IT...
IS YELLOW NO GOOD?

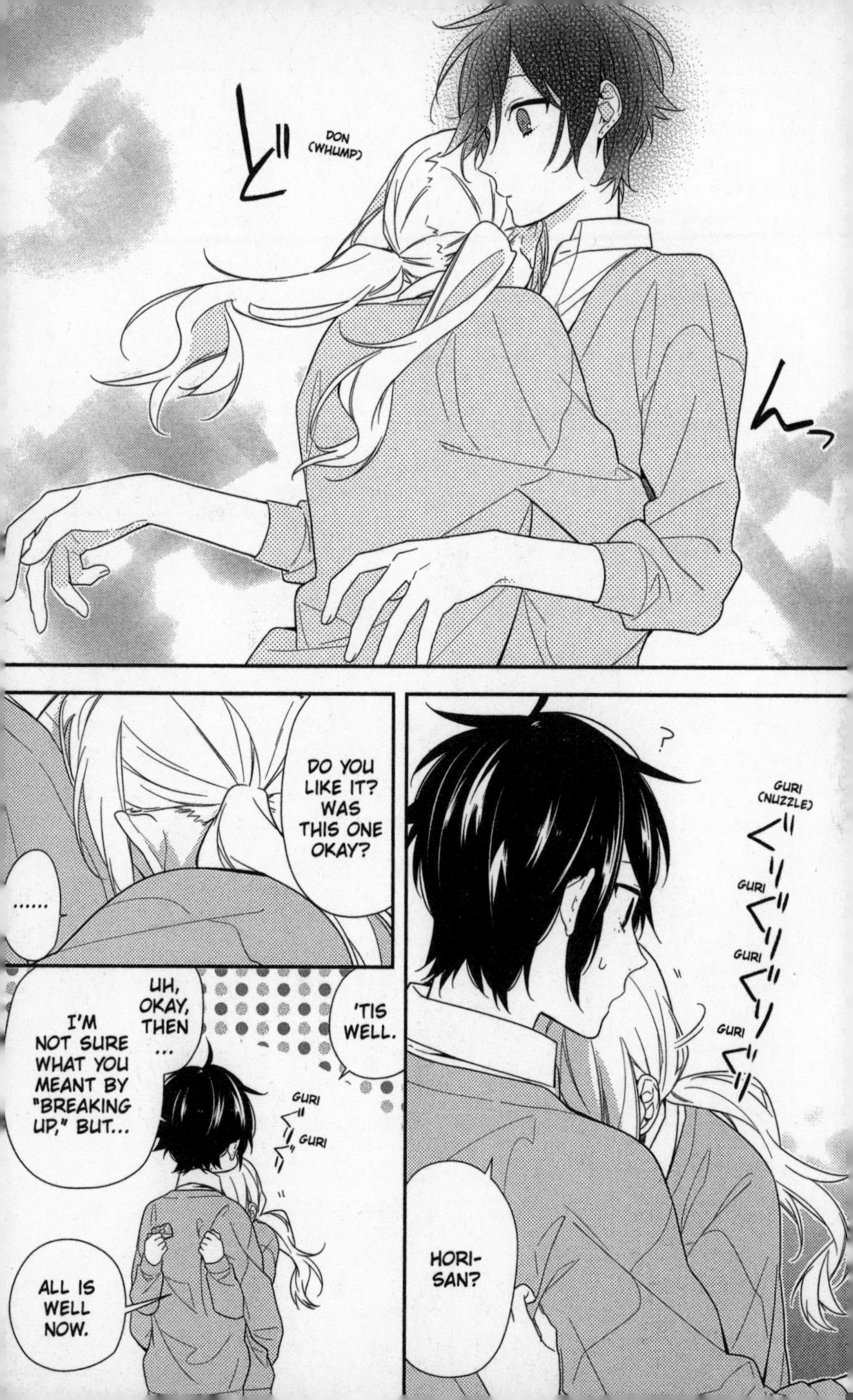
ど
DON (WHUMP)
んっ
?
GURI (NUZZLE)
ぐり
GURI
ぐり
GURI
ぐり
GURI
ぐり
HORI-SAN?
DO YOU LIKE IT? WAS THIS ONE OKAY?
......
'TIS WELL.
UH, OKAY, THEN...
I'M NOT SURE WHAT YOU MEANT BY "BREAKING UP," BUT...
GURI
GURI
ALL IS WELL NOW.

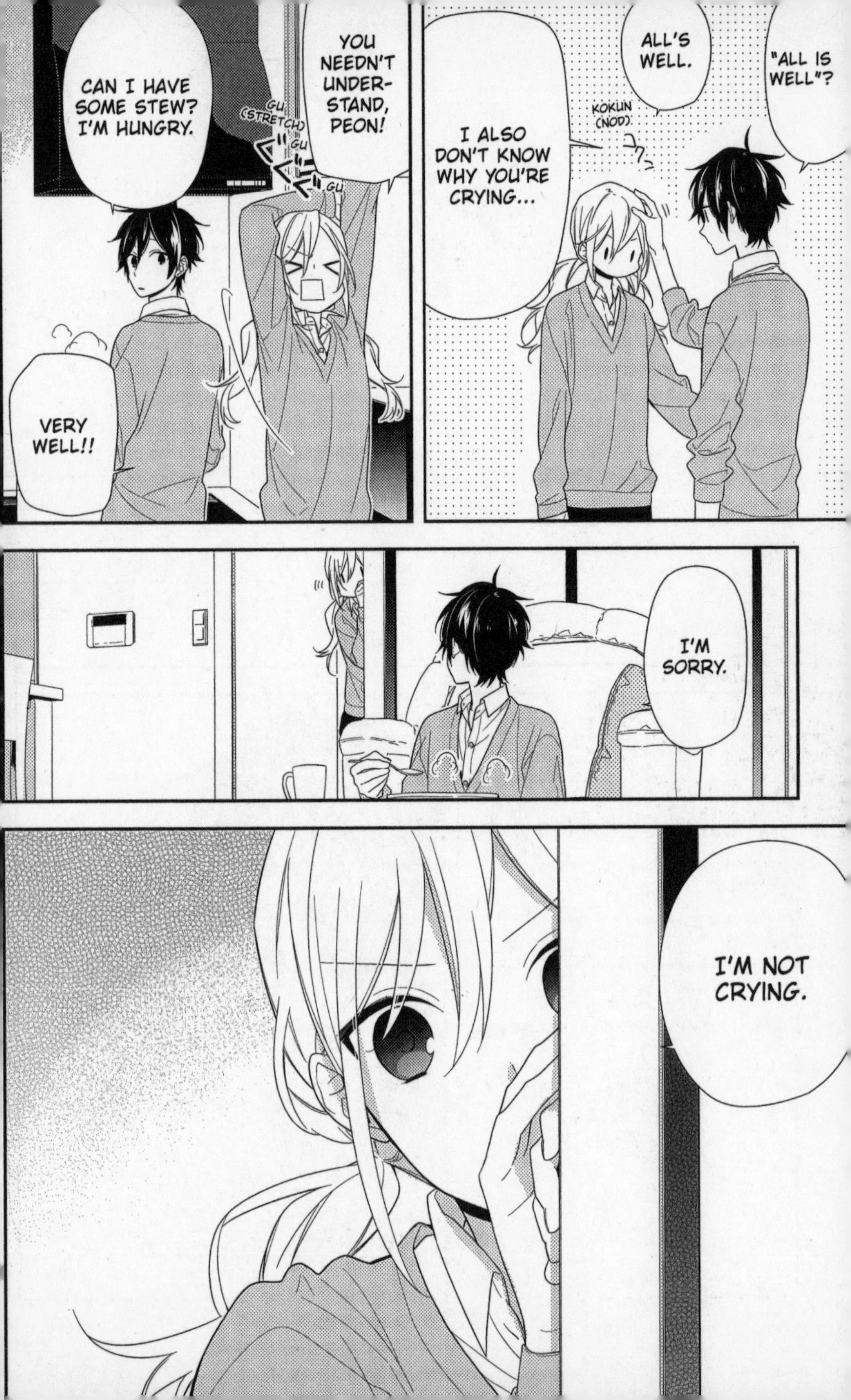
"ALL IS WELL"?
ALL'S WELL.
KOKUN (NOD)
I ALSO DON'T KNOW WHY YOU'RE CRYING...
YOU NEEDN'T UNDERSTAND, PEON!
GU (STRETCH) GU GU
CAN I HAVE SOME STEW? I'M HUNGRY.
VERY WELL!!
I'M SORRY.
I'M NOT CRYING.

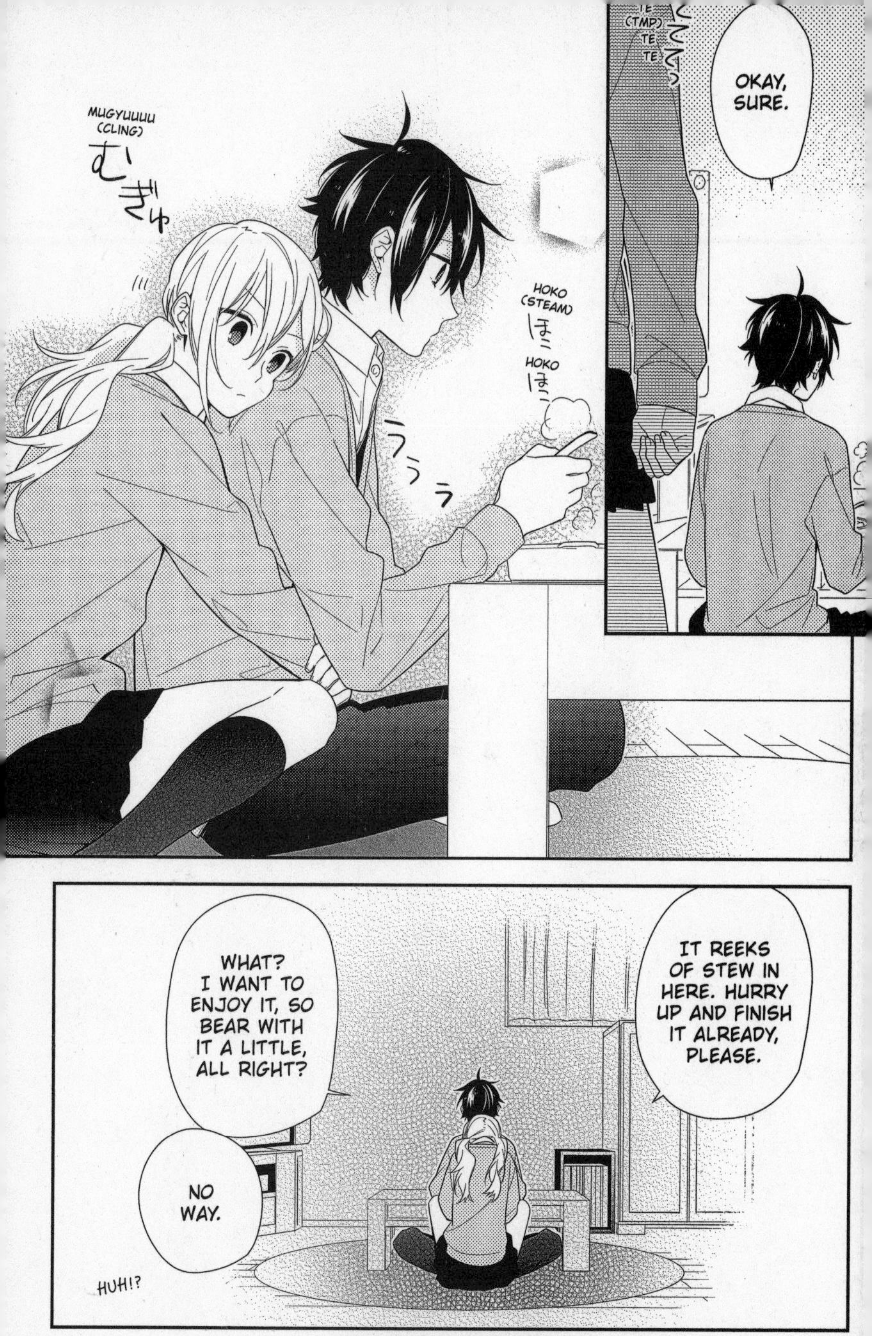
TE (TMP) TE TE
OKAY, SURE.
MUGYUUUU (CLING)
むぎゅ
HOKO (STEAM)
ほこ
HOKO
ほこ
ラララ
IT REEKS OF STEW IN HERE. HURRY UP AND FINISH IT ALREADY, PLEASE.
WHAT? I WANT TO ENJOY IT, SO BEAR WITH IT A LITTLE, ALL RIGHT?
NO WAY.
HUH!?

**HORIMIYA 8 END**

*To Be Continued...*

# BONUS MANGA: MYAMURA ⑦

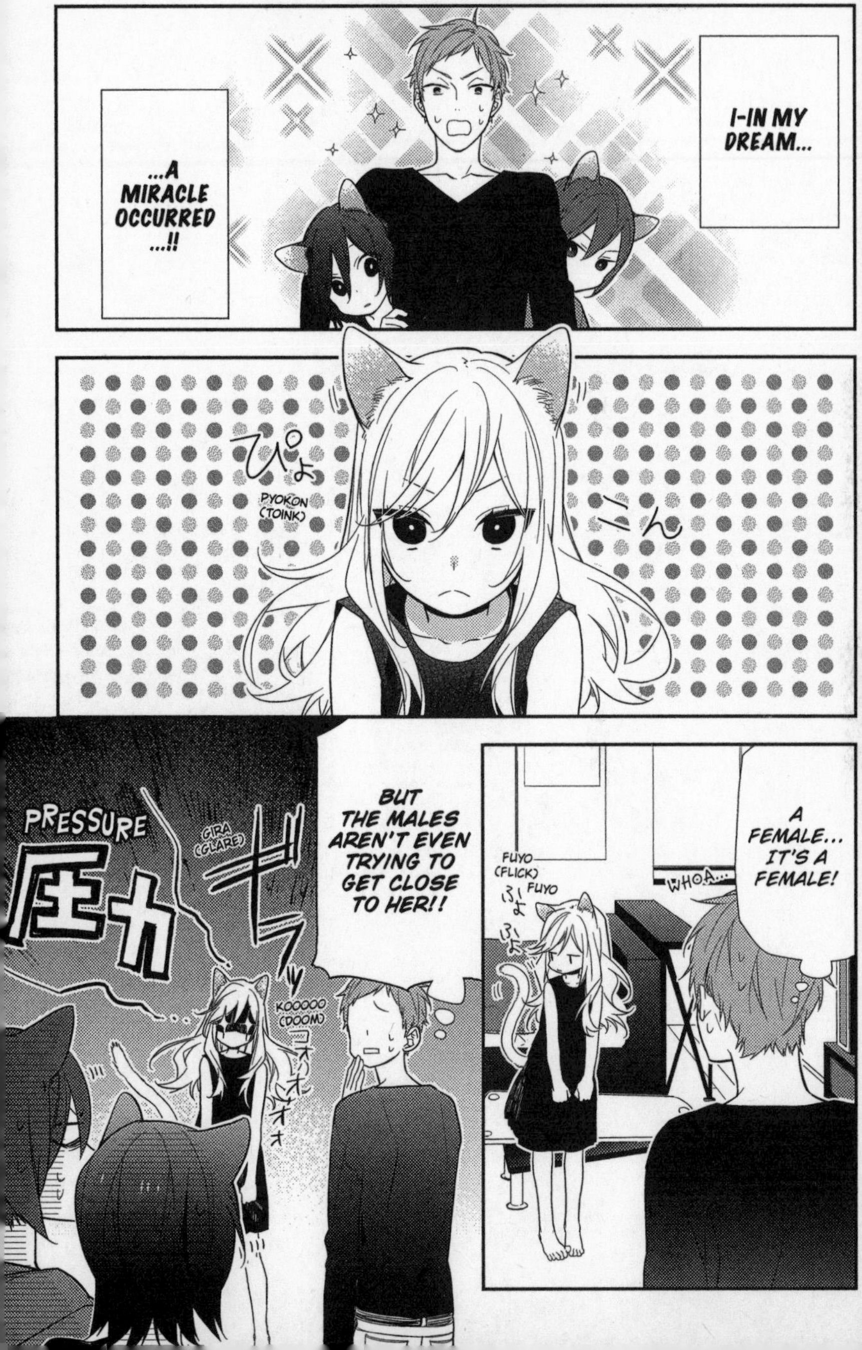
I-IN MY DREAM...
...A MIRACLE OCCURRED ...!!
ぴょこん
PYOKON (TOINK)
A FEMALE... IT'S A FEMALE!
WHOA...
ふよふよ
FUYO FUYO (FLICK)
BUT THE MALES AREN'T EVEN TRYING TO GET CLOSE TO HER!!
ギラッ
GIRA (GLARE)
圧力
PRESSURE
KOOOOO (DOOM)

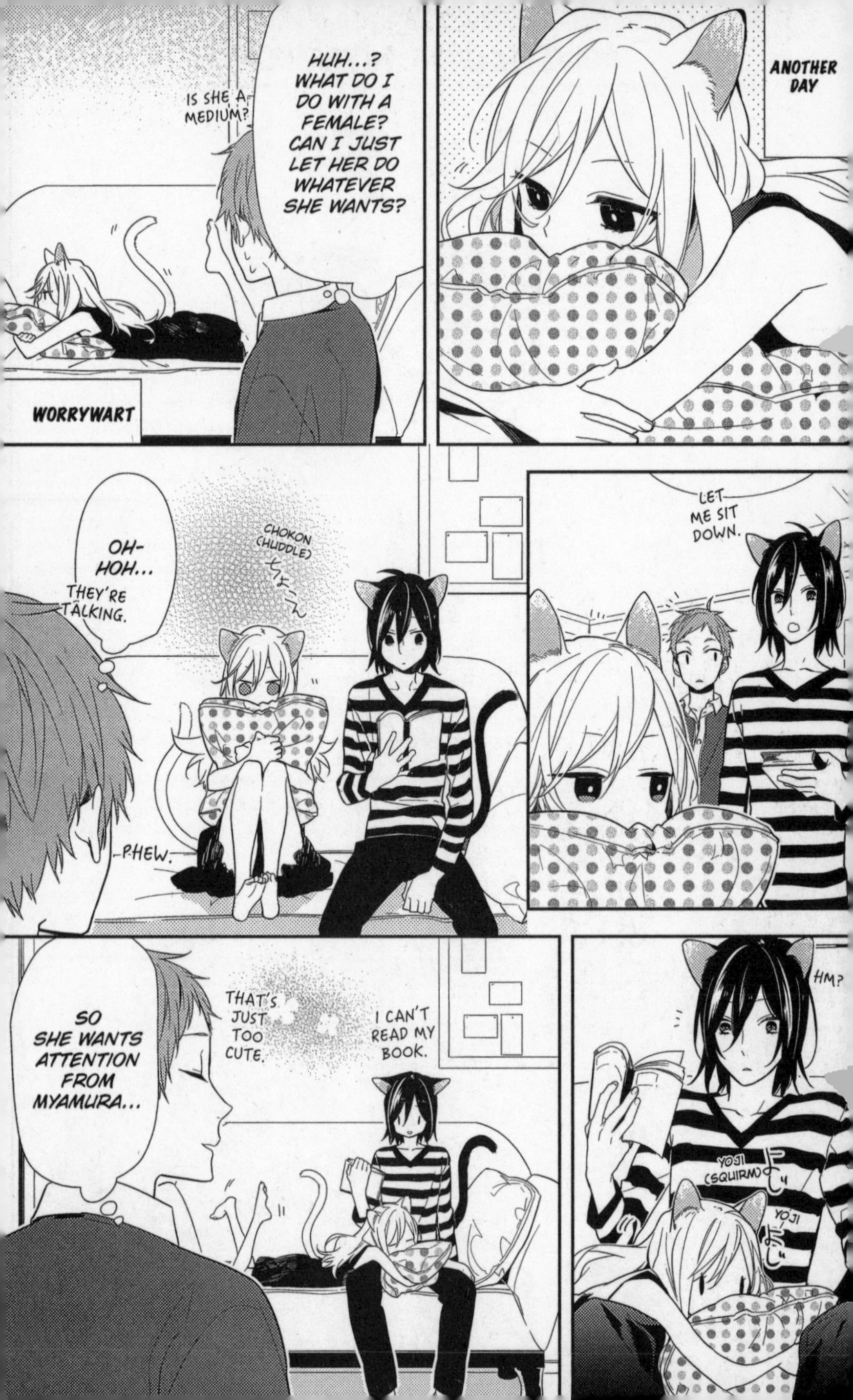
ANOTHER DAY
HUH...? WHAT DO I DO WITH A FEMALE? CAN I JUST LET HER DO WHATEVER SHE WANTS?
IS SHE A MEDIUM?
WORRYWART
LET ME SIT DOWN.
CHOKON (HUDDLE)
OH-HOH...
THEY'RE TALKING.
PHEW.
HM?
YOJI (SQUIRM)
YOJI
I CAN'T READ MY BOOK.
THAT'S JUST TOO CUTE.
SO SHE WANTS ATTENTION FROM MYAMURA...

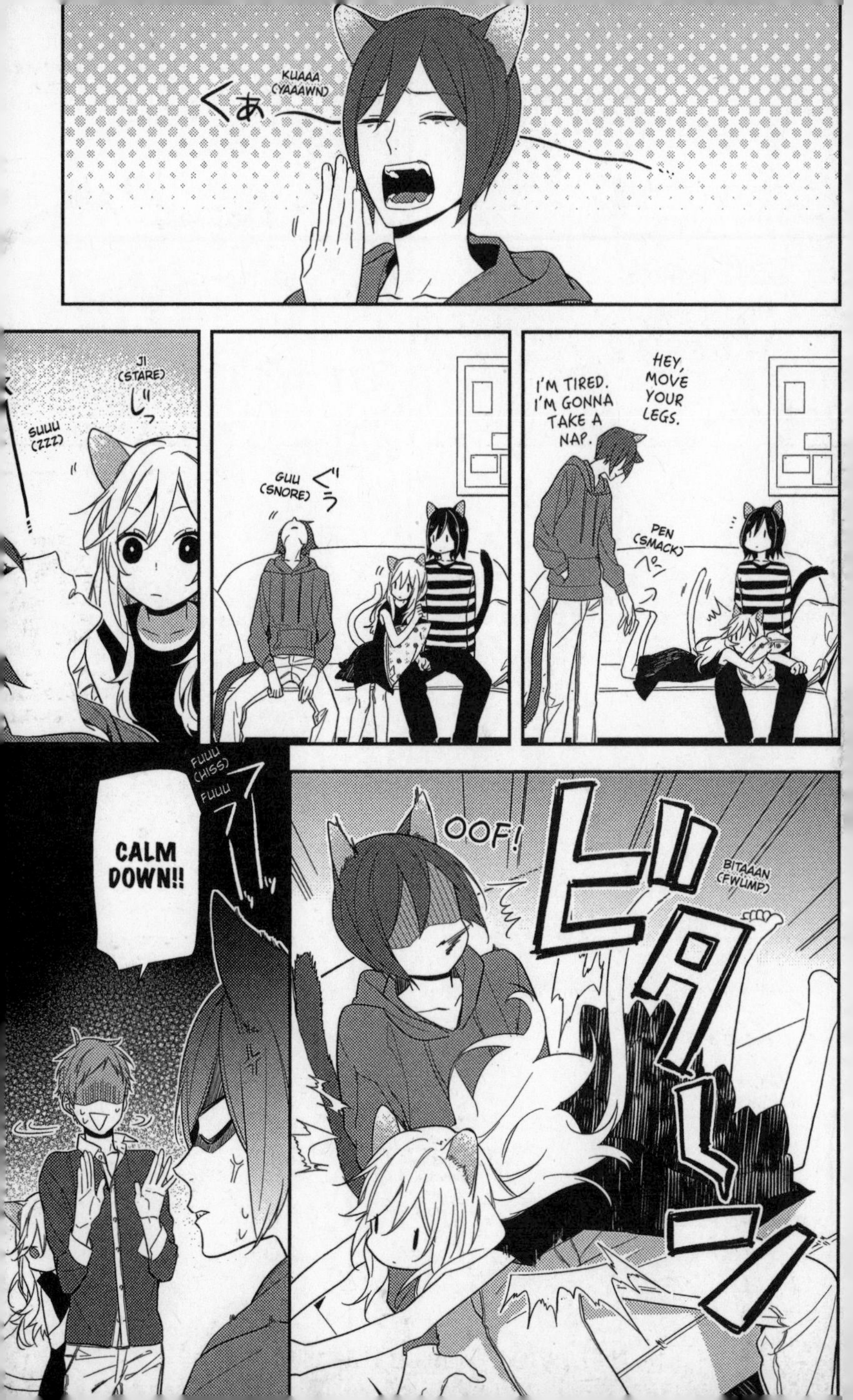

KUAAA (YAAAWN)
くあ
HEY, MOVE YOUR LEGS.
I'M TIRED. I'M GONNA TAKE A NAP.
PEN (SMACK)
GUU (SNORE)
ぐう
JI (STARE)
じっ
SUUU (ZZZ)
BITAAAN (FWUMP)
OOF!
ビタ
FUUU (HISS) FUUU
CALM DOWN!!

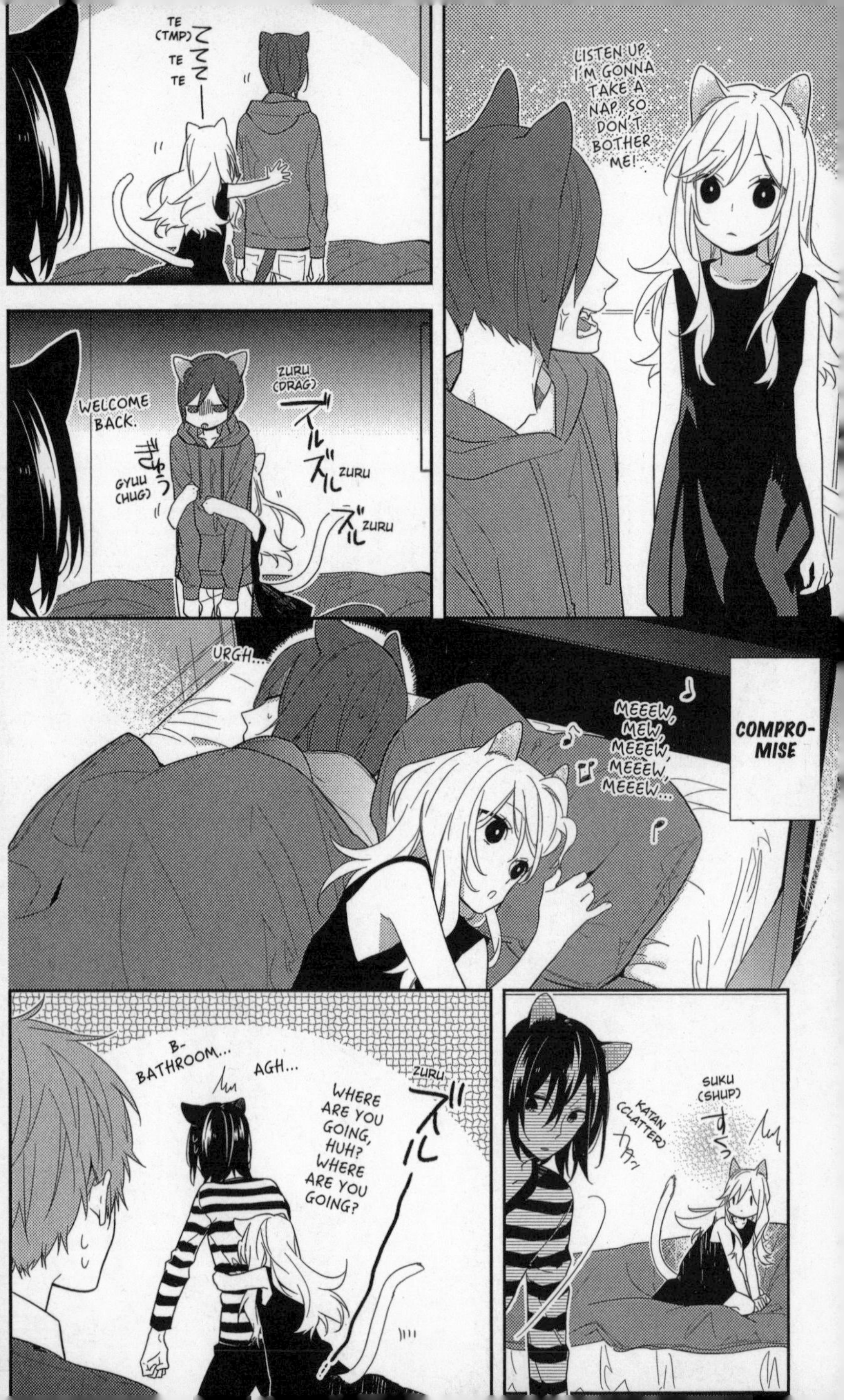

LISTEN UP. I'M GONNA TAKE A NAP, SO DON'T BOTHER ME!
ててて
TE (TMP) TE TE
ズル
ZURU (DRAG)
ズル ZURU
ズル ZURU
WELCOME BACK.
ぎゅう
GYUU (HUG)
COMPROMISE
MEEEW, MEW, MEEEW, MEEEW, MEEEW...
URGH...
SUKU (SHUP)
すくっ
KATAN (CLATTER)
カタッ
ZURU
ズル
WHERE ARE YOU GOING, HUH? WHERE ARE YOU GOING?
AGH...
B-BATHROOM...

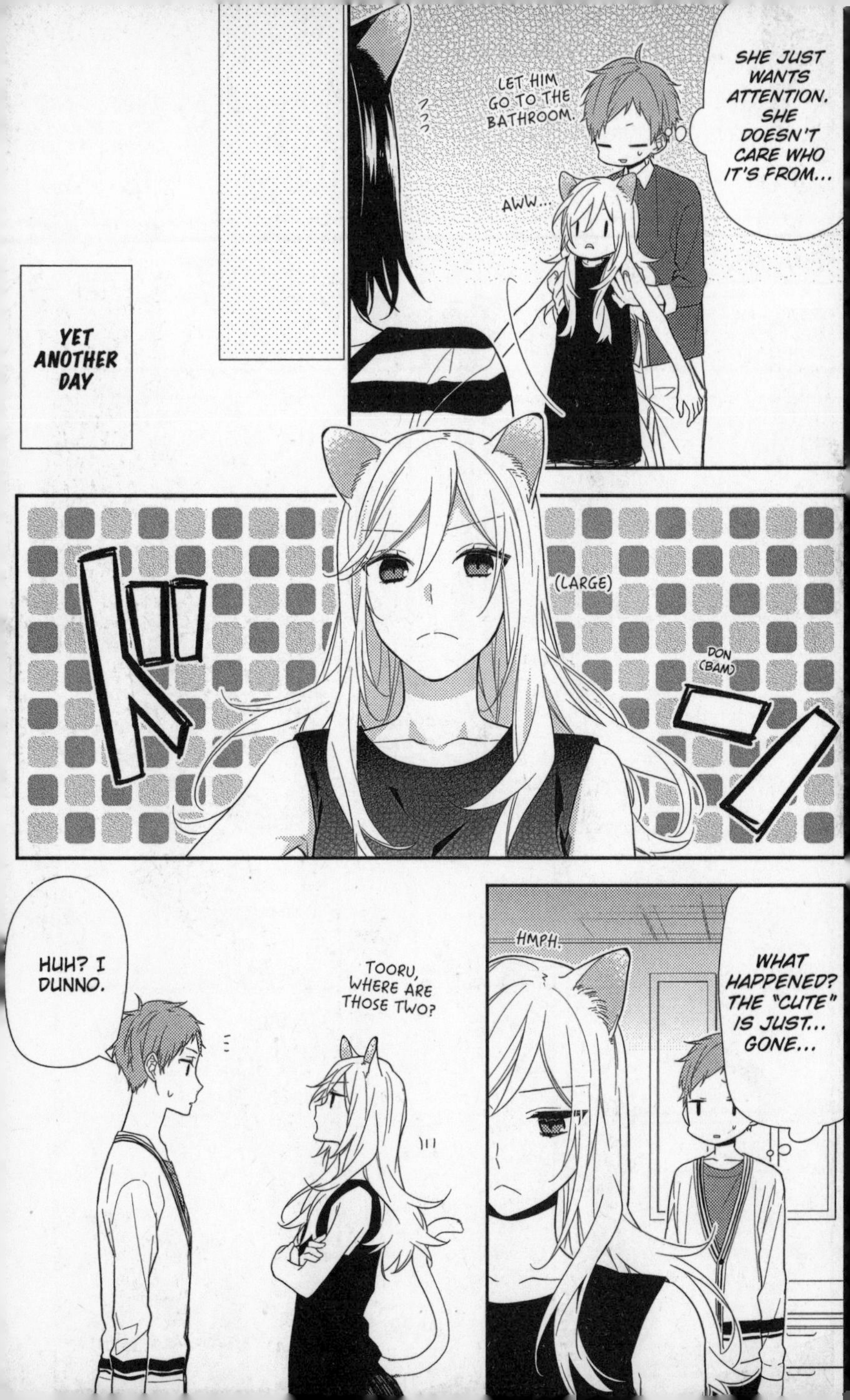
SHE JUST WANTS ATTENTION. SHE DOESN'T CARE WHO IT'S FROM...
LET HIM GO TO THE BATHROOM.
AWW...
YET ANOTHER DAY
(LARGE)
DON (BAM)
WHAT HAPPENED? THE "CUTE" IS JUST... GONE...
HMPH.
TOORU, WHERE ARE THOSE TWO?
HUH? I DUNNO.

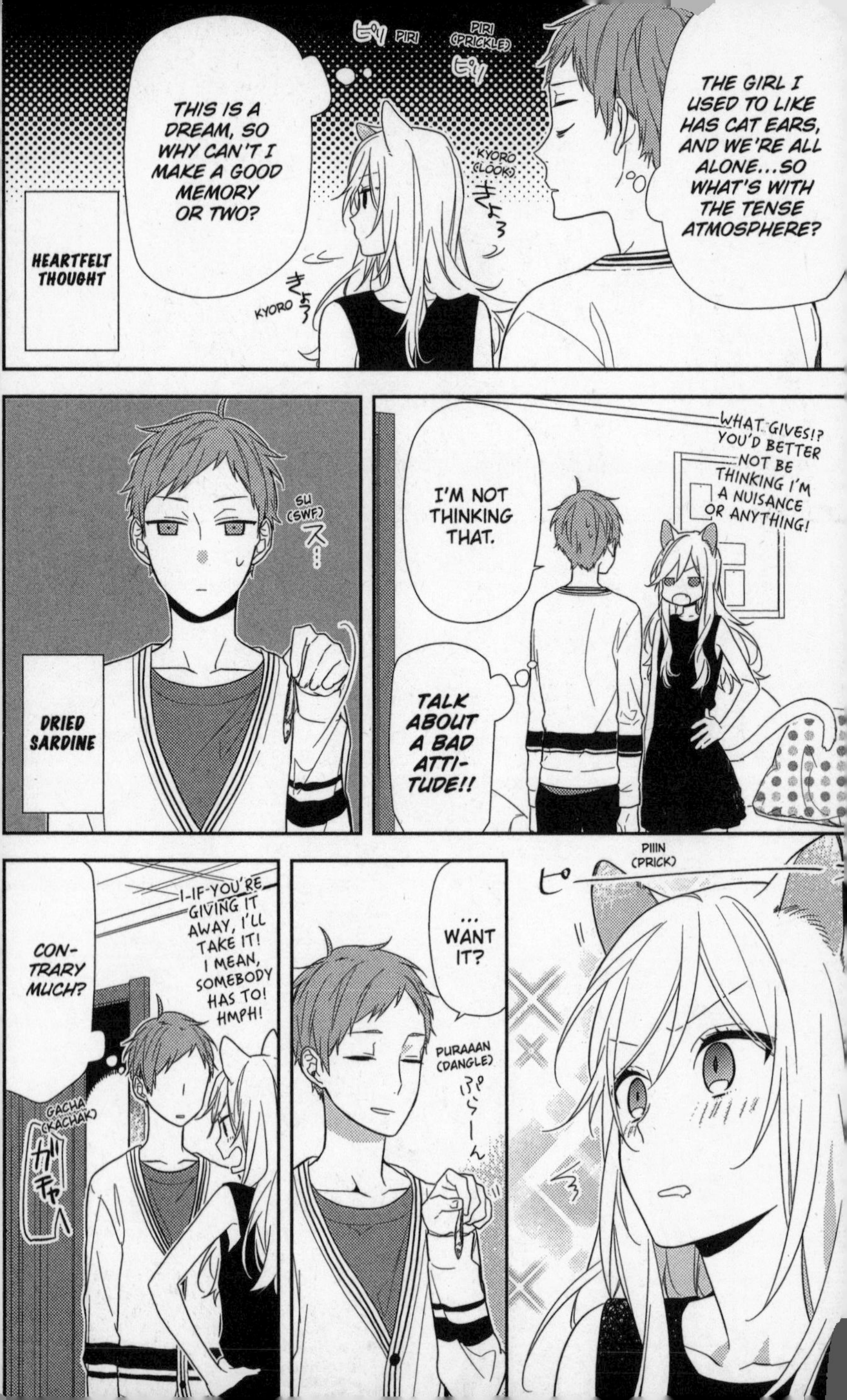
THE GIRL I USED TO LIKE HAS CAT EARS, AND WE'RE ALL ALONE...SO WHAT'S WITH THE TENSE ATMOSPHERE?
PIRI (PRICKLE)
PIRI
KYORO (LOOK)
THIS IS A DREAM, SO WHY CAN'T I MAKE A GOOD MEMORY OR TWO?
KYORO
HEARTFELT THOUGHT
WHAT GIVES!? YOU'D BETTER NOT BE THINKING I'M A NUISANCE OR ANYTHING!
I'M NOT THINKING THAT.
TALK ABOUT A BAD ATTI-TUDE!!
SU (SWF)
DRIED SARDINE
PIIIN (PRICK)
... WANT IT?
PURAAAN (DANGLE)
I-IF YOU'RE GIVING IT AWAY, I'LL TAKE IT! I MEAN, SOMEBODY HAS TO! HMPH!
CON-TRARY MUCH?
GACHA (KACHAK)

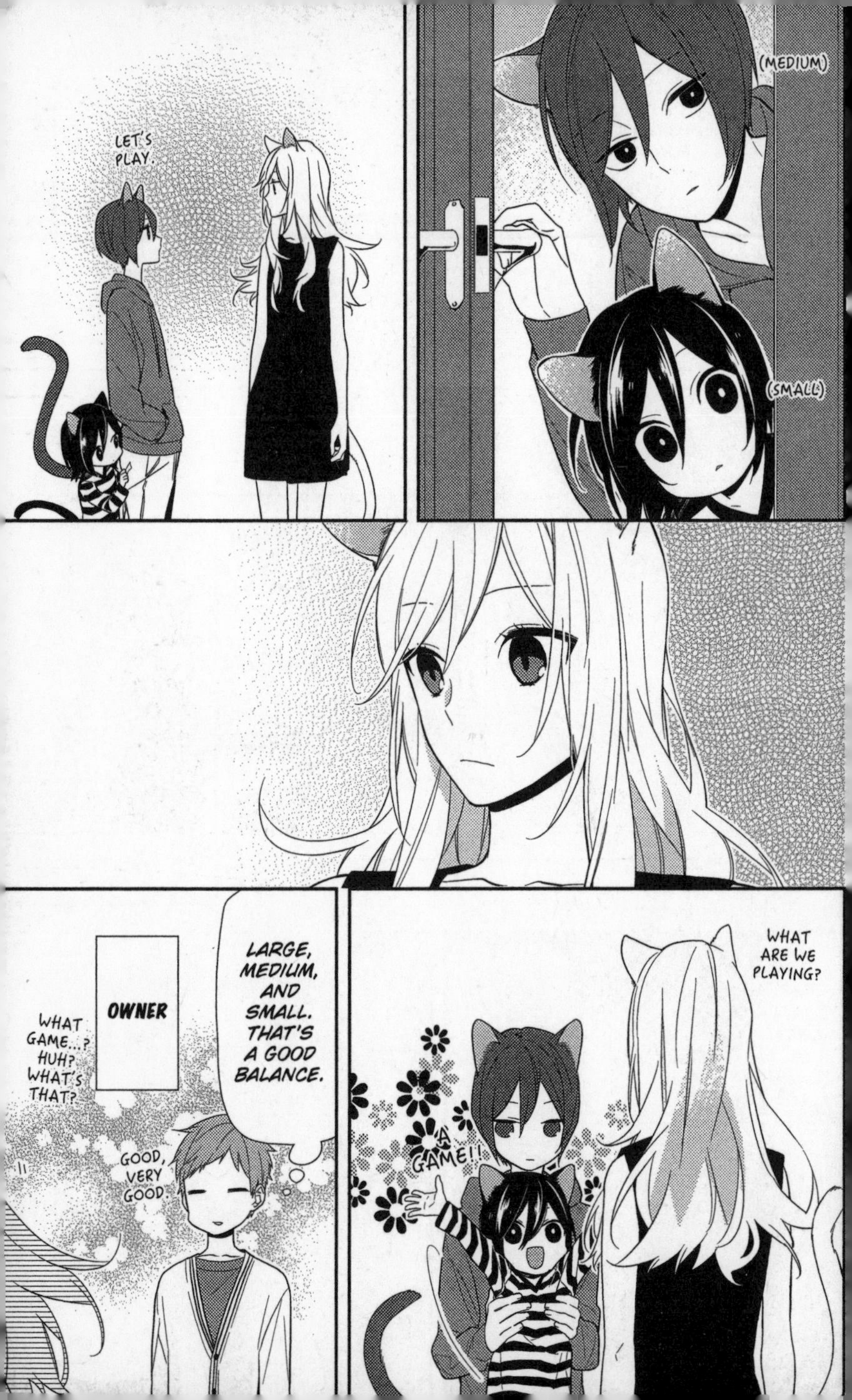
(MEDIUM)
(SMALL)
LET'S PLAY.
WHAT ARE WE PLAYING?
A GAME!!
LARGE, MEDIUM, AND SMALL. THAT'S A GOOD BALANCE.
OWNER
WHAT GAME...? HUH? WHAT'S THAT?
GOOD, VERY GOOD.

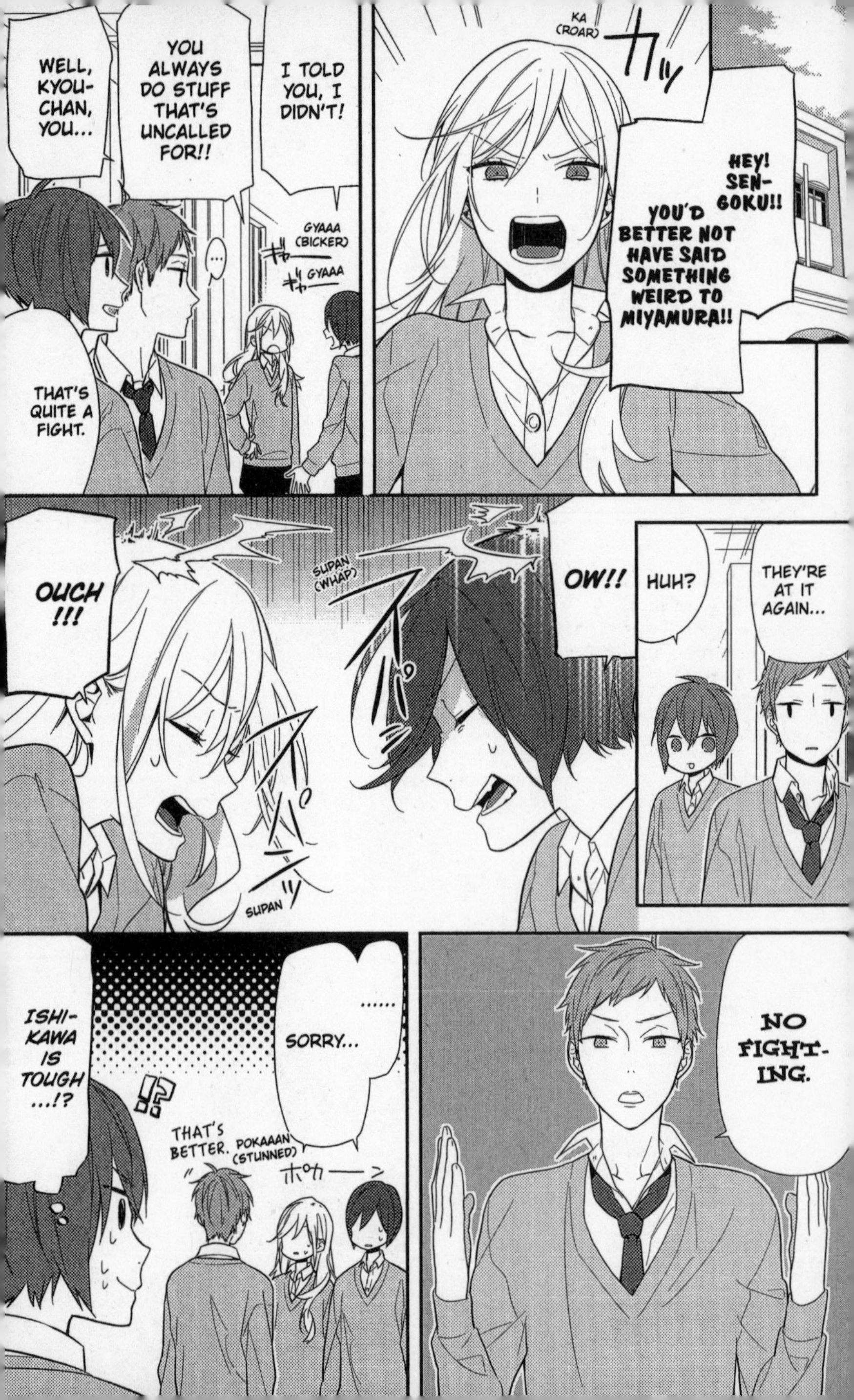
KA (ROAR)
HEY! SEN-GOKU!!
YOU'D BETTER NOT HAVE SAID SOMETHING WEIRD TO MIYAMURA!!
I TOLD YOU, I DIDN'T!
YOU ALWAYS DO STUFF THAT'S UNCALLED FOR!!
WELL, KYOU-CHAN, YOU...
GYAAA (BICKER)
GYAAA
...
THAT'S QUITE A FIGHT.
THEY'RE AT IT AGAIN...
HUH?
OW!!
SUPAN (WHAP)
OUCH!!!
SUPAN
NO FIGHT-ING.
......
SORRY...
POKAAAN (STUNNED)
THAT'S BETTER.
!?
ISHI-KAWA IS TOUGH...!?

## STAFF

**★ ORIGINAL WORKS ★**

HERO-sama
"Hori-san and Miyamura-kun"

**★ EDITOR ★**

Ishikawa-sama
Thanks for everything!!

**★ SPECIAL THANKS ★**

To the members of the editorial
department, the printers, everyone
involved with this story, my
family, my friends, and everyone
who picked up this book—

THANK YOU!!

## Translation Notes

**Page 9 – "I want to become a shell..."**
Sengoku is greatly exaggerating the misery of his conscription and forced labor. This is a famous line from a semi-autobiographical book by Tetsutarou Katou about a barber who was drafted into Japan's military during World War II, released from the army after the war, and then arrested as a war criminal for wounding an Allied soldier—his superior had ordered him to execute the soldier, but he couldn't bring himself to do it—and given the death penalty. In his will, the man writes, "I never want to be born as a human again. If I'm reborn, I want to become a shell at the bottom of the deep ocean."

**Page 39 – Clapping**
Traditionally, you clap your hands together before praying at Shinto shrines. If the teacher feels this is an urgent request or that she's asking a lot, she may be mimicking this gesture to show how much she means it.

**Page 77 – Gakuran**
A very common type of boys' school uniform in Japan. It's usually an all-black top and bottom, with buttons up the front of the jacket and a high collar. They're generally believed to have been modeled on Prussian military academy uniforms.

**Page 87 – Enka**
A type of Japanese folk music. It's described as "sentimental ballad music" and is considered to be closer to traditional Japanese music than most other genres. It isn't terribly popular with high schoolers.

**Page 89 – Corn soup**
A typical "hot" vending machine offering in Japan. When sold as a beverage, it's usually creamy, smooth, and very lightly seasoned, and it's treated a bit like hot chocolate.

**Page 140 – Tapirs**
The animals walking around Hori are Malayan tapirs. Tapirs in general are viewed as being connected to supernatural entities from Chinese folklore called baku, which were believed to eat nightmares. Because actual tapirs match the physical description of the mythical baku to some extent, they were named after them, and the same kanji character is used for the names of both creatures.

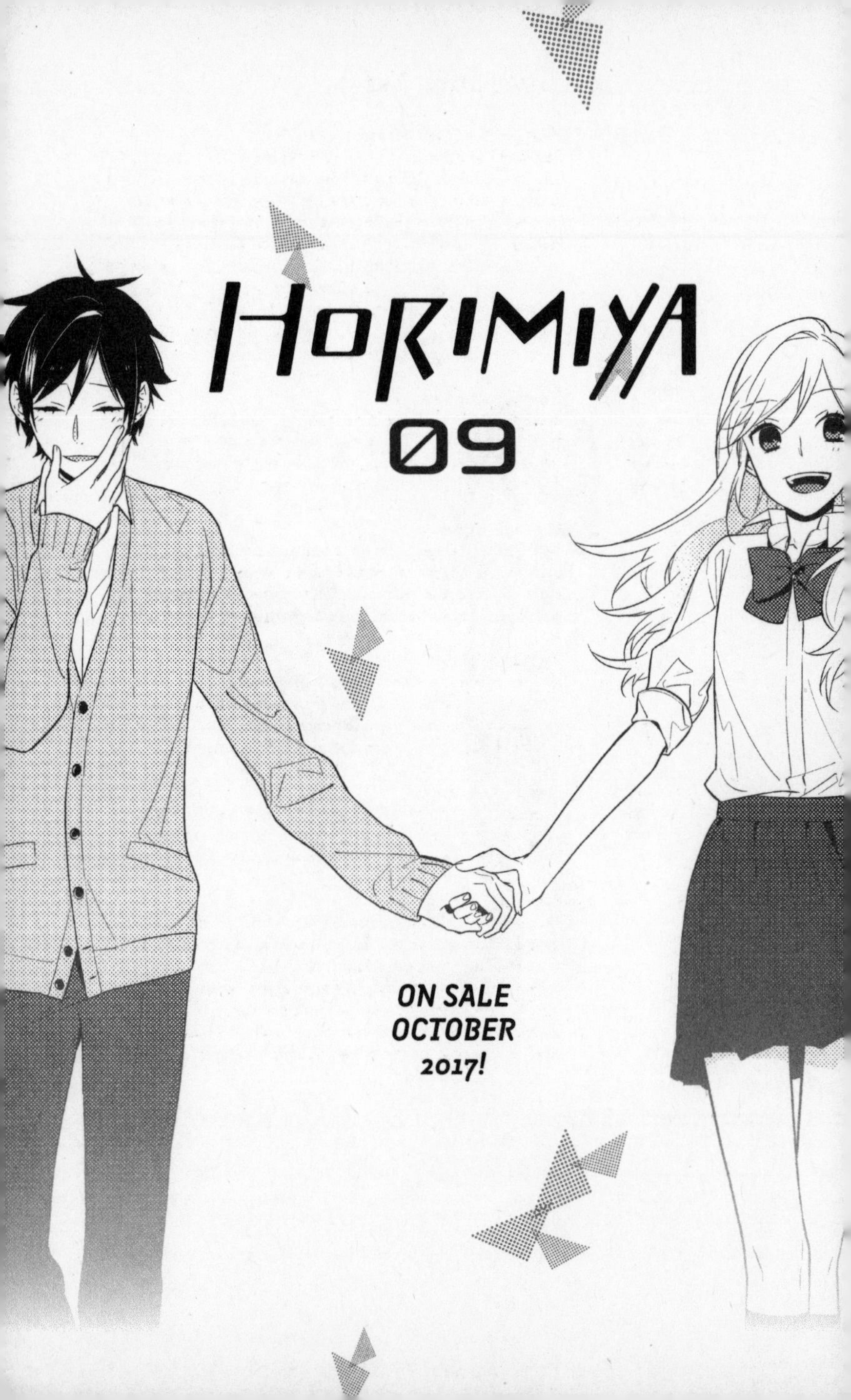
HORIMIYA
09
ON SALE
OCTOBER
2017!

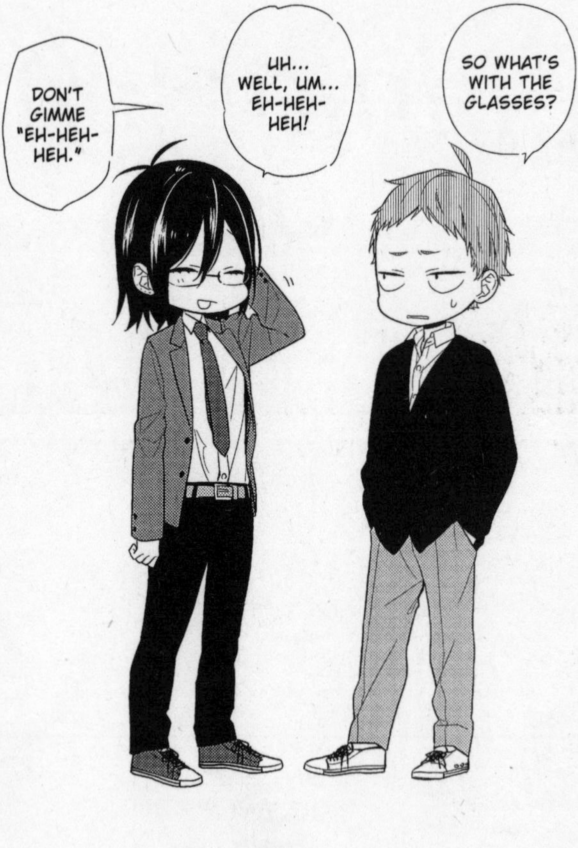
SO WHAT'S WITH THE GLASSES?
UH... WELL, UM... EH-HEH-HEH!
DON'T GIMME "EH-HEH-HEH."

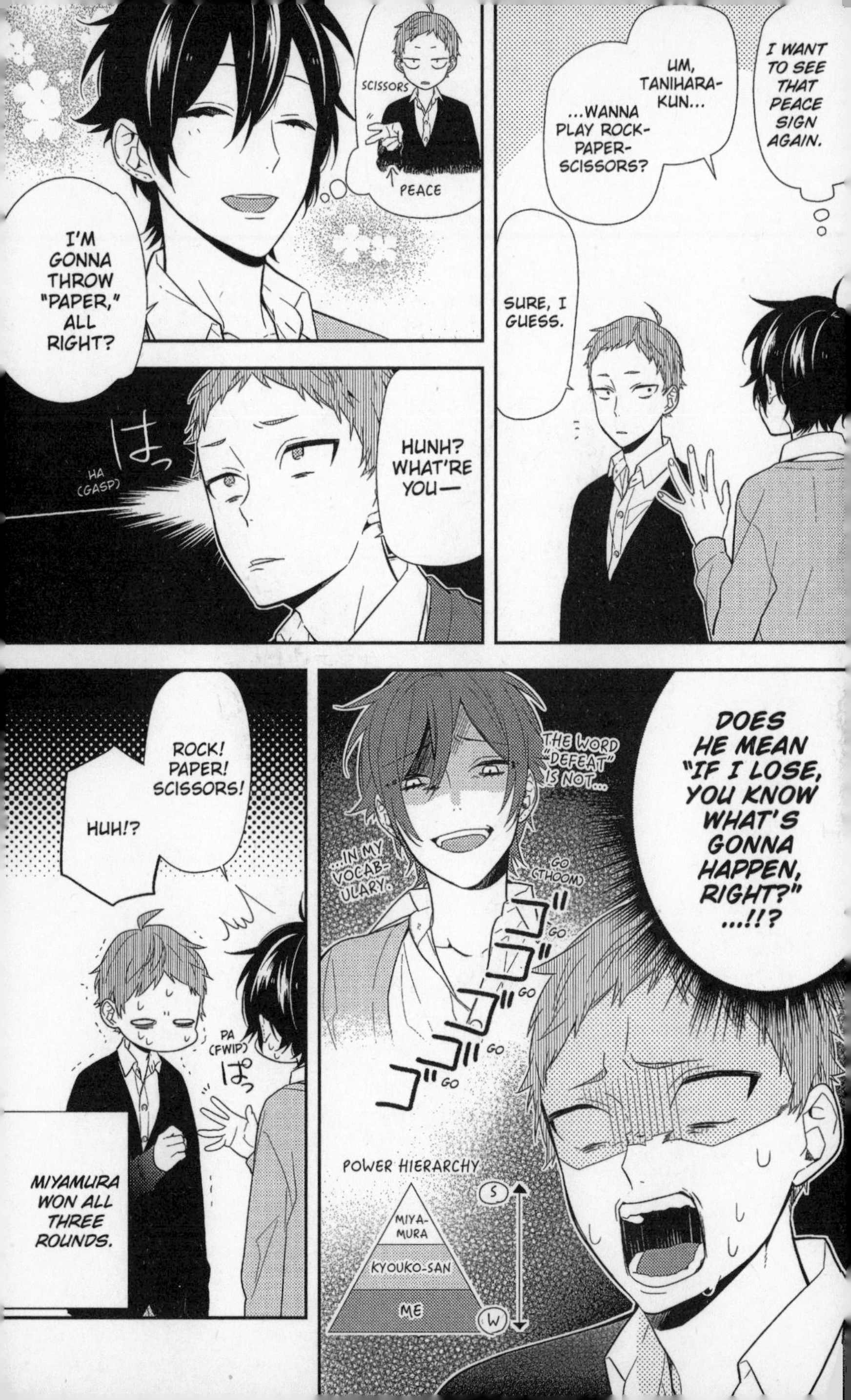
I WANT TO SEE THAT PEACE SIGN AGAIN.
UM, TANIHARA-KUN...
...WANNA PLAY ROCK-PAPER-SCISSORS?
SURE, I GUESS.
SCISSORS
PEACE
I'M GONNA THROW "PAPER," ALL RIGHT?
HUNH? WHAT'RE YOU—
はっ
HA (GASP)
DOES HE MEAN "IF I LOSE, YOU KNOW WHAT'S GONNA HAPPEN, RIGHT?" ...!!?
THE WORD "DEFEAT" IS NOT...
...IN MY VOCABULARY.
ゴ GO (THOOM)
ゴ GO
ゴ GO
ゴ GO
ゴ GO
POWER HIERARCHY
S
MIYAMURA
KYOUKO-SAN
ME
W
ROCK! PAPER! SCISSORS!
HUH!?
ぱっ
PA (FWIP)
MIYAMURA WON ALL THREE ROUNDS.

HORIMIYA

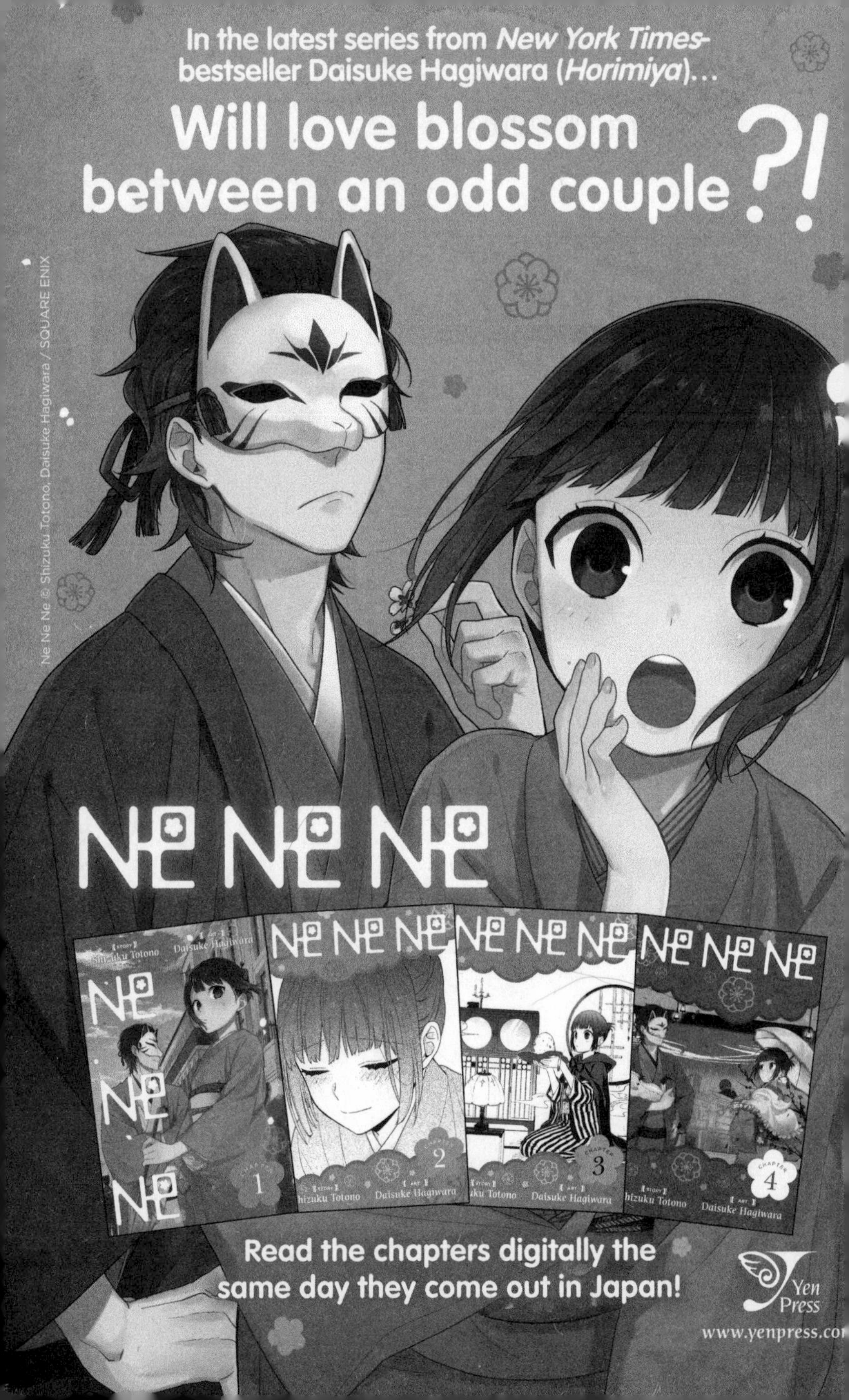
In the latest series from New York Times-bestseller Daisuke Hagiwara (Horimiya)...
Will love blossom between an odd couple ?!
Ne Ne Ne
Ne Ne Ne © Shizuku Totono, Daisuke Hagiwara / SQUARE ENIX
Read the chapters digitally the same day they come out in Japan!
Yen Press
www.yenpress.com

## HERO × Daisuke Hagiwara

*Translation: Taylor Engel*
*Lettering: Alexis Eckerman*

HORIMIYA vol. 8
© HERO • OOZ
© 2015 Daisuke Hagiwara / SQUARE ENIX CO., LTD. First published in Japan
in 2015 by SQUARE ENIX CO., LTD. English translation rights arranged with
SQUARE ENIX CO., LTD. and Yen Press, LLC through Tuttle-Mori Agency, Inc.

English translation © 2017 by SQUARE ENIX CO., LTD.

Yen Press
1290 Avenue of the Americas
New York, NY 10104

Visit us at yenpress.com • facebook.com/yenpress •
twitter.com/yenpress • yenpress.tumblr.com •
instagram.com/yenpress

First Yen Press Edition: July 2017

Yen Press is an imprint of Yen Press, LLC.
The Yen Press name and logo are trademarks
of Yen Press, LLC.

The publisher is not responsible for websites
(or their content) that are not owned by the
publisher.

Library of Congress Control Number:
2015960115

ISBNs: 978-0-316-56019-1 (paperback)
978-0-316-43970-1 (ebook)

10 9 8 7 6 5 4 3 2 1

BVG

Printed in the United States of America